Theory and Interpretation of Narrative
James Phelan and Peter J. Rabinowitz, Series Editors

the real

THE REAL, THE TRUE, AND THE TOLD

Postmodern Historical Narrative and the
Ethics of Representation

ERIC L. BERLATSKY

 THE OHIO STATE UNIVERSITY PRESS • COLUMBUS

For Jennie, Katie, and Julia

Copyright © 2011 by The Ohio State University.
All rights reserved.

Library of Congress Cataloging-in-Publication Data

Berlatsky, Eric L., 1972–
 The real, the true, and the told : postmodern historical narrative and the ethics of representation / Eric L. Berlatsky.
  p. cm. — (Theory and interpretation of narrative series)
 Includes bibliographical references and index.
 ISBN-13: 978-0-8142-1153-3 (cloth : alk. paper)
 ISBN-10: 0-8142-1153-4 (cloth : alk. paper)
 ISBN-13: 978-0-8142-9254-9 (cd)
  1. Historical fiction—History and criticism. 2. Postmodernism (Literature) 3. History—Philosophy. 4. Historiography. 5. Woolf, Virginia, 1882–1941—Criticism and interpretation. 6. Swift, Graham, 1949–Criticism and interpretation. 7. Rushdie, Salman—Criticism and interpretation. 8. Spiegelman, Art—Criticism and interpretation. I. Title. II. Series: Theory and interpretation of narrative series.
 PN3441.B47 2011
 809.3'81—dc22
          2010033740

This book is available in the following editions
Cloth (ISBN 978-0-8142-1153-3)
CD-ROM (ISBN 978-0-8142-9254-9
Paper (ISBN: 978-0-8142-5614-5)
Cover design by Becky Kulka / Designsmith.
Text design by Jennifer Shoffey Forsythe.
Type set in Adobe Minion Pro.

∞ The paper used in this publication meets the minimum requirements of the American National Standard for Information Sciences—Permanence of Paper for Printed Library Materials. ANSI Z39.48-1992.

CONTENTS

Acknowledgments		ix
Introduction	Memory as Forgetting: Historical Reference, Ethics, and Postmodernist Fiction	1
Chapter 1	The Pageantry of the Past and the Reflection of the Present: History, Reality, and Feminism in Virginia Woolf's *Between the Acts*	39
Chapter 2	"A Knife Blade Called Now": Historiography, Narrativity, and the "Here and Now" in Graham Swift's *Waterland*	77
Chapter 3	"What's Real and What's True": Metaphors, Errata, and the Shadow of the Real in Salman Rushdie's *Midnight's Children*	109
Chapter 4	"It's Enough Stories": Truth and Experience in Art Spiegelman's *Maus*	145
Conclusion	Expanding the Field	187
Notes		197
Works Cited		217
Index		237

ACKNOWLEDGMENTS

There are a wide variety of people who can take credit for this book finally reaching fruition. They are, of course, not to be blamed for its shortcomings. First, and foremost is my wife, Jennie, who has been reading this book, in one version or another, for almost ten years—two-thirds of our married life. It is a testament to her patience and love that she has done so with an absolute minimum of complaint. If there is anyone who is happier that the project is complete than me, it is certainly she. The support she provided was not only emotional and intellectual, but also, for my years in graduate school, financial. In addition, she has proven willing to pick up and move far from family, friends, comfort, and security on my behalf. This book is as much hers as it is mine. I must also thank my daughters, Katie and Julia, who occasionally provided me with quiet and time to work, and more often provided a welcome distraction. Katie's capacity for prodigious napping in her earliest years was especially notable in allowing me to complete the dissertation from which this book developed. My parents, Joel and Teddi, and my brother, Noah, are also due thanks for support of various kinds, including blind faith balanced by masked concern. My grandmother, Raedina Winters, always admonished me to make the book "sexy." If I failed to comply, it is through no fault of hers. I am only sorry and saddened that she did not live long enough to see its publication. I would also like to thank Jennie's sprawling family. While they often have only the vaguest idea what I actually do, they never fail to provide support and congratulations when and if I actually achieve something. No doubt, this will be no different.

The book has origins at the University of Maryland graduate program in English, particularly in the classes of Brian Richardson, Susan Leonardi, Kandice Chuh, and Jonathan Auerbach. All of these professors nurtured and contributed to transforming a variety of half-baked ideas into a bona fide book, introducing me to the concepts of narrative theory, life writing, critical race theory, and postmodernism that were the backbones of this project. I would also like to thank William Cohen for being the first in a long line of people who contributed titles that I shamelessly stole and for giving me the opportunity to hone my research skills. Also at the University of Maryland, I would like to thank fellow students-cum-professors who workshopped my dissertation. In particular, Steve Severn and Ryan Claycomb saw things through to their ultimate conclusion, and Ryan has continued to provide me with useful and insightful feedback to the developing book in postgraduate years. Thanks also to an old and dear friend, Donjiro Ban, who, many years ago, before scanners were on every desk and in every English department, scanned some images from Spiegelman's *Maus* for me. I am still using those scans, perhaps for the last time. I would also like to thank him for taking time out of a pretty busy day to try to make me look good on the back-cover photograph for this book. The blame for any failure to do so must fall upon the subject, not the photographer.

Finally, I would like to thank my colleagues and students at Florida Atlantic University, many of whom have contributed to the revision and development of this book. In particular, both undergraduate and graduate classes of Postcolonial Literature contributed mightily to the *Midnight's Children* chapter, and participants in the Comics and Graphic Novels course(s) were instrumental in revisions to my ideas about *Maus*. Two separate Virginia Woolf graduate seminars also made it possible to position my ideas about *Between the Acts* in relation to the remainder of the Woolf corpus. Special thanks are due to those who scheduled these courses, Johnnie Stover and Wenying Xu. Their flexibility in course schedule allowed me to teach these courses and therefore remain connected to my research. As chairs, Wenying Xu and Andy Furman also deserve special thanks for encouraging and facilitating the research of junior faculty like myself. I would also like to acknowledge the importance of The Dorothy F. Schmidt College of Arts and Letters, who allowed me to "finish" the book (for the second or third time) by granting me a Scholarly and Creative Achievement Fellowship (SCAF) in 2006–7. FAU has been a welcoming and receptive place, despite budgetary and institutional obstacles, and for that I thank the above people as well as the faculty and students at large.

At The Ohio State University Press, I must thank Jim Phelan and Peter Rabinowitz for their lengthy and painstaking efforts to push this book in the right direction. I would also like to thank the anonymous reviewer, whose comments helped me reshape it (for the third or fourth time). Sandy Crooms is also due thanks for her efforts in shepherding the project to the starting gate and the finish line. Although I sometimes like to construct a narrative of myself working in an antisocial vacuum of sorts, the above indicates how reliant I actually am on the strength and wisdom of others. Thank you all.

• • •

Portions of the introduction and chapter 4 were previously published in substantially different form in "Memory as Forgetting: The Problem of the Postmodern in Kundera's *The Book of Laughter and Forgetting* and Spiegelman's *Maus*." *Cultural Critique* 55 (Fall 2003): 101–51.

Much of chapter 2 was previously published as "'The Swamps of Myth . . . and Empirical Fishing Lines': Historiography, Narrativity, and the 'Here and Now' in Graham Swift's *Waterland*." *Journal of Narrative Theory* 36.2 (Summer 2006): 254–92.

A tiny segment of chapter 1 was published previously as "The Pageantry of the Past and the Reflection of the Present: History, 'Reality,' and Feminism in Virginia Woolf's *Between the Acts*." *The Twelfth Annual Conference on Virginia Woolf Proceedings: Across the Generations*. Eds. Merry Pawlowski and Eileen Barrett. Bakersfield, CA: The Center for Virginia Woolf Studies, 2003. 170-76. http://www.csub.edu/woolf_center/open.html (Publications).

Thank you to *Cultural Critique* and *The Journal of Narrative Theory* for the right to reprint those portions of the above that were published in their pages.

I gratefully acknowledge Random House, Inc., for permission to reprint from the following:

- *Maus I: A Survivor's Tale/My Father Bleeds History* by Art Spiegelman, copyright © 1973, 1980, 1981, 1982, 1984, 1985, 1986 by Art Spiegelman. Used by permission of Pantheon Books, a division of Random House, Inc.
- *Maus II: A Survivor's Tale/And Here My Trouble Began* by Art Spiegelman, copyright © 1986, 1989, 1990, 1991 by Art Spiegelman. Used by permission of Pantheon Books, a division of Random House, Inc.

INTRODUCTION

Memory as Forgetting

Historical Reference, Ethics, and Postmodernist Fiction

> Can't bring back time. Like holding water in your hand.
> —James Joyce, *Ulysses* (168)

> Art and morality are, with certain provisos ... one. Their essence is the same. The essence of both of them is love. Love is the perception of individuals. Love is the extremely difficult realization that something other than oneself is real.
> —Iris Murdoch, "The Sublime and the Good" (215)

Milan Kundera's *The Book of Laughter and Forgetting* opens in Prague, with two scenes that send contradictory messages about the possibility and necessity of recovering and representing the past. In the first, set in 1948, Kundera relates the largely true story of Gottwald and Clementis, both Communist leaders. Gottwald delivers a winter speech with Clementis by his side. In a gesture of solidarity Clementis removes his hat and places it on Gottwald's head. The moment is reproduced copiously and, "[o]n that balcony, the history of Communist Bohemia began" (3). Four years later, however, Clementis is charged with treason and eventually hanged. At this point, "The propaganda section ... made him vanish from history and ... from all photographs.... Nothing remains of Clementis but the fur hat on Gottwald's head" (3–4). *The Book* here highlights the inherent possibility of, and concomitant danger in, the effacement of historical fact. Here and elsewhere, the novel asserts the necessity of retaining the reference to historical truth outside of merely competing subjectivities. The meeting of Gottwald and Clementis is not presented as merely one view of events that can be countered on equal epistemological grounds by the propaganda section that rewrites history. Rather, the event occurred, insists the novel, a fact that must be maintained if political domination is to be resisted.

In the second scene, set in 1971 during Gustav Husak's presidency, Mirek saves his diary, correspondence, and minutes of meetings despite the possibility that the documents may later be used against him as evidence of subversiveness. In justification, Mirek asserts that the "struggle of man against power is the struggle of memory against forgetting" (4), indicating that power can be resisted only as long as the past is recalled accurately. In this, Mirek echoes the narrator, asserting the necessity of reporting the historical truth despite institutional forces that attempt to erase it. Immediately, however, the very possibility of holding on to the past is undercut, as Mirek destroys items that he does not wish to accept as part of his personal identity. In particular, he embarks on a quest to destroy the love letters he had sent to a woman named Zdena, removing his love for her from his life's narrative. Kundera's reputation as a master ironist is built on such moments as these, as Mirek struggles against the effacement of history by institutional power, while asserting similar power in his personal life.

> He wanted to efface her from the photograph of his life not because he had not loved her but because he had. He had erased her . . . as the party propaganda section had made Clementis disappear from the balcony. . . . Mirek rewrote history just like the Communist Party, like all political parties, like all peoples, like mankind. They shout that they want to shape a better future, but it's not true. The future is only an indifferent void no one cares about, but the past is filled with life, and its countenance is irritating, repellent, wounding. . . . We want to be masters of the future only for the power to change the past. (30–31)

There are, of course, multiple ways of reading this juxtaposition. It is possible to see Mirek's political goals as admirable and his personal behavior as hypocritical. That is, we might see the truth of the past as clearly accessible and any effort to rewrite it, change it, or use it for one's own purposes to be merely an abuse of power. However, Kundera's insistence that *all* parties, *all* people, and "mankind" itself rewrite history makes such a view of the situation problematic. If all treatments of the past are "rewrites," if, in fact, we can "change the past" through our retrospective emplotment of it, then Mirek, ironically, is correct in his treatment of his letters to Zdena and wrong in his attitudes towards his political documents. That is, if the rewriting of the past is an unavoidable universal impulse, Mirek's claim to struggle "against power" in the interests of objectivity can only be a self-deception. Instead, Mirek's attempts at objective history must be seen as an effort to assert subjective power against another equally subjective, if inarguably stronger, attempt to do so. While the Communist Party creates a narrative of infallible benevolence, Mirek constructs his own exclusionary life story. These narratives explain the past in ways congenial to their narrators, oppressing those who, like Zdena, do not conform to their plots. They do not, however, tell the historical "truth."

The Book of Laughter and Forgetting, then, teaches us not to trust the simplistic dichotomies it initially presents. "Memory" cannot be easily opposed to "forgetting" since the former also involves selection, erasure, and elision for ideological purposes. Likewise, resistance cannot be simply opposed to "power," since such resistance is itself inevitably a power play. Finally, objectivity cannot be easily opposed to subjectivity, since Mirek's "objective" memories are revealed as efforts to construct subjectivity. This dissolution of binaries and denaturalization of seemingly given categories, combined with the exploration of the vexed nature of historical reference, is what has earned *The Book* the slippery label of "postmodern."[1]

Defining and Redefining Postmodernism

Invoking a term like "postmodern" is, of course, problematic given the wide variety of definitions already available. However, the balance of this book provides yet another effort to redefine and reexamine the postmodern and particularly its relationship to historical reference. Because it is impossible to question or reject previous definitions without identifying what they are, I will briefly discuss the various "postmodernisms" that I interact with and challenge in this book, including a look at poststructuralism and its relationship to postmodernism.

Jean-François Lyotard's aptly named "Answering the Question: What Is Postmodernism?" provides one of the most influential definitions, and his claim that the postmodern takes place in the "withdrawal of the real" (*Postmodern Condition* 79) is appropriate to my reading of Kundera thus far. *The Book* initially depends on the ethical necessity of referencing historical "reality," but then "withdraws" any comfort we may have in doing so, reminding us both of the manipulability of supposedly referential technology (the photograph) and of the inevitably ideological nature of all histories. Lyotard's claim that "[m]odernity cannot exist without a shattering of belief and without discovery of the 'lack of reality' of reality, together with the invention of other realities" (*Postmodern Condition* 77), is another useful version of the same claim. For Lyotard, modernism and postmodernism are merely variations on one another, with the former nostalgically longing for a time when "belief" and "reality" seemed available, and the latter content to acknowledge, and even embrace, a lack of moral, ethical, and ontological compass (*Postmodern Condition* 79–81). To affirm the "'lack of reality' of reality" is to realize that our "common-sense" notion of what is "real" is not real at all, but a construction of a variety of things: language, discourse, technological media, "conventional wisdom," etc. Reality, if it exists, says Lyotard, is "sublime" or "unrepresentable" (*Postmodern Condition* 80), and our acknowledgment of this troubling truth ushers us into the modern *and* the postmodern age.

Perhaps even more well known is Lyotard's claim that (post)modernism is foundationally constituted by "incredulity toward metanarratives" (*Postmodern Condition* xxiv), disbelief in or skepticism toward any "master discourse" (religion, science, Marxism) that would adequately explain and validate all experiences. Without a "metanarrative" to adjudicate between different "truths, "realities," or "language games," we are left adrift in a sea of competing subjectivities and discourses, with no objective or external validation for any of them. Using these definitional touchstones, it is possible to see a "family resemblance" between Lyotard and a number of other influential theorists, as well as a link to poststructuralism.

The definition of poststructuralism is, of course, less contested, and I will not here attempt a complete recapitulation of continental philosophy after Ferdinand de Saussure (and/or Ludwig Wittgenstein). Instead, I will try to establish what the relationship of poststructuralism to postmodernism might be said to be and why I return to the ideas of Jacques Derrida, Michel Foucault, Jacques Lacan, and other theorists over the course of this book. Poststructuralist thinkers rarely, of course, assay their own definitions of the postmodern. Insofar as its ideas are important to the "withdrawal of the real," however, poststructuralism is a primary philosophical contributor to postmodernism as Lyotard defines it. Poststructuralism, and indeed, structuralism before it, are, of course, crucial elements in the philosophical "linguistic turn," wherein, in the wake of Saussure's *Course in General Linguistics*, language is seen as "bracketed" from the referent, generative of meaning without specific reference to the "real" world it had previously been said to describe. This influential unmooring of language from its supposed object of reference is congenial to Lyotard's notion of the "'lack of reality' of reality," since what we call "reality" comes to be seen by the (post)structuralists as a *product* of language, not as an "object" that language describes. It is for this reason that Foucault, at the end of *The Order of Things*, can declare that "man is a recent invention" and "one perhaps reaching its end" (386–87), since in his typically reversed poststructuralist logic, it is the language and "discourse" *about* humanity that actually *produces* the "thing" itself, which we then erroneously take to be real. Likewise, Derrida's well-known assertion that there is "no outside the text" (*Of Grammatology* 158) is a means of asserting that there is no reality independent of signs and discourse. Instead, what we take to be reality is constituted by and in language, a problem compounded by Derrida's assessment of language's fundamental errancy. Richard Rorty's claim that "language goes all the way down" ("Nineteenth-Century Idealism" 139) is the analytic philosopher's version of this "linguistic turn." For Rorty, too, there is nothing "real" or "true" *beneath* language "since truth is the property of sentences, since sentences are dependent . . . upon vocabularies, and since vocabularies are made by human beings" (*Contingency* 21).

The linguistic turn within philosophy is not, however, the only contributor to the "withdrawal of the real." Another important element is the rapid development of global capitalism, mass media, and technology, all of which many theorists see as contributors to the dissolution of the notion of the "authentic," the "original," and (therefore) the "real." Walter Benjamin, for instance, is frequently identified as a theorist of the postmodern *avant la lettre* and is in fact mentioned prominently by Lyotard (*Postmodern Condition* 74). Benjamin's 1936 discussion of the ways in which capitalism and the technology of "mass production" (photography, film) have made the distinction between the real, the authentic, and the supposed "copy" or "representation" untenable may be the earliest important contributor to this trajectory ("Work"). Benjamin's unorthodox Marxism also prefigures that of Jean Baudrillard who argues that capitalism, technology, and media have removed the real altogether, reducing all representations *and* experiences to "simulacra" that masquerade as reality, or produce "reality," without ever actually laying claim to it. Fredric Jameson's definition of postmodernism dovetails with the excesses of Baudrillardian rhetoric when he argues that reality, history, and even politics have been reduced to objects for sale, and "exchange value has been generalized to the point at which the very memory of use value is effaced" (*Postmodernism* 18). For Jameson and Baudrillard (and Guy Debord), things, people, and events are no longer valued or identified by their "use" but merely for their monetary "exchange" value. Since money itself is an illusion (and credit even more so), no longer tied to anything real (like the gold standard, or labor, or use value), the infinite exchangeability of capital is, like the infinite chain of signifiers in Deconstruction, an indicator of the impossibility of encountering the real (or referent).

Outside of the realms of philosophy and economic/political theory, Einstein's relativity theory, Werner Heisenberg's uncertainty principle, and the subsequent advances in quantum physics give a scientific reason for us to be less than certain about the nature of (or existence of) reality, but none of these discourses addresses postmodern literary practice exclusively or directly. While Lyotard and Jameson discuss literature, it is not, in this context, their primary concern, and defining literary postmodernism from their perspectives may therefore be problematic. Brian McHale's influential *Postmodernist Fiction* attempts instead to define postmodernism from a strictly literary perspective, by distinguishing it pointedly from its modernist precursor. McHale's definitions do, however, also intersect with Lyotard's notion of the "withdrawal of the real." He argues that modernist fiction is characterized by an "epistemological dominant," and postmodernist fiction by an "ontological dominant" (10). That is, for McHale, modernism is preoccupied with questions of "how we know" and frequently complicates and undercuts the possibility of "true" knowledge. Postmodernism, however, focuses on questions of ontology and on interrogating or undermining the nature of reality and/or existence, perhaps influenced by recent philosophical, economic, or scientific developments.

Also preoccupied with aesthetics, and especially fiction, Linda Hutcheon coins the term "historiographic metafiction" to define her version of postmodernism. Historiographic metafictive texts, argues Hutcheon, both recount historically "real" events and administer a "denaturalizing critique" of them (*Politics of Postmodernism* 3), reminding the reader of the subjective, ideological, and linguistic contributors to the historical text's constructedness. In a variety of books and articles, Hutcheon argues that the self-reflexivity of much postmodern fiction reminds the reader not only of the constructedness of the text they are reading but also of the constructedness of all histories, contributing to the undermining of accepted histories and of hegemonic "reality." With Lyotard, Hutcheon assumes that "reality" and history as we typically see them are not "true," and that postmodern fiction *reminds* us of this "lack of reality," opening up a critical discourse about history itself, which always merely masquerades as reality. While Jameson sees contemporary art and literature as symptoms of the disappearance of reality itself under late capitalism, Hucheon sees postmodern literature as a potentially salutary reminder of the ways in which "reality" has *always been* subjective and ideological.

It is worth noting, then, that despite the wide differences between the social analysis of Baudrillard, Jameson, and Benjamin, the more strictly literary/aesthetic viewpoints of McHale and Hutcheon, and the rarefied air of poststructuralist philosophy, there is a generally implicit agreement that "reality" itself is in withdrawal in "postmodernism," whether the term refers to *all* texts produced by a particular type of society (à la Jameson), or to specific kinds of texts with specific formal features (à la Hutcheon and McHale). Whether the assertion of the "withdrawal of the real" is seen as a universal "truth" (that the only truth is the absence of truth), or as a result of the proliferation of images, discourses, and commodities in an age of postindustrial capital, none of these theorists are willing to insist that reality is accessible, or that postmodern literature attempts mimeticism, or an accurate representation of "reality" in a material, historical, or existential sense. It is this tacit agreement that I wish to challenge.[2]

Even Hutcheon, who identifies postmodernism as "historiographic," insists that what separates it from more traditional historical fiction is that it always reminds the reader that, despite its efforts to represent the historical past, it, in fact, cannot ever do so accurately. *The Book,* in this regard, seems to fit her model since it continually reminds the reader of the degree of construction and ideology in any supposedly objective historical reportage, including its own. The novel not only presents characters and governments whose ideology governs their retelling of history, but it also includes an intrusive narrator, dreamlike anti-realistic episodes, and Kundera as a character, all of which remind the reader of the text's constructedness and its complicity.

It is because of aesthetic features such as these that Hutcheon asserts that postmodern fiction's political impact is necessarily limited. While it may be capable of critiquing putatively objective discourses, it is manifestly incapable, says Hutcheon, of offering an alternative to established or dominant histories. It has no way to "enable[. . .] a move into political action" (*Politics of Postmodernism* 3) because of its admitted incapacity to reference the historical real. From this vantage point, Mirek's efforts to take a political stand are invalidated by his complicity. He has no recourse to truth, but only to his ideological appropriation of the traces of the past.

Within Hutcheon's model, then, *The Book* and postmodern texts like it serve a significant ethical purpose in their capacity to denaturalize (or "de-doxify") discourses once taken to be referential and objective. At the same time, it is filled with a referential, and therefore ethical, despair that contradicts its initial movement. While Mirek and the narrator insist on the necessity of historical referentiality for ethical and/or political resistance, the postmodern reading of the novel marks objective historical reference as impossible and therefore resistance as untenable, at least in the way Mirek suggests. While it is undoubtedly useful to identify ideology and power in the purportedly objective representation of the past, to deny the possibility of historical reference entirely is to abandon a cornerstone of ethical response. Is this really what Kundera's novel suggests? Even as it asserts the necessity of referring to the past, does it, in fact, deny the possibility of such reference and, if so, does this mark postmodern literature more generally as apolitical and nonethical? I begin this book with the assumption and the assertion that such a reading of postmodern fiction is unsatisfactory and that, despite the questions these texts raise about historical reference, "history" and "reference" are categories they nevertheless maintain and redefine out of political and ethical necessity.

It is undoubtedly the case that postmodern texts like Kundera's challenge any possibility of a transparent representation of reality in textual form. However, this complication of reference does not necessarily mean that all access to the real is foreclosed in favor of the models of endless textuality familiar from poststructuralist theory. Instead, I argue that texts like Kundera's complicate and problematize notions of reference precisely in order to suggest a subtler, and therefore more compelling, model of mimesis. In doing so, I do not, however, wish to make a blanket claim about all texts considered postmodern by one critic or another, some of which may in fact suggest the impossibility of historical reference. I follow Hutcheon in my interest in the relationship of postmodernism to history, and I focus closely on that relationship in order to reevaluate it. I do, however, caution against the tendency to view *all* texts with certain characteristics, self-reflexivity foremost among them, as illustrating a particular attitude toward historical referentiality or towards the "real" as generally conceived. For this reason, I call the texts I consider in this study, and others like them, "postmodernist historical fiction," emphasizing their continuity with a tradition of historical fiction that assumes the capacity for historical reference and distinguishing them from this tradition by their deployment of postmodern formal features. These texts are drawn together by three important characteristics, all evident in *The Book:* 1) their commitment to locating the truth of past events, despite their acknowledgment of the manifold barriers to doing so; 2) their use of a variety of innovative formal features, particularly nonnarrative devices, deployed not only to highlight the barriers to transparent reference, but also to theorize and overcome such barriers; and 3) their expression of the ethical necessity to find the real. *The Book* provides, in this introduction, a test case for reevaluating postmodern fiction as a self-theorizing historically referential medium.

In this context, it is important to see that in the opening episodes of *The Book* there is not only an ironic critique of those who claim objectivity while asserting their own ideology, but also a privileging of historical truth for its own sake. Kundera, after all, saves his most savage attacks for those who reject history altogether. Among these is Gustav Husak, labeled the "President of Forgetting" (217) for his role in driving 145 historians from research institutes and universities. In response, the displaced historian Hübl asserts,

"You begin to liquidate a people . . . by taking away its memory. You destroy its books, its culture, its history. . . . Then the people slowly begin to forget what it is and what it was. The world at large forgets it faster" (218). Hübl here expresses the belief that it is possible to connect with the past and to maintain the truth of history. If Husak is to be condemned for his actions, an alternative must be held forward as an inherent possibility. Historians are configured in this episode as the guardians of truth, history, and objectivity, and their disappearance is alarming. Associating *The Book* with a postmodernism that configures "history" as mere signification cannot account for the force with which the novel asserts the ontological "givenness" of the past and its accessibility.

History and the Linguistic Turn

Whereas Linda Hutcheon defines postmodernism by its relationship to history, Fredric Jameson criticizes it for its tendency to merely provide the past as "pastiche," to replace "real" history with a collage-like "pastness" (*Postmodernism* 19). In both cases, it is clear that history, as a purportedly real and referential discourse, and postmodernism, as that which withdraws the real, have a vexed relationship. It is no surprise, then, that poststructuralist and postmodern theorists often discuss the philosophical notion of history, nor that historians eventually find themselves compelled to discuss postmodernism and the linguistic turn. It is necessary to explore both to contextualize my own discussion of postmodernist historical fiction.

While it would be foolish to link postmodern theory to Stalinism, the threat of "forgetting" history that Hübl and Kundera articulate is nevertheless present in both. While Husak (and Stalin) works to erase and replace specific historical facts for ideological purposes, postmodern theory operates from the opposite direction, questioning and redefining the whole notion of what history and memory can be said to be. For this reason, recent efforts in postmodern historiography[3] have, in the wake of foundational postmodern thinkers like Lyotard, and poststructuralists like Derrida, Barthes, and Foucault, questioned the relevance of the entire field of inquiry. In *Why History?*, for example, Keith Jenkins advocates dismissing both the term and the discipline of history altogether (193). For Jenkins, the past is gone and cannot be retrieved, and the desire to do so is merely an attempt to shore up faulty and creaky institutions like the historical profession itself. Elizabeth Deeds Ermath similarly argues that the notion of an objective recovery of the past is inherently false and only illusions remain: "There is *only* subjectivity. There are *only* illusions. And every illusion, because it has no permanently objectifying frame, constitutes reality and hence is totally 'objective' for its duration" (111).

How do Jenkins and Ermath arrive at the notion(s) that history must be abandoned and that any claim to objectively represent (or know, or see, or recount) the past is a fool's errand and a reactionary one? It is, after all, only 120 years since Leopold von Ranke became the most influential historical theorist when he argued that the historian "should wipe himself out" and Fustel de Coulanges similarly declared: "Gentlemen, it is not I, but history that is speaking to you!" (Ankersmit, *History and Tropology* 20). Ranke's promise to present history, "*wie es eigentlich gewesen*" ("as it actually happened"), became the basis for "that noble dream" of historical objectivity that soon dominated the profession, at least in the United States.[4] As Nietzsche's "On Truth and Lie in an Extra-Moral Sense" indicates, however, objections to any simple notion of historical objectivity were already in circulation long before they become the subject of widespread concern in the historical profession. Indeed, Nietzsche's identification of the barriers between language and truth becomes central to the linguistic turn that follows. As Nietzsche notes, "'the thing itself' . . . is quite incomprehensible to the creators of language" (45) and truth is merely a "mobile army of metaphors . . . : illusions about which one has forgotten that this is what they are" (46–47). In this separation of the "thing itself" from its linguistic representation, Nietzsche prefigures the concerns of the (post)structuralists. Not only can language not represent reality, argues Nietzsche, but also the attempt to do so is a lie that serves hegemony. For Nietzsche, "to be truthful is to lie herd-like in a style obligatory to all" (47).

If being truthful in the historical sense is merely to lie about the past in the conventional way, the very basis for the historical profession in its Rankean mode is put into radical question. In fact, the signifier "history" already reveals this problem, as Hegel, Michel de Certeau, and Hayden White have all noted. "History," after all and in several languages, refers both to "the past itself" and to its retelling. While Hegel sees this dual meaning as "of a higher order than mere outward accident" (White, "Value of Narrativity" 11), for White the deployment of two meanings in a single term is purely rhetorical. For White, linguistically eliding the distinction between the past and its representation tacitly makes an argument that these two things *are* the same, an argument White categorically rejects (see also Certeau 21).

The notion that history is merely a linguistic product that has no direct relationship to the "real" of the past is elaborated upon in Roland Barthes's influential "Le discours de l'histoire" ("The Discourse of History," 1967), one of several (post)structuralist statements on the problem of history. Barthes claims, "[H]istorical discourse does not follow the real; rather, it merely signifies it, constantly repeating *this happened,* without this assertion ever being anything but the signified *wrong side* of all historical narration" ("Discourse of History" 139; emphasis in original). Like Saussure, Barthes "brackets" the historical real from the signs that lay claim to it. History is a textual effect, says Barthes, a product of symbolic systems that combine arbitrary signifiers and differential matrices to create a socially constituted meaning. Again, the "linguistic turn" takes place when we see history as a product of historical discourse as opposed to an accurate reflection of what actually occurred.

In fact, however, it is not merely the contention that language cannot refer to the past "objectively" that is of central concern to poststructuralist and postmodern thinkers. For theorists like Certeau and Foucault, in particular, it is more important that history uses its discursive authority to manage and control the present. Certeau argues that history uses language and structure to create the illusion of unity and order. History, he argues, "customarily began with limited evidence ... and it took as its task the sponging of all diversity off of them, unifying everything into coherent comprehension" (78).[5] While a complete and unified understanding of the past might seem to be a laudable goal, Certeau suggests that such a history is that which gives the dominant society of the present a way to define itself against that past. In this, he reveals how a dream of objective and complete comprehension is a means of domination and manipulation. "[I]ntelligibility is established through a relation to the other; it moves (or 'progresses') by changing what it makes of its 'other'—the Indian, the past, the people, the mad, the child, the Third World" (3). In this, Certeau notes how history defines the contemporary world through discourse about the "other" of the past. This definition is then deployed in an effort to define, constrain, and discipline various "others" in the present. Kundera's presentation of Clementis and Gottwald makes a similar point. The Communist Party of the present erases Clementis in order to maintain the unity of their historical narrative. The past "truth" becomes merely an "other" at the service of present ideology, with all notions of objectivity transformed into ideology. While Certeau speaks of power structures that are less vertical and less explicit than those explored in *The Book,* Kundera's novel simplifies and clarifies some of the subtleties of Certeau's claims.

Certeau's position has much in common with the work of Michel Foucault, particularly in his "middle period," encompassing *The Archaeology of Knowledge, Discipline and Punish,* the first volume of *The History of Sexuality,* and "Nietzsche, Genealogy, History." In the last of these, Foucault points to the ways in which origins, truths, and facts are impossible to uncover and argues that history is not the recounting of past events, but mere interpretation without a historical object: "If interpretation were the slow exposure of the meaning hidden in the origin, then only metaphysics could interpret the development of humanity. But if interpretation is the violent or surreptitious appropriation of a system of rules, which in itself has no essential meaning, in order to impose a direction, to bend it to a new will . . . and to subject it to secondary rules, then the development of humanity is a series of interpretations" (86). Foucault's dismissal of metaphysics, a typical poststructuralist position, combined with his denial of any "origin" in philosophy or history, leads to an understanding of all discourse as ideological and therefore perpetuating social domination. History, as one species of "interpretation," serves to establish and circumscribe the rules of society in the name of objective representation. In "Nietzsche, Genealogy, History," then, "[s]tatements do not represent the world but rather bring to light the conditions of emergence of the object of study" (Wyschogrod 35). Like Jenkins some twenty-five years later, Foucault advocates for the dissolution of traditional history, advocating instead a "genealogical" approach that "introduces discontinuity into our being" ("Nietzsche" 88), exposing discourses of power precisely *as* discourse, not as truths.

Following Nietzsche, Foucault identifies the "will to knowledge" (95) with the "will to power," claiming that any effort to understand people or events is necessarily an attempt to dominate those people or control events for one's own purposes. If "all knowledge rests upon injustice" (95), as Foucault claims, then genealogical history is a process of "unknowing," denying the possibility of historical truth. Again, *The Book* reflects Foucauldian critique.[6] Whether it is the erasure of Clementis, or Mirek's treatment of Zdena, journeys into the past in the novel seem always and only to be acts of domination in the present.

A look at how historians have reacted to theorists like Foucault at once affirms poststructuralism's influence and throws some of its more radical assumptions into question. While Foucault has been supremely influential in literary studies for the past twenty-five years, the historical profession's linguistic turn took more time to develop and has only hit its stride in the past fifteen years. Hayden White remains its most influential figure, however, with the publication of his *Metahistory* some thirty-five years ago.[7] What makes the historians' version of the linguistic turn unique is its focus on narrative. Drawing from Barthes's remarks in "The Discourse of History,"[8] White launches an assault on the form that proves enlightening.

Before White's intervention, the historical profession still operated largely under a mimetic model, whereby history was said to reflect, present, or provide the truth of what occurred in the past. As such, the theorization of history was primarily a theorization of research methods, an examination of how best to make use of the archives and unearth the relics of the past.[9] That is, graduate-level historical instruction began, and often ended, with a consideration of how best to obtain and to use sources. It is true that such discussions were sophisticated and did not treat such sources as transparent windows into the past. Nevertheless, once analysis of sources was complete, attention was rarely paid to the role of the historian in retextualizing, or "writing up" the findings derived from the facts or the archives. White's innovation was to consider more closely what occurs after the sources are gathered, in the writing process itself. In doing so, he notes that "we do not look at the past *through* the historian's language, but *from* the vantage point suggested by it" (Ankersmit, *History and Tropology* 65; emphasis in original). In 1996, twenty-three years after the publication of *Metahistory*, White was still noting how "in conventional historical inquiry, the facts established about a specific event are taken to *be* the meaning of that event. . . . But the facts are a function of the meaning assigned to events, not some primitive data that determine what meanings an event can have" ("Modernist Event" 70). Like Foucault, White claims that what we take to be facts are generated by the formal qualities of historical discourse. The form *is* content and, in fact, constructs the facts normally taken to precede it. For White, "form," in this context, typically means narrative.

Narrative and History

Before more clearly defining the critique of narrative undertaken by White and its potential impact on the interpretation of postmodern fiction, it is necessary to provisionally define what "narrative" itself means. Tzvetan Todorov provides a useful beginning when he argues that "there are two types of episode in a narrative: those that describe a state (of equilibrium or of disequilibrium) and those that describe a transition from one state to the other" (51). He additionally argues that narratives typically begin and end in equilibrium, but these states of quiescence are often not identical. Therefore, he insists that "sequence" is essential to narrative, since transitioning from one "state" to another requires a series of chronological events whose relationship is a matter of some debate.

In *Aspects of the Novel*, E. M. Forster influentially tries to identify two different kinds of relationships between sequential events, separating "story" from "plot." Forster argues that while a story is a sequential series of events, a plot is such a series causally connected (86). Applied to Todorov's definition, this would mean that a "plot" suggests that the events narrated would definitively *cause* the transition from one state of affairs to another, while a "story" would merely present a *sequence* of events without necessarily linking them causally. A transition would still occur, but the reader would not necessarily be able to identify the cause. Stories, for Forster, answer the question "and then?" while plots additionally answer the question "why?"

For Forster, plot then serves to *explain* events, bringing them into comprehensibility and order, while story merely presents chronology without explanation. Later developments in narrative theory, however, serve to render the distinction problematic, if not moot. Seymour Chatman explains how any linear presentation of events leads the reader to *assume* causality, even where it is not explicitly stated. In fact, Chatman argues that no chronological presentation can exist without the implied specter of causality haunting it (45–48). The mere process of selecting two events to juxtapose implies that *someone* believes that the two events, while perhaps on the surface merely sequential, have some other (possibly causal) relationship. This is perhaps why Gerald Prince begins his definition in his *Dictionary of Narratology* not with the events narrated but with the origin of the narration. Narrative, for Prince, is, "The recounting (as product and process, object and act, structure and structuration) of one or more real or fictitious events communicated by one, two, or several . . . narrators" (58). In Prince's definition, the "recounting" is central, since it is in the telling that causality, structure, and therefore meaning, are explicitly or implicitly attached. Although these definitions of narrative are capable of capturing a wide variety of "stories," they all imply structure and meaning, in part by reference to the teller, narrator, or author who has selected the material from a potentially infinite morass of real or imagined alternatives.

In the context of narrative history, then, Lawrence Stone offers that "[n]arrative is taken to mean the organization of material into a chronologically sequential order and the focusing of the content into a single coherent story, albeit with subplots" (3). "Material" here implies the raw material of "history" itself, or real events, something not necessary for narrative fiction but assumed (at least provisionally) for history. Stone focuses not on this "material," however, but on its "organization." For Stone, although the linear presentation (*sjuzet* or discourse) of material may not be strictly necessary, the procession of events (the story itself or *fabula*) should be presented to the reader as a chronological series that is invested with meaning, deriving principally from causality and conclusion. Stone, like Prince, focuses on narrative as a structuring principle that omits all events or information that do not fit into its "coherent story." It is this focus on organization and coherence that becomes a central subject of debate for narrativist historiographers like White, along with Forster's nagging question of causality.

According to White, historical narrative, because of its chronological presentation and either explicit or implicit arguments for causation, allows for the interpretation of the past as a plot with inherent meaning. White's central claim, however, is that the past did not occur in this way. Rather, the conglomeration of historical detritus cannot have meaning independent of its narrativization. That is, for White, "reality wears the mask of meaning" in that it appears to have coherence, even deliver a message, but such an appearance conceals the truth. He argues that "the plot of a historical narrative is always an embarrassment and has to be presented as 'found' in the events rather than put there by narrative techniques" ("Value of Narrativity" 20). In this, White asserts that a historian must comb through sources and claim to "find" a pattern or plot that explains past events. In fact, the plot is imposed by the historian, indicating that the narrative form itself is that which removes "history" conceived as discourse from "history" conceived as the past itself.

While elsewhere, White seems to refer to "reality" as a mere articulation of the discourse that discusses it, here he takes a less extreme position by referring to reality as if it does have independent existence, even as narrative "masks" it. Masked within White's own position, however, is the assertion of one truth from which his entire argument follows: that reality is unstructured and therefore meaningless. His division of historical narratives into various distinct "emplotments" then becomes a description of the ways in which the truth of historical meaninglessness is converted into various falsehoods of intelligibility. It is no surprise then, when White shows a marked preference for nonnarrative modes of historical discourse.

The postmodernist historical fiction I will examine over the course of this study similarly critiques narrative's tendency to obscure our access to the past. However, although this fiction is frequently read as if it promotes a thoroughgoing relativism, I argue that it suggests alternative forms as more effective means of accessing the real. In this context, White's preoccupation with annals and chronicles is a useful starting point,[10] for although White insists that these discursive forms also merely present the past "as if" their modes are true, his implication that formlessness is, ironically, the true form the past takes, infers that there are better, more accurate, means of constructing histories than narrative provides. White claims that our notions of historical reality are themselves constructed from the form in which they are most typically offered (narrative) and that our conception of what reality is would be completely different if we operated in a society in which annals or chronicles were the preferred form of presentation. Yet, White's own intimation that narrative cannot be truthful in its account of the past indicates the degree to which perceptions of reality *can* actually differ from the discourses that purportedly produce them. In this, there is the possibility that reality itself may actually govern White's (and therefore anyone's) claims about narrative's interactions with it. Similarly, postmodernist historical fiction plays with form, and particularly with models of narrativity, not merely to expose history's discursivity but to more accurately represent the past itself.

In *The Book*, for instance, a close look at Clementis's hat and Zdena's love letters suggests how reality may not be merely a discursive byproduct of narrative. Instead, reality appears to resist narrative's attempts to explain it. While it is undoubtedly the case that the government attempts to erase those, like Clementis, who do not fit into their "plot" of Czech history, it is equally true that there are truths of the past that are not integrated into that plot and which therefore resist it. The Communist plot is not that which creates reality but that which distorts or effaces it, without ever being able to do so completely. Clementis's hat is the clearest example of this possibility since, despite the efforts of the propaganda machine, it remains "in the picture."

If one considers, however, Hana Píchová's account of *The Book*, the hat seems to be just one more example of a manipulation of reality, not an indicator of its "objective" presence. Píchová notes that the photograph was recently reproduced in its original form in the Czech journal, *Kmen*. In the photo, both Clementis and Gottwald have their own hats, and while Clementis *was* erased from the photo, his hat was as well, leaving (in Kundera's terms) *no* trace of the former leader. Píchová sees Kundera's misrepresentation as part and parcel of his commitment to a postmodern aesthetic that denies the possibility of truthful historical reference, noting that Kundera is here "faithful to infidelity" (102). On the contrary, however, the substantial truth of Kundera's account is proven by Píchová's research. While the hat itself was more fully erased than Kundera claims, it did exist, as does the history of Clementis' presence on the balcony. The discourse of latter-day Communist Bohemia does not create *or* destroy Clementis and his hat. Instead, Clementis' existence eludes its narrative appropriation to such a degree that first *Kmen* and then Píchová herself can reclaim the facts, even if Kundera does not accurately provide them. The hat in *The Book* is paradoxically an indicator and theorization of referentiality, despite, or perhaps because of, its historical inaccuracy.

Kundera, then, describes the past as "irritating, repellent, wounding" (30) precisely because of its capacity to resist narrativization. Clementis is erased in order to construct a narrative that makes sense of Communist rule, but it is always possible that the moment on the balcony will be recovered, resisting its later emplotment. Mirek's final fate illustrates this notion as well, since he is finally jailed for his subversive activities. Rather than be dismayed at this punishment, however, he is satisfied because his mere presence in the prison will resist the Communist vision of an "unstained age of unstained idyll" (33). The Czech government's self-representation is of a beautiful unity, a utopia in which everyone is happy and satisfied. The mere presence of a prison for dissenters exposes the falsehood of this narrative. As such, "Mirek is going to land his whole body on the idyll, like a stain" (33).

Mirek's resistance is not configured as simplistically outside of narrative, discourse, and ideology, however. Rather, he envisions his incarceration as part of an alternative narrative, the story of his own life. In fact, he "could not imagine a better ending to the novel of his life" than his own imprisonment (33). He sees his punishment as precisely that which gives his life meaning, the ending that explains all that precedes it. In this moment, he is able to (re)define his own life as one of idealistic and disinterested resistance, creating a narrative that satisfies his vision of himself, even as he resists the "plot" of his enemies. Once again, however, Mirek's narrative is subverted by Zdena, for although Mirek imagines discarding his love letters to her into a garbage can "as if [they] were besmirched with shit," he cannot do so because she refuses to give them up (24–25). The existence of these letters becomes "unbearable" to Mirek. His past (and potentially present) love for Zdena remains, as does textual evidence of it, despite his efforts to delete it or shape it to his needs. It is clear here that it is not narrative or discourse that constructs the reality in which these characters live. Instead, narrative is merely a strategy they deploy to encompass and explain the real that inevitably exceeds that form. These moments of disjunction between ideological narrative and past experience are, in fact, the moments that the novel suggests are most proximate to the real itself. Clementis' hat, Mirek's imprisonment, and the packet of love letters refer to past moments not fully explicable within their narrative redeployment and, as such, they quietly insist upon the possibility of historical reference. It is true that narrative continually incorporates and subsumes past experience in *The Book,* but it is also true that the real always leaves a "leftover" that cannot be thrown so easily into the garbage can of history. As Nina Pelikan Straus argues, "Kundera is continually referring the reader to an outside-of-the-discourse" that can only be described as the real (71; see also Caldwell 51).

Nowhere is this clearer than in the two connected accounts of the life of Tamina. Like Mirek, Tamina is engaged in the retrospective construction of the past, but unlike him, Tamina does not have an easily identifiable ideological agenda. Rather, she seems to attempt to recall Pavel, her husband, merely for the purpose of keeping his memory alive.[11] Ironically, however, while Mirek wants to forget Zdena, Tamina wishes to remember Pavel. Unfortunately, "her husband's image was irrevocably slipping away" (117). She wishes to recover notebooks she kept during their marriage in order to recapture their past, but when her efforts to do so fail, her subjectivity recedes and she eventually retreats from the world altogether to the oneiric island of children. While Mirek rewrites the past as an act of domination, Tamina's inability to perform such a rewriting leads to a near complete loss of identity, placing humanity itself in an almost untenable position. Memory is faced with the choice of either erasure or ideological emplotment.

In the second section involving Tamina, this double bind of memory is ultimately rejected, however. Tamina finally leaves the small town wherein she spends her exile from Prague. Driven by a man named Raphael, Tamina has committed herself to finally abandoning her husband's memory and, in fact, to forget her forgetting, the empty place her memory once filled (224). Unexpectedly, however, the past reasserts itself. "The landscape took Tamina back to the area of Bohemia . . . where her husband . . . had found his last job. . . . She once went out there to visit him, and they took a walk through a landscape very much like this one. . . . They walked side by side in rubber boots that slipped and sank in mud. They were alone in the world, filled with anguish, love, and despairing concern for each other" (228–29). At the outset of their relationship, Tamina attempts to "keep a diary that would record their life" in chronological and sequential fashion, and after her husband's death she divides a school notebook into eleven sections in an effort to recall and reorder each year of their life together. These attempts at sequential and narrative reconstruction fail, however, and Tamina is about to give up when the memory of their walk leaps up to confront her. She is "thrilled . . . to find . . . a lost fragment of her past" and Tamina comes to realize, too late, that "her husband was still alive" in the sadness that she has at his loss and that "she must go in search of him" (229). Rather than hoping the memories find her, Tamina resolves to voyage "all over the immense world" to locate them (229).[12] This spatialized account of the recovery of the past is contrasted with the textual/sequential attempts in the diary and notebooks, suggesting that the real cannot be found in narrative ordering but only in the contingent and the fragmentary.

Inherent to this encounter with Tamina's past is the distinction between Hegelian "recollection" and memory itself. For Hegel, if memory (or intuition) is the images and feelings that exist in our past and in "the dark depths of our inner being," recollection is that process by which these memories become "our actual possession," are integrated into the ego, and become part of subjectivity (§454). Tamina's effort to "recollect" her past life with her husband fails, but her memory persists, indicating a link to her past that exceeds any attempt to integrate it. Tamina's experiences reflect the distinctions made between involuntary, spontaneous, or unconscious memories and those intentionally brought to consciousness by the subject. In psychoanalytic discourse, involuntary memory is considered most trustworthy because it is not "worked over" by conscious subjectivity. Such distinctions are important in modernist masterpieces like Proust's *À la recherché du temps perdu* (see especially Proust 44–48) and Joyce's *Ulysses* (Rickard 61) but are often considered less important in a postmodernism that assumes that there is no truth independent of signification and therefore that even involuntary memories are not "true" in any essential sense. However, despite the metafictional content of *The Book,* which continually reminds the reader of its constructedness, Tamina's involuntary memory is depicted as a fleeting vision of the real, at least somewhat free of semiotic and ideological appropriation.

Indeed, *The Book,* like Tamina, who is described as both its protagonist and its audience (227), is perpetually in search of such moments, inassimilable to narrative and ideology, and therefore identifiable as real. Within this context, the formal construction of *The Book* indicates its aversion to narrative, and may also be seen as an attempt to avoid the kind of "recollection" that transforms memory into (oppressive) discourse. The narrator describes the book as "a novel in the form of variations" (227). Divided into seven sections, *The Book* does not follow one set of characters through a chronological narrative that would explain them or Prague, the city to which they all are connected. Instead, some characters (Mirek, Zdena) are confined to single sections, while other characters (Tamina, Kundera himself) recur in two sections. Titles of two sections repeat, while three sections' titles do not. There is, of course, design in this organization, but it is not a narrative: a chronological series of events unified into explanation and meaning. Instead, as with the connection between Tamina's present and past, it is a contingent and fragmentary design.

Likewise, Kundera refuses traditional conceptions of history without abandoning the concept of referentiality entirely. In discussing the "historical" importance of the blackbirds' invasion of European cities, for example, Kundera observes, "no one dares to interpret the last two centuries as the history of the invasion of man's cities by the blackbird" (268). However, he argues, this is only because of "a rigid conception of what is important and what is not, and so we fasten our anxious gaze on the important, while from a hiding place behind our backs the unimportant wages a guerilla war, . . . changing the world and pouncing on us by surprise" (268). Tamina's memories "pounce" on her in the fashion of this metaphorical guerilla war. Again, the novel suggests that history, or the real itself, is not the "narratable" actions typically labeled "important" but is that which rises up to take us by surprise and which therefore has the capacity to change the "rigid conception[s]," or dominant discourses, of society. *The Book* is structured in order to allow this kind of "pouncing" to take place. Instead of moving readers linearly toward a clear conclusion, *The Book* provides variations on similar scenes and themes, searching for the real even as it reveals the ideological component of all representations.

If we return, then, to the mechanics of White's critique of narrative, it is clear that he acknowledges that the sequential nature of annals and chronicles do, *per* Chatman, produce a de facto kind of narrative, just as *The Book,* despite its form, can be said to "mean" despite its avoidance of conventional narrative. Nevertheless, unlike typically defined narratives, it is clear that annals (like *The Book)* leave gaps that they make no attempt to fill. That is, annals list years for which there are no corresponding events. In this, White pinpoints narrative's function—to pull together disparate events and to give the impression that they are all related and form a whole: "[T]he presence of these blank years in the annalist's account permits us to perceive, by way of contrast, the extent to which narrative strains to produce the effect of having filled in all the gaps, to put the image of continuity, coherency, and meaning in place of the fantasies of emptiness, need, and frustrated desire that inhabit our nightmares about the destructive power of time" ("Value of Narrativity" 11).

White's view of narrative reflects the view of history presented by Franz Grillparzer, the Viennese dramatist, cited by Nietzsche: "What is history but the way in which the spirit of man apprehends *events impenetrable to him:* . . . substitutes something comprehensible for what is incomprehensible?" (Nietzsche, "On the Uses" 91; Lane 456; emphasis in original).

Central here is the idea that events are inherently impenetrable and that history merely futilely attempts to make them comprehensible. What White reveals, however, is how *narrative* performs this deception while other forms may be less deceptive and therefore less oppressive. That is, annals, chronicles, or themes and variations may confer meaning in a less totalizing way than narrative, and in doing so may reveal more of the "impenetrable" truth of the past itself. While White never commits to such a claim explicitly, it is implicit in his discussion of the ways in which narration takes part in the production of "law, legality, legitimacy, or, more generally *authority*" ("Value of Narrativity" 13; emphasis in original). Narrative's capacity to make what may be random or ideological choices of events for presentation *seem* natural and whole is, to White, a means of naturalizing the social order, or of legitimizing the law. Narrative is, then, a function of "the impulse to moralize reality" (14).

The notion that the narrative form is a means to affirm conventional morality may be a questionable one, since inevitably events might be selected and placed into a narrative in such a way as to promote the immoral or amoral. White's broader point, however, is more compelling. The unifying tendency of narrative, its capacity to exclude and select while simultaneously providing the impression of natural and transparent meaning, obfuscates the barriers to accessing the past and, in so doing, may provide an even stronger such barrier. That is, by obscuring the large degree of selection, exclusion, elision, and erasure of which any account of the historical past must necessarily partake, narrative discourages the pursuit of knowledge of those events and personages that have been excluded. Likewise, events recovered and presented within a narrative form must be made to fit a broader explanation to which they might otherwise be inimical. From here, it is a small step to suggest that narrative has the capacity to falsify real events, although again White never quite makes this assertion.[13] By contrast, *The Book* makes statements both true and false, both fictional and factual, but by self-reflexively highlighting its own constructedness, it encourages interrogation and excavation of additional truths.

While there have been spirited defenses of both the possibility of historical objectivity and narrative's capacity to transmit such objectivity, what is of central interest to me here are the ways in which postmodernist historical fiction expresses a skepticism similar to White's toward narrative's capacity to represent the past. The common critical approach to such skepticism is to see these texts as denying the possibility of historical reference *in toto*, instead of focusing on its critique of the narrative mode in particular. In this, White's own critical fortunes mirror that of the novels I will discuss. White is excoriated by his critics and praised by his fellow travelers for denying the possibility of historical objectivity, when this is not necessarily his primary interest. Instead, there is at least as strong a current in his work that is focused on critiquing a particular form of representation, narrative, and on advocating alternative forms. White argues strongly that narrative not only provides our sense of what reality is, but, in fact, also distorts the truth of that reality. Likewise, he argues that historical discourse should reflect the knowledge of this distortion and not ignore it. It is not surprising, then, that White's greatest reception has been among literary scholars who see such self-awareness in the metafictional historiography of much postmodern fiction and not in the typically less self-canceling texts of the historical profession.

The clearest expression of White's argument for alternative, nonnarrative, forms occurs in the early "The Burden of History" (1966). White argues in this essay not for the mere identification of modes of historical emplotment later undertaken in *Metahistory*, but for a "liberation of the present from *the burden of history*" (41; emphasis in original). In this, White argues that the myth of objective presentation has confined the writing of history to a realistic framework that identifies "the *sole possible form* of historical narration" as that used in "the English novel as it had developed in the late nineteenth century" (41; emphasis in original). White's critique of outdated "realism" leads to his advocacy for historians' employment of the "techniques of literary representation" of the great modernists, encouraging the use of "surrealistic, expressionistic, or existentialist historiography" (43) and the "plunder of psychoanalysis, cybernetics, game theory, and the rest" (47). White calls for these experimental innovations as a means of acknowledging the futility of recapturing the past in a "literally truthful" manner and instead claims that history "can be judged solely in terms of the richness of the metaphors which govern its sequence" (46). He promotes history, then, as literature, to be judged not by its capacity for objectivity, but for its linguistic richness.[14]

This 1966 essay is not, however, an isolated instance in which White expresses a preoccupation with modernist form. Thirty years later, in "The Modernist Event," White returns to this issue, but with a difference. In discussing the traumatic events of the twentieth century, White again critiques narrative by arguing that "the threat posed by the representation of such events as the Holocaust . . . , the assassination of . . . Kennedy, or Martin Luther King, or Gandhi, . . . [is none other] than that of turning them into the subject matter of a narrative" (81). That is, while narrativization "might very well provide a kind of intellectual mastery" of these events, "insofar as the story is identifiable as a story, it can provide no lasting psychic mastery" (81). While narrative may seem to provide a means of coping with traumatic events, our inherent knowledge that such narratives are "mere stories" prevents them from actually serving this purpose. For this reason, "the kinds of antinarrative nonstories produced by literary modernism offer the only prospect for adequate representations of the kind of 'unnatural' events . . . that mark our era" (81). What precisely White means by "adequate representation" is not fully explained, but it is clear that he is privileging nonnarrative representations over narrative ones. White recommends the "psychopathologies" of modernist writing, including "artificial closures, the blockage of narrative, . . . deformation and formal compensations, [and] the dissociation or splitting of narrative functions" (82; Jameson, *Sartre* 210). White's advocacy of alternative forms here exceeds a preference for "linguistic richness." Rather, nonnarrativity is "adequate" to the presentation of history, whereas narrative is not, and what can "adequate" mean in this context except for the truthful portrayal of real (historical) events? Kundera implicitly makes a similar claim in the critique of narrative appropriation of history as performed by Mirek, the Communist Party, and even Tamina, combined with the nonnarrative form of *The Book* and Tamina's brief, and unexpected, encounter with her past.

Nonnarrative, Antinarrative, and the Historical Sublime

Reading White as an advocate of a particular form of historical writing places postmodernist fiction in a new light. Indeed, much of this fiction, like White's work, advocates for different linguistic forms, and particularly nonnarrative approaches, as more effective means of accessing the real of the past. As such, quotation marks around the term "real," standard for any discussion of reality in a postmodern context, are perhaps not as necessary as they appear, and I will henceforth dispense with them in most cases. The postmodernist historical fiction I analyze in this study suggests that where narrative obscures reality while laying claim to it, models of nonnarratability and antinarrativity give us such access without claiming unity and coherence, thus avoiding the type of obfuscation White, Barthes, and other narrativist theorists of history find to be inherent to the form. Each text I discuss provides a different model of nonnarratability or antinarrativity, and all critique narrative's influence on historical referentiality, despite their inevitable dependence upon it to tell their own "stories."

As I have endeavored to provisionally define narrative, it is also necessary to define terms such as antinarrativity and nonnarratability. Simplistically, of course, a definition of these terms should consist of a point-by-point rejection of a definition of narrative. In light of the several definitions offered above, this might mean the rejection of: 1) sequential organization; 2) the frequently asserted fundamental separation of past from present; and 3) any notion of progress, teleology, or closure. Also, what I am calling nonnarrative and/or antinarrative texts may refuse the principles of selection, elision, and erasure that allows for the homogenization of disparate elements of the past into a single, unified story. While the texts I will discuss cannot, of course, include *every* event or personage in a particular segment of the past, they work diligently to present alternative events to traditional histories and/or events that are not easily integrated into a singular narrative. Here, again, *The Book* proves a useful test case, in its nonlinear and disconnected form, its inclusion of events not found in most histories, and in the connection of past to present that Tamina fleetingly locates.

Throughout this study, I use several terms to delineate separate elements or specific characteristics of nonnarratability, in order to explore them more fully. In particular, I separate the term "nonnarrative" or "nonnarratable" from "antinarrative." For nonnarratability, I draw principally from D. A. Miller (*Narrative*) and Peter Brooks (*Reading*), both of whom assert, in the wake of Todorov, that in order for a narrative to commence, an event must occur that brings instability or disequilibrium into a previously stable situation. As such, it requires life-altering circumstances that separate the moment narrative begins from its nonnarratable past. These moments need only be *relatively* life-altering, however, and need not be on a grand scale. In historical discourse, of course, instability is often measured on a "historical" scale, but even this varies depending on the kind of history being told and the kind of historian telling it. One strategy used in postmodernist historical fiction is to focus on the nonnarratable, the period devoid of life-altering events, or focusing on the degree of continuity between past and present as opposed to assuming the kind of discontinuity that is normally a prerequisite to narrative.

By contrast, I use the term *antinarrative* to refer to events so strange, incomprehensible, or inexplicable that they are impossible to comfortably fit into the unity, coherence, and comfort of narrative. While narrative is stimulated by life or world-altering events, narrative also functions by providing mastery over such events, wrestling them through its mechanisms of causality and conclusion into meaning of some kind. As White suggests, however, some events cannot be explained by narrative and do not fit easily into the "conclusions" provided by narrative closure. In the primary texts I read closely, both Virginia Woolf's "moments of being" and Graham Swift's "Here and Now" focus on the capacity of real events to exceed the discourse engendered to contain and explain them. In this, the typical linguistic "turn" seems unsatisfactory in its claims that discourse and language define for us precisely what reality can be said to be. Rather, these novels offer that what is real is precisely that which cannot be rendered satisfactorily in discourse, or at least in narrative.[15] Instead, they suggest alternative modes in which history can be "made present." While narrative theorists have divided the nonnarratable in different ways, this binary division serves my purposes, at least for the moment.[16]

My discussion of antinarrative moments in postmodern fiction dovetails with recent discussions of the historical sublime, invoked by critics like Ann Rigney and Hans Kellner. In defining the sublime, Kellner refers to the inexplicability of certain events, actions, and their causes and, like White, notes the responsibility of the historian to express that opacity in both form and content. He refers negatively to the "beautification by explanation" inherent to narrative (592), but never suggests that avoiding such beautification may lead us closer to the real. Kellner, like White, critiques narrative but does not claim the inherent historical accuracy of nonnarrative techniques, advocating a form of antinarrativity inspired by the historical sublime without giving it epistemological privilege. Postmodernist historical fiction like Virginia Woolf's *Between the Acts* and Graham Swift's *Waterland* does, however, give it that privilege and presents a compelling logic for doing so.

The notion of the historical sublime has become an increasingly fertile one for theorists like Slavoj Žižek, Dominick LaCapra, and Frank Ankersmit. LaCapra, in particular, warns against an overly enthusiastic embrace of trauma, or the sublime unsymbolizable moment, as the only subject of historical investigation (*Writing History* 77; *History in Transit* 11). He acknowledges the necessity of focusing on "sublime moments" but insists that we not allow them to define our encounter with the past, as they do in the models of some theorists.[17] Ankersmit's discussion (*Sublime Historical Experience*) also highlights some of the problems with recent discussions of historical sublimity. Ankersmit defines "sublime historical experiences" as those that constitute "ruptures" between the present and the past and therefore both highlight the gulf between then and now and also engender the efforts to overcome it. This definition illustrates how even definitions of the sublime, often depicted as that realm of experience that resists plotting, take part in the logic of narrativity. Narrative, after all, requires the "transition from one state to the other" (Todorov 51) and comes into being through a kind of "rupture" which destabilizes a previous situation. From this perspective, the "rupture" Ankersmit identifies is merely a prerequisite for narrative and hardly the resistance to it. I suggest, then, that it is more useful to think of sublimity as a connection of present to past, a view to which Ankersmit's theory is ultimately not antithetical.

Keeping in mind the objections to sublimity posed by LaCapra, I position the sublime as only one type of antinarrative strategy. Another type can be seen in my reading of Salman Rushdie's *Midnight's Children*, wherein Saleem's focus on the "errata" generated by his narrative indicates a skepticism towards the capacity of narrative to reproduce the past in its fullness, engendering a need to include events, personages, or ideas that are outside of the unifying narrative construct, or are "disnarrated." While some of these errata may encompass sublime moments, others are largely irrelevant. By mentioning them, however, Rushdie avoids the "beautification" of narrative, constructing a book as messy and inconsistent as the past itself.

While forms antithetical and inimical to narrative take a central role in the depiction of the historical real in postmodernist historical fiction, all of the texts I consider also deploy narrative, the narratable, and the hypernarratable as points of contrast. If an event is narratable when it stimulates narrative desire, creates the disequilibrium necessary to generate a story, and fits easily into a unified sequential progression, it is hypernarratable if its narratability is parodically extreme, stimulating a wealth of stories, or providing the fulfillment of coherence too easily. In particular, both Swift and Rushdie make use of the hypernarratable to provide a stark contrast to their nonnarrative and antinarrative strains, contributing to their theorization of the historical real and the establishment of an ethics that accompanies it.

Ethics and History

The very idea of ethics is, of course, problematic in light of developments in the theorization of postmodernity. That is, in a postmodern world, ethics can no longer mean something as simple as a listed code of behaviors based on judgments derived from previous experience. Indeed, the injunction to follow another's fully articulated code of ethics often strikes postmodern and poststructuralist thinkers as tantamount to violent subjugation. For example, in "Force of Law," Jacques Derrida shows how any assertion of judgment or justice is always and already an expression of violence, both epistemological and literal. If this is the case, any traditional concrete ethical rules, like the Ten Commandments, or Kant's categorical imperative, must, of necessity, also be violent in some fashion, and therefore be unethical. Likewise, in *The Gift of Death* and elsewhere, Derrida notes how "ethics" rests upon notions of "responsibility," but that following an ethical "code" is precisely the opposite of "responsibility," since a person can merely follow "rules" without feeling the weight of, or taking responsibility for, any difficult decision (*Gift* 60–68; see also Bennington 42). If (traditional) ethics is itself unethical (or irresponsible), ethics is nothing but a dead end, or in poststructuralist *parlance,* an "aporia." The Derridean exposé of ethics *as* violence seems, indeed, always to be lurking on the fringes of contemporary ethics, making theorists think twice about articulating what, precisely, we should be *doing* in social practice. Judith Butler, for instance, in "Ethical Ambivalence," asserts, "I've worried that the return to ethics has constituted an escape from politics, and I've also worried that it has meant a certain heightening of moralism and this has made me cry out, as Nietzsche cried out about Hegel, 'Bad Air! Bad Air!'" (15). Butler's own denaturalization of "given" gender categories is a significant blow against patriarchal discriminations that have been based upon essentialist definitions of gender. Her radical politics is then based on destabilizing established "rules" and she understandably expresses discomfort and skepticism towards the notion that "ethics" (behavioral rules) can somehow be helpful in fighting patriarchy.

In this light, Butler, like Derrida and so many other contemporary ethicists, turns to Emmanuel Levinas as a touchstone, reenvisioning Levinas's injunction of openness to the demands of the ("face" of the) Other, without voicing precisely how the Other should be treated, who the Other might be, and what this might mean for daily or historical behavior. "The ethical relation is that of a passivity beyond passivity, one that escapes from the binary opposition of passive and active; it is an 'effacement,' a 'bad conscience,' a primordial exposure to the Other, to the face of the Other, to the demand that is made by the face of the Other" (Butler 27n2). For Levinas, the ethical is a matter of response to the Other's "right to be—not by reference to the abstraction of some anonymous law, some juridical entity, but in fear of the Other" ("Bad Conscience" 38). This ethics is not, then, ethics in any traditional sense, but is rather an effort to imagine an ethics, perhaps a postmodern ethics, when traditional approaches become impossible.[18]

It may be, in fact, the anxiety about the possibility of the loss of ethics that has engendered the recent "ethical turn" in the humanities. That is, ethics becomes a subject of fascination precisely because of its theoretical impossibility. While some ethics studies discuss the (im)possibility of defining the term in an age of postmodernity, others suggest that we have now reached a time beyond (or "post") the "postmodern," where ethics can once again take a central role. Even in these latter cases, however, it is rare to find a theorist whose "post-postmodern" claims include a substantial rejection of poststructuralism. The challenge, instead, is to articulate the possibility of an ethics within, or following, such philosophy.

Perhaps this quandary is best expressed by looking at the origins of the recent "ethical turn." Martha Nussbaum has observed how the humanities' revived interest in the ethical corresponds in large part not with a turn *against* poststructuralist "relativism," but precisely in a turn *by* poststructuralism towards ethics, particularly in the wake of Paul de Man's posthumous exposure as a one-time Nazi sympathizer. Barbara Johnson's *A World of Difference*, J. Hillis Miller's *The Ethics of Reading*, and Derrida's *Politics of Friendship*, in light of the de Man affair, all mark attempts by some of the foremost poststructuralist theorists to claim poststructuralism *as* a frequently misconstrued ethical discipline (Nussbaum 29; Parker 32).[19] In fact, Derrida's interest in Levinas dates back to at least 1964 (the French publication date of "Violence and Metaphysics") making a clear narrative of his progress towards ethical concerns problematic. It is true, however, that Derrida's late focus on ethics is indicative of a broader "ethical turn," even if Derrida may most often be invoking ethics in order to deconstruct it.[20]

Despite the increased *interest* in ethics, then, thinkers influenced by poststructuralism are not everywhere jettisoning their avowed critiques of reference, objectivity, and Enlightenment rationality in order to return to a codified, "reasonable" collection of rules. Rather, this branch of the ethical turn insists on either configuring hermeneutic indeterminacy *as* an ethics in itself (as in Levinas) or in reevaluating what ethics *can* be if we assume all of the problems of reference, objectivity, and rationality that poststructuralist thought has brought to bear. That is, the ethical turn is largely not a turn *against* poststructuralism, but is rather a turn *within* it that attempts to articulate how it may be possible to have both an inveterate skepticism towards universality and reference and a commitment to ethical causes and political action.[21]

For this reason, the discussion of ethics within the context of history is so often not, as one might expect, a discussion of the ethical (or unethical) behaviors of the past and how they might apply to our present. Such discussions run aground for all of the reasons discussed above. If Mirek's divisions of "men against power" and "memory vs. forgetting" are false because "man" is always asserting power and "memory" is merely a reconstruction that simultaneously forgets and oppresses, then ethics built upon historical experience must be rejected. That is, if we cannot say with any confidence what actually occurred in the past, but only what discursive constructs are present in that past's multitudinous texts, it becomes much more difficult to determine if the human actions taken were, or are, ethical. Likewise, even if making such an ethical judgment about past actions is deemed possible, the notion of transferring such lessons to our present in the form of a concrete set of rules is rejected in much contemporary ethical theory due to the irreducibility of the singular event and the epistemological violence it would take to wrestle certain lessons from one context into another.

Within this framework, it is not surprising to note that the editors of a recent collection, *The Ethics of History,* find the common link between the essays to be what one would at one time have been a distinctly antihistorical approach. "Explicitly or implicitly, each [author] accepts Michel de Certeau's thesis of an unbridgeable gap between the past and the historian's present account" (Carr, Flynn, and Makkreel ix). Because of this, each author wishes to revise "the popular appeal to historical *objectivity*" (ix; emphasis in original). That is, where once the "noble dream" and the ethical commitment of the historical profession was to represent the past with the greatest degree of objectivity (despite consistent acknowledgment of the difficulty of this venture), now the "ethical" endeavor is to reject such an attempt as impossible.

Paradigmatically, Edith Wyschogrod, a contributor to the anthology, defines history not as objective description but as a "double passion; an eros for the past and an ardor for the others in whose name there is a felt urgency to speak" (*Ethics* xi). "Because the past is irrecoverable," Wyschogrod asserts (xii), the practice of history is described as speaking in the "stead" of the "others" that cannot speak. Wyschogrod defines history as an ethical practice only insofar as it acknowledges the impossibility of "recovering," knowing, and reporting the past in any complete fashion, while expressing a passionate desire to do just that. As such, history is impossible from its inception, and it is this impossibility that somehow constitutes its ethics.

Wyschogrod's ethics, while compelling, is comprised of acknowledged "lies" to the dead (the "nameless others") in the form of an assertion of truth ("I, here, now vouch for what I say" [xiii]). But from what position can this historian vouch for what she says, when "truth" is already a rejected category? For Wyschogrod, this vouchsafing derives from the commitment and positionality of the "heterological historian" whose passion for the recovery of lost voices exceeds any account of the objective past. The heterological historian "is a radically new persona" (38) that acts along the lines of a Borges *ficcion*. "The premises, the metaphysical conceits of a narrative, are exhibited in the narrative itself, a disclosure that brings to the fore the discursive practices in which the narrative is embedded" (39). Like Foucault, says Wyschogrod, a heterological historian will combine speaking "for the nameless others" with an effort to expose and enumerate discourses of power. This latter will be accomplished by self-consciously "bringing to the fore" the underlying ideology and assumptions of her own discourse. That is, the heterological historian will act in the fashion of a postmodern writer of metafiction. Passion for the unreachable "others" of the past, self-reflexivity, and an acknowledged rejection of objectivity are, for Wyschogrod, the new version of historical ethics. In fact, Wyschogrod, like Butler, reflects the common trend in recent criticism to champion Levinas as the principal touchstone for ethics. Levinas's insistence on acknowledging the "Other" as inalterably other, and therefore inassimilable to the knowledge or subjectivity of the self, acts as a counterbalance to the threat of knowledge as an unavoidable assertion of power. The postmodern "withdrawal of the real" becomes the ethical itself.[22]

Wyschogrod here expresses some of the difficult contradictions of postmodern thought. She expresses an ethical commitment to fighting ideological oppression and to giving a voice to many who have been denied one. At the same time, because of her allegiance to poststructuralist philosophy, she acknowledges the impossibility of recovering and recounting the facts or "truth" of past oppression. In a central example, Wyschogrod insists upon the ethical imperative to give voice to those exterminated during the Holocaust, but she must finally admit the impossibility of recovering the event itself, and its participants, in an objective, truthful, or factual way.

From the point of view of someone like Wyschogrod, influenced heavily by poststructuralism and by middle-period Foucault, the insistence on such outmoded concepts as objectivity, truth, or facts can only be read as signifiers of a retrograde and reactionary politics. From this perspective, the discourse of truth is merely a way of exerting power over others. However, this vision of epistemology, while rhetorically useful, cannot completely account for the utility of terms like "truth" and "knowledge" for a radical or oppositional politics.[23] In fact, historical accuracy may well be a necessity for attacks on essentialism of other kinds. Certainly, a naïvely traditional approach to history that views its standard presentation as transparently mimetic does not allow for the exposure of rhetoric, propaganda, and ideology often just beneath its surface. It is, however, equally problematic to categorically deny the possibility that an accurate presentation of the past is possible. As Norman Geras argues in *The New Left Review*, "If there is no truth, there is no injustice . . . if truth is wholly relativized or internalized to particular discourses or language games . . . there is no injustice. . . . The victims and protestors . . . are deprived of their last and often best weapon, that of telling what really happened. They can only tell their story, which is something else. Morally and politically . . . anything goes" (110, 125). Here Geras insists that the first step to fighting injustice is not merely identifying and deconstructing dominant discourses, but is rather in uncovering and affirming the existence of oppressive behavior. As Geras indicates, it is imperative to be able to say what really happened, even if our only accounts of those events are from the oppressor. In fact, far from undermining hegemonic discourse, Lena Petrovic expresses concern that the postmodern "withdrawal of the real" contributes to it: "[W]hen . . . as counterstrategy to the terror of the political logic of the same, the postmodern theorists prescribe a universal multiplicity—of language games, of free interpretations, of subject positions, none of which lay claim to superior truth or justice—they end up as champions of compulsory epistemological and ethical relativism that is fatal . . . to one of the strategies of self-defense against the power of dominant culture" (57).

In this light, I want to point to the possibility that, paradoxically, poststructuralist denaturalization and antifoundationalism may *need* some recourse to objective historical reference, even as such discourses busily reject it. For third-wave feminist theory, for instance, the category of "woman" can only be a functional one because of *historical* divisions between genders, both discursive and experiential. It is ironically because of the history of oppression that feminists can articulate women as a group engaged in liberation, even as third-wave feminists question or undermine the essential definition of "woman." If we cannot rely on history as something identifiable, locatable, and confirmable, then such radical discourses are subtly, but significantly, undermined.

Similarly, as bell hooks notes in "Postmodern Blackness," the resistance to postmodernism in the African American community has come largely from a fear that a rejection of an essential black identity will necessarily lead to a loss of history and, therefore, communal identity. "The unwillingness to critique essentialism on the part of many African-Americans is rooted in the fear that it will cause folks to lose sight of the specific history and experience of African-Americans and the unique sensibilities and culture that arise from that experience" (2483). In fact, however, an insistence on the identifiable history of the African American community can provide an alternative definition of race that rejects essential definitions based on "one drop of blood," skin color, or parentage. A definition that is based on historical experience, and is therefore diachronic and continually adjustable, can then replace definitions that are fixed and synchronic. As hooks notes, "We have too long had imposed upon us from both the outside and the inside a narrow, constricting notion of blackness" (2482). The history of the black "race" has enough variety and complexity to conquer this problem, but only if history can be said to be accessible, not merely in the discourses that construct race, but also in the black experience. Neil Gotanda's separation of the singular term "race," into several alternative definitions indicates the importance of history to racial construction. For Gotanda, "formal-race" refers to the external, supposedly neutral, phenotypic characteristics ascribed by societal discourse, while "historical race" refers to the combination of societal inscription and communal identification that has created race as currently constituted (257). By pointing out the key distinctions between essentialist and historical definitions, Gotanda indirectly indicates how approaches that relativize history may undermine potential redefinition and liberation of oppressed peoples. This is not to say that we must claim that reference to the past is simple and transparent, but that accepting its impossibility as an article of faith is equally problematic.

In their treatment of ethics, then, radically postmodern approaches to history lose their utility. Keith Jenkins exemplifies such an approach through his interpretation of Levinas, Derrida, and Lyotard. He defines ethics by the traditional definition of a series of rules for behavior, but insists that in order for an act to be "moral" it must be unique and personal. From this perspective, no decision can be moral if it merely refers to a series of already established rules. Therefore, "ethics (ethical systems) flounder before the unique choice. It is no good having a history here to 'tell you what to do,' to apply one of its 'lessons'" (*Why History?* 21). Instead, as Derrida argues in *The Gift of Death* and elsewhere, "[a] decision that didn't go through the ordeal of the undecidable would not be a free decision" ("Deconstruction of Actuality" 30). In this context, Jenkins argues that the present moment, the moment of the ethical decision, cannot be dictated by a series of rules derived from the observation of history. His reasons for this are manifold but rest primarily on the notion that the past is inexplicable, sublime, and therefore inaccessible in the kind of rational discourse that would be required to articulate its lessons. That is, although it may be possible to have cognitive or empirical knowledge about the past, these can have no relationship to "regulative and normative notions" that would give us ethical rules (*Why History?* 81).

According to Lyotard, any effort to "equate" cognition with regulation and to "learn from history" is a "category mistake," or a "negative lesson on the sheer contingency of all such events" (Lyotard, *Postmodern Explained* 12–15). That is, because each event is unique, a "singularity," turning to the past to make ethical decisions in the present is fruitless. A view of the past as inalterably "past," and beyond interpretation leads to the notion that the past has no utility for us, and "morality" can only be based on the "madness" of the present decision (Jenkins, *Why History?* 21, 49; Laclau 53; Derrida, *Gift of Death* 66). While this claim may be theoretically helpful in its interrogation of specific ethical systems, to reject history carte blanche in terms of its usefulness for making moral or ethical judgments is unsubstantiated. While it is true that no contemporary event will *exactly* reproduce the circumstances of the rise of Nazism and the Final Solution, or the initiation of the slave trade, or the extermination of the native inhabitants of the Americas, our knowledge of such events *may be* helpful to us in opposing atrocities in the future.

When a rhetoric of extreme nationalism, accompanied by arguments for racial purity, arise in a contemporary situation, for instance, we would do well to hark back to Europe's fascist past and take it as a warning against the questionable actions that might follow the rhetoric. To say that our approach to the contemporary event must be made on the basis of an ungrounded "madness" seems unwise, since the past does provide us with indications of (at the very least) things of which to be leery, even if there is no guarantee that the results of somewhat parallel events will be identical. From this perspective, the recent U.S. intervention in the Persian Gulf has been justifiably critiqued precisely because of the similarities between these actions and those in Vietnam forty years previous. Ethical atrocities may arise out of unpredicated circumstances, but to claim that the past has *no* relevance to ethical decisions in the present is irresponsible. After all, we have nothing else with which to make judgments, and surely the ethical thing is to do our best to achieve a desirable outcome given the information we have. To ignore the information seems not "moral," in Jenkins's terms, but exactly the opposite, making decisions willy-nilly, with potentially disastrous results. That is, to completely sever the relationship between cognition and action is to advocate random and irrational decision making. This is, of course, part of the point of much postmodern theory, where Enlightenment reason is frequently under attack, but an antipathy to Rationalism writ large need not lead to the abandonment of individual decisions based on past experience, as if they were somehow identical. To make this claim is to not only undermine the basis of oppression but also that of resistance. As such, the dissolution of history, materiality, and ethics that Jenkins advocates should be reexamined and rejected, as the texts I discuss in this book largely do.

Indeed, it is important to acknowledge that even those thinkers most committed to indeterminacy and who consider the turn to ethics as potentially "Bad Air!" must, in the end, admit their own investment in concepts of ethics, morality, and justice, which, in turn, rely upon seemingly outmoded concepts of historical reference. Butler, for instance, argues that any purportedly universal ethics is inevitably a particularist one that reflects traditional and oppressive ideology. While this may be the case, reversing the relevant terms reintroduces the necessity of ethics even in its repudiation. That is, if we are to come to any conclusions about the necessity of opposing both the ideology and the deeds of longstanding power structures like bourgeois patriarchy, heteronormativity, whiteness, etc., we can only do so from an ethical/moral position that indicates that the "right" thing to do is to work against oppressive power. Ethics is already present in Butler's case against it, something she finally admits, precipitating her turn to Levinas.

Levinas himself is not, however, free from this contradiction. The "passivity beyond passivity" that he invokes is, indeed, difficult to define, and does not always align with pacifism, or even inaction, as such. Levinas asserts in "Judaism and Revolution" that, "Unquestionably, violent action against Evil is necessary" (*Nine Talmudic Writings* 109). This firm claim is not based, however, on what he asserts as his own ethics, the confrontation with the face of the Other. Rather, as Robert Bernasconi notes in his discussion of Levinas, the face of the Other does not tell one what to do in any given situation. Instead, it "simply establishes a responsibility that one cannot evade" (33). This whole species of thought is connected to that avoidance of traditional ethics that Jenkins advocates, wherein the "impossibility of ever knowing what the right thing to do is combined with the impossibility of being indifferent so that one must do something" (Bernasconi 33). While there is some wisdom in the notion that we may be wrong no matter what we choose to do, it is precisely here where knowledge of the past is most useful to us and can help us make choices. Knowing the right thing to do may never be a sure thing, but becomes more possible within the context of historical knowledge. How else can Levinas claim that violence against evil is necessary? Surely it is only in the context of past events, undoubtedly Nazi aggression among them, that Levinas confidently asserts that violence is, in certain instances, necessary.

I do not suggest, then, that one can ever be completely sure of what, in all circumstances, can be considered ethical, but that ethics is a precondition for action, not an avoidance of it, and as such, it is not inimical to politics as Butler initially suggests. Ethics and politics are, rather, inextricably related, and morality, while a more tainted term,[24] is bound to them as well. In all cases, however, maintaining the possibility of accessing and representing our past, as well as our present, is necessary for any discussion and delineation of these terms. That is, a refusal of the possibility of accessing history is a simultaneous refusal of ethics and morality: an unacceptable refusal, certainly. I do not wish, in this claim or in this study more generally, to unlearn the lessons of poststructuralism. The complication of linguistic reference, along with the revelation of ideology beneath seemingly naturalistic and transparent discourse is essential to the construction of ethics and morality, not inherently opposed to them. Žižek's refusal to abandon either term of the either/or question of "Class Struggle or Postmodernism?" is instructive. Like Groucho Marx, and perhaps Karl as well, Žižek responds to this question with "Yes, please!" asserting a fundamental need for both linguistic skepticism and class struggle, even though the latter is based upon materiality and postmodernism is frequently defined as its dissolution.

Remembering as Forgetting

Throughout this book, then, I argue that it is crucial to see that Mirek may be right, despite his own compromised subject position. The fight against power is predicated upon the accessibility of the past, even if those accessing it may also be guilty of asserting discourses of power. Kundera's own assertion of ethics, both in *The Book* and elsewhere, however, initially seems to more closely resemble that of poststructuralist thinkers than a more traditional model of a guidebook for prescribed behaviors. In *The Art of the Novel,* for instance, Kundera champions the novel form precisely because of its capacity to deny notions of metaphysical truth and to instead insist on "relativity, doubt, questioning" (14). Indeed, in that book Kundera argues for seeing the "world as ambiguity . . . not a single absolute truth but a welter of contradictory truths" (6–7). In this, the only "certainty" is the "wisdom of uncertainty" (7). Kundera's "wisdom of uncertainty" sounds strikingly similar to contemporary ethicists' injunctions to acknowledge the otherness of the Other. That is, if the Foucauldian "will to knowledge" is a "will to power," the only ethical response is an acknowledgment of the degree to which we cannot "know" things in their entirety, to resist totalization, or, for Kundera, "Totalitarian Truth" (*Art of the Novel* 14).

A similar position is forwarded in *The Book,* where the "circle-dance" is a recurring image of an agreed-upon univocal meaning that excludes and/or oppresses any Other who is not part of the dance. For Kundera, those who put their faith in Communism are victims of ideological essentialism, or, in his more user-friendly terms, are "circle-dancers." While Kundera acknowledges the attractions of essentialist ideological discourse ("I too once danced in a ring" [91]), he clearly rejects it when he describes the idyll, another version of the circle-dance.

> I emphasize: *idyll* and *for all,* because all human beings have always aspired to an idyll, to that garden where nightingales sing, to that realm of harmony where the world does not rise up as a stranger against man and man against other men, but rather where the world and all men are shaped from one and the same matter. There, everyone is a note in a sublime Bach fugue, and anyone who refuses to be one is . . . caught and crushed between thumb and finger like a flea. (11)

The attempt to reduce the Other to the self is clearly seen here, as anyone who refuses to be subsumed within the singular discourse, narrative, or circle-dance is eliminated. Kundera, then, seems to deny any totalizing narrative, even a master narrative premised on equality ("justice for all"), because the closed circle of the idyll will "crush" those it does not encompass.

For Kundera, however, this rejection of a singular vision of Truth is not inherently linked to a rejection of historical reference. Instead, the historical real, as we have seen, is precisely that which slips through the proverbial fingers of ideological unity. Mirek's imprisonment eludes the idyll of Communist Bohemia, just as Zdena's letters elude Mirek's. In this, the "wisdom of uncertainty" is itself linked to materiality. It is the truth of past events that prevents the circle from being irremediably closed. In fact, as in White's theory, the only truth of reality is its resistance to such attempts at unity.

It is perhaps for this reason that *The Book* ends with a meditation on "the border" between the postmodern "withdrawal of the real" and the confident assertion of Truth. On one side of the border resides "love, convictions, faith, history," while on the other side these things "no longer ha[ve] meaning" (281). This meditation repeats the comparison of angelic laughter with its diabolic counterpart earlier in the novel. Angelic laughter is configured as a celebration of "how well ordered, wisely conceived, good, and meaningful everything is" (87), while devil's laughter "refuses to grant any rational meaning to that divinely created world" (86). While much of this section of *The Book* seems to be dedicated to the mockery of the angelic laughers, just as much of the novel is devoted to a critique of idylls or circle-dances, here, as in the final section, the Kundera-narrator insists not only that if "there were too much incontestable meaning in the world, . . . man would succumb under its weight" but also that if "the world were to lose all its meaning . . . we could not live either" (86). Postmodern meaninglessness, then, comes under a critique equal to the attack on totalizing meaning. Indeed, the claim that there is no meaning, no truth, and no reference is a version of totalization that denies the tools we do have both to access the past and to construct an ethics in response to our encounter with it.

Like Mirek, in fact, Kundera insists upon the capacity of language to represent the past, although he does so in a less binary and simplistic fashion than his character. In *Testaments Betrayed* (1993), Kundera asserts that "[w]e know reality only in the past tense. We do not know it as it is in the present, in the moment, when it's happening, when it *is*. The present moment is unlike the memory of it. Remembering is not the negative of forgetting. Remembering is a form of forgetting" (128). It would be easy to read this statement as a simply "postmodern" one, asserting, even mourning, the "withdrawal of the real," but to do so would be to deny the statement itself, as well as the subject matter of the essay in which it appears. Rather than offering that the evanescent "present" is the real and the past is irretrievably missing, Kundera asserts the opposite, that the present is unknowable but that reality *is* knowable, if only in its past form. While Kundera does observe the instant conversion of present materiality into "abstraction" (or, perhaps, signifying practices), he simultaneously sees literature as a variably successful effort to resist the "loss of the fleeting reality of the present" (129). All of this is part and parcel of Kundera's assertion that literary criticism, in imposing moralizing or theoretical homogenization on literature, reduces it to kitsch, "throw[ing] a veil of commonplaces over the present moment, in order that the face of the real will disappear" (146). For Kundera, the "face of the real" is found in literature, and particularly, the novel, while theory inevitably totalizes meaning, even when it is a theory that denies totalization. As such, he would no doubt object to my effort to see literature in the context of historiographic theory. Nevertheless, I argue that postmodern literature is dedicated to unveiling the "face of the real" and not to merely declaring that there is nothing beneath the veil. Indeed, Kundera's conception of the "present moment" as a crucial element in revealing reality is addressed by both Woolf and Swift, who try not merely to recover the present, but to establish its peculiar character.

The Real, The True, and The Told, then, operates from the assumption that the ties between ethics and history are not merely ones derived from despair at the impossibility of reference. While it may be "ethical" within the historical profession to acknowledge the impossibility of complete, transparent reference to the past, the ethics of history should go beyond the ethics of the practice of history and also entail some understanding of how, in a more general sense, ethics can only be derived from past experience. Since the present is so fleeting as to be gone the instant it has arrived, the past becomes that vast repository for nearly all human experience, and the capacity to access that past and to base future actions upon them is not a combination of reactionary politics and epistemological impossibility, but is instead a difficult necessity.

The mere necessity for the capacity to transfer both observations about the world and construct a workable ethics based upon that observation does not, of course, guarantee that such reference is possible. I do not then suggest that the texts I study here guarantee the possibility of reference, but that they both insist upon it and offer new ways to think about it that contribute to the discourse about these matters in important ways. The theoretical hegemony of poststructuralism has led to the widespread interpretation of postmodern texts as merely rearticulating poststructuralist dogma in regard to historical reference. These texts do no such thing. Instead, the postmodernist historical fiction I analyze takes both political and ethical positions based upon the events of the past, but does so only after acknowledging the barriers to historical reference and theorizing some possible ways to overcome these barriers, particularly that of narrative. The first three chapters of this book look closely at novels that offer versions of nonnarrative or antinarrative as a means of accessing the past. Woolf's *Between the Acts* focuses on women's oppression at the hands of patriarchal history and narrative and offers alternative forms of historical representation as a means of telling the truth about women's oppression. Similarly, Swift's *Waterland* explores how narrative works to repress the past of the working class, as well as of traumatic events, and offers representational forms that might ethically recover such events. Finally, Rushdie's *Midnight's Children* provides a critique of both colonial England's and Indira Gandhi's management of the historical truth. Rushdie takes the ethical position that a truer history can, and must, be told, through a critique of these hegemonic narratives, and a turn to alternative forms of historical representation. Like White, these authors critique narrative as a form that misrepresents the past, but do so from a position that insists that a more accurate version of the past is both possible and ethically necessary.

In chapter 4, I turn to a discussion of the single most debated area of historical representation, that of the Holocaust. Through a close reading of Art Spiegelman's *Maus,* I explore recent theoretical models, like that of Frank Ankersmit, which advocate historical representation as a means not merely of presenting epistemological truth but also as a medium for conveying the affect of past experience. Ankersmit's division of truth and experience helps explain why a text like *Maus* can be dedicated to an ethical witnessing of the Holocaust, while simultaneously highlighting its own distance from and mediation of that event. From this perspective, I will indicate how postmodern form can be read as a type of mimeticism in relation to the Holocaust, and how this model might be applied to historical studies more generally. To read postmodern fiction (and, in this case, nonfiction) as mimetic, and as theorizing mimeticism, may be counterintuitive, but it has the advantage of revealing both the ethical imperative in these texts and the dependency of ethics upon reference. While I do not, then, claim that these writers have untied the Gordian knot of historical reference, these works do have much to teach us about the social, political, and ethical importance of accessing the materiality of the past, and about the formal capacity for doing so. Each chapter of this book, then, suggests how the text in question has been typically read as postmodern in its complication and ultimate rejection of the possibility of historical reference. By contrast, I argue that these books deploy nonnarrative and antinarrative strains in order to critique narrative as a means of accessing the past, while proposing alternative means to historical referentiality, particularly out of ethical necessity. These texts highlight the degree to which narrative itself may be seen as a barrier to historical accuracy and suggest several different ways of hurdling that barrier.

CHAPTER 1

The Pageantry of the Past and the Reflection of the Present

History, Reality, and Feminism in Virginia Woolf's
Between the Acts

> [I]s it not possible . . . that things we have felt with great intensity have an existence independent of our minds: are in fact still in existence?
> —Virginia Woolf, "A Sketch of the Past" (*Moments of Being* 67)

> *[T]he present itself is only the most contracted level of the past.* . . . *it is pure present and pure past, pure perception and pure recollection as such, pure matter and pure memory* . . .
> —Gilles Deleuze, *Bergsonism* (74; emphasis in original)

Written by one of the most canonical modernists, Virginia Woolf's final novel, *Between the Acts* (1941), has been more recently identified as a forerunner of postmodernism, and particularly of postmodern attitudes towards history. In fact, as Werner Deiman notes, it has "an almost obsessive preoccupation with history on virtually every page" (56). However, as in most of Woolf's work, locating one position that the novel takes on the conceptualization of history is extremely difficult, as she is a master of ambiguity, playing each character's perspectives off of all the others. What is clear, however, is that the novel does not accept traditional histories uncritically, equating their representations with the truth of past events.

Over the course of this chapter, I will show how *Between the Acts* both foresees and challenges the problems of historical representation outlined in the introduction. In the novel, Woolf muddies distinctions between fact and fiction, art and history, and memory and narrative in order to question, problematize, and deconstruct public discourse about the most proper and accurate modes of historiography. In doing so, however, she does not, as some have suggested, abandon the possibility of accurate historical representation altogether, nor does she champion ambiguity as an ethics in itself. Long before Hayden White, Woolf's novel rejects narrative as the ideal mode of historical representation. Instead, it insists on nonnarrative, using the present itself as a theoretical building block and focusing on moments "between the acts" as opposed to the climactic actions that generate narrative. These strategies contribute to Woolf's feminist vision of a world not dictated by patriarchal forms and therefore open to the possibility of peace.

The Picture and the Portrait

Between the Acts takes place on the day of an annual village pageant, presenting "Scenes from English History" (81). Well before the reader knows the subject of the pageant, however, "history" is introduced. Lucy Swithin is seen reading an *Outline of History*,[1] which describes an antediluvian London populated by "the iguanodon, the mammoth, and the mastodon; from whom . . . we descend" (8–9). Lucy's long view of time is complemented by the more traditional accounts of national history in the pageant, and a comic look at the family history of the Olivers.

The last of these is emphasized by the two portraits at the top of the stairs in Pointz Hall: a "long lady" and a "man holding his horse by the rein." The lady is described as a "picture," purchased for aesthetic reasons, while "the man was an ancestor. He had a name" (36). The juxtaposition of the two paintings initially seems to offer the reader the typically "modernist" distinction between art and life, with the former an independent and autonomous project, and the latter linked to history and politics.[2] In Allen McLaurin's discussion of the novel, he uses the two paintings to focus on Woolf's formalism, asserting that Woolf approves of the independent artistry of the "picture" because of its "pure form" while disapproving of the contamination of the portrait by social and worldly concerns. McLaurin allies Woolf's aestheticism with the formalism of her friend and fellow member of the Bloomsbury circle, Roger Fry, who insists that "the essential aesthetic quality . . . has to do with pure form" and that "the value of the aesthetic emotion" is "infinitely removed from . . . ethical values and likewise from the concerns of history and politics" (54).[3] The "picture," from this perspective, is a floating signifier with no referent, while the portrait signifies something beyond itself: the external world, or reality.

No sooner, however, is this separation of art and life introduced than it is undermined. Although the ancestor has all the weight of reality and history initially attached to him, the reader soon learns that the portrait excludes, omits, and deletes elements of his past in an effort to configure it as history. While Buster the horse is included in the portrait, Colin, the "famous hound," is omitted because the "Reverend Whatshisname" would not allow him at the sitting. Immediately, Colin's exclusion puts the mimetic claim of the portrait into question, as it only selects certain elements of the ancestor's life and personality. It later becomes clear, however, that Colin has not been lost to history but has been amply recorded elsewhere. Bartholomew Oliver, Lucy's brother, asserts, "The dog has a place in history" (48), noting how one text's process of selection and excision is not the limit of history's resources.

Lodged within the lighthearted discussion of Colin is a commentary on the nature of historical representation. The dog's situation indicates the propensity for historical representation to exclude, omit, and select elements of the past, determining what is to be considered "important." Likewise, because the ancestor records Colin's existence elsewhere, his absence from the portrait becomes a central fact of the ancestor's history, leading Lucy to identify the ancestor purely by his desire to be painted with the dog (48–49). In fact, while Colin's name is emphasized, the ancestor's individuality recedes, left unnamed, and determined by the absence of his pet. In this microcosm, it is clear that historical discourse makes what is selected *seem* essential, while omitting other potentially important facts.

Seeing how the ancestor's portrait is constructed, framed, and manipulated for aesthetic and ideological content, one might then be tempted to see it as essentially identical with the lady's picture, as two examples of "art" or even "fiction." There are still, however, substantial differences between the ancestor's portrait and the lady's picture. As David McWhirter observes, the lady has more in common with Colin than she does with the ancestor, due to her lack of social power. In fact, her "formal perfection—the objectification of her beauty in the male artist's 'picture'—is inseparable from her gendered powerlessness, her absence from history and its discourses" (806). While the portrait is revealed to be closer to "art" than to objectively referential "history" in its posed, mediated, and constructed form, the supposedly "pure" form of the picture is revealed as a reflection of the struggles, oppression, and power relations of historical existence. When paired with the portrait, the picture reveals how men's stories and patriarchal pursuits (in this case, hunting) are considered worthy of historical consideration, while women are reduced to objects of the male gaze, worthwhile only to the degree to which they give aesthetic pleasure.[4]

Rather than call for a separation of art from history, then, *Between the Acts* presents the telling of history itself as an artistic creation, while aesthetics cannot help but bear the imprint of history. Beyond the family history of the paintings, Miss La Trobe's pageant dominates the novel, foregrounding how one artist, or historian, "creates" history, recording, selecting, erasing, and editing vast expanses of time in order to construct a unified text. In this, the novel presages the postmodern theorization of the discursive and textual construction of history. In addition, the pageant confuses and conflates English history with the nation's literary history, presenting pastiches of historical literary styles like the Renaissance drama and Restoration comedy *as* history itself. La Trobe's pageant, like the two paintings, puts pressure on the division between fact and fiction. The dissolving of this boundary is central to Linda Hutcheon's definition of the postmodern, in which "the familiar separation of art and life . . . no longer holds" (*Poetics of Postmodernism* 7), and leads some recent criticism of the novel to place it in the postmodern camp.[5]

The clearest example of the dissolving of the art/life distinction occurs after the pageant has ended and Miss La Trobe retires to the local pub, entertaining a vision of her next artistic creation. "There was the high ground at midnight; there the rock and two scarcely perceptible figures. Suddenly the tree was pelted with starlings. She set down her glass. She heard the first words" (212). At first, this passage seems to be a simple description of artistic inspiration. At the novel's close, however, Giles and Isa Oliver confront one another angrily after a day in which Giles has engaged in adulterous flirtation. Isa "let[s] her sewing drop" and the couple are described "against the window" merging into the natural outside world and the prehistoric past. "It was the night that dwellers in caves had watched from some high place among the rocks. Then the curtain rose. They spoke" (219).

This closing passage does more than close the book on the Olivers' contentious relationship for the day; it also puts their status as independent agents into question. The reference to the "high place" reflects the "high ground" that La Trobe foresees, while the "two figures" in her vision are almost certainly versions of Giles and Isa. When the final sentence encloses the Olivers on a stage where the curtain rises, we are presented with the possibility that Giles and Isa are part of a play, rather than merely its observers; that they are artistic creations and not "real people," refusing their status as ethically autonomous subjects. They are certainly seen here as creations of another, whether it be Miss La Trobe or Woolf herself, or both. Just as the two paintings at first seem diametrically opposed with one representing art and the other reality, the actions that take place within the pageant initially seem to be art, while those between its acts seem representative of life. This division is, however, destabilized when a theatrical curtain rises on Giles and Isa, exposed as actors in a play and, of course, characters in a novel.[6]

While the dissolution of art/life boundaries may suggest an advocacy of an incipient postmodernism, several of Woolf's essays caution us from jumping too quickly to that conclusion. In "Modern Fiction," "Phases of Fiction," and "The Narrow Bridge of Art," Woolf maintains the distinction between art and reality and identifies the central problem of artistic creation as the difficulty in maintaining unity, order, and coherence while also representing the real world accurately. "[S]tyle, arrangement, [and] construction, . . . put us at a distance from the special life and . . . obliterate its features; while it is the gift of the novel to bring us into close touch with life. The two powers fight if they are brought into combination" ("Phases" 101). Woolf here notes that unity and order are not to be found in the real world and that these provinces of art are in natural opposition to the truth-telling duty of the novel.

The difficulty of trying to maintain order, unity, and coherence in a real world antithetical to these concepts is illustrated also in *Mrs. Dalloway*, wherein Clarissa desperately tries to sustain them at her party. When she hears of Septimus Smith's suicide, she thinks, "Oh! . . . in the middle of my party, here's death" (183). The unity and order of the party is shattered by the intrusion of the chaos and despair of Septimus's world, the real world. However, far from choosing artistic form over the accurate portrayal of reality, Woolf, in "Modern Fiction," praises Joyce's *Ulysses* not for its unifying mythic structure, à la Eliot, but for its capacity to disregard structural concerns in favor of the "flickerings" of real "life" (126). While Woolf is often taken, in this essay, to be promoting an aestheticism divorced from the materialism of the "real world," her praise of Joyce reveals a commitment to accuracy in content over and against beauty in form.

Between the Acts is also characterized by the tension between the unity of artistic achievement and the chaos of reality. Lucy, for instance, is prone to "one-making," the attempt to draw everything in her surroundings into one central meaningful order, while Miss La Trobe attempts to do the same with her pageant. The tension between unity and the inevitable reality of dispersal are also expressed explicitly by La Trobe's gramophone. When there is an unexpected gap in the unified whole of her play, La Trobe, like Clarissa Dalloway, bemoans its loss: "Illusion had failed. 'This is death,' she murmured, 'death'" (140).[7]

As in Woolf's analysis of the disjunction between reality and art, Hayden White and other postmodern historians see the shaping unity, coherence, and emplotment of historical narrative as incompatible with reality's chaos and uncertainty. From this perspective, La Trobe can be seen both as a historian in the White mode and as an artist in Woolf's theory of fiction. In fact, for constructivist historiographers like White, the distinction between artistic creation and historical discourse is obscure, since both take raw material and shape it into the form of a narrative through exclusions, erasures, and selections, fictionalizing that which has any purchase on empirical reality. La Trobe's pageant is then both a work of art and a historical text and, like White's account of the historian, she desperately attempts to create unity out of contradictory raw material. This attempt at ordering, often through narrative, leads the historian/artist increasingly further away from representing reality in Woolf's and White's theories. Woolf, too, undertakes a critique of narrative in an effort to expose and overcome its nonmimetic properties.

The Pageant, Patriarchy, and Deconstruction

Like much later feminist thought influenced by poststructuralist theory, *Between the Acts* and the slightly earlier *Three Guineas*[8] expose how history is not merely a representation of past reality, but is also a discursive production of a patriarchy that defines what is important enough to be considered history. As Woolf points out in *Three Guineas*, it is a masculinist paradigm that defines the great "acts" of great men, particularly in the field of battle, as the appropriate subject matter for historical narrative. In fact, she argues that it is impossible to prevent war as long as battlefield exploits are immortalized in history. "We should not believe in war," argues Woolf, suggesting that it is only through the expurgation of violence from the mind and from signification that peace can emerge (97).

This critique of patriarchal discourse and its domination of historical narrative is also present in *Between the Acts*, wherein traditional historical subject matter is either absent or is deflated with parody. Colonel Mayhew complains, for instance, of the notable excision of all military history from the pageant. "What's history without the Army, eh?" (157). Through Mayhew, Woolf emphasizes the ways in which history has been inextricably defined by acts of violence and oppression. Likewise, La Trobe's omission of the British Army suggests that there are other stories to be told, or that an absence of "stories" may be preferable.

What makes *Between the Acts* particularly insightful in this context, however, is not merely its exposé of the ideological component of historical narrative. Rather, its close focus on the difficulty of stepping outside patriarchal discourse and offering an alternative is most striking. Indeed, patriarchal discourse is depicted as nearly all encompassing, permeating every element of life. The pervasiveness of patriarchal discourse is seen both in traditionally textual media like the pageant and in the outer frame, or the novel's "real world." In this, *Between the Acts* predicts many of the insights of poststructuralism, and reading these insights back into the novel also proves useful. In particular, the novel's treatment of history *as* discourse prefigures Foucault's thought and productively interacts with Derrida's proclamation that there is no "outside the text" (*Of Grammatology* 158).⁹ This dictum does not indicate merely, of course, that the search for an extratextual referent is impossible but that reality itself is composed of discourses, signs, and contexts. Derrida's term, archi-writing (*archi-écriture*), or the "general text" (*le texte en général*), refers to the "text" of the world itself, the network of signifying practices that comprise our real-life experiences (*Of Grammatology* 26). It "implies all the structures called 'real,' 'economic,' 'historical,' socio-institutional . . . : all possible referents" (Derrida, *Limited Inc.* 148).

It is clear that *Between the Acts* similarly suggests that the everyday world is an "archi-writing" that can be read and, perhaps, deconstructed like any text, including the novel itself or the pageant within it. The pageant illustrates how patriarchal and imperialist discourse dictates what is presented as history while dictating the behavior of those within it. The reader is signaled not to confine her reading of these discourses to the pageant itself, however, by the use of the above-mentioned framing devices. When the "curtain rises" on the Olivers, we understand that they are trapped within a patriarchal archi-writing that is similar to that of the pageant itself.

While the embodied symbol of Enlightenment Reason and the Victorian policemen in the pageant transparently vocalize historically imperialist and sexist points of view, Isa and Giles act out the same roles outside the pageant, with Giles as violent dominator and Isa as oppressed homemaker, albeit both with a layer of complexity not afforded their counterparts. They are the new pageant, which will repeat the same dialogues and social scripts as the previous one unless something occurs to change them. Likewise, just as the Olivers are the audience for the pageant, so we, as readers, observe the Olivers. Like them, we are not "outside the text." We too live in a world of signs and discourses; the curtain is also around us.¹⁰

This is, of course, Woolf's preoccupation in *Three Guineas* as well, wherein she refuses to take a stridently anti-Nazi or pro-British nationalist position as World War II approaches because she sees the deep and pervasive parallels between Nazi ideology and the nationalist patriarchal structure of England.¹¹ She warns against viewing Britain as outside of the network of discourses that comprise "Hitlerism," instead asking her readers to see their own complicity in the creation of the Nazi menace. Likewise, while Woolf calls for women to form a "Society of Outsiders" that rejects patriarchal culture, she acknowledges their part in that culture.[12]

Similarly, in *Between the Acts,* Woolf, through the medium of Mrs. Swithin, notes that the contemporary English are hardly different from their Victorian ancestors or their Nazi contemporaries in their valuation of social status, violence, and domination. As Woolf offers in *Three Guineas,* "it seems as if there were no progress in the human race, but only repetition" (120). Similarly, Mrs. Swithin notes that the Victorians are just "you and me and William dressed differently" (175).[13] Isa also reflects upon the burden the past inflicts upon women who have suffered generations of patriarchal inscription. "'Kneel down,' said the past. 'Fill your pannier from our tree. Rise up donkey. Go your way 'til your heels blister and your hoofs crack.' That was the burden . . . laid on me in the cradle; . . . crooned by singing women; what we must remember; what we would forget" (155). The desire to "forget" oppression is strong, but remembrance remains a necessity for resistance in the present.

The parallels between the pageant and the world outside it are too plentiful to comprehensively enumerate, but reviewing a few can reveal how the novel configures the social text of patriarchy and imperialism. The depiction of the patriarchal tendency to value violence and domination of colonized cultures is particularly clear when Budge the policeman refers to the "*white man's burden*" (163; emphasis in original) and when Reason asserts how her ideology is built upon the sweat of the "*savages*" (123; emphasis in original). The same values are expressed outside the pageant when Bartholomew daydreams about "himself, a young man helmeted . . . and in his hand a gun," linking youth, violence, and implicitly sexual power (17).

When Isa "interrupts" his reverie, Bartholomew mentally accuses her of "destroying youth and India" (18) just as the possibility of a world shaped equally by women would destroy the world in which Bartholomew lives and the prerogatives he enjoys. Although his youth and gun are gone, the ideology of patriarchy and imperialism remain of value to him. Similarly, as Christopher Ames observes, the children in the pageant's Victorian skit reiterate their stodgy parents' prejudices: "When the young couple flee together to become missionaries, they carry on the imperialist project associated with their parents' generation" ("Modernist Canon Narrative" 397). The seemingly inescapable patriarchal and imperialist discourses may be a source of humor in the pageant, but it is also an ominous commentary on the world that produces it.

Like the young Victorians, Giles follows in his father, Bartholomew's, footsteps. Both fearful and angry at the impending war in Europe, Giles nevertheless participates in the violence it promises. When he comes across a snake choking with a toad in its mouth, Giles thinks, "it was birth the wrong way round—a monstrous inversion. So raising his foot, he stamped on them" (99). Like Europe, the snake and the toad are killing one another, but the only solution Giles can arrive at is one of bloodshed. While his action solves no problems, it is clear that the audience partakes in a patriarchal ideology that valorizes violence as heroism. Just as the pageant opens with a song about Rhoderick, "Armed and Valiant/Bold and blatant" (79), so too is Giles seen as a "hero" by both Mrs. Manresa (107) and William Dodge, the homosexual whom Giles disdains (110). Even as Woolf asserts in *Three Guineas* that, "if we knew the truth about war, the glory of war would be scotched and crushed" (97), in *Between the Acts* it is clear how difficult knowing that truth actually is, even by those, like Manresa and Dodge, who are more likely to be the victims of patriarchy than to be rewarded by it.

Just as men's discursive and ideologically defined roles are highlighted in the pageant and reflected in the world outside of it, so too are women's. Even though Isa sees through Giles's image as heroic figure, she cannot completely abandon the tendency to celebrate what he symbolizes. While she internally tells Giles, "I don't admire you. . . . Silly little boy, with blood on his boots" (111), she nevertheless retains a part of herself that insists on loving him because he is, "'[t]he father of my children' . . . slipping into the cliché conveniently provided by fiction" (14). As David McWhirter notes, Isa is able to identify the clichés that dictate her behavior, but "she cannot escape the restrictive identity—wife, mother, 'Sir Richard's daughter'—she has internalized" (795).

Likewise, despite Catherine Wiley's claims that the pageant "bears a distinctly feminine face" (13), the women in it are consistently associated with the domestic and defined by their need to marry and reproduce, even when such roles are mocked and parodied. The Victorian valuation of feminine domesticity is asserted most clearly by Budge: "*For it's 'Ome ladies, 'Ome gentlemen. Be it never so humble, there's no place like 'Ome*" (172; emphasis in original). Despite their acknowledgment that La Trobe critiques this "Angel in the House" ideology, many in the audience still do not wish to relinquish it. "'Oh but it was beautiful,' Mrs. Lynn Jones protested. Home she meant; the lamplit room; the ruby curtains; and Papa reading aloud" (173).

Similarly, the marriage-for-money plot that is depicted in the pageant's mock-Restoration comedy is reflected in the "real world" by Mrs. Manresa's marriage to Ralph, the wealthy Jew. Likewise, the cross-dressing and gender bending of the mock Renaissance comedy is wrestled into order and conventional heterosexual couplings at its conclusion, just as the lesbian Miss La Trobe and the gay William Dodge are mocked and marginalized by the larger community. The enforced heteronormativity, economically determined heterosexual relationships, and feminized domesticity mocked in the pageant are nevertheless reflected in its audience. In this context, Isa sees her own life as "abortive" (15), since she never realizes her potential but instead follows the roles others have written for her.

It is clear, then, that the novel reflects the critical act of deconstruction and, at least initially, repeats some of its problems. Because Derrida's philosophy denies the possibility of an external vantage point to critique a particular text or a broader social context, all deconstructions are, by definition, *within* the text they critique: "double readings." The deconstructive critic first repeats "the dominant interpretation" (*Limited Inc.* 143) of a text and then proceeds to a process of "opening a text up to the blind spots or ellipses within the dominant interpretation" (Critchley 23). That is, a deconstructive reading proposes a text's central structures and beliefs before outlining how it is inconsistent or blind to its own metaphysics, inevitably unraveling itself.

Between the Acts certainly supplies such a "double reading." Initially, it presents the traditional account of patriarchal history, through Mr. Budge's policeman, the young Victorians, and the voice of Reason, but it also reveals the contradictions within that history by showing, for instance, the greed at the center of marriage in the Restoration comedy and the possibilities of gender and eroticism foreclosed in the Renaissance playlet. The pageant reveals the ways in which "history" and contemporary political practice are contradictory. Like deconstruction, however, it does not seem to offer an alternative history or discursive practice, since all it has to work with is the "text" of patriarchy itself. In providing a double reading, it destabilizes patriarchal discourse, "opening it . . . onto an alterity which goes against what the text wants to say" (Critchley 26–27). It is valuable, of course, to see how patriarchy cannot fulfill its own purported ideology, but doing so still avoids the question of an alternative (feminist) ideology.

This description of deconstructive "double reading" described by Simon Critchley is remarkably similar to Hutcheon's assessment of "postmodern parody," which she defines as a "double process of installing and ironizing . . . signal[ling] how present representations come from past ones and what ideological consequences derive from both continuity and difference" ("Politics of Postmodern Parody" 225). Hutcheon suggests that parody in the postmodern era derives from the repetition of historical representations with irony in order to comment on the status and function they have in the contemporary world. Certainly, Woolf's pastiches of the Renaissance drama, the Restoration comedy, and the Victorian family picnic function in this way, repeating the basic form and message of these texts along with an ironic commentary on their (lack of) relevance to contemporary society. The impact of postmodern parody in the Hutcheon mode is, however, still ethically and politically limited in its tendency to stop at the point of denaturalization and critique, and its refusal to offer a stronger alternative, or indeed to acknowledge that the history "represented" is not only politically damaging and exploitative but also factually inaccurate.

While patriarchal history is revealed to be a construction of ideological hegemony in postmodern parody as Hutcheon describes it, the problematic nature of all representations is highlighted as well. Therefore, while we are taught to doubt the "truth" presented by hegemonic power, we are also taught that truth in relationship to historical representation is inaccessible. "The postmodern condition with respect to history might well be described as one of the acceptance of radical uncertainty" ("Politics of Postmodern Parody" 227).[14] It is this movement to displace the real completely into the purview of representation that is ultimately denied by Woolf's novel. While *Between the Acts* does function in the fashion of a postmodern parody, revealing the discursively oppressive nature of patriarchal history, it also anticipates the problems with stopping there and moves more firmly toward an ethical stand based on a reference to the real.

Irruptions of the Real

What makes the reading of *Between the Acts* presented thus far troubling is the way in which it seems to preclude an ethical dimension. While the novel does provide a detailed and chilling diagnosis of the pervasiveness of patriarchal discourse, it does not seem to offer its readers a way to fight against patriarchy or the connected threat of fascism. Because Woolf presents the world outside the pageant as a mirror to the patriarchal and imperialist ideology within it, and because both of these texts reflect the primitive behavior of the hunters and gatherers in the prehistoric London of the *Outline of History*, there is a sense that there is nothing but repetition in history and that this repetition is caused by the internalization of patriarchal discourse.[15] An ethical movement that denies the extreme ramifications of this reading emerges, however, when, at several moments, there are irruptions of chaos and dispersal that challenge the unity and coherence of the patriarchal historical plot.

The first such irruption occurs when Isa reads of the rape of a girl by barracks officers at Whitehall.[16] The soldiers, unavoidably symbols of British patriarchy, tell the girl of a horse with a green tail, making Isa imagine a fairy-tale story of romantic knights and fantastic adventure. What follows, however, is a gang rape that is anything but romantic and fantastic. Instead, "That was real; so real that on the mahogany door panels she saw the Arch in Whitehall; through the Arch the barrack room; in the barrack room the bed, and on the bed the girl was screaming" (20). The reality of the rape gives Isa a vision of the horrific encounter, which, although mediated by the newspaper story, also exceeds it.[17] Like Giles, the soldiers are symbols of heroism not in spite of, but because of, their link to violence and conquest. The "horse with a green tail" likewise invokes fairy-tale images of a rescued "damsel in distress," a traditionally patriarchal plot. In this case, however, the fact of the rape cannot be reconciled with such a narrative. Instead, the event "alerts Woolf's readers to the side of war that is rarely historicized" (Wiley 13). Importantly, the reason it is not historicized is because of the difficulty in fitting it into the patriarchal metanarratives that constitute "history." Within the disjunction between the singular event and the ideological cultural narrative is what Isa identifies as "real."

The curious beginning of *Three Guineas*, lauding both the newspaper and the photograph, makes a similar point.[18] Although both of these media are prone to heavy mediation, deformation, and manipulation, Woolf presents them here as symbolic of the access to the real that is possible. The daily paper is called "history in the raw" (7), and photographs are described as "pictures of actual facts . . . statements of fact addressed to the eye" (10). While she notes the ways in which soldiers not yet at war valorize violence, the photographs of the Spanish Civil War present a very different picture: "photographs of dead bodies" so "mutilated" they could be mistaken for the "body of a pig" (11).

Later in the essay, Woolf voices extreme skepticism towards newspaper "objectivity"[19] and her play with photographs in the mock-biography *Orlando* indicates a similar awareness of their manipulability. Nevertheless, it is clear that she distinguishes between the stories told about war and the facts of war, or the real as defined by the photographs. It is, indeed, this reality that becomes the basis for Woolf's ethical stand for pacifism in *Three Guineas*.[20] Isa's encounter with the rape functions similarly, as an access to the reality of oppression that cannot be reconciled with the stories of the glories of war and patriarchal history. There is little doubt in *Between the Acts* that actual events can be adapted to and transformed into narrative, discourse, and ideology. It is also true, however, that the novel points us toward the possibility that these events, and their photographs, may exceed and resist the narratives in which they are embedded.

A second irruption of the real occurs towards the end of the pageant, when Miss La Trobe attempts to release her hold on its unity and coherence and to present the real of present time itself. Like John Cage's musical experiments,[21] she presents nothing on the stage and instead attempts to "douche" the audience "with present-time reality. But something was going wrong with the experiment. 'Reality too strong,' she muttered. 'Curse 'em!'" (179–80). La Trobe, like Clarissa Dalloway, again correlates reality with "death . . . when illusion fails" (180). Several critics suggest that the pageant's failure to achieve formal unity functions as a critique of fascist and patriarchal politics, but few note that the disruption of this concord is achieved by reality itself. Patricia Joplin, for instance, asserts that La Trobe "bears a striking resemblance to a petty dictator in her will to re-impose unity on her fragile, dispersed, uncontrollable work of art" (88). However, Joplin reads the novel as one which "celebrates rather than mourns the impossibility of final meaning" (89), configuring it as antifascist due to its postmodern assertion of the impossibility of metanarratives. Then, in a somewhat commonplace critical maneuver, Joplin analogizes a faith in linguistic reference with political authoritarianism: "Woolf's last work becomes a meditation on the proximity of artist to dictator . . . when language is used as if there were no gap between . . . sign and referent" (89). While it is certainly true that Woolf is critical of authoritarianism, reference to the real, as in the case of the rape, is presented as crucial to resisting it, not as its metaphorical reiteration. While Pamela Caughie claims that the novel treats "truth and reality as negotiable concepts" (*Virginia Woolf and Postmodernism* 54), the novel actually insists upon our capacity to access the real precisely for political and ethical reasons.

While it is clear that *Between the Acts* juxtaposes chaos with order and dispersal with unity, it does so by analogizing the chaotic and the dispersed with the real itself. La Trobe encourages the intrusion of the real in the final act of the pageant despite her anxiety, and Isa gets a glimpse of the real when reading the newspaper. That there is often a gap between "sign and referent" is emphasized repeatedly in the novel, but there is also a tendency to insist on the possibility of factual accuracy and that some truths are not negotiable, as in the cases of the bomb victims and the rape. This tendency is the building block of Woolf's feminist ethics in the novel, an ethics that also relies on the rejection of narrative and the turn to nonnarrative forms.

The Problem with Plot

While definitions of narrative have a long critical history,[22] a common thread within that history is the claim that there must be some action or event that sparks narration, making something "narratable," or worth narrating. That is, something, some "action," must occur in order to stimulate a reader's "desire" for explanation. *Between the Acts'* focus on "acts" and "actions," suggests the degree to which the novel may be read as a commentary on narration, particularly given several comments by its characters on the nature of plot.

While narrative typically predicates itself upon action, much of Woolf's work is built precisely on questioning that notion. Although *Between the Acts* only rarely comments on narrative explicitly, its abstraction from specific acts to a more theoretical concept of "action" correlates with her attempts to theorize narrative in earlier essays and fiction. When Giles crushes the snake, "action" is explicitly brought to the fore: "But it was action. Action relieved him. He strode to the barn, with blood on his shoes" (99). Giles's violence is defined *as* action through a curiously metonymic logic. It is "action" in a general sense that relieves him, but the *specific* action that does so is one of violence. In this case, the specific comes to stand for the more general, as if this particular violent "act" is shorthand for "action" itself. From this perspective, the action that is, in much narrative theory, merely necessary to raise narrative interest is redefined as always and already violent. Action may spark narrative desire, but in *Between the Acts* it is precisely that which we must not (ethically) desire.

In fact, the "acts" referred to in the title of the novel have multiple significations, each reflective of Woolf's critique of patriarchy. The most literal and obvious of these is the sense that the "real" story of the novel takes place not in the pageant but between its theatrical acts. As we have seen, the actions in the pageant are reflective of accepted patriarchal historical discourse. The notion of a place *between* these "acts" may then refer to a women's history and a reality obscured by the actions of men. Likewise, the title refers to the novel's setting between the two world wars. Published in 1941, the novel is set in 1939, before England joins in the fight against the Nazis: "the last interval of 'normal' life before Britain ceased to be a spectator and became an actor in the war" (Joplin 92). Patricia Joplin's choice of a theatrical metaphor here reflects Woolf's own use of action versus its lack in the novel. The correlation of the wars with "acts" contrasts "active" violence with nonviolent pacifism. In tying this pacifism to nonnarrative, we may note that whereas action is the prerequisite for narrative itself, the title of the novel suggests the difficult necessity of avoiding acts and instead finding the spaces "between" them. In doing so, the novel makes an attempt to imagine a world without plot or patriarchy.

As Aristotle paradigmatically argues, plot should be "complete and of a certain magnitude" (*Poetics* VII.52), proceeding to emphasize the importance of "unity" as that which excludes the irrelevant and focuses solely "around a single action" (VII.52). Says Aristotle, "the events which are the parts of the plot must be so organized that if any one of them is displaced . . . the whole will be shaken and put out of joint" (VII.53). The corollary of the "unified" and complete nature of narrative is also important; that is, the removal of anything unnecessary. In this regard, Roland Barthes offers that "art does not acknowledge the existence of noise" ("Introduction" 245), or, in a different translation, "art knows no static" (Carr, *Time, Narrative, and History* 13–14). That is, where life contains many insignificant and irrelevant actions, these events must either be excluded from a proper narrative or invested with symbolic meaning so as to include them (13–14, 58). In fact, for critics like Paul Ricoeur and Peter Brooks, the act of emplotment is a "configurational act" that "grasps together" various elements and creates a unified whole by looking at the series of events from their end point. "[R]eading the end in the beginning and the beginning in the end, we also learn to read time itself backwards" (Ricoeur 1:105; see also Carr, *Time, Narrative, and History* 64 and Brooks 18). Barthes's claim is similar, since he notes that the mere inclusion of events in a narrative means they must be read *as* significant, whereas in life they might not be. In either case, while actions occur in time, the plotting of these events is the order imposed upon them either dynamically or retrospectively. Those actions that are extraneous to the plot are eliminated, leaving only a unified structure.

Although these definitions of narrative and plot seem merely structural, and therefore politically and ethically innocuous, Woolf's novel serves both to destroy our sense of what we should expect from a narrative and to advocate for a mode of nonnarrativity that leads us away from the ethical and political conclusions offered by plot as defined by Aristotle, Brooks, Carr, and likeminded theorists. I am not, of course, the first to note Woolf's aversion to narrative. Previous analyses in this regard often link Woolf's writing to the "lyric," however, a claim I find definitionally problematic, as I discuss later. In either case, Woolf's critique of plot is not original to *Between the Acts*. In "Modern Fiction" (1919; 1925) for instance, Woolf objects to the necessity of narrative, arguing that plot is a mere convention that fixes fiction in a deathlike state, "embalming" it with "probability" (105–6). Here and in "Mr. Bennett and Mrs. Brown" (1923), the critique is formal and mimetic, but seems apolitical. In *A Room of One's Own* (1929), however, the antagonism to plot contributes to a social and political argument. As Susan Stanford Friedman notes, "Woolf's advocacy . . . of a feminine style and sequence conflates feminism and modernism in a radical way" (162). In *A Room*, Woolf not only criticizes plot but also suggests that it is antithetical to a women's state of mind. When she argues that women must "break the sentence" and "break the sequence" (81) of a progressive and unified plot, she is insisting on not only an explosion of the narrative form, but also a rejection of patriarchy.

Given these claims, it is no surprise that Woolf's fiction expresses a similar antipathy to action-oriented plot both in form and content. In the impressionistic stories of *Monday or Tuesday* (1921), Woolf includes sketches like "Blue and Green" and "Monday or Tuesday" that include no human "characters" and no "actions" that could be considered "narratable" (*Complete Shorter Fiction* 137, 142). In "A Mark on the Wall," the narrator displays a "contempt for men of action" and contrasts them with "something definite, something real" that gives "proof of some existence other than ours," indicating both a desire for the real and a skepticism towards narrative's role in portraying it (*Complete Shorter Fiction* 88). Even in her first novel, *The Voyage Out* (1915), which is more dependent upon narrative conventions, Woolf explicitly critiques sequentiality, unity, and plotted history. In that novel, Richard Dalloway defines the great achievements of England precisely in terms of sequence, tacitly linking narrative form to imperialist domination: "'It's the continuity' said Richard sententiously. A vision of English history, King following King, Prime Minister Prime Minister, and Law Law, had come over him. He ran his mind along the line of conservative policy, which . . . gradually enclosed . . . enormous chunks of the habitable globe" (48). Insofar as "sequence" is inextricable from narrative, the ironic mockery of the "sententious" Dalloway also encompasses plot itself. Dalloway likewise asserts that his "ideal" is "Unity. Unity of aim, of dominion, of progress. The dispersion of the best ideas over the greatest areas" (61–62). Again, Woolf's critique of sequential "progress" is combined with an examination of narrative's configurational aspects that "unify" and control disparate peoples and territories within a single "story." In *The Voyage Out*, patriarchy is also closely linked to the marriage "plot" by which Rachel Vinrace is consumed.

Mrs. Dalloway too is marked by the contrast between (narrative) sequential time, linked to Big Ben as a symbol of patriarchal dominance, and the nonsequential, potentially nonnarrative streams of consciousness of its characters. These streams combine with the preoccupation with "exquisite moments" to emphasize the importance of the single instant (29). *To the Lighthouse* is also more interested in the moment ("little daily miracles" [161]) than in the progression of time, despite the fact that the "Time Passes" section transforms such moments into a narrative of sorts.[23] This narrative, however, is one in which the human actions that construct most patriarchal plots (war, marriage) are made literally parenthetical (see Delorey). The satirical portrayal of Mr. Ramsay's preoccupation with a rigid philosophical "sequence" from A to Z (33) likewise illustrates Woolf's critique of narrative form.

The height of Woolf's critique of narrativity, however, may well be *The Waves*, whose series of lyric monologues undercuts chronological character development and teleological progression without dispensing with them altogether. Indeed, the two epiphanic "moments" that the six friends/ narrators experience at Hampton Court are explicitly configured both as moments of ecstatic connection and as moments of nonnarrativity wherein "the miracle had happened . . . and life were stayed here and now" (225). As Tamar Katz argues, the moment's "involutions halt the flow of narrative for the reader, reenacting and reconfirming the moment's separation from linear narrative" (190). History too is dissolved at this moment as "the lighted strip of history is past and our Kings and Queens; we are gone; our civilization" (*Waves* 225). While it is true that time, narrative, and history all resume, the wonder of the singular moment is contrasted with the oppressiveness inherent to plotting. When Bernard, for instance, encourages the others to "crawl under the canopy of currant leaves, and tell stories" (22), it is clear that for him, such "stories" are imperialist plots of violence and domination. "[I]n a malarial jungle. There is an elephant white with maggots, killed by an arrow shot dead in its eye. . . . This is our world. . . . We are giants, lying here, who can make forests quiver" (22–23). The sense that this jungle is now "our universe" (22), owned by the "giant" storyteller and colonial explorer, links conquest with the stories it produces. This is even clearer in the story Bernard constructs of Percival's conquest of India, complete with "innumerable natives in loin cloths" (136) and concluded "[b]y applying the standards of the West" so that "in less than five minutes . . . [t]he Oriental problem is solved" (136). This simple ending, incorporating the "saving" of the heathens and the "civilizing" of the natives, is clearly both oppressive and inaccurate, linking narrative closure with falsification and dominance.[24]

Bernard's narratives consistently redefine and co-opt others' stories for his own purposes in this fashion, but often on a more individual level. In describing Bernard, Neville asserts, "Let him describe what we have all seen so that it becomes a sequence. Bernard says there is always a story. I am a story. Louis is a story" (37–38), noting how these stories are inadequate to the reality they attempt to subsume. In fact, Neville refuses to share his love of Percival with Bernard precisely because Bernard would "make a story" of it, rather than appreciate it in its full intensity (51). As Neville says, "We are all phrases in Bernard's story. . . . He tells our story with extraordinary understanding, except of what we most feel" (70). Bernard eventually realizes the failings of narrative when he attempts to locate "the true story, the one story to which all of these phrases refer" (187), but cannot do so. In this light, he soon begins to question his decision to "impose my own arbitrary design" and to "select this, out of all that—one detail" (188), reminding us again of the narrativist historiographer's focus on selection and erasure as the deforming element in historical narrative. Bernard finally concludes that he is "tired of stories," principally because "none of them are true" (238). He longs, in fact, for a means of nonnarrative expression that will bring him more "in accordance with those moments of humiliation and triumph that come now and then undeniably" (239). Like Clarissa Dalloway and Miss La Trobe, Bernard's final confrontation with "Death" reflects his seemingly failed attempt to abandon form, linking the nonnarrative real to mortality itself.

The link of mortality and nonnarrative is also evident in the barely articulated suicide of Rhoda (281). It is no surprise, then, that Rhoda is the least assimilable to Bernard's stories, the least described of the six friends, and the least willing to allow the figural (the narrative, the metaphor) to obscure the real. Her possible lesbianism (see Oxindine), like that of Miss La Trobe, places her firmly outside of patriarchal plots like Bernard's, and may also allow her to separate discourse from that which it represents. "'Like' and 'like' and 'like'—but what is the thing that lies beneath the semblance of the thing" (163), she asks, noting how Percival's death (another link of nonnarrative to mortality) has given her "the gift" of being able to see "the thing" itself (163) as opposed to metaphoric substitution. Bernard too eventually acknowledges, "How much better is silence," resolving to "sit here for ever" with "things themselves" (295). In all of this, *The Waves* asserts nonnarrative's supremacy in representing "life," even as it configures the encounter with the real as traumatic, an idea that recurs in *Between the Acts*.

Between the Acts' antagonism to narrative is expressed most explicitly by Isa, who, in observing the convoluted plot of the pageant's Renaissance playlet, thinks, "Did the plot matter? . . . The plot was only there to beget emotion. There were only two emotions: love and hate. There was no need to puzzle out the plot" (90). Whereas plot is normally seen as central to any assessment or understanding of a work of narrative, Isa observes that "what happens" and how it is tied together is irrelevant. In referring to the playlet's cacophony, Isa thinks, "There was such a medley of things going on . . . that she could make nothing of it" (90). At this moment, the playlet fails to meet the requirements of an Aristotelian ideal plot, including the static that does not have direct relevance for the meaning and/or resolution of the story.

It is, however, this deviation from plot that allows Isa to have insight into the relative insignificance of the depicted actions and instead place emphasis on the emotions invoked. Even here, however, Isa is constrained by the patriarchal plots she has witnessed both inside and outside of the pageant, identifying only two possible emotions, each stemming from traditional patriarchal plots, the marriage plot (love) and the plot of masculine competition (hate). It is only when the scene comes to a conclusion that Isa identifies a third possible emotion, stemming, it seems, from a lack of plot: "Peace was the third emotion. Love. Hate. Peace. Three emotions made the ply of human life" (92). Intriguingly, Isa identifies an emotion not normally conceived to be an emotion at all and one associated not with patriarchal action but with the feminist pacifism advocated in *Three Guineas*. In seeing beyond the male plots of the pageant, Isa gets a glimpse of the peace for which the novel expresses hope, if not confidence.

The inclusion of "static" in the playlet is then repeated and redeployed in the novel as a whole. As any cursory reading will show, *Between the Acts* is full of ambient noise: snippets of conversation among the audience members, natural sounds of animals and birds, and, at one crucial moment, the sound of airplanes flying. While it might be possible to extract elements of this noise and identify it as important to a particular strand of plot, much of it seems included merely to indicate atmosphere and at times obscures the plot more than it contributes to it.[25]

> Then when Mr. Streatfield said: One spirit animates the whole—the airplanes interrupted. That's the worst of playing out of doors. . . . Unless of course she meant the very thing. . . . Dear me, the parking arrangements are not what you might call adequate . . . I shouldn't have expected either so many Hispano-Suizas . . . That's a Rolls . . . That's a Bentley . . . That's the new type of Ford. . . . To return to the meaning—Are machines the devil or do they introduce a discord. . . . Ding dong, ding . . . by means of which we reach the final . . . Ding dong. . . . Here's the car with the monkey . . . Hop in . . . And good-bye, Mrs. Parker . . . Ring us up. Next time we're down don't forget . . . Next time . . . Next time. . . . (200–201; ellipses in original)

Although some of this passage might be said to integrate clearly with the novel's themes, the effect is of a random collage of static that exceeds any unifying narrative trajectory.[26]

The aversion to narrative is also clear in several other symbolic moments in the novel, particularly the comparison of the two paintings discussed above and the legend associated with the Pointz Hall lily pool. Both these episodes contrast narratable stories with alternatives in closer contact with the real. It is initially clear, for instance, that the ancestor in the portrait is representative of history, while the painting of the lady is merely an example of disinterested art. Not coincidentally, the portrait of the male ancestor is also symbolic of patriarchy, while the picture encapsulates its feminine opposite. Finally, the portrait is linked with narration, while the picture is associated with nonnarratability. The portrait is a "talk producer" (36), providing the impetus for the stories of the hound and the horse. The picture, on the other hand, suggests the very opposite of narration, "Empty, empty, empty; silent, silent, silent" (36), which itself echoes Bernard's, "Silence falls;

silence falls," at Hampton Court (*Waves* 225). Also similar to *The Waves* is the depiction of the picture as outside of temporality, "The room was a shell, singing of what was before time was" (36–37). This contrast of the portrait with the picture conveys how Woolf's stand against war and patriarchy must be carried out not through historical stories that counter traditional patriarchal narratives in content, but through nonnarrative expressions that more closely approximate the real. While the image of the "silent" woman can be integrated into any number of patriarchal plots, her image also refuses the temporal progression that would make such appropriation possible. Woolf continually provides nonnarrative representations that are configured as more historically accurate than their narrative counterparts.

As noted above, several critics have configured Woolf's exploration of alternatives to plot as "pre-Oedipal," linked to the lyric form, and therefore not with the materiality of the historical real. Honor McKitrick Wallace's definitions of narrative and lyric are indicative of this view: "narrative is the formal expression of linear, teleological movement that is . . . linked to . . . masculine desire, while lyric is the attempt to subvert narrative's linearity by positing a timelessness linked to feminine desire" (177). It is clear that this definition of lyric intersects with and illustrates both the lady's picture and the lily pond in *Between the Acts,* especially through their connection to timelessness and silence. The lyric approach to these passages may obscure Woolf's crucial claims to historical materiality, however, since entry into the Oedipal triangle is frequently conceived not only as entry into the world of heterosexual desire but also as entry into the world of the linguistic, the social, and the political. Positioning Woolf's work as lyric, then, may suggest that it is not concerned with "real-world" politics and material history, but with an ahistorical pre-Oedipal union with the mother: a utopia detached from social praxis. As such, we might do better to avoid such a label, given Woolf's engagement with contemporary social and political issues. The term does, however, suggest the ways in which Woolf's antagonism towards plot is linked to her concern with love and solidarity between women, and a more broadly conceived feminism. More flexible definitions of the lyric, and its relationship to narrative, may therefore be applicable.[27]

Associating Woolf's aversion to narrative with feminism is not to say, however, that women in the novel cannot be at the center of narrative. The lily pool behind Pointz Hall, for example, is a site that is "talk producing." The legend, perpetuated by the servants, is that in the "deep centre" of the pool a "lady" drowned herself. Ten years later, the pool is dredged and a sheep's thigh bone recovered (44). The "stories" of the lady's suicide are contrasted with the reality of the dead sheep. In this it is clear that narration is constructed from the desire to uncover and explain "secrets," even if the secrets themselves must be fabricated retrospectively.

These "stories" may be contrasted with the description of the lily pool itself:

> There had always been lilies there, self-sown from wind-dropped seed, floating red and white on the green plates of their leaves. Water, for hundreds of years, had silted down into the hollow, and lay there four or five feet deep over a black cushion of mud. Under the thick plate of green water, glazed in their self-centered world, fish swam—gold, splashed with white, streaked with black or silver. Silently they manoeuvered in their water world, poised in the blue patch made by the sky or shot silently to the edge.... (43)

The effect of the passage is of a painting observed, with beautiful colors silently integrating with one another, balancing and moving without explanation, eternally and naturally maintaining a unity without linear progression. Renée Watkins sees in the pond one of the central ideas of the novel: "the study . . . of the moment, . . . the observation of its many dimensions, as they interlock." Woolf, Watkins says, "looks outside society, to nature, in hopes of finding reliably real things" (364). Watkins points to how *Between the Acts* tries to locate a real "outside the text" of a society that is dominated by patriarchy. While art may at first seem to be an appropriate alternative to the discourses that construct reality, Woolf's treatment of the pageant indicates how art is more likely to repeat, reflect, and even generate the plots of lived history than to be exclusive of them. In Watkins' view, nature offers an alternative nonnarrative "reliably real thing," but even something mysterious and silent like the lily pool produces narration through the story of the lady's ghost. While the picture and the lily pool offer possibilities for nonnarration, they can only have limited success in countering the imperatives of narration. Both are integrated and explained in some of the most common patriarchal plots, especially in the tendency to define women as "silent," "inexplicable" and "beautiful."

Bergson's Present and Woolf's "Moments of Being"

The lily pond and the picture reject narrative in their retreat from linear temporality and their embrace of the present moment. This present is not defined merely as an evanescent, fleeting nonpresence, however, or as a timeless paradise that prefigures narrative temporality. Instead, it is a moment of significant promise and substantial materiality. To fully understand the novel's treatment of the present, it is productive to both reposition Henri Bergson's oft-cited influence on Woolf and to counter recent rejections of that influence.[28]

In particular, Ann Banfield seeks to displace Bergson by turning to Bertrand Russell and the Cambridge philosophers with whom Woolf was more personally familiar. As Banfield is quick to point out, Woolf declared that she had never read Bergson in a 1932 letter, although she had certainly been exposed to at least the general contours of his philosophy (Banfield, "Tragic Time" 45). While Woolf's exact reading on philosophical debates about time is unclear, Banfield's case against Bergson's influence focuses principally on *Time and Free Will* (1889) to the exclusion of his later philosophy. It is, however, the later philosophy that proves more relevant. Banfield configures Bergson as a philosopher who posits time, change, and motion without any matter that moves through it. Russell asserts that Bergson imagines "a flight but no arrow," whereas Zeno once imagined an "arrow but no flight" (Banfield, *Phantom Table* 103). In *Time and Free Will,* Bergson observes that in watching a clock he "does not measure duration" but "merely count[s] simultaneities" because outside of consciousness "in space, there is never more than a single position of the hand and the pendulum, for nothing is left of the past positions ... and hence no duration" (107–8). This seems to displace the notion of "duration" to a place within consciousness and not "out there" in the material world. Bergson then appears to Russell (and Banfield) to be an idealist, since movement of matter seemingly only occurs in the mind.

It is for this reason that Banfield asserts that Bergson's dualism (of time and world, or matter and memory) is "the prelude to the rejection of one side" of each of these pairs ("Tragic Time" 67; *Time and Free Will* 495). Russell, on the other hand, purportedly maintains the "A" series of time's movement and the "B" series of individual sequential moments, or "both the arrow and its flight" (Banfield, *Phantom Table* 103; *Time and Free Will* 479–86). I do not wish to refute Russell's relevance, but it is important to reject the depiction of Bergson as a thinker who erects temporal dualism merely to reject one of its terms. Perhaps this is somewhat true of *Time and Free Will,* but in *Matter and Memory* (1896), Bergson advocates an acknowledgment of both duration and matter. In fact, Bergson's dualism focuses heavily on the materiality of the present moment, something central to Woolf's thought on temporality, and rejected by Russell (see Banfield, "Tragic Time" 54).

Bergson, of course, insists that both time and consciousness can be intuitively conceived of as pure continuity, in a constant state of flux and impossible to divide into definable and stable moments. Because time *is* motion (although spatial movement is not equivalent to time) and because each present moment eclipses the one previous to it, matter itself seems eclipsed, as in the example of the clock. However, the Bergson of *Matter and Memory* also insists on the central presence of matter and the substantiality of the natural world as independent from consciousness. "My brain is a part of the material world; therefore it is absurd to suppose . . . that it produces, or is a condition of, all other images: if we cancel the world we cancel the brain along with it" (Kolakowski 39). The philosophical contradiction here seems evident, as Bergson suggests that there are two modes of existence: one, constantly moving, of memory, consciousness, and time and one of solidity and matter that is of an entirely different order.[29] These roughly equate to the "A" series and the "B" series discussed by Russell, and both he and Bergson actually believe that they can be "correlated" (Banfield, "Tragic Time" 46).

In order for the "enduring mind and an enduring world" to come together, "without getting caught up in the one-upmanship of trying to reduce the origins of either one to the other" (Mullarkey 33), the present moment is indispensable. As Gilles Deleuze points out, in Bergson's philosophy "the present itself is *only the most contracted level of the past*. . . . [I]t is pure present and pure past, pure perception and pure recollection as such, pure matter and pure memory . . . and thus rediscover[s] an ontological unity" (74; emphasis in original). That is, while matter and memory seem to be fundamentally different, they come together in the present. While time eclipses the matter of the previous moment, it is in the present that consciousness, as memory, meets matter, transforming it from the latter to the former. Bergson writes, "the present is that which interests me, which lives for me, . . . which summons me to action; in contrast my past is essentially powerless" (*Matter and Memory* 137). Here, Bergson identifies a moment of an "ideal present" that separates the past from the future, but at the same time he notes the impossibility of such a moment (137). His conceptualization of an "ideal present" is undercut by his assertion that such a present cannot exist due to time's perpetual motion. Still, for Bergson the present *does* exist, is material, and is always present, if just out of our grasp. In fact, the fluidity and continuity of time implies that the past too is always present, merging its materiality with that of the present moment. This is not merely a matter of abstract philosophical pondering, but is also an important statement about the possibility of human freedom and of social, political, and ethical change.

As Leszek Kolakowski writes, the importance of Bergson's present is that "each moment carries within it the entire flow of the past and each is new and unrepeatable" (3). That is, while the present moment bears the burden of the entirety of the past (to which Isa attests), it is also the one moment that is not purely part of the past, not strictly a part of consciousness, but is also part of the world of matter, on the order of the real, and is therefore the one moment when true freedom is possible, the freedom to move beyond our own history, our repeated social plots, and to instead create and experience something new. "In real time, in the life of consciousness, . . . our self is at every moment . . . in a state of being born, absorbing its past and creating its future" (*Matter and Memory* 21). While each moment in consciousness is then a freedom from the past, each of these moments is only free in the present moment, in the precise moment where consciousness meets matter itself. Freedom does not depend, then, only on "free play" in the abstract realm of consciousness or signification but must, of necessity, equally rely on the materiality of the present.[30] While there are some similarities between Bergson and Russell, Russell mutes the enthusiasm that Bergson has for the present by granting that the future, if viewed spatially (à la Einstein), is in some sense "determined" (Banfield, "Tragic Time" 53). On the other hand, Bergson's resistance to spatialized time derives from his commitment to free will. If the "line" of time already exists, the future is not a series of successive (if inevitably merged and continuous) "presents" of limitless possibility, but a place whose spatial location is already decided. Despite Russell's dismissal of the link between spatialized time and human autonomy, Woolf's preoccupation with the present suggests that her depiction of time is more linked to the Bergson of *Matter and Memory* than to Russell.[31]

Like Bergson (if not identically so), Woolf theorizes and shows a version of life that is not *completely* dominated by the plots of the past and gives us the possibility of a present that exceeds the scripted plots of daily reality. In this, she offers a way to form an ethics counter to that generated by the plots of patriarchal and imperialist society. Her theorization of such a possibility is most clearly elaborated in the long autobiographical fragment, "A Sketch of the Past," written almost contemporaneously with *Between the Acts* in 1939–40.

In "A Sketch of the Past," Woolf asserts that most of daily life is cut off from "reality" but, at rare moments, receives a shock. These shocks, or "moments of being," are, according to Woolf, "a token of some real thing behind appearances" (*Moments of Being* 72). In this, Woolf offers the possibility of a vision "behind the scenes" of discourse even when she seems to deny that possibility through her layering of narrative frames. The application of "moments of being" to *Between the Acts* is evident if we return to the novel's rare and fleeting irruptions of the real. Isa gains a vision of the real beyond the archi-writing of patriarchy when she sees the rape, and for her this is a moment of being, a vision of the "real thing."

Many readings of Woolf's vision of "moments of being" see them as a "vision of reality as a timeless unity which lies beneath the appearance of change, separation, and disorder that marks daily life" (*Moments of Being* 18): that is, as a moment of unity inherent to reality, when the world, to all appearances, is disjointed and disconnected. In fact, Woolf, in both "A Sketch of the Past" and *Between the Acts,* does not suggest that "unity" is exclusively that which is beautiful and timeless. Rather, it is clear in the novel that if the chaos and disorder of daily existence are unified, it is because it is permeated by patriarchal oppression. Likewise, "moments of being" like those experienced by Isa introduce discontinuity into this pattern. While the lily pond and the lady's picture may, in one sense, be beautiful unified visions, they are, in another sense, that which is discontinuous with the unified plot of patriarchal "reality." It is this vision of "moments of being," as precisely discontinuous, nonunified, and therefore fundamentally chaotic, that lends the novel's vision of the real a frightening and dystopian edge.

In "A Sketch of the Past," moments of being are, in fact, both encounters with the real and experiences of the unified and transcendent. In "a revelation of some order" (*Moments of Being* 72), Woolf describes a flower, a vision of perfect unified beauty, saying that "we—I mean all human beings—are connected with this; that the whole world is a work of art; that we are parts of the work of art" (72). In this, Woolf sounds a bit like Reverend Streatfield and his interpretation of the pageant. "Each is part of the whole. . . . Scraps, orts, and fragments! Surely we should unite!" (192). Streatfield, however, is described as "a piece of church furniture . . . a butt, a clod, laughed at by looking-glasses; ignored by the cows, condemned by the clouds" (190). The circulation of the collection baskets that transforms the pageant into a fundraising opportunity further undermines Streatfield's vision and credibility. However, another description of a moment of being in "A Sketch of the Past" suggests alternative possibilities. Woolf recalls herself, the young Virginia Stephen, fighting her brother, "pommelling each other with our fists." However, just as she is about to strike Thoby again she "felt; why hurt another person? I dropped my hand instantly and let him beat me." The result is "hopeless sadness," as she becomes "aware of something terrible: and of my own powerlessness" (*Moments of Being* 71).

It is not easy to correlate this scene with the vision of the flower, the painting, or the lily pool, but it is clear that the episode reflects a vision of an ethics that resides outside the dominant cultural symbolic of patriarchy as Woolf conceives it. That this moment of past experience is a moment of pacifism, and is discussed near the outbreak of World War II, contextualizes this memory both as a political construction *for* the present *and* as a belief in an ethics that resists and transcends social scripting. While Thoby "acts" within the patriarchal social plot, his sister frees herself from it, preferring to take a beating rather than to actively participate in violence. Woolf's "moment of being" here reflects the Bergsonian present in its correlation with a reality behind the scenes of daily existence, a solid and perceivable instant where matter and truth itself are visible. In this "moment" there is the freedom to ignore past plots and make a new choice, an active decision in the material world that changes both one's own consciousness and the world it encounters. Woolf, like Bergson, extends the present into the past, but in a different way. Rather than acknowledging the past's inevitable presence in the connected flow of time, Woolf locates moments of antinarrativity that exceed hegemonic plotting, revealing their status as real.

Earlier in "A Sketch of the Past," Woolf wonders "is it not possible . . . that things we have felt with great intensity have an existence independent of our minds; are in fact still in existence" (*Moments of Being* 67), reflecting Bergson's insistence on material presence, even as she rejects the notion that the past is irremediably gone and removed from present access. In referring to the "peculiar horror and . . . physical collapse" of these moments, she notes how the human capacity to "provide an explanation blunts the sledgehammer blow" of the real. Here, Woolf offers narrative's role in "explaining" as that which prevents moments of being from continually hurting us, but also that which obscures the past itself (72).

In this context, the account of the fight with Thoby offers a precise opposite to the "explanation" Streatfield provides. Streatfield attempts to "read time itself backwards," by placing a unifying plot upon the pageant after its conclusion. He claims "that we are members of one another. Each is part of the whole. . . . We act different parts; but are the same" (192), but in the middle of his speech, in the middle of a word, twelve RAF airplanes in formation streak across the sky, drowning out his voice. These planes are often taken to be a pessimistic undercutting of the Reverend's attempt to provide a unifying vision,[32] but in another way these planes underscore the Reverend's message, as he attempts to unify and homogenize into a single plot the disparate "orts, scraps and fragments" of the pageant, just as Hitler attempts to unify Europe into the plot of German superiority. Although Woolf is clearly attracted to unified visions throughout her career, in *Between the Acts* (and *The Years*) she also expresses the ethical and political dangers of trusting such a vision, sustained by narrative. In a "Sketch of the Past," Woolf offers past moments both as real and as a rejection of the unification that Streatfield attempts to inflict upon the fragments of the past. Unification, then, is not always shorthand for beauty, but is also often a plot that marginalizes and oppresses that which is outside its borders.

Although "A Sketch of the Past" focuses on past moments with presence, Woolf, like Bergson, is often more concerned with capturing the meaning and materiality of the present. While Woolf's impulse and desire to identify "atomistic" and isolated moments that encounter the real is antithetical to Bergson's rejection of atomism in favor of "flow," her focus on the materiality of the present is akin to Bergson's argument in *Matter and Memory*. This is particularly the case in *Orlando* (1928), another novel concerned with the possibility of historical representation. Like *Between the Acts*, *Orlando* provides an overview of British history from the Renaissance to the present moment, while enacting an ironic and parodic version of a mimetic medium. The earlier novel treats biography in ways that are similar to the treatment of history in *Between the Acts*, consistently pointing to the degree of selection and erasure evident in contemporary biographies and how their supposed referentiality is easily exposed as questionable at best. The proto-magical realist cold snap of the novel's opening chapter, combined with Orlando's sudden sex change, and his/her incremental aging as centuries pass signal that the definition of accuracy in this "biography" will be a loose one. The narrator/biographer insists vociferously on the "Truth" while reporting impossibilities that can only be based on "burnt papers and little bits of tape" and result in "tantalizing fragments which leave the most important points obscure" (126).

While it is not my purpose here to discuss the relationship of truth, history, and narrative in *Orlando* fully, it is worthwhile to note that even as the attempt to pinpoint truth in history fails in the novel, this failure is associated with the imperative of transforming life into narrative. Near the close of the novel, Orlando is doing nothing, or nothing narratable, and the biographer notes how she is powerless in the face of such inaction. "Life it has been agreed . . . is the only fit subject for the novelist or biographer; life, the same authorities have decided, has nothing whatever to do with sitting still in a chair and thinking" (267). The biographer then begins to imagine how much better it would be for Orlando to get up and kill a wasp. "Then, at once, we could out with our pens and write. For there would be blood shed. . . . And if killing a wasp is the merest trifle compared with killing a man, still it is a fitter subject for novelist or biographer than this mere wool-gathering" (267). While the biographer goes on to note that "love" can substitute for bloodshed in the case of women, Orlando's resistance to both of these "plots" makes her "no better than a corpse" for the story the biographer is attempting to tell (269).

Indeed, the trajectory of the novel is from the intensely narratable masculine Orlando's fantastic adventures with both bloodshed and love to the increasingly nonnarratable androgynous Orlando's efforts to encounter "life" in the mundane and everyday. The young boy Orlando begins the book by "slicing at the head of a Moor which swung from the rafters" (13), but the novel ends with the grown woman's extended encounter with "the eleventh of October. It was 1928. It was the present moment" (298). This "moment" lasts for thirty pages, wherein variations on the term "present" are often repeated (305, 320–21, 329). Likewise, this moment is described as a "terrifying revelation" and as a "shock," tying it closely to the moments of being later described in "A Sketch of the Past." This trajectory allows Woolf to move from mocking efforts to represent the historical real to an attempt to do so herself.[33]

The Pageant and the Present

The present that features so centrally in the last sections of *Orlando* and *The Years* is, if anything, even more important to *Between the Acts,* which stages the ideal present as a separate Act of the pageant. During the final intermission, La Trobe takes great pains to present a nonnarrative situation wherein nothing occurs on the stage and the audience members are left to contemplate a lack of action: "All their nerves were on edge. They sat exposed. The machine ticked. There was no music. The horns of cars on the high road were heard. And the swish of trees. They were neither one thing nor the other; . . . Tick, tick, tick, went the machine . . . nothing whatsoever appeared on the stage" (178–79). La Trobe's ticking machine dramatizes the passage of time without action, temporality without a unifying plot to give it purpose. While the audience waits for the plot to resume, Woolf, who has already put into question the ethical and moral efficacy of a dependency on plot, shows the uneasiness associated with its lack.

La Trobe's stage notes read: "try ten mins. of present time. Swallows, cows, etc." (179). Although the introduction of reality into the pageant is, in fact, La Trobe's goal, she is not prepared for the discomfort associated with it. When she finds "Reality too strong" (179), she experiences the same "hopeless sadness" and "powerlessness" that Virginia Stephen does after being beaten by Thoby. Whereas action, control, and unity are the configurational acts of patriarchal plotting, letting go of the power to form and unite is uncharted and uncomfortable territory: "panic seized [Miss La Trobe]. Blood seemed to pour from her shoes" (180).

The sense of death she experiences is not, of course, biological, but is similar to what Slavoj Žižek, following Lacan, calls a "*symbolic suicide:* an act of 'losing all,' of withdrawing from symbolic reality, that enables us to begin anew from the 'zero point,' from that point of absolute freedom" (Žižek, *Enjoy Your Symptom!* 43; emphasis in original). To describe this, Žižek calls upon the Rosselini film *Stromboli,*[34] wherein Karin jettisons herself from the patriarchal social relations on the titular island. When faced with "the primordial power of the volcano, all social ties pale into insignificance, she is reduced to her bare 'being there.'" Likewise, she is confronted with something "more horrifying, the *Real*," followed by a moment of "supreme bliss," that occurs after "*we renounce all symbolic ties*" (Žižek, *Enjoy Your Symptom!* 42–43; emphasis in original).

La Trobe's ten minutes of "nothing" parallels Karin's experience in their mutual rejection of the prescribed symbolic, plot, or archi-writing of her community. Latrobe's "symbolic suicide" reduces her to "being there," an experience she also attempts to confer upon her audience. In the attempt, she feels the "horrifying" effects of removal from "symbolic ties." In fact, she sees herself, from the audience's perspective, as abject Other. "She felt everything they felt" (180), but at the same time wishes to disassociate herself from them: "Audiences were the devil. O to write a play without an audience" (180). Her initial reliance on the audience's affirmation prevents a complete symbolic suicide, but once she passes through this moment and "renounces all symbolic ties," her experience begins to resemble "supreme bliss."

As the patriarchal plot of linear order and unity is dissolved through the inaction of the pageant, a new order starts to form as it begins to rain (180). La Trobe begins to believe that her decision to act in the open air has paid off, dissolving the anguish she experiences when she fails to connect to the audience. Isa experiences the rain as if "they were all people's tears, weeping for all people," just as La Trobe analogizes the rain to "all the people in the world weeping (180).[35] The connection achieved between La Trobe and Isa is followed by the sound of a gramophone record employed earlier in the pageant, playing "*The King is in his counting house / Counting out his money, / The Queen is in her parlour*" (181; emphasis in original). These lines have been used previously in the pageant to parody its patriarchal plots. The King is configured as an active acquisitor of capital in the public sphere, while the Queen remains "'ome" performing her "feminine" domestic duties. Now, however, the lines take on a different valence. Isa experiences the recording as if "it was the other voice speaking, the voice that was no one's voice. And the voice that wept for human pain unending" (181).

The notion that these simultaneously conventional and oppressive lines from a nursery rhyme can be read not as part of the symbolic creation of "human pain" but as pain itself, and sympathy, speaks to the dissolution of the patriarchal "general text" under which such lines have been created and traditionally understood. Language itself loses its conventional meaning and undertakes a new one; one of pacifism, community, and empathy, particularly between La Trobe and some members of the very audience that she had previously chosen to condemn and abandon. Isa too wishes for what La Trobe has momentarily achieved when she murmurs, "O that my life could here have ending" (181). Her wish is not necessarily for physical death but is an embrace of the symbolic passing that places her outside the pageant's historical plot.[36] Woolf outlines this experience in *A Room of One's Own* when she notes that women may shift from "being the natural inheritor of . . . civilization" to "outside of it, alien and critical" (97).

Although the experiences of La Trobe and Isa resemble Lacanian symbolic death, there is at least one crucial difference that is essential to the ethical/political ramifications of the novel. Lacan sees the act of symbolic suicide as solitary, one which affirms the uniqueness of the individual at all costs and "against the community" (J. Lee 130), emphasizing the fundamental isolation of one who jettisons herself from the social symbolic. Certainly, La Trobe feels traumatic isolation, but Isa's connection and response to the pageant indicates that even beyond the restrictions and bounds of traditional language, communication and connection are possible. The connection between La Trobe and Isa resembles an effort to access a communal voice that may replace the idea of the controlling, individualist narrator, which La Trobe herself embodies in her earlier efforts to control the pageant completely. The possibility of such a communal voice is explored by Susan Lanser who, in commenting on Monique Wittig's *Les Guérilleres*, observes that the women in the story decide that their "own discourse" is "outworn" and that "everything must begin over again" (271). La Trobe and Isa explore this possibility when they redefine words and phrases, making resistant connections. The joining of the two women in a place outside of patriarchal language resembles Woolf's hope in *Three Guineas* for a female Society of Outsiders, who, despite their status as exiled, independent, and fundamentally other, nevertheless can connect with one another.[37]

The likelihood of two people transforming the nursery rhyme from one of rigid gender roles and male domination into one of fundamental human sympathy, community, and pacifism is radically unlikely, requiring, as it does, a new language, even "words without meaning" (212), but the connection Isa has to La Trobe offers the possibility of a communal bliss after "all symbolic ties are broken." It is perhaps here that *Between the Acts* most achieves the goal Woolf sets for it in an April 26, 1938, diary entry: "why not Poyntzet Hall: a centre: all lit. discussed in connection with real little incongruous living humour; & anything that comes into my head; but 'I' rejected: 'We' substituted: [. . .] 'We' . . . composed of many different things . . . we all life, all art, all waifs and strays—a rambling capricious but somehow unified whole [. . .]?" (*Diary* 5:135). In *Between the Acts*, "we" substitutes for "I" in the narrative sense, and although a "unified whole" may be achieved, it is only after a dissolution of narrative and social plot, with a new unity being "rambling and capricious," not linear and progressive.[38]

The Pageant and the Present (Take 2)

La Trobe's depiction of the present does not end with the ten minutes of silence. As Christopher Ames points out, the final act is, in fact, divided into three stages: "ten minutes of silence, the actors approaching the audience with fragments of mirrors, and the actors chanting bits and pieces of their earlier lines" ("Modernist Canon Narrative" 400). Ames does not include in his list the brief interlude in which a ruined wall is rebuilt by "woman handing bricks . . . black man in fuzzy wig; coffee-coloured ditto in silver turban" taken by a reporter to be symbolic of the rebuilding of civilization by the League of Nations (181–82). The audience responds to what they see as a "flattering tribute to ourselves" (182), but in light of what has gone before and what is to follow, it is clear that this episode calls for a dissolution of what is currently "civilization" and a rebuilding under more egalitarian terms, such that the League of Nations may have symbolically promoted but did not achieve.[39] The unity of the rebuilt wall is, indeed, soon met by discordance and discontinuity, indicating how its "wholeness" is another plot of achievement, civilization, linear progress, and imperialism that must be interrupted, in this case when the music "changed; snapped; broke; jagged," creating a "cackle, a cacophony" in which "nothing ended" (183). Nothing could be more opposed to the unifying vision of plot and of the wall of civilization than this music, its aural discontinuity matched by the return of the cast members using pieces of glass and mirrors to reflect fragments of the audience.

The Lacanian notion of mirror images being constitutive of a false unified subjectivity is, in this scene, reversed (Lacan 1–7). Instead, *these* mirrors, or fragments of mirrors, refute any notion of a unified self. With the fragmented mirrors, La Trobe encourages her audience to abandon the coherent narratives of their own lives and to acknowledge instead the fundamentally fragmentary and multiple nature of their identities (183–84). From the point of view of various unidentified audience members, the reflections are "distorting," but the audience expresses discomfort not only because of this distortion but also because the mirrors reflect them "as they are" before they have a chance to "assume" poses, plots, or identities.

For Lacan, the wholeness of the self as seen in the mirror during the formative "mirror stage" is defined as "Imaginary," a delusion of wholeness and self-presence that is revealed as such over the course of the rest of the subject's existence. Once the self is revealed to be fragmented, it must enter the domain of language, the Symbolic, in order to attempt a reunification through the construction of a life narrative. Because, for Lacan, identity is, by its nature, never unified, it sparks the need for narratives, which, constructed retrospectively, attempt to approximate a wholeness that never existed (and never will).[40] The conclusion of the life "story" invests the self with meaning, as in much theorization of narrative that attributes particular interpretive importance to a story's end. For this reason, it is significant that "nothing ended" (183) in the discordant music near the pageant's close. The lack of an ending necessarily leaves the history told in the pageant unintelligible. The introduction of discontinuity and the lack of closure are a concerted effort to remove or counter the (ironic) meaning of the pageant's plot, that of the achievements of patriarchy and imperialism. If we, as readers and audience, cannot know where this "plot" ends, we cannot attribute it a clear meaning, whether positive or negative. Likewise, while the mirror fragments subvert the imaginary wholeness of the self, wholeness is not then reconstituted through language, as it is in Lacanian theory. Instead, the words of the pageant are re-presented in random and incoherent order, freed of their original context and the signals and markers of progressive narration (184–85).

The fragments of speech spoken by the actors are not limited to those previously performed in the pageant, however, but expand to include additional texts, colloquialisms, rhymes, and phrases. Again, Woolf emphasizes how the pageant is both a repetition and representation of the "general text" of the world outside of it, with the words, phrases, and commonplaces of one bleeding into and out of the other. Plots are not merely repeated, however, but are reordered into incoherent fragments that refuse narratable temporality. If human identity and history itself are understood as only explicable through narration, Woolf's novel suggests that this understanding of them is both factually inaccurate and unethical. La Trobe's final speech to the audience both draws together the parallel between human identity and history and emphasizes its continuing ramifications. "Look at ourselves, ladies and gentleman! Then at the wall; and ask how's this wall, the great wall, which we call, perhaps miscall, civilization, to be built by . . . orts, scraps, and fragments like ourselves?" (188). While the audience sees the complete and unified wall of civilization as representative of the unity, coherence, and power of their culture, La Trobe explicitly puts this notion into question, indicating how it is all but impossible that such a unity could be built by individuals who are as fragmented, discontinuous, and divided as the audience members. It is, in fact, the distance between the communally assumed unity of identity and history and their actual fragmentation that renders any faith in unified civilization problematic, if not delusional. Such delusions, predicated on the expunging of those people and ideas that do not fit the preconceived unity, make any actual attempt at social and political universality ungraspable. La Trobe's attempt to reveal the distance between (unified) perceptions and (fragmented) actuality mark an effort to escape patriarchal and hegemonic "plots" into an as-yet-unarticulated nonnarrative reality.

Despite the utility of Lacan's "mirror stage" in understanding the final stages of La Trobe's pageant, it is important to identify some crucial differences between Woolfian notions of temporality and history and Lacanian ones. It is clear, for instance, that the novel articulates the Bergsonian "present" as a moment of *being* and not as a moment of "lack" or emptiness as is more common to Lacanian thought.[41] While Lacan discusses the importance of narrative in constructing subjectivity within the Symbolic, he also insists that any accurate account of subjectivity must acknowledge the Symbolic's limits, and the need to move beyond it into the register of the Real, wherein the impossibility of a unified self is revealed. As such, narrative is ultimately rejected, as it is in the final scenes of *Between the Acts*. However, for Lacan, the rejection of narrative is not linked to an acknowledgment of materiality. Instead, "the authentic realization of temporality . . . would recognize . . . the inescapable emptiness, *béance,* gap, or gulf around which the human subject builds a false identity" (J. Lee 81). Because "identity," in Lacanian psychoanalysis, is constructed as a narrative that must have a beginning, middle, and end, we have no choice in analysis but to arbitrarily choose an end point from which to construct our life story retrospectively. This arbitrariness, however, reveals Symbolic identity to be merely a comforting story, neither rooted in the "presence" of an arrested, graspable, and ontological "present," nor true, since the ending that confers its meaning is not really an end, but is chosen, almost at random, from a never-ending stream. The rejection of the Symbolic (and narrative) and the turn to the Real is not, for Lacan, a turn to material "reality" or "authentic" identity, but is merely an acknowledgment of the impossibility of such a turn, since stopping time at a "present" moment (or a moment of conclusion) is impossible.

This assessment of temporality has relevance beyond a philosophical understanding of subjectivity, however. In his extended treatment of Heidegger's *Being and Time,* Derrida notes that time carries with it many dependents, including "*Dasein,*" "finitude," and "historicity," all of which have significant impact on political and ethical concerns ("*Ousia*" 64). In "*Ousia* and *Grammé,*" Derrida deconstructs the notion of material "presence" (in history, in being) because of the term's link to the temporal "present." For Derrida, like Lacan, the present is never categorically "here" and is never therefore a guarantor of material existence or fundamental essence. Derrida argues that, "Being, the present, the now, substance, essence, are all linked in their meaning to the form of the present participle" (40), and this tying of materiality to something as fleeting as the present moment serves to unmoor substance itself (Being/history) from the solidity it implicitly claims. It is for this reason, says Derrida, that thinkers like Hegel have tried to remove the idea of "presence" from the idea of the temporal "now" and to place it in an "Eternal" realm outside of time. This, however, presents the problem that "Being is nontime, time is nonbeing insofar as being already, secretly, has been determined as present, and beingness (*ousia*) as presence" ("*Ousia*" 51). Derrida here reveals how Hegel refuses "presence" in the temporal present, moving it to a realm outside time, and in doing so, implicitly refuses concepts (like history) that depend upon substance and materiality in the real world, which is unavoidably temporal. Derrida's deconstruction of "presence" relies, however, on the conception of the "present" as nonpresent, always fleeting and evanescent and never "there."

While Woolf's novel has much in common with deconstruction as "double reading" and with Lacan's treatment of subjectivity, it is in the understanding of temporality that such parallels fail. The Lacanian and Derridean approaches to time seize strongly upon one half of Bergson's dialectic, configuring time as continually moving and the present as an impossible moment that is always already passed, making presence, substance, and materiality impossible. Bergson, however, also insists upon the concept of the present as the intersection of time/consciousness and space/matter. In doing so, he does not reject time as pure continuity but insists that both pure continuity *and* material presence exist simultaneously. In these terms, the oppressive Symbolic, plot, and general text can be dissolved without presence itself being reduced to "lack." If narrative is defined as temporality tied together by action, with both a beginning and an end, its subversion can be achieved not only by a never-ending pure continuity without beginning or end, but also and simultaneously by the arresting of time, the conceiving of an ideal present "moment." In this case, ontological presence may accompany the fragmentation of plot. It is for this reason that La Trobe's insertion of ten minutes of "unplotted time" is not purely characterized by absence or lack. Rather, it also carries with it the materiality of a "reality too strong" to be plotted into a familiar Symbolic. We may call these "moments of being" or antinarrativity, wherein material presence is felt most strongly. These moments, like Bergson's present, embody the convergence of matter and memory, rooting resistance to hegemonic discourse in materiality as opposed to "emptiness, *beancé*, gap" or "lack."[42]

Plot's Return

Throughout this chapter, I have highlighted Woolf's resistance to patriarchal discourse and her construction of theories of time and history that allow that resistance to be based not merely on alternate discourses but also on referentiality and truth. There are, of course, always multiple discourses operating at a particular time, and feminist ones certainly existed in 1941, some influenced significantly by Woolf's own work.[43] It would be possible, then, to merely argue that Woolf participates in an alternate discourse to the one dominant in her society without necessarily referring to the "truth" itself. To do so, however, would be to support the popular critical position that truth is merely a byproduct of discursive formations and not productive of them. This critical environment derives principally from the pervasive influence of middle-period Michel Foucault, who, despite his acknowledgment of multiple discursive frameworks, denies truth-value to any of them. Instead, Foucault, when at his most relativistic, asserts that all statements claiming truth are results of various loci of power that define the "true." To explain the presence of multiple discourses, but the impossibility of acting outside of them, Foucault introduces the notion of an episteme, which he describes as "the total set of relationships that unite, at a given period, the discursive practices that give rise to epistemological figures, sciences, and possibly formalized systems ... the totality of relations that can be discovered, for a given period" (*Archaeology of Knowledge* 191).

As Reed Dasenbrock discusses in *Truth and Consequences,* Foucault needs the notion of an episteme in order to retain his claim that there is no such thing as truth, but only "regimes of truth," which "each society . . . accepts and makes function as true; the mechanisms and instances which enable one to distinguish true and false statements, the means by which each is sanctioned" (115). If society is to have a shared sense of what counts as "true," then there must be an episteme under which various competitive discourses function. Under this logic, under one episteme, the rape of the girl at Whitehall would be a romantic and loving gesture, under another an act of violence and domination, and under a third no rape could be said to have occurred at all. The truth of each of these statements cannot be measured against the world, as such, but only judged within particular epistemes. In *Power/Knowledge,* Foucault argues for an almost purely social conception of truth and a nearly complete lack of agency for the subject: "we are forced to produce the truth of power that our society demands" (93).

As Dasenbrock points out, the Foucault on display here is similar to the Stanley Fish who asserts that we are all merely products of interpretive communities, or the Thomas Kuhn who argues that each scientific paradigm is properly considered "true" for the time period in which it operates, but none can be considered objectively valid.[44] What none of these theories (often identified as "postmodern") can explain adequately, however, is how epistemes change, paradigms shift, or new interpretive communities develop. To explain this, Dasenbrock invokes Donald Davidson, who refuses the notion that scientific paradigms (or epistemes) are hermetically sealed ways of producing different epistemic worlds. Rather, he argues, they are competing means of explaining a single world. Therefore, when we encounter data, language, or communication that we cannot comprehend, we develop a "passing theory" to help cope (Dasenrock 73). A new theory is then created, which may become influential, depending on its utility for coping with new data and situations.

In the notion of the "passing-theory," Davidson introduces two concepts anathema to Foucault and Fish at their most relativistic. First, there is the notion of the individual as more than the subject of discursive discipline or interpellation. As discussed above, in *The Order of Things*, Foucault defines "man" as an articulation of discourse who is "in the process of disappearing" (*Order* 385). Similarly, Fish denies the existence of both subjects and objects in *Is There a Text in This Class?* (332). On the contrary, Davidson insists that new ideas can arise out of encounters between individuals holding differing beliefs. People are not merely products of discourses; rather they are also capable of producing them. Second, Davidson's idea that "data," "language," or even "truth" can confound a particular episteme and its participants implies that not all data, language, or truth is integrated to that episteme. For epistemes to shift there must be something to shift them, something *outside* the oppressive system, demanding a reorganization of discourses. That is, inherent to the intensely constructivist notions of multiple interpretive communities, multiple paradigms, and multiple epistemes is the necessity of something outside of them, which we might tentatively call the real.

Davidson further notes that there must be some statements that are true, since there is a world that we all share (and not merely competing interpretations). Crucially, however, although "we may discover the truth, we can never be certain we have discovered it" (Dasenbrock 168). That is, truth must be separated from certainty, since one is possible and one is not. Notions of truth allow for the "disconfirmation" of things once held to be true, but which do not stand up to the present data, but they do not necessarily allow for complete confirmation of new theories that match data. From the perspective of a world on the brink of World War II, wherein the quarrel over colonialist acquisition led to the Great War, the Victorian belief in the moral and ethical imperative of imperialism displayed in La Trobe's pageant might be said to be potentially disconfirmed. Likewise, the real evidence of the rape can be seen as evidence for the disconfirmation of the general wisdom and superiority of patriarchal structures. None of this gives complete certainty to Woolf's models of time and history, but the possibility of truth allows for a critique of dominant paradigms from a perspective that exceeds mere disagreement.

The "shocks" of being that jettison La Trobe and Isa from the dominant social symbolic indicate the capacity for new data, new information, and new language to introduce discontinuity into a dominant episteme. That such "shocks" are associated with the materiality of the present and not merely with an alternate discourse is crucial not to an insistence that we can know the "truth" in all cases, but that we can know things that are *not* true, like the "history" presented in the pageant. The possibility of an encounter with "present" truths that become the basis for ethical resistance is seen most clearly in the moment following the radical fragmentation and reordering of the pageant in the voices of its actors. At this precise moment, "The hands of the clock had stopped. . . . It was now. Ourselves" (186).

Certainly in any naturalistic reading of the novel, it would be impossible to say that time actually stops for the actors and the audience. However, it is clear that both Woolf and La Trobe wish to give the audience, and the reader, the sensation, and the knowledge, of the ideal present, wherein ontological existence can be felt with all of its force. That nearly everyone in the audience cannot confront his or her own reality illustrates the difficulty in jettisoning ourselves from the plots we have adopted. "All shifted, preened, minced; hands were raised; legs shifted. . . . All evaded or shaded themselves" (186). Mrs. Manresa uses the mirrors to "make up" a new identity, powdering her nose rather than facing herself as reality.

Woolf's incisive and deep probing of the pervasive influence of discourse and social plotting are then balanced, if not undercut, by the tripartite attempt to theorize the present as something that can subvert plot and that exists in material fashion, even as it continually passes us by. In this sense, while we may experience life as a plot as David Carr and similar thinkers argue, and while discourse and social text may pervade every corner of our lives, it is possible to seize the present moment as present to us and to remove ourselves from the plot of our life and our culture, even if doing so feels like a kind of death. The novel, then, is more than a "crazy quilt of discursive and aesthetic forms" (McWhirter 803); it is also an examination of how to remove oneself from that quilt.

Likewise, Woolf sees the immense power of society to transform and recuperate symbolically suicidal acts into its own repetitive plots. It is for this reason that Judy Little can see the novel both as celebratory of the possibility of regeneration and mournful of the ways that "such regeneration is thwarted" (36). Following the transformative effects of La Trobe's performance, Reverend Streatfield attempts to unify the fragments once again. It is not only Streatfield, however, who returns the world of Pointz Hall to its usual plots. La Trobe herself reunites her fragmented players and audience by returning to a simple tune, linear and orderly, like an "ideal" Aristotelian narrative, "The tune began; the first note meant a second; the second a third. . . . but not the melody . . . alone controlled it; but also the warring battle-plumed warriors. . . . To part? No. . . . they crashed; solved; united" (189).

La Trobe, after metaphorically halting time itself, departing from the symbolic, and exploding narrative, winds up the clock and re-forms plot, both in her pageant and in the general text outside of it. It is significant that it is not purely the linear, orderly melody that reunites the pageant and its audience but the "battle-plumed warriors," the symbols of patriarchal violence. It is clear here that Woolf is aware of the limited sociopolitical force a single work of art is capable of generating, and that it takes very little for discursive power to be reasserted. It is for this reason that La Trobe can "say to the world. You have taken my gift," and also begin to believe that it "meant nothing," lasting only "for one moment" (209). La Trobe's subversion of plot, after all, seems possible only within a controlled environment like an artistic creation.

It is important to recall, however, that Woolf has already illustrated the parallels between the world outside the pageant and that within it. Through this layering of frames, Woolf encourages her readers not only to read the world as a text and to do so ironically and skeptically but also to imagine a different type of text, a different language that may result in peace. Many have read *Between the Acts* as a final pessimistic resignation to the inexorable progress towards World War II or as a final statement of the possibility of artistic unity that may protect us from the real world.[45] In fact, it is the unity and progress of a particular *type* of plot that makes World War II seem inevitable. That Woolf can see the possibility, if not the likelihood, of a break in that plot is a reserved but insistent affirmation of hope.

CHAPTER 2

"A Knife Blade Called Now"

Historiography, Narrativity, and the "Here and Now" in Graham Swift's Waterland

> To articulate the past historically does not mean to recognize it "the way it really was." ... It means to seize hold of a memory as it flashes up at a moment of danger.
> —Walter Benjamin, "Theses on the Philosophy of History" (257)

> We're cutting back on history.
> —Graham Swift, *Waterland* (5)

In *Between the Acts,* Virginia Woolf builds a case against plot and advocates the possibility of an access to the materiality of the past achieved through a theorization of the present. In this critique of narrative form and its crippling effect upon the ideology and accuracy of historical representation, Woolf foresees contemporary debates about narrativist historiography and the ethics of postmodernism despite preceding them by several decades. As such, any discussion of Woolf's connection to postmodernism happens retrospectively, through a critical lens provided by our present. Written some forty years later, Graham Swift's best-known novel, *Waterland,* not only tackles the same issues but also seems clearly conscious of the academic debate over relativist historiography. In fact, *Waterland* has been almost inevitably discussed within this context, with references to Hayden White dominating the critical conversation.[1] Like White, Swift's novel illustrates the failures of narrative in representing the historical truth, while recommending nonnarrative forms that offer new possibilities for historical reference. As such, any reading of *Waterland* should not only consider how it expresses skepticism toward the possibility of accurate narrative history (a commonplace in Swift criticism), but also the ways in which it insists upon alternative forms in order to achieve such accuracy.

Set in the East Anglian fens over the past 250 years, *Waterland* focuses on the struggles of Thomas Crick, a history teacher, to come to grips with his sordid personal and family history, England's national decline, and the ontological status of "history" itself. The competition of the adolescent Crick, his brother Dick, and their friend, Freddie Parr, over the affections of Mary Metcalf lead to the trauma of Mary's backwoods abortion, Dick's murder of Freddie, and Dick's eventual suicide. Crick retells these traumatic events to his class in lieu of lessons on the French Revolution as a means of understanding both his own life and the national history of which his family is a microcosm. Like *Between the Acts,* then, *Waterland* portrays history in all of its forms and theorizes the importance of nonnarrativity for historical accuracy.

In fact, *Waterland* opens not with an introduction to its characters or in the midst of its plot but with a dictionary entry for "*Historia*" that defines history as "1.) inquiry, investigation, learning 2). a) a narrative of past events, history, [or] b) any kind of narrative: account, tale, story." While these definitions begin with a practicing historian's search for material accuracy, they end with the revelation, in entry 2b, that there is no substantial difference between a "story" and a "history." This point is emphasized when Crick declares that "the more you try to dissect events, the more you lose hold of them—the more they seem to have occurred largely in people's imagination" (140). In this, he echoes White's contention that there are no stories "found" in the past. Rather, plots are imagined and constructed later by historians struggling to understand incomprehensible and inaccessible events. Likewise, when Crick's student, Price, sarcastically replies, "Should we be writing this down sir? The French Revolution never happened. It only happened in the imagination?" (140), he sounds like the voice of materialist reason, puncturing theoretical relativism with the necessity of the retention of hard facts.

This debate between teacher and student is importantly not conducted in an apolitical theoretical context but against the political and social backdrop of the rights of the people and the oppression of the working class that is an undercurrent throughout the class discussion of the French Revolution. While Crick speculates about the semiotic slippage involved in the popular utterance "*Vox populi, vox Dei*" ("the voice of the people is the voice of God") (139), noting how difficult it can be to find a referent behind the signifier, "the people," Price insists on that referent in order to create a political affiliation. In doing so, Price calls to the reader's attention "the unnumbered corpses [of the French . . .] Italians, Austrians, Prussians, Russians, Spaniards, Portuguese, Englishmen—which were to be strewn over the battlegrounds of Europe" (141) after the revolution. Price, then, foregrounds the materiality of history and the human suffering that can be neglected if it is viewed purely as a realm of text and discourse.

Nevertheless, presumably because of Crick's status as narrator, *Waterland* has often been interpreted not only as a comment on postmodernist historiography but also as an expression of it. Paradigmatically, Linda Hutcheon closes her discussion of the novel with a claim that Crick is an "allegorical representation of the postmodern historian," citing as exemplars White, Dominick LaCapra, Raymond Williams, Foucault, and Lyotard (*Politics of Postmodernism* 56). Elsewhere, Hutcheon links *Waterland* with the postmodern desire to "contest the ground of any claim to [. . . empirical] validation of history" (*Poetics of Postmodernism* 123). Explicitly following Hutcheon, Alison Lee labels the novel as "historiographic metafiction" and positions it as a deconstructor of the truth claims of realist discourse (40–46). Also in this tradition,[2] Robert Irish focuses on the novel's exploration of the limits of signification in representing the historical real, comparing Crick's historiography to that of White. While Irish asserts that the novel exposes how "history cannot be rendered reliably in narrative form" (929), he never acknowledges the degree to which *Waterland* asserts the referential capacity of nonnarrative presentation.

These readings of *Waterland* are not surprising given Crick's perspective. When Price sarcastically asks if "we can find whatever meaning we like in history" (140), Crick's internal response echoes and reiterates those of narrativist historians like White: "I do believe that. I believe it more and more. History: a lucky dip of meanings. Events elude meaning, but we look for meaning. Another definition of Man: the animal who craves meaning—but knows—" (140). The suspension of Crick's internal monologue at this point indicates the unspeakable possibility that historians like White have been offering, that history itself, if we understand it as the material past, has nothing to teach us. That is, even as we crave meaning, we intuitively "know" that history is meaningless, devoid of progress and teleology, and irremediably beyond our grasp. Like White, Crick focuses on the role of narrative in presenting history, noting how its central function is to provide meaning where none exists, and to provide comfort in explaining traumatic events. Crick, like David Carr and similar thinkers, suggests that narrative is hardwired into the human condition, and "man" is identified as the storytelling animal. "Wherever he goes he wants to leave behind not a chaotic wake, not an empty space, but the comforting marker-buoys and trail signs of stories. He has to go on telling stories.... As long as there's a story, it's all right" (63). However, while Crick's focus on the comforting, if misleading, aspects of historical narrative allies him with constructivist historiographers, the novel itself does not reject referentiality. Instead, it insists upon it by offering the two versions of nonnarratability discussed briefly in the introduction: non-narrative and antinarrative.

For both D. A. Miller and Peter Brooks, the nonnarratable is that which cannot stimulate readers' interest or spark a narrative: the stable, sufficient, or just plain boring. While Miller and Brooks associate this term explicitly with the ending of a narrative, wherein desire is satisfied (at the narrative/sexual climax), *Waterland* explores the possibility of nonnarration more thoroughly and productively, not merely as the byproduct and conclusion of narrative, but as an independent state worthy of investigation in two distinct modes.

The first of these modes is the presentation of situations and processes that cannot spark narrative interest: what I will call nonnarratability. While the novel does partake in sequential and progressive narration in its presentation of the history of Crick's maternal ancestors, the Atkinsons, equally important is its indirect presentation of the nonnarratable history of the Cricks, his paternal progenitors. While the Atkinsons are characterized by the capitalist/imperialist "progress" consistent with Western historical narrative, the Cricks participate in the day-to-day activity of dredging, distinguished by "process," as opposed to progress.

In addition, while White focuses on the ways in which narrative incorporates events into a story that conveys meaning, Swift suggests, through his formulation of the "Here and Now," that certain traumatic occurrences, while narrated, nevertheless exceed narrative's capacity to bestow them with meaning. These antinarrative events exceed the comfort and meaning that narrative provides and allow access to the materiality of the present itself through a failure of symbolization. That is, "reality" is not here merely an articulation of narrative, as in the characterization of some historical theorists under the sway of the linguistic turn, but is precisely that which exceeds narrative, or cannot be explained by it. As in Woolf, the "cotton wool" of daily life is described as the "history lesson" that makes up nine-tenths of life in *Waterland*, while "life is one-tenth Here and Now" (61), like Woolf's "moments of being." Through these dual stratagems, and in opposition to its own protagonist, *Waterland*, with Price, refuses to present history as fictionalization. Instead, ethical resistance is tied to the real in order to counter narrative's tendency to obscure the histories of the working class and to exalt imperialism.

Progress and the Atkinsons

Throughout *Waterland*, Crick longs for and argues in favor of a type of historical narration that will provide comfort and meaning in a world that lacks these commodities. However, it would be incorrect to wed Crick's early insistence on a totalizing and unifying history to an attempt by the novel to go back to this Enlightenment, or "classical" model.[3] In fact, everything in the novel suggests that Crick's longing is a desperate one that is already antiquated before it is voiced. While *Waterland* does engage with a model of classical history, it is a model that has proven, in late twentieth-century England, to be an abject failure. British imperialism and its accompanying narrative of seriality and progress is shown both in its period of ascendancy and in its inevitable decline through the brewmaking Atkinsons. However, by the time Crick begins recounting this story, he is on the verge of being made redundant from his job, not, supposedly, because of his unorthodox teaching methods or because of his wife's abduction of a baby in a supermarket, but because history is no longer a subject worth studying. As Lewis Scott, the headmaster, puts it, "we're cutting back on history" (5).

Crick's dream of a totalizing History that explains the trauma of his personal and national past is thus exploded both from within and from without, through the restructuring of British public education and the fall of the British Empire. With the dissolution of Empire, its totalizing narrative of progress is also dismantled. It is this narrative that underpins the novel's longest chapter, "About the Rise of the Atkinsons" (63–105), revealed, by chapter's end, to be a house of cards, not the "complete and final version" of history that Crick desires (8).[4] While the narrative of progress once provided communal identity and reassurance to Britain's hegemony, with its loss, history becomes "pointless information" with no "practical relevance" (25).

Throughout *Waterland*, Thomas Crick, like Miss La Trobe in *Between the Acts*, offers both a traditional narrative of causality and progress and withdraws it. In doing so, he presents, as Linda Hutcheon has observed, a history both complicit in its reenactment of traditional narrative and its deconstructive critique. Narrative, because defined partially by its sequentiality, implies progress, both in (explicitly) temporal and (implicitly) thematic fashion. The novel's progressive narrative traces the history of the East Anglia fens from the arrival of the Dutch Cornelius Vermuyden in 1655, through the efforts of the "water people" Cricks who participate in land reclamation. It moves on to the hiring of the Cricks by the Atkinsons, who embody the progress of capitalism by founding breweries and transporting beer to customers. The rise of the Atkinsons is also detailed patrilineally, with each member of the family dynasty profiled both in his capitalist successes and the "begetting of heirs" (69) to inherit the family business.

In this way, *Waterland* pinpoints the narrative of progressive history within a male English power structure (complicated only somewhat by the reigning Queen). The parallel of the Atkinson rise to the rise of Empire is indicated by the occasions for which the Atkinsons brew "special" versions of their heralded beer. "'The Grand '51'; 'The Empress of India'; 'The Golden Jubilee'; [and] 'The Diamond Jubilee'" (93) are all celebrations of imperial success. Crick even goes so far as to make the link of Atkinsons to Empire explicit:

> Have they not brought great improvement to a whole region, and do they not continue to bring it? Do they not travail long and indefatigably in the council chamber . . . for the welfare of the populace? Have they not established . . . an orphanage, a town newspaper, a public meeting-hall, a boys' school, . . . a bath house,—a fire station? And are not all these works . . . proof of that great Idea . . . ; proof that all private interest is subsumed by the National Interest and all private empires do but pay tribute to the Empire of Great Britain? (92)

Clearly, the metanarrative of History provides confidence and reassurance for England through the great Idea of "Progress" (identified explicitly as such in the previous paragraph) to those who profit by it. The passage also shows that this Idea, reminiscent of how the same word is deployed in Conrad's *Heart of Darkness,* excludes many others, particularly women, who are absent from the schools, and colonized peoples whose private interests are sacrificed. Indeed, Crick's story follows a Foucauldian trajectory in more ways than one, as two of the subjects of Foucault's primary studies have a prominent but marginalized role in the Atkinson family narrative. The Atkinsons found a mental institution in an effort to contain and institutionalize their family matriarch Sarah Atkinson and, later, Crick's father, Henry. Likewise, via their incestuous affair, Crick's mother (Helen Atkinson Crick) and her father (Ernest Atkinson) fall squarely into the realm of the perverse, the specification of which Foucault sees as central to the construction of Victorian sexuality. In these stories, the reader is encouraged to note how the Victorian narrative of progress is far from universal and instead necessitates the isolation of certain elements of the family and the nation for its narrative of wholeness to be comforting.[5]

It is, of course, a commonly voiced truism that History is told by the victor and that those excluded are the stories of the oppressed or defeated. As Walter Benjamin puts it, "One asks with whom the adherents of historicism actually empathize. The answer is inevitable, with the victor. . . . Whoever has engaged victorious participates to this day in the triumphal procession in which the present rulers step over those who are lying prostrate" ("Theses" 256). For Benjamin, history is not a recounting of universal progress but is the narrative of class conflict, which always includes both dominators and dominated. Through this Marxist perspective, it becomes clear why Ernest, already identified as perverse, is also the only Atkinson who is vocally anti-imperialist (156–62), further cementing his position as outside the narrative of capitalist progress. Ernest's presence suggests the possibility of a counter-narrative that critiques the remaining Atkinsons' "dreams of inflated and no longer tenable grandeur" (161).

By including those elements of history that do not typically feature in a unifying progressive narrative, Swift exposes the flaws not only in *this* narrative but also with the narrative form itself, which must exclude certain "others" in order to convey its unifying meaning. In *Waterland*, however, the identification of such a limited perspective is not left only for the reader to infer. Instead, Crick indicates its contingent, constructed, and provisional nature in his efforts to identify the precise apex of the Atkinson family fortune: configuring a self-conscious narrative through the building of drama, climax, and denouement. Crick muses upon the precise date of the height of the Atkinson family fortune, concluding with, on one hand, 1872, the year the family ale is exported to India, and on the other, 1874, the year Arthur is elected to parliament, the Atkinsons build their asylum, Sarah Atkinson dies, a great flood waters down the beer, and Ernest Atkinson is born. As White suggests, history is not "found" in the sense that the important events are immanent and incontrovertible. Rather, Crick, as historian, constructs the climax by choosing among possible climaxes, providing no fewer than five dates (1849, 1851, 1846, 1858, and 1862) before narrowing it to one of the two above (91). The Atkinson family history is self-consciously constructed retrospectively to fit a typically Victorian narrative of progress.[6] By bringing this to our attention, Crick exposes that narrative not as concrete and referential but as more "story" than fact.

In addition, Slavoj Žižek argues that "the past exists as it is included, as it enters (into) the synchronous net of the signifier . . . and that is why we are all the time 'rewriting history,' retrospectively giving the elements their symbolic weight by including them in new textures—it is this elaboration which decides retroactively what they 'will have been'" (*Sublime* 56). In accordance with many of the principles of the linguistic turn, Žižek here notes that history can only be given its meaning by looking back at an event through the prism of currently dominant "regimes of truth," or in Žižek's Lacanian terms, the Symbolic register. In fact, Žižek's extreme rhetoric indicates that the past, as such, does not exist until it is integrated into a broader system of signification. It is this notion that prompts David Price to claim that *Waterland* asserts that "[o]ur truths . . . lie (in every sense of the word) in language" (*History Made* 252). This view of history as inevitable lies derived from the instability of language is propagated by Crick's self-conscious suggestion that narratives are made, not found, and are part and parcel of the "postmodern" view that posits all histories as articulations of discourse without recourse to the referent. *Waterland*, however, refuses to settle for a mere deconstruction of historical narrative.

Before exploring *Waterland*'s alternatives, however, it is useful to see how the novel uses the discourse of psychoanalytic discourse to cement its critique of narrative. In Freudian thought, of course, traumatic events are integrated into the story of a person's life, ideally allowing the person to finally encounter his or her (often traumatic) past and understand it, resulting in a healthier subjectivity. This therapeutic view of narrative is echoed both by Crick and his mother, Helen Atkinson: "she believes in stories. She believes that they're a way of bearing what won't go away, a way of making sense of madness. . . . And out of this discovery she evolves a precept: No, don't forget. Don't erase it. You can't erase it. But make it into a story. Just a story. . . . What's real. All a story" (225). Here, Helen, a nurse in a post–World War I convalescent hospital, voices an instinctive Freudianism in which traumatic events, personal and historical, must be integrated into comforting narrative.[7]

Hayden White, not surprisingly, transfers this logic from the micro-level of the subject to the macro-level of history, asserting that historical events must also be integrated (emplotted) into a narrative in order for them to be understood:

> [Emplotment] is not unlike what happens, or is supposed to happen, in psychotherapy. . . . The problem is to get the patient to "reemplot" his whole life history in such a way as to change the meaning of those events for him. . . . Historians seek to refamiliarize us with events which have been forgotten through either accident, neglect or repression . . . by showing how their developments conform to one or another of the story types that we conventionally invoke to make sense of our life stories. ("Historical Text" 86–87)

White stresses the necessity of integrating historical events into narratives that utilize forms familiar from fictive writing, explaining those events through the form itself. The familiarity of these forms has nothing to do with their referential capability but with their recognizable conventions. While, then, the emplotment of historical events is necessary for the present's therapeutic understanding of the past, this understanding is largely a false (or at least fictional) one because the emplotment of events transforms "historical texts" into "literary artifacts."[8] From this it is clear that in each of these theoretical frameworks (Žižek's Lacanian and White's Freudian), it is assumed that the past, in itself, either does not exist or is inaccessible until it is integrated into a narrative or some other system of symbolization. The former claim is a radical stance that is not taken seriously by any theorist but is deployed instead, as by Žižek, for rhetorical effect. However, the distinction becomes practically unimportant if any attempt to access and/or represent that past is fruitless. Through an analogy between Crick's personal psychology and history on a broader scale, *Waterland*, like White, manages to link personal trauma to the historical trauma of the lost referent, and provides a meditation on both.

Crick's discussion of the Atkinsons indicates his own knowledge that the history he tells is not found, but is retrospectively dictated by the Symbolic in which he operates. In this case, the important events of the narrative are determined to be so by the larger Victorian narrative of progress. Crick's explicit exposure of the backward-looking narrativization of the Atkinson story indicates skepticism towards the immanence and material presence of the imperialist narrative that it parallels. Britain's rise seems only to exist through a retroactive glance from Crick's position in post-Empire decline. Progress, then, only exists from the vantage point of its opposite and appears to the reader as a (linguistic, discursive) construction that dissolves into the series of selections and erasures that characterize the Atkinson history. From this perspective, critics seem justified in associating *Waterland* with White and narrativist historiography.

While it is clear that Crick's theorization of history is similar to White's, it is equally clear that Crick does not always disapprove, as White most often does, of the deforming nature of historical narrative. He, like his mother, also embraces the necessity of narration as a therapeutic remapping of the chaotic and disquieting otherness of the past. Crick's recounting of the Atkinson history both indicates a self-reflexive acknowledgment of the constructedness of historical progress and embraces the story as a comfort that helps him define his own life, explaining his impending unemployment and his wife's insanity. Crick acknowledges imperial progress as an ideologically narrow myth, but he also willingly incorporates it into the national and personal narratives necessary for his sanity and survival.

The notion of history as myth is not, however, without its troubling elements for Crick, who is not quite willing to concede that historical reference is mere storytelling, no matter how comforting doing so might be. At one point, for example, Crick explicitly insists on separating myths from history: "There are times when we have to disentangle history from fairy tale. There are times . . . when good dry textbook history takes a plunge in the old swamps of myth and has to be retrieved with empirical fishing lines" (86). The question of what precisely Crick (or Swift) could be said to mean by "myth" is ambiguous, but in the context of the rise of the Atkinsons, it almost certainly has much in common with the way Roland Barthes deploys the term in the closing essay of *Mythologies*. According to Barthes, the "very principle of myth" is that "it transforms history into nature" (129). That is, it takes specific historically and ideologically motivated events and makes us view them as natural and inevitable. Barthes, not coincidentally, uses French imperialism as his example, but his observations apply equally to the Atkinsons and the British Empire, whose superiority, through myth, is transformed from historically contingent military and economic superiority into "natural" moral and intellectual preeminence. Barthes concludes that "the myth exists from the precise moment when . . . imperiality achieves the natural state" (130), a claim supported by Crick (and Swift). Crick's self-reflexive highlighting of narrative choices, along with his insertion of women, the mad, the perverse, and the working class, indicates a resistance to any narrative that would naturalize Atkinsonian bourgeois hegemony.

While Crick does, at times, embrace history as comforting delusion, he is not always willing to relegate history to the domain of mere myth. In fact, unlike White, Crick is in this instance careful to separate the history and myth with "empirical fishing lines," asserting the possibility of extricating the past as referent from the myths surrounding it. In this, *Waterland* is not merely content to expose certain versions of history *as* myth but wishes also to separate material history *from* its mythic transformation or, at the very least, acknowledge that history itself is dialectically *both* truth *and* ideological obfuscation, not merely the latter.

Process and the Cricks

While Crick is quick to recount narratives of historical progress and even to define humanity itself, or at least "man," by his desire for narration and storytelling, he is simultaneously drawn to the opposite argument: that narrative obscures the truth and, as such, conceals and falsifies history without lending sufficient "meaning" or comfort. The confrontation of these opposing viewpoints is carried out through conversations between Crick and Price. While Crick supports narration as a therapeutic explanation of events, Price argues the opposite, insisting instead on historical reference. Price asserts vociferously that, "explaining is a way of avoiding the facts while you pretend to get near to them. . . . [P]eople only explain when things are wrong, don't they, not when they're right? So the more explaining you hear, the more you think things must be pretty bad" (167). Here, Price expresses D. A. Miller's view. In this reading, explanation and narration become not merely indicators of the resolving of instability and lack but also signifiers of their presence. Narration is seen not as a means to access the facts but as a means of avoiding them, not as a means to provide comfort but as a signifier of disquiet and the "pretty bad" nature of the world. The notion that an alternative to narrative is unnecessary is punctured here. If narrative neither provides historical accuracy nor soothes disquiet, surely an alternative *is* important to locate.

In response, the novel offers a mode of historical presentation that is not narratable, shying away from explanation in the narrative mode. Whereas narrative is linked explicitly to progress, causality, and teleology, the symbolic process of land drainage provided in *Waterland* provides an alternative to such storytelling commonplaces. While the Atkinsons oversee dredging and brewmaking in their progressive rise up the Gildsey social ladder, the Cricks perform the day-to-day activity of drainage and "human siltation," characterized almost completely by a lack of progress. In fact, Crick explicitly compares the process of land drainage to teleological and progressive histories, noting their fundamental differences: "forget, indeed, your revolutions, your turning-points, your grand metamorphoses of history. Consider, instead, the slow and arduous process, the interminable and ambiguous process—the process of human siltation—of land reclamation" (10). While "revolutions," and "grand metamorphoses" spark narrative desire, they are here countered by the lack of such desire, or the nonnarratable itself.

The rejection of historical "progress" is accomplished through a focus on "[s]ilt: which shapes and undermines continents: which demolishes as it builds; which is simultaneous accretion and erosion: neither progress nor decay" (9). While narration and "progress" are associated with retrospective construction, fabulation, and, even falsification, the "process" of drainage is linked to reality itself: "To live in the Fens is to receive strong doses of reality. The great flat monotony of reality: the wide empty spaces of reality" (17). As Crick notes:

> Reality's not strange, not unexpected. Reality doesn't reside in the sudden hallucination of events. Reality is uneventfulness, vacancy, flatness. Reality is that nothing happens. How many of the events of history have occurred, ask yourselves, for this and for that reason, but for no other reason fundamentally, than the desire to make things happen? I present to you History, the fabrication, the diversion, the reality-obscuring drama. History, and . . . Histrionics. (40)

In this passage, Crick offers History, in the upper case, as the presentation of intensely narratable events that stimulate interest. As suggested here, the desire for the narratable not only obscures reality in its representations, but it also encourages people to "make things happen" in order to meet its demands, expressing, like Woolf, the ways in which real actions and events are not necessarily "outside the text" of historical discourse but are often performed in order to conform to it. History, then, is not characterized by its referentiality but by its "reality-obscuring" drama. However, this does not mean that reality itself is inaccessible as it is in the formulations of extreme postmodern historiographers. Instead, reality is characterized by the nonnarratable: the flat, the quotidian, the boring, and the repetitive. Not coincidentally, the progress and movement of narrative is associated with the retrospectively questionable politics of empire, while nonnarratability (and dredging) is explicitly separated from imperialism. "My humble model for progress is the reclamation of land. Which is repeatedly, never-endingly retrieving what is lost. . . . But you shouldn't go mistaking the reclamation of land for the building of Empires" (336). While Crick identifies siltation as "neither progress nor decay," here dredging *is* a kind of progress, but a progress toward the real, not toward empire or explanation.

While History and progress are connected to the corpses strewn across Europe, not to mention those in Asia, America, and Africa, drainage finds its progressive nature precisely in its deviation from this course. Inherent to the novel's claims for the nonnarratable access to the real is a political claim for the acknowledgment of the working class. History as "reality-obscuring drama" is contrasted with the Fens as reality itself, emphasizing the importance of the working-class Cricks over and against the bourgeois Atkinsons.

In this redefinition of progress, *Waterland* makes its key intervention, rejecting versions of constructivist historiography that present the past as irreversibly passed and unavailable in its materiality. As we have seen, White's psychoanalytic construction of "history" assumes that the present is separated from the past by a traumatic chasm and that narration attempts to make this chasm less painful by "explaining" the past in ways that make sense of the present. This view is similar to and supplemented by Michel de Certeau's definition of history. Certeau argues that historical discourse normally creates what is to be defined as "the real" through acts of division that "separates its present time from a past" (36). According to Certeau, however, this act of separation allows for the revelation of two versions of the real. The first is the material reality of the past itself, always "other" from the present. This "other," like any other group defined as such, helps the present subject define himself (3). As with White, then, for Certeau the real exists only in the past but provides a means of coping in the present.

By contrast, the second version of Certeau's historical real is the *process* of historical discourse itself "insofar as it is entangled with the scientific operations" (35). In this binary division, Certeau plays upon the two meanings of the word "history": past reality itself, and its telling (21). Certeau then offers that both of these signifieds ("history" and "history") are, in fact, "poles of the real" and that the most accurate history is that which plumbs the depths of the schism between them. "Historical science takes hold . . . in their relation to one another, and its proper objective is developing this relation into a discourse" (35).

Self-reflexivity and the repeated reference to a text's own textuality are, of course, standard hallmarks of postmodern literature, historical or otherwise. Here, however, Certeau indicates that it is the intersection of the reality of the past, however inaccessible it may be, *with* a self-reflexive investigation of the production of historical discourse that allows access to the real, indicating that the discursive process must be combined, juxtaposed with, or read alongside material reality itself. Despite Certeau's acknowledgment of both "poles" of the real, however, he is careful to keep them separate and to insist upon the past as an "other" that cannot be made present. In this, he, like White himself, takes part in the logic of narrativity. That is, both Certeau and White explain history and the real precisely through the "great events" and wide-scale changes that create narrative and narrative desire. In their accounts of the separation of present from past, there is, at minimum, the "transition from one state to the other" (51) that Todorov identifies as narrative's minimal definition, if not outright progress from past to present.

Both White's and Certeau's accounts of the transformation from material past to historical discourse *are* then narratives in their insistence on the "transition" from materiality to discursivity. *Waterland*, however, suggests that this faith in "progress" and narratability is not the real at all. Indeed, lack of change and stasis, the forward and retreat of siltation is real, implying that, in fact, the past is not irremediably passed but is always at least partially present not only through its discursive traces but also in its materiality. In this view, the large changes that make the past seem impossible to recover are more narratable deformations of the real than its accurate presentation. The logic of progressive historical narrative that declares the past inaccessible is substantially belied, then, by the concept of process, which asserts that at least some of the actions of the past are actually repeated in the present and that they, therefore, may not be completely lost, epistemologically speaking, after all. While Certeau discusses "process" as a key element of the real, he associates it only with the processes of the production of historical discourse, and *not* with the processes of past actions or events. It is Swift's expression of the materiality of the past *as* a process through the metaphor[9] of dredging that allows him to bring Certeau's "poles of the real" together, insisting on a historicity that is accessible to our present.

The association of the Cricks with nonnarratability and the Atkinsons with narrative is problematized, however, by the claim that the "Atkinsons made history, the Cricks spun yarns," (17) implying that the Atkinsons are those who "act," while the Cricks are those who narrate. This dichotomy is shown to be false, however, if we recall Helen Atkinson's capacity for storytelling and the fact that it is quite possible that her husband's tendency to narrate may merely reflect hers (2). In actuality, Helen's stories have more in common with the conception of narrative as a soothing explanation of reality than Henry's, using them explicitly "to make me sleep at night" (2). Henry's stories, however, are "[m]ade-up stories, true stories; soothing stories, warning stories; stories with a moral or with no point at all; believable stories and unbelievable stories; stories which were neither one thing nor the other" (2). While some of Henry's stories contain a moral, an explanation, or the capacity to soothe, others are pointless or unclassifiable: perhaps not narratives at all. The Crickian "yarns" refuse to conform to a single type, while the Atkinsons "make" history, in action and narration.[10] Likewise, while the Cricks may tell stories, it is manifestly difficult to tell any stories *about* them. It is only after the Cricks and Atkinsons intermarry that the Cricks become susceptible to narrative representation.

"A Knife Blade Called Now"

Although the correlation of the real with the repetitive and mundane process of daily labor is essential to the understanding of historical reference in *Waterland*, it is not the only avenue to the real that the novel explores. Rather, the first indication that there is another version follows closely upon the first description of the real as a "grey flat empty space" (17). In the wake of this definition it is quite surprising to find Crick asserting its seeming opposite, "Reality's so strange and unexpected" (25). Nevertheless, this countervailing trend in the definition of reality continues throughout the novel and becomes clearer in the subsequent chapter, which takes place during Crick's teen years in the summer of 1943. Here, the young Tom, with the help of his father and brother, fishes the body of Freddie Parr out of his father's sluice. In this extraordinary circumstance, seemingly the essence of narrativity, the Crickian process of pumping and drainage is parodically repeated when Henry attempts to revive the long dead Freddie through the "Holger-Nielsen Method of Artificial Respiration": "what else was my father doing on that July morning than what his forebears had been doing for generations; expelling water? But whereas they reclaimed land, my father could not reclaim a life" (32).

Whereas the repetitive and laborious process of drainage has been previously defined as the real itself, Crick notes that this attempt at drainage is just the opposite: "Dad labours to refute reality, against the law of nature, that a dead thing does not live again" (32). The real here is not, however, merely the material presence of death itself, but is rather the extraordinary and dislocating event that makes Crick aware that he is not merely a part of a story or dream but is inexpressibly in "the present," or the "Here and Now." It is not upon seeing the dead body of Freddie Parr that Crick experiences this sensation, but in the contingent and unsettling moment when the boat-hook catches under Freddie's jaw and rips upwards through the cheek, eye-socket, and temple, while Freddie's body drops back into the water and bursts forth with a new layer of blood: "a dark, sticky, reluctant substance, the colour of black-currants" (30). At this moment, "I came out of a dream.... I realized I was looking at a dead body. Something I had never seen before" (30). Crick is, in this moment, able to see the grim reality his father attempts to ignore in his efforts to pump the water out of Freddie. This reality is not merely the prospect of mortality, but the realization of one's own existence outside of a scripted, easily explained Symbolic, a momentary sense of uniqueness and presence not easily explained or transformed into narrative, and which gives the sense of one's own participation in the world, not merely as an observer. Crick describes the feeling of an encounter with the real. Interestingly, this encounter is accompanied by an insight into more conventional areas of truth, as he notices the bruise on Freddie Parr's face that is *underneath* the bruise inflicted by the boat hook. That is, Tom discovers a truth that no one else has realized: that Freddie was murdered with a blunt object, not drowned. It is undoubtedly true that this murder becomes the impetus for the most compulsively narratable element of the novel (the detective story of Freddie's murderer), but Crick's capacity to read a "truth" previously unavailable from the "text" of the corpse indicates the possibility of encountering the past through its representations, despite the obscuring power of narration (35).

It is true that the reality of Freddie's body being pulled by the boat hook is quickly subsumed by the needs of narration. However, while the novel acknowledges that "the reality of things ... only visits us for a brief while," (33) it is also the case that, in *Waterland*, "history is a thin garment, easily punctured by a knife blade called Now" (36). While History is the "reality obscuring drama" that converts traumatic events into a comforting and comprehensible narrative, it also becomes clear that the "Here and Now," can, at times, intrude and puncture its narrativization, bringing the sense of reality back even where it is most actively suppressed (and repressed) during the course of a narrative. It is this experience that I label antinarrative.

It is also here that the novel's deployment of psychoanalysis again emerges. While psychoanalysis frequently attempts to find integration and coherent narrativization of foundational and/or traumatic events, it is true that some versions of psychoanalytic theory posit the impossibility of subsuming and reintegrating traumatic events into a coherent narrative or subjectivity. Traumatic events are, in fact, often those elements that resist symbolization and continue to "return" in different forms, never quite disappearing, yet never retaining a consistent symbolic value or place in the subject's life-narrative.

The Lacanian version of this traumatic moment is identified with the Real register, a useful turn of phrase.[11] From this perspective, a traumatic event, like the retrieval of Freddie Parr, is first experienced as inexplicable or beyond explanation (Žižek, *Sublime Object of Ideology* 61). While the recurrence or repetition of such a traumatic occurrence (through memory, through retelling, through narrativization) allows it to "find its place in the symbolic network" (61), there is always some portion of that intrusion of the Real that remains unexplained and which retains its contingent nonsymbolized status. As Žižek asserts, the capacity for a "retroactive modification of the past" has its limits, "it stumbles on to a rock upon which it becomes suspended. This rock is . . . the Real, that which resists symbolization: the traumatic point which is always missed but none the less always returns," despite our attempts " to neutralize it, to integrate it into the symbolic order" (69). Žižek indicates that despite the tendency to explain traumatic events, there are always elements of those events that resist such incorporation.

Although Lacan speaks principally of the construction of subjectivity and not of historical reference, this explanation of the Real helps to understand historical reality as conceptualized in *Waterland*. The extraction of Freddie Parr, which I referred to as a "dislocation" above, actually provides a momentary "location" of Crick outside of narrativization and, instead, in a material reality that functions as an indicator of material presence. Such antinarrative moments recur infrequently in *Waterland,* but they do recur and are given the name of the "Here and Now" by Price. In *Waterland,* it is these momentary encounters with the real, that prevent a completely constructivist view of history for Crick. "I believed . . . that history was a myth. Until a series of encounters with the Here and Now gave a sudden pointedness to my studies . . . informed me that history was no invention but indeed existed" (62).[12]

While History in the upper case is referred to as "the Grand Narrative, the filler of vacuums, the dispeller of fears in the dark," or the narratives and stories that fend off and explain the real, history in the lower case is identified with the real itself: not an invented story but a material presence that sparks fear and dis-ease rather than dispelling them. In this sense, as Crick suggests, "all stories were once real. And all the events of history, the battles and costume-pieces, once really happened . . . were once feelings in the guts" (297).

Central also to Crick's encounter with Freddie's body is the way in which Crick describes himself as "awakening from a dream." Likewise, in a later traumatic episode, the backwoods abortion of his child, Crick asserts that "there are things which happen outside dreams that should only happen in them" (308). In this, Crick once again reflects Lacanian thought. As Žižek explains, the Lacanian Real is not that which awakens us from our dreams, but is instead that fundamental traumatic part of our past reality that defines us and our desires. It is that which, in Freudian terms, reveals the unconscious and "which announces itself in the terrifying dream" (*Sublime Object of Ideology* 45). In this context, as Crick observes, dreams are not a fantastic escape from reality but are more real than reality itself. Whereas reality, as it is commonly defined, is our own Symbolic reimagining (or narrativization) of the traumatic "kernel" of our identity, the trauma itself exceeds the narrative it engenders to normalize it and often reappears in dreams.

Likewise, although the "Here and Now" does not share the idea of process with the drainage of the Fens, it does serve to collapse the separation of present and past, stressing the ways in which time is recursive, repetitive, and cyclical, ushering the past into the present and vice versa. This strange effect of the traumatic real is clear during the backwoods abortion of Mary Metcalf's child, before which Martha Clay instructs Crick to go outside and pluck a duck.

> His head starts to spin. The duck he's holding in his hand isn't a duck, it's a hen. He's sitting in the sunny space between a chicken coop and the kitchen door, where Mother stands, in her apron. But the hen's not dead, it's still alive. Its wings start to flap and it starts to lay eggs. . . . A copious unending stream of eggs, so many that he has to collect them with the help of his mother and her apron. But Mother says they're not really eggs, they're fallen stars. And so they are, twinkling and winking on the ground. We carry the fallen stars into the chicken coop. Which isn't a chicken coop at all. It's the shell of the old wooden windmill by the Hockwell Lode. And Mary's inside lying naked with her knees up. Mother discreetly retires. And Mary starts to explain about her menstrual cycle and about the wonders inside her hole and how babies get to be born. She says, "I've got eggs, you know." And he, ignorant but eager to learn, says, "What

like hens?" And Mary laughs. And then she screams and then she says she's the mother of God—I drop the duck I'm holding. . . . It's not a dream. What you wake up into can't be a dream. It's dark. I'm here; it's now. (307–8)

The passage entails not only the merging of reality and dream but also of the past and present. The present plucking of the duck is transformed into the childhood plucking of the hen, while the hen's eggs are transformed into Mary's ovarian eggs during their mutual exploration of "holes and things" at the Hockwell Lode. This is, in turn, transformed into the novel's obvious religious iconography, with Mary as the mother of God and Dick as the parodic "Savior of the World." This iconography is further crystallized by the oaths Mary swears: "HolyMaryMotherofGodHolyMaryMotherofGodHolyMaryMotherof—" (308).

In its theorization of the "Here and Now," *Waterland* indicates how, on a broader scale, lived experience is recursive and repetitive, repeating and reliving foundational trauma and unconsciously revisiting the past in the present. Tom and Mary's experience of losing a child recurs often in their later lives, as they obsessively seek out and obtain child substitutes in various attempts to cover over this trauma. Price, their dog, and the baby Mary kidnaps from the supermarket all, at various times, fulfill this symbolic role. What this passage indicates, however, is how both Tom and Mary are obsessed with the symbolic significance of reproduction long before their own child is aborted, and how this traumatic moment exceeds their mutual capacity to explain or narrativize it while taking them both back into the past and forward into the future. The passage lends weight to Crick's theorizing about history in which he claims, "It goes in two directions at once. It goes backwards as it goes forwards. It loops. It takes detours. Do not fall into the illusion that history is a well-disciplined and unflagging column marching unswervingly into the future" (135). Instead, it seems that Crick's traumas are not merely produced by his narrative but actually "return" in a material/historical sense. In this, we have not only the "return of the repressed" but also the "return of the referent" as the past becomes present not only discursively, but also in Tom and Mary's repeated actions.

Curiosity and Dick Crick

Peter Brooks analogizes narrative with male sexual desire, wherein the narrative middle is associated with a prolonged desire that is ultimately consummated in the narrative climax (103). This vision of narrative is undercut by *Waterland*'s dual modes of nonnarrativity, which focus both on the flaccid boredom of the fens and on inexplicable moments that are neither "realized" nor consummated by narrative climax. In addition, Brooks' conception of narrative is parodied in the personage of Tom Crick's brother, Dick. Dick is, of course, a colossal phallic symbol, not only through his name and his size but also through the continual reference to his oversized penis. In Freudian terms, of course, the phallus is the master signifier, that which confers meaning to the Oedipal narrative and which is always ultimately desired. In *Waterland*, however, Dick's penis takes on explicitly contradictory import, never serving to confer meaning or to satisfy desire (two important functions of narrative). The unmasking of Dick's erection at a Hockwell Lode swimming competition is followed not by sexual climax but by rapid detumescence. "The monstrous swelling, that trapped baton—he no longer pushes it before him. It is gone—sunk" (190). Likewise, his prodigiousness does not contribute to his sexual potency, instead making him "too big" to be able to procreate (58, 261).[13] The size of Dick's penis is first noted at the swimming contest, but when the huge member is finally revealed, it does not hold the magical power or the symbolic significance that readers (and Mary) expect.

Dick's connection to Freud is further sealed by the fact that he is the product of the incestuous union of Helen and Ernest.[14] Incest is, of course, the narrative compulsively told within psychoanalytic discourse, with all sexual desire defined as displaced desire for the mother. If, as Brooks suggests, narrative is nothing if not desire, and for Freud all desire is originally incestuous, Dick can easily be read as the grotesque byproduct of narrative itself.[15] The fact that Dick's ridiculous phallicism is impotent and that his position as "Savior of the World" (a sobriquet given him by his father/grandfather, Ernest) can only be read as ironic, indicates how the novel positions itself against narratability as such, at least insofar as narrative can contain the historical real. Where narrative is said to explain the inexplicable, Dick is presented as a failure of explanation.

If, as Brooks asserts, we should see "the narratable as a condition of tumescence, appetency, ambition, quest" (103), Dick's detumescence at the swimming contest indicates the novel's interest in the nonnarratable, or the foiling of traditional narrative interest. This frustration of the narratable does not, however, fully explain why Crick insists that this 1940 episode is "tense with the present tense" and "fraught with the here and now" (207). It is not merely the presence of Dick, nor the revelation and withdrawal of his symbolic phallus, that brings the scene into the realm of the real, but also the comparison of that failed symbolic with the reality of the four other exposed penises in the scene. The swimming contest is engendered by a challenge from Mary Metcalf to five boys (including Freddie, Tom, and Dick). After exposing her breasts, Mary offers to remove her knickers as well, if the boys do the same. When the boys finally do so, their penises "droop so plaintively" upon inspection that Crick offers several (narrative) explanations to mitigate his failure to "rise to the occasion" (207). Despite his efforts, however, it is clear that there can be no symbolic weight attached to the pedestrian penises of the four boys. Indeed, these penises merely *are,* with no "appetency" promising future narrative interest: "Four wrinkled irresolute and slightly sticky members revealed, amidst nests of incipient pubic hair; which attempt to stand up, go limp and stir again feebly" (184). While Mary's sexual curiosity and the reader's narrative desire are piqued by the contest, what is finally (not) revealed suggests a parallel to the comparison of the Cricks and Atkinsons. What is real here is not the satisfaction of narrative desire, but the impossibility of realizing that desire, signified ironically by the (flaccid) penis itself. Because of this encounter, Crick is led to "escape[. . .] to his story-books" in an effort to provide a buffer between himself and the real (207).

Mary's sexual curiosity closely parallels Crick's narrative curiosity, especially in his attempt to discover the truth behind Freddie's murder. The desire to uncover a secret is often at the center of plot-driven stories (detective fiction, gothic novels, horror tales) and "the secret" is itself a synecdoche of plot itself in theories, like that of Brooks, which see a sustained and unrealized desire as the center of narration. As Brooks discusses, via Barthes, plot is defined by its near identity with the "hermeneutic code," the code of enigmas and answers, as opposed to the proairetic code, the code of actions. "The hermeneutic code concerns . . . the questions and answers that structure a story, their suspense, the partial unveiling, temporary blockage, eventual resolution. . . . The clearest and purest example . . . would undoubtedly be the detective story" (Brooks 18). Although action is necessary to ensure narrative's progress, mystery is necessary to provoke a reader's desire and stimulate narratability. Crick's explicit analogizing of historical research with "detective work" indicates the dependency of history upon narrative, just as Crick's pursuit of Freddie's killer shows itself to be committed to one of the most typical models of narration: the revelation of a secret. Swift partakes heavily of the long history of secret-driven fiction, and particularly that of the eighteenth-century gothic novel, by having Crick uncover the existence of the secret in a chest hidden in the attic of the family home. Within the box is not only a hidden stash of Ernest Atkinson's Coronation Ale (made, appropriately, with a "secret recipe"), but also the Atkinson family history as told by Ernest.[16] Within the family history is the secret(s) towards which much of the narratable plot of the Atkinsons leads. Both Dick's murder of Freddie and the secret of his parentage are revealed.

As discussed above, within certain contexts Dick is nothing but the logical conclusion of a typically Freudian narrative desire. The fact that "incest" additionally becomes the pursued object of the hermeneutic code merely solidifies Dick's connection to narratability. Likewise, the identification of Dick as "The Savior of the World" links him to the teleological narrative *par excellence*, that of Christianity and the Second Coming. Despite the overdetermination of Dick's link to narrative, Crick suggests the opposite about Dick's incestuous origins. "[W]hen fathers love daughters and daughters love fathers it's like tying up into a knot the thread that runs into the future, it's like a stream wanting to flow backwards" (228). That is, despite incest's status as eminently narratable in Freudian parlance, it cannot be a plot in the conventional sense in that it does not "progress" forward but runs only backwards into the past. Ernest and Helen try to deny this element of their relationship by affixing the Christian teleological label onto Dick, but his status as an incestuously produced "potato-head" indicates his incapacity to provide salvation, meaning, and truth, and therefore also the failures of teleological narrative.

Waterland's critique of desire is not universal, however. Rather, it is limited to the particular form of masculine sexuality that is marked by incipience, delay, and climax. This masculine desire is, in fact, continually contrasted in the novel with a more varied erotics, identified as "curiosity." "Curiosity drove her [Mary], beyond all restraint to want to touch, witness, experience whatever was unknown and hidden from her. . . . Curiosity, which bogs us down in arduous meditation and can lead to the writing of history books, will also, on occasion . . . reveal to us that which we seldom glimpse . . . the Here and Now" (51). While "desire" is a model of narration, Mary's "curiosity" is not structured merely around a particular climax-oriented satisfaction. That is, it does not seek a single response to a single desire (as in Crick's search for Freddie's murderer). Instead, it wishes to reveal anything that might be hidden, and, in doing so, may provide a glimpse of the "Here and Now." When this happens, "everything is open, everything is plain: there are no secrets, here, now, in this nothing-landscape" (52). Mary's tendency to want to share everything with Tom and to satisfy all curiosities, even the secrets of her monthly period, is analogized to the Fens themselves in which everything is flat and open to inspection, "the wide empty spaces of reality" (17). Here again the nonnarratable real makes an appearance, not as the satisfaction of a particular narrative desire but as an encounter with an ontological "space," the "empty vessel" described earlier (42): reality itself.[17]

Mary's sexual curiosity clearly deviates from the masculine model of narrative offered by Brooks. Likewise, Crick discusses curiosity as multiple and complex erotics that have little to do with the "progress" toward climax and achievement seen in traditional historical representation.

> Supposing it's revolutions which divert and impede the course of our inborn curiosity. Supposing it's curiosity—which insures our sexual explorations and feeds our desire to hear and tell stories—which is our natural and fundamental condition. Supposing it's our insatiable and feverish desire to know about things, . . . which is the true and rightful subverter and defeats even our impulse for historical progression. Have you ever considered that why so many historical movements . . . fail at heart, is because they fail to take account of the complex and unpredictable forms of our curiosity? Which doesn't want to push ahead, which always wants to say, Hey, that's interesting, let's stop awhile, let's take a look-see, . . . What's the rush? Let's *explore.* (194; emphasis in original)

Crick here refuses the dichotomy of narrative vs. nonnarrative that has dominated this discussion thus far. Instead, he echoes the many feminist narrative theorists who see the masculine model of narrative desire as reductive, limiting, and (even) unnatural.[18] In Robyn Warhol's discussion of soap operas, for instance, she invokes the possibility that all desire in narrative is not and cannot be defined, as Brooks suggests (103), by a Freudian death drive that is realized in the story's explanatory climax. Brooks's model privileges narrative conclusion as analogous to the "death" of the orgasm, justifying and explaining all of the "foreplay" leading up to it. Instead, Warhol points out that in the viewing of soap operas no end is wanted or needed, and that narrative desire can rather be sustained by the desire for a continuous deferral of conclusion, allowing for "narrative climax after narrative climax" ("Guilty Cravings" 353). The exploration, with no conclusion, that Crick advocates similarly reorients textual erotics, but asserts this curiosity not only as pleasurable but also as both "natural" and "true." Crick, in fact, eventually argues for what might be considered a "deviant" or "perverse" desire in the historical field: a desire not for one story but for infinite explorations. His model for this type of curiosity is the "natural history" of the search for the origins of *anguilla anguilla,* or the common eel.

Crick's radical deviation from his central plot to tell the tale of the search for the eel's origins is a model of the tangential curiosity that the novel advocates. As Crick explains, the journey of the eels from Europe to the Sargasso Sea and back again is "more mysterious, more impenetrable perhaps than the composition of the atom" in its accomplishment of "vast atavistic circles" (204). A contrast is again offered between the inexplicable, unsymbolizable, and circular and the linear, progressive, and explicable, with the latter seeking conclusions while the former pursues curiosity for its own sake. The linear search for history seeks "[r]eality. Reality made plain. Reality with no nonsense. Reality cut down to size. Reality minus a few heads" (206). What Crick suggests, however, is that the reality that reduces, eliminates nonsense, and cuts things down to size is the opposite of the "really" real as it has been defined elsewhere in the novel: the quotidian, the unsymbolizable trauma, and the "unsolved mystery of mysteries" like the mating pattern of the eels. The role of the eels in the novel's opposition to the Freudian is sealed by the myth that "a live fish in a woman's lap will make her barren" (18). The fact that Freddie Parr drops an eel down Mary Metcalf's knickers indicates how the novel jokingly refers to the attempt to halt masculine and/or reproductive narrative desire and replace it with an alternative eel-like curiosity that "weds us to the world" (206).[19] The eel's own status as phallic symbol is similarly undermined by the failure to explain its origins. The novel continually mocks the linear and/or phallic explanation, whether in the form of Dick's "eel" or in the eels themselves.[20]

Reproduction, Representation, and the Reality of the Real

The contrast *Waterland* erects between the nonnarrative real and meaning-making narrative is perhaps best seen in the marriage of Crick and Mary Metcalf that follows the trauma of the backwoods abortion. Mary is, for much of her marriage, brave enough to face the reality of her lost child without affixing some retrospective meaning to the event. That is, she is able to acknowledge the historical truth of the abortion (and the murder of Freddie, and Dick's suicide) without requiring it to fit amiably into a larger narrative that justifies it. She "did not believe any more in miracles and fairy-tales nor . . . in New Life and Salvation" (127). In this, she comes to a "knowledge of the limits of our power of explanation" (108) that Crick claims is the ultimate goal of history itself. Unlike Crick, she is able to "lay aside dreams, moonshine, cure-alls, wonder-workings, pie-in-the-sky—to be realistic" (108). "To be realistic," it appears, is to confront the reality of events without transforming them into Symbolic "explanation." This very notion of a real without signification denies the more extreme formulations of the linguistic turn, in which "truth itself is finally reduced to one of the style effects of the discursive articulation" (Žižek, *Sublime Object of Ideology* 153).

In an effort to arrest such poststructuralist excesses, Slavoj Žižek finds in the Lacanian notion of the Real something oppositional to other versions of poststructuralism and something congenial to his own class politics. Lacan, claims Žižek, allows for a truth beyond discourse, even if that truth is unsymbolizable or cannot be fully accessed or occupied. "Metalanguage is not just an Imaginary entity. It is *Real* in the strict Lacanian sense—that is, it is impossible to *occupy* its position. But Lacan adds, it is even more difficult to simply *avoid* it. One cannot *attain* it, but one can also not *escape* it" (*Sublime Object of Ideology* 156–57; emphasis in original). Analogously, the historical real may be impossible to present completely, in all of its plenitude and fullness, but it also cannot be banished to the realm of discourse. Rather, it always returns, like the psychoanalytically repressed. The link between individual trauma and historical event that *Waterland* maintains indicates how the historical past, while impossible to occupy completely, is nevertheless always present. Again, the concept of antinarrative is useful here. Where narrative is aligned in the novel with progress, linearity, and teleology, these moments of encounter with the unsymbolizable real, like the long periods of nonnarratable repetitive dredging, refuse the simplicity of sequential temporality. Likewise, where narrative is consistently tied to the soothing of fears and the use of explanation to quell disquiet, these moments of traumatic fright exceed narrative's capacity for comfort. Mary's refusal to be comforted by narrative or explanation marks an attempt on her part to confront the real.

Crick, on the other hand, and as we have seen, has a tendency to need the escape of storytelling. Because of this, it is Crick who leans on Mary in facing their mutual trauma. While Crick is forever attempting to replace the lost child with his students, she "made do . . . with nothing . . . , the empty space of reality" (126). In doing so, Mary even rejects adoption because "adoption is not the real thing" (127).[21] This acceptance of the real and the facing of the truism that "you cannot dispose of the past" (126) is, however, finally too much for Mary to bear as she turns towards one of the most tried and true of teleological metanarratives, that of religion, adopting the metaphorical role of "mother of God" that her name suggests. Like Ernest and Helen Atkinson, who configure Dick as the "Savior of the World," Mary declares that the supermarket baby is given to her by God, and the baby's return to its mother sparks Mary's own consignment to an insane asylum. Whereas Mary is once upheld by Crick as an exemplar of the bravery needed to confront the reality of the past and its present presence, she soon becomes yet another example of those who succumb to the compulsion to narrate.

Mary's short-lived capacity to make do with "nothing" is indicative of *Waterland*'s ambivalent orientation towards narrative. While the nonnarratable and nontraditional forms of narration are forwarded as necessary in accessing the historical past, the novel does not advocate the elimination of narrative from history, or from our lives, since doing so leads to madness. Indeed, Crick's continual assertion that history and storytelling are necessary means of coping with trauma should not be dismissed as merely fetishistic disavowals of the real. Rather, as Dominick LaCapra has discussed, it is not an effective means of dealing with the world to allow trauma to merely "repeat" itself "in a melancholic feedback loop" (*Writing History* 21), a description which may well describe Crick's own behavior at times in *Waterland*. Rather, LaCapra, like Crick, advocates the exploration of various modes of "working through" the trauma of past experience, allowing us to maintain sanity in our present. Unlike radically constructivist historiographers, however, LaCapra refuses the notion that the "medium" of the working-through inevitably defines the past events with which it grapples. Rather, the events themselves have a significant role in governing their retrospective shaping.

Even Hayden White, who is well known for arguing that "a historian could choose to plot any series of . . . events with any given plot structure or mode," is forced to reverse fields when faced with a trauma of sufficient strength (LaCapra, *Writing History* 17–18). White asserts, "In the case of the events of the Third Reich in a 'comic' or 'pastoral' mode, we would be eminently justified in appealing to 'the facts' in order to dismiss it from the lists of 'competing narratives'" ("Historical Emplotment" 40).[22] In this, he acknowledges the presence of past events even in and through their representation. It is perhaps for this (unacknowledged) reason that he argues for the use of "surrealist, expressionistic, or existentialist historiography" ("Burden of History" 43), for it is these forms that might be said to have the trauma of modern history impressed upon them. *Waterland*, like many (post)modernist texts, is likewise characterized stylistically by its rejection of linear, realistic narrative and its embrace of recursive, circular, self-reflexive, and heavily subjective narration. Rather than see these as merely self-regarding acknowledgments of the novel's fictional status, however, it is more productive to see them as formal reflections of the novel's historical moment, as well as the traumas discussed in its content. If "the facts" resist certain types of emplotment, surely they may demand alternative forms.

Swift's novel, then, insists both on LaCapra's warning against the valorization of the sublime *and* on Žižek's injunction against the erasure of the real through symbolization. *Waterland* continually refers to the therapeutic power of narrative, but it simultaneously points to the presence of the historical past and how an overdependence upon narrative may obscure that reality. Crick indicates the interdependence and inextricability of story and the real when he offers, "First it was a story—what our parents told us, at bedtime. Then it becomes real, then it becomes here and now. Then it becomes a story again" (328). Although Crick inverts the materialist assessment of the relationship of the real to its symbolization by claiming that the story comes first, this is not a causal claim that the story somehow engenders reality. Rather, a sequence is presented without clear causality, loosening the intricate link between "story" and "plot," and disallowing a simple explanation of one in terms of the other. This sense is compounded when Crick reverses his previous statement, saying, "First, there is nothing; then there is happening. And after the happening, only the telling of it. But sometimes the happening won't stop and let itself be turned into a memory" (329). Here, Crick shifts the primacy to two versions of the real (nothing and happening), while telling takes a tertiary role. Even so, there is the insistence that there are some (antinarrative) events that resist their transformation into symbolization, even as they "won't stop" recurring and are therefore always present.

Crick's continual combination and recombination of versions of storytelling with versions of the historical real indicates the degree to which they are interdependent and not reducible to one another in any simplistic or straightforward way. As Richard Terdiman notes in his study of memory in the modern age, there is a continuous tension and balance between memory as "*the absolute reproduction of unchanging contents*" and memory as the "*mobile representation of contents transformed*" (288; emphasis in original). *Waterland* asserts that the same is true of history, as it alternates between these extremes: the reproduction of traumatic events that retain their presence despite being past, and the representation of stories of the past as a therapeutic salve for the lack of meaning in the present. The claims of the linguistic turn in historiography and elsewhere overemphasize one half of this dialectic, too frequently asserting that historical discourse is only representation without any reproductive element. *Waterland* insists, however, that both sides of this dialectic be maintained, asserting the possibility of nonnarrative encounters with the real, even within a broader narrative.[23] The marriage of the Atkinson family to the Cricks indicates the novel's commitment to the notion of these two conceptual strands, as well as to their inextricability. Likewise, in its insistence upon the presence of the past, *Waterland* makes it possible to build our ethics upon an encounter with the real, and not merely upon our acknowledgment of the impossibility of that encounter.[24]

Trilobites, Ichthyosaurs, and Anagrams Made Flesh

In this chapter, I have highlighted the ways in which *Waterland* posits the possibility, even inevitability, of accessing the real of history. Although it presents narrative as a complex and subtle barrier to historical reference, it refuses to see history as a mere textual byproduct. Like *Between the Acts,* it elaborates the complexity of signification, including a focus on its ideological component, not in order to deny the possibility of seeing the real but in order to critique certain modes of representation that serve hegemonic interests.

While Woolf focuses on the patriarchal construction of history as part and parcel of material oppression, Swift's treatment of the Atkinsons, and their link to imperialism, functions as a critique of bourgeois historical representation, not merely as a disavowal of any possibility of history. Through these examples I wish to suggest a reorientation toward postmodern fiction that examines the purposes and effects of metafictional and self-conscious techniques not only as a reflection of a postmodern world wherein the real is perpetually withdrawing but also as a critique of that world and a suggestion of alternative modes of representation.

Within this context, Swift's other novels are also instructive, as several predict or expand upon the concerns highlighted in *Waterland*. *The Sweet-Shop Owner* (1980) uses the notion of the "Now" in roughly equivalent ways to the "Here and Now" in *Waterland*, while *Out of This World* (1988) investigates the capacity of photography to distill the real, even as it acknowledges the role of representation in the form. Likewise, in *Shuttlecock* (1981), Prentis investigates the impact of the past upon the present and considers the advisability of concealing the "facts" of his father's past within a more comfortable and comforting narrative. It would be impossible here to give a complete treatment of each of these novels, but in terms of Swift's treatment of narrative, reality, and history, it is worthwhile to look at *Ever After* (1992), the novel that, other than *Waterland*, deals most extensively with these issues. Like the earlier novel, *Ever After* works rigorously to point to the ways in which all elements of the world that we perceive to be real are, in fact, constructions, substitutes, and representations. The narrator, Bill Unwin, is a false academic, attaining his position not through merit but through a fellowship funded by his stepfather, Sam Elliot. Sam himself is a self-proclaimed "substitoot" for Bill's "real" father, who committed suicide. However, even the father whom Bill had always taken to be his biological progenitor is not "real," as Bill learns. He is, instead, the product of his mother's affair with an unnamed railroad man. Origins, then, are displaced, life-narratives are revealed as fictions, and notions of biological identity are replaced by social/textual constructions of subjectivity.

The radical questioning of reality is further emphasized in the fact that Bill's "true love," Ruth, is a famous actress who is paid to counterfeit love on stage and screen, leaving Bill to wonder if the foundation of his marriage is built upon false premises. His claim that their love continues happily "ever after" (until Ruth's death) is also exposed as fairy tale, with Bill continually stifling his suspicions of Ruth's infidelity. Indeed, Bill's suspicion of Ruth seem inevitable, given the fact that nearly everyone and everything in the book seem "untrue," including a variety of other extramarital affairs. Sam's work in the plastics industry highlights the ways in which the authentic seems inaccessible, and we are left with only the plastic, the "substitoot" and the second-order representation, as critics have been quick to point out.[25]

Within this context, *Ever After* treats notions of history directly in Bill's recovery of notebooks and letters written by his great-great-grandfather, Matthew Pearce. While Michael Potter, a colleague in the history department, self-interestedly offers to publish the material, Bill is more concerned with uncovering and accessing the real of Pearce's life, encountering its materiality and truth, than he is in conventional academic goals. As Bill says, "I am not in the business of strict historiography." Rather, he undertakes "a presumptuous task: to take the skeletal remains of a single life and attempt to breathe into them their former actuality" (100).

The idea of accessing Matthew's "presence," however, is clearly spawned by Bill's desperate desire to do the same for both his father and Ruth, who recently died of cancer. Because of the transparency of his motives, Bill's "recovery" of the past seems to serve the purpose of providing a salve for the trauma of the present and, because of its close links to Bill's self-interest, has no clear or transparent connection to the historical truth. As in *Waterland*, however, what makes Bill's encounter with Pearce interesting is not the ways in which he is able to appropriate Pearce's life in order to ease the pain of his own but rather the reverse: the ways in which Pearce's life is difficult to mold to this purpose.

Like Bill, Pearce has a love affair that is as close to the "real thing" as the world offers. Unlike Bill, however, Pearce does not desperately cling to his wife and child but abandons them because he loses his religious faith. Despite protracted discussions with his father-in-law in which he attempts to reconcile himself to Christianity, Pearce's encounter with a fossilized ichthyosaur, combined with his reading of Darwin's *Origin of Species*, provides an insurmountable obstacle to his happiness. Just as Bill attempts to integrate Pearce's life into his own, Pearce attempts to integrate the ichthyosaur into the narrative of Christianity that had always been central to his own subjectivity. Nevertheless, "within sight of the plump hills of Dorset and the ruffled waters of Lyme Bay, was the thing itself. . . . Here. Now. Then. He stood face to face with the skull of a beast that must have lived . . . unimaginably longer ago than even the most generous computations from the Scripture allowed for the beginning of the world" (111). The reprisal of "Here, Now" specifically sends the reader to *Waterland*'s construction of the term, although the addition, "Then," suggests a further connection with the material past. More than this, however, the description of the ichthyosaur is contrasted with nearly everything else in the novel, in which the "thing itself" has proven to be so elusive. As in *Waterland*, the "Here, Now" is characterized by its incapacity to be integrated into narrative. Pearce "pretends [to believe in God] so hard that one day, perhaps, he will forget he is pretending" (113). Pearce wishes desperately to be able to believe in biblical narrative and to remain married to his wife, but the brute factuality of the ichthyosaur disrupts every element of his life, prompting a final argument with his father-in-law and his departure.

Pearce's notebooks prove equally difficult for Bill, who cannot understand how an encounter with a fossil can interrupt love and life so fully. Of course, many of Bill's contemporaries have no trouble reconciling religion with ancient fossils, and the efforts to do so by the likes of Philip Henry Gosse in the years immediately following Darwin's revelations indicate how the effort to incorporate "the thing itself" into dominant cultural narratives is always underway. What Bill does have trouble reconciling, however, is how Pearce could have left his happy and comfortable existence over such a triviality as religion. Pearce's behavior, while perhaps occupying a narrative of its own, is impossible to integrate into Bill's. While Bill is frustrated by his incapacity to "explain" Pearce's behavior, it is precisely his inability to do so that is a signifier of the historical real in Pearce's life and letters.

Although Bill repeatedly and self-consciously draws attention to his own role in retrospectively constructing Pearce's life, it still proves intractable to his purposes. Indeed, Bill wonders why and how "a book" like Darwin's should make "so much difference in the world" (195). The question Bill asks next is a provocative one: "Did people have souls until 1859, when Darwin published his momentous work, then suddenly cease to have them?" (195). Within a radically "postmodern" system of thought, wherein truth is a mere byproduct of discursive or epistemic articulation, "souls" are real only as long as discourse asserts their existence, while dinosaurs too are only real if discourse grants them truth value. Clearly, however, in *Ever After*, the question is an ironic one. Pearce's encounter with "the thing itself" insists that Darwin did not destroy the notion of souls with his book. Rather, they never existed. Evolution was grinding on quietly and painfully long before Darwin came along to label it. Interestingly, Pearce has both paradigms, religious and evolutionary, available to him at this junction in history, and he tries desperately to hold onto the former. It is reality itself that prevents him from doing so. As Bill later observes, "Life isn't a theatre, is it? Life is a back-stage business. A struggle for existence" (231). Like *Waterland*, then, *Ever After* does not expose reality and history as fictions, nor does it assert a naïve mimeticism. Instead it advocates a treatment of history that dialectically combines Terdiman's notions of representation and reproduction. Bill notes that from the notebooks comes "a complete yet hybrid being, part truth, part fiction" and refuses to find that being to be completely "false" (100).

It is important, then, to see the metafictional self-reflexiveness of these novels not as an effort to put all notions of truth and reality into question but as an attempt to expose the various barriers to encountering reality and, in so doing, allowing such an encounter to take place. *Ever After*'s overlaying of the false, the fictional, the substitute, and the plastic serves not only to make us question the ideologies and narratives of the world in which we live, but also works to highlight and bring attention to the encounter with the ichythyosaur and the notebooks: the real itself. Conceiving of such formal features in this way allows us to reexamine many postmodern texts. In fact, prehistoric fossils prove to be a recurrent metaphor, particularly in British postmodernism, with fossils acting as texts that gesture to the real even within the most self-reflexive fiction. Jeanette Winterson's *Lighthousekeeping* (2004) is merely one of the more recent examples of postmodern novels that present the earth-shaking encounter of faithful Victorians with the reality of the fossil record.[26] In this novel, Babel Dark, the conflicted Victorian preacher, is told by Darwin himself that "[n]othing can be forgotten. . . . The universe itself is one vast memory system. Look back and you will find the beginnings of the world" (167). Despite Winterson's consistent thematizing of stories and storytelling, Dark's encounter with a cave full of marine fossils, like Pearce's encounter with the ichtyhosaur, is configured as a meeting of past and present: "everything was very still; he felt that he had disturbed some presence, arrived at a moment not for him" (117). The moment he arrives at is one from millions of years ago and refutes his "knowledge" that "the earth was 4,000 years old" (117).

Within this context, both *Ever After* and *Lighthousekeeping* implicitly refer to John Fowles's *French Lieutenant's Woman* (1969), whose protagonist is also a fossil hunter in Lyme. Significantly, *The French Lieutenant's Woman*, like these later novels, disorients its characters and its readers away from transparent conceptions of reality precisely in order to reveal the real, contrary to the many critical accounts of its postmodernism.[27] Fowles's (in)famous thirteenth chapter is inevitably the centerpiece of such discussions. In this chapter, Fowles intrudes as narrator, explaining that "these characters I create never existed outside my own mind" (95), while later Fowles metaleptically appears as a character, rewinds time, and allows the final chapter's events to be repeated and changed. Certainly, Fowles throws the "reality" of his fictional world into sharp question with these techniques, and, in doing so, might be said to make us question the reality of our own world. Still, Fowles performs these alienating techniques not merely to make us acknowledge the fictionality of our own experiences but also to free us from those fictions. Immediately after explaining that he is the creator of his characters, Fowles asserts that one of them, Charles Smithson, has already begun to disobey him. "It is not only that he has begun to gain an autonomy; I must respect it, and disrespect all my quasi-divine plans for him, if I wish him to be real" (97). All of this seems contradictory, as Fowles almost immediately admits (97), but he enacts this contradiction in order to lead his readers into a realization of their own reality and freedom. To do so, he addresses the reader directly, asserting, "You do not even think of your own past as quite real; you dress it up, you gild it, or blacken it, censor it, tinker with it . . . fictionalize it, in a word, and put it away on a shelf—your book, your romanticized autobiography. We are all in flight from the real reality. That is a basic definition of *Homo sapiens*" (97; ellipses and emphasis in original). Here, Fowles's narrator predicts Crick's claim of "man" as "the storytelling animal," but, as in the later novel, Fowles points out our "flight from the real reality" in order to orient us towards it. While we all perform roles in our own fictions, seeing that this is the case makes it possible to free ourselves from those roles. As Fowles asserts, "There is only one good definition of God: the freedom that allows other freedoms to exist" (97).

In this context, it is quite possible to read Sarah Woodruff's attempt to jettison herself from Victorian society as a kind of "symbolic suicide," similar to that experienced by Miss La Trobe in *Between the Acts,* while her manipulation of Charles is designed to bring him to the same encounter with the real. Unlike Pearce and Dark, however, Charles is never quite aware of the significance of his encounters with fossilized trilobites (49). The fact that there is no God, no author of our existence, is a prerequisite for a radical existential freedom in Fowles's oeuvre, but Charles does not understand this immediately. Instead, the elaborate "godgame" undertaken by Sarah serves to bring Charles into an encounter with the real and gives him the opportunity to reject the social scripts he initially inhabits. Through Sarah's manipulation, Charles loses his class position, his status as "gentleman," and his potential marriage. The fact that a "god" of sorts is needed to bring Charles into a realization of his own reality is problematic, of course, but the eventual withdrawal of Sarah from Charles's life indicates that once a realization of the pervasive discursivity of existence is achieved, an ethical encounter with the world is possible. By the conclusion of the novel, Charles has, it seems, "found an atom of faith in himself, a true uniqueness, on which to build" (467) when he leaves Sarah, although there is some ambiguity as to whether or not he is, at this moment, still fooling himself, still performing a role in a cultural narrative. Even if this is the case, the novel's self-reflexivity encourages its readers to consider their own confinement in social text and to do what Charles, perhaps, cannot. Fowles's address to the reader in chapter 13 is designed to spur the reader into an encounter with the real, not to lead us into a postmodern web of textuality from which we can never emerge.[28]

The same is true of Fowles's earlier novel, *The Magus.* In *The Magus,* too, there are the self-reflexive metafictional gestures that frequently garner the postmodern label. It is true, of course, that the novel's main characters, Nicholas and Allison, are not real, and Fowles draws attention to the artifice of their final moments together, wherein we are left to wonder whether they will reconcile or separate forever. "She is silent, she will never speak, never forgive, never reach a hand, never leave this frozen present tense" (656). As in the dual endings of *The French Lieutenant's Woman,* Fowles leaves the ultimate choice of what Nicholas and Allison will do to the reader who *can* choose. In Brechtian fashion, Fowles's foregrounding of artifice serves to remind readers of the distinction between these characters and themselves. While Nicholas and Allison may escape from the fictions imposed upon them by Conchis (and by more widely conceived social expectations), the fact remains that they are mere textual features, not "anagram[s] made flesh" (655).[29]

As James Phelan discusses in *Reading People, Reading Plots,* Fowles's foregrounding of the "synthetic" (clearly constructed) element(s) of his narrative(s) allows him to speak simultaneously to a "narrative audience" following the developments of character and plot, and an "authorial" audience alert to more formal and thematic concerns (83–106). In metafictively reminding his readers that they are reading a constructed narrative, the distance *between* such a "synthetic" narrative and "flesh and blood" readers' real lives is emphasized. Unlike Charles and Sarah, the reader is not a character in a Fowles novel and actually *does* have choices of the kind only thematized in the novel's multiple endings. As Phelan points out, while Fowles may *claim* his characters have the freedom to act against his will, the authorial audience, which "takes as a first principle... that the whole narrative is itself a synthetic construction" (Phelan, *Reading People* 93) will be well aware that such claims are false. However, by invoking such existential "freedom," Fowles invites the reader to consider and embrace their own relative freedom.

The highlighting of artifice in postmodern narrative may be read as a revelation of the artifice of our daily lives. At the same time, however, it reminds us of the distinctions between fictional narrative and life experience. Nicholas, Alison, Charles Smithson, and Sarah Woodruff have no *real* choices, since they are mere creations of their author. Readers, however, *do* have such choices, particularly if they realize that the plots they inhabit are not inevitably sequential and progressive. By "freezing" the conclusion of *The Magus,* Fowles invokes something similar to Swift's "Here and Now," a moment of an encounter with the real that cannot be integrated into an explanatory narrative and in which an ethical choice can, and must, take place.

CHAPTER 3

"What's Real and What's True"

Metaphors, Errata, and the Shadow of the Real in Salman Rushdie's Midnight's Children

> ... the past is a country from which we have all emigrated ... its loss is part of our common humanity.
> —Salman Rushdie, *Imaginary Homelands* (12)

Both *Between the Acts* and *Waterland* evince the historical referentiality of nonnarrative forms by pitting narrative (the pageant, the Atkinsons) against its opposite ("between the acts," the Cricks) and by showing how antinarrative events can exceed and defeat the narrative that attempts to represent them. However, to conceive of Salman Rushdie's *Midnight's Children* in similar terms is problematic for several reasons. First, *Midnight's Children* positively "teems" with narrative, as Rushdie himself notes (*Imaginary Homelands* 16), continually offering story after story, history, fantasy, (auto)biography, fable, and myth. This virtuoso display of storytelling is unlikely to yield an antipathy to the narrative form, and, at least initially, it makes more sense to read the novel as a celebration of narrative rather than as a critique. Still, insofar as *Midnight's Children* is not merely a group of fantastic stories, but is also a history of modern India with an allegiance to historical reference, its embrace of narrative is always qualified by the acknowledgment that narrative demands a kind of formal unity that may violate the imperatives of veracity suggested (if rarely achieved) by the term "history." Rather than focus on the plotless or unplottable, then, Rushdie employs what Gerald Prince has labeled the "disnarrated" in order to supplement narrative's failings with an alternative form.

"Disnarration," according to Prince, refers to "those passages in a narrative that consider what did not or does not take place" ("Disnarrated" 1).[1] The disnarrated typically refers to events or circumstances that the narrator tells the reader, but which did not actually occur in the world of the story. Either one of John Fowles's endings to the *French Lieutenant's Woman* could, for instance, have been "disnarrated" if the narrator had finally revealed that one of them was actually the "real" ending. Doing so would remove the other ending from the narrative proper. In fact, Fowles actually does provide a disnarrated ending earlier, in which Charles marries Ernestina and they live "happily ever after." When the narrator reveals that "the last few pages you have read are not what happened, but what Charles spent the hours between London and Exeter imagining might happen" (339), he disnarrates part of the previous chapter.[2] Similarly, in *Midnight's Children,* Rushdie provides both a central narrative and a series of disnarrated events, which he elsewhere labels "errata," because they reveal errors in the narrative. Interestingly, however, the disnarrated "errata" are frequently attached to real-world historical events, supplementing the errors and excesses to which the narrative proper is prone, and suggesting that the narrated world is, at times, disconnected from the historical real. In this way, Rushdie explores the value of narrative, while also examining its referential shortcomings. In doing so, and in similarly reevaluating figurative language, Rushdie does not undermine historical reference (as critics frequently suggest), but reimagines it.

Mistakes and Lies

By providing both a narrative proper (a narrative "whole") and a series of disnarrated "extra parts" (the errata), *Midnight's Children* enacts a vacillation between the unity of form and its opposite in fragmentation that is similar to what we have observed in both *Waterland* and *Between the Acts.* The dynamic relationship between part and whole, form and fragmentation, is, in fact, a dominant theme in the novel, as several critics have discussed.[3] Saleem Sinai, in particular, is consumed with the desire to narrate his entire life and that of his nation if he is to "end up meaning—yes meaning—something" (4). Saleem feels that he must complete his story, providing closure to his life's narrative, while also noting how comprehensibility (or "meaning") can only be generated from a completed whole, or a unified form. It is certainly this urge that leads him to attempt to create a comprehensive history that "swallows" the multitude of possible stories: "[T]here are so many stories to tell, . . . an excess of intertwined lives. . . . I have been a swallower of lives; and to know me, . . . you'll have to swallow the lot as well . . . guided only by memory of a large white bedsheet with a roughly circular hole . . . cut in the centre" (4).

The internal contradictions of *Midnight's Children,* of Saleem, and of India itself are all contained quite startlingly in this passage. Saleem declares the multitude of divergent tales that his personal (his)story will contain, including the seemingly incompatible "improbable and the mundane" (4). Nevertheless, he asserts that his life *will* encompass them all, "swallowing" them into his singular body and his singular story, providing a unity of form and content that seems unlikely from such divergent source material. Ironically, however, the "open-sesame" that allows Saleem access to a historical past he has not himself lived is one of the novel's most obvious symbols of fragmentation: the holey bedsheet that plays such a central role in the courtship of Dr. Aadam Aziz and Naseem, Saleem's maternal grandparents.[4] The sheet prevents Aziz from viewing his patient's whole body, protecting purdah during a medical exam. He is allowed, then, only to view seven-inch portions of her body, and he falls in love piece by piece. Ironically, this symbol of fragmentation allows Saleem to unify his narrative, "filling in the gaps in [his] knowledge" (14). Through the hole, then, Saleem makes his history "whole."

The focus on the wholeness of form is reflected in Nadir Khan's roommate "whose paintings had grown larger and larger as he tried to get the whole of life in his art" (49), in Lifafa Das, the peepshow proprietor, who invites people to "see the whole world" in his postcards (81), and in Saleem himself when he asserts, "Everything has shape if you look for it. There is no escape from form" (259). He likewise asserts that the urge to find form and unity is "an Indian disease" (82), a "national longing for form," and that "form lies hidden within reality" (344). These urges towards an all-encompassing formal unity are contrasted with the equally prevalent images of fragmentation: the slow dissolution and eventual fragmentation of Saleem's body into millions of pieces,[5] Amina's resolve to fall in love with Ahmed Sinai piece by piece, and the splintering of the Midnight's Children Conference. As discussed above, within Hayden White's model of constructivist historiography, the urge to unify and explain that is indicated in a "national longing for form" is actually a barrier to historical reference, while the fragmentation of that unity may be the means to access the real. From this perspective, the filling of gaps that Saleem undertakes is a transformation from a referential vision of history, always contingent and meaningless, into a "meaningful fiction" with themes, storylines, and moral content.

In this context, it is important that the unity for which Saleem strives in his story is generated by his efforts to correlate himself with India as a whole, leading him to manipulate personal and political chronology in order to make them correlate. This project also generates the multitude of historical errors. In the essay entitled "Errata," Rushdie argues that the function of these mistakes is not only to mark Saleem's narration as unreliable but also to highlight the inevitability of unreliability as such (*Imaginary Homelands* 22). In "Imaginary Homelands" Rushdie reminds his readers that *Midnight's Children* is a novel of memory (explicitly opposed to "history") and is thus inevitably selective and inaccurate. In this, Rushdie reflects the ideas of theorists like Pierre Nora who separate memory from history by offering memory as a personal and liberating alternative to oppressive "official" or institutional history. Rushdie's memories become an alternative narrative dedicated to "denying the official, politicians' version of the truth" (*Imaginary Homelands* 14), a sentiment that Saleem echoes almost verbatim in the novel (242).

That is, by Rushdie's account, Saleem's mistakes underscore a denaturalization of historical discourse, emphasizing its fallibility, construction, and inaccuracy, and therefore asserting how any claim to the past has limited access to the real and is subject to both personal and ideological manipulation. This may explain why Saleem makes so many historical errors, but it does not fully explain why he is so *aware* of and troubled by them. In fact, a closer look at these mistakes reveals that they assert the possibility of accurate historical reference despite Rushdie's explicit claims to the contrary. Most important to this alternate reading is the simple assertion that, in pinpointing Saleem's errors and correcting them both in the novel and in the later essay, Rushdie asserts the existence of a factual accuracy that exceeds, or lies outside of, his protagonist's narration. The correction of Saleem's errors cannot help but remind us of the disnarrated truth(s) that he obscures, elides, and displaces in the narrative proper.

From this perspective, it is important to recall that most of these errors are generated by Saleem's efforts to correlate his own life with that of his country. Saleem's belief in his own centrality derives from the letter he receives from Prime Minister Nehru once he is found to be the child born closest to the precise moment of Indian Independence (139). Because of Saleem and India's shared birth date/time, the reader is led to read the novel as an allegory of subcontinental history. At the same time, however, *Midnight's Children* functions as a parody of that history, not least because Saleem's purported status as "midnight's child" is erroneous, since he is switched at birth with Shiva, the knock-kneed untouchable. The ridiculously elaborate structural framework Saleem needs to make all events in his personal life relevant to national affairs makes the parodic element even clearer: "I was linked to history both literally and metaphorically, both actively and passively, in what . . . scientists might term 'modes of connection' composed of 'dualistically-combined configurations' . . . : actively-literally, passively-metaphorically, actively-metaphorically and passively-literally" (272–73).

Both the pseudoscientific language and the convoluted path Saleem takes to prove himself "inextricably entwined with my world" (273) points the reader away from taking his claims too seriously. No doubt, with such an elaborate rubric, *anyone* could find correspondence between national history and their own lives, and this, among others, is a point the novel makes. More important than this fairly banal observation, however, is the implication that Saleem's elaborate structuring sacrifices referentiality for unity. The most significant example of the disjunction between historical accuracy and Saleem's model occurs when he hears of the assassination of Mohandas Karamchand Gandhi while viewing his Uncle Hanif's film, *The Lovers of Kashmir*. To the uninitiated, nothing seems amiss, but Saleem soon realizes he has made an "error in chronology," misplacing the date of the Mahatma's murder (189–90). Here, the novel metaphorically infers that it is not now the "right time" for Gandhi to die. Still, there is more to this error than a commentary on the tragedy of the murder. Saleem, in fact, seems less concerned with the tragedy itself than he is with his own mistake. At this moment he begins to doubt the validity of his entire narrative: "Am I so far gone, in my desperate need for meaning, that I'm prepared to distort everything . . . to place myself in a central role?" (190).

In this passage, Saleem begins to suspect that his "modes of connection" are stretching the limits of historical accuracy beyond their breaking point. The inconsistency *does* threaten his structural framework, but, ironically, by introducing the real date of the event, a disnarrated sliver of reality itself. That is, the true date of the assassination is *not* part of Saleem's narrative, but it is nevertheless expressed clearly in the novel in the form of an acknowledged mistake. While most accounts of Rushdie's errata identify this merely as a self-reflexive signal to the reader of the inevitable inaccuracy of all historical narration, this same reflexivity reminds readers of the real itself, providing us with a glimpse of the (accurate) history that Saleem is *not* telling. The other mistakes to which Rushdie points in "Errata" likewise come as a result of Saleem's efforts to integrate his life with that of his nation, but they function not as an index of the fundamental impossibility of accurate representation, but as an injunction to the reader to find a version more accurate than Saleem's.[6]

From this perspective, David Carroll's claim that a coherent national story naturally contributes to and supports a unified and healthy individual subjectivity is undercut (112; Srivastava 67–68). Rather, in *Midnight's Children*, the two narratives, personal and national, push and pull at one another, generating errors in either or both in Saleem's effort to make them continuous. It thus becomes difficult to believe Rushdie's advice to always trust the relative truth of one's own memories. Rather, it becomes clear that Saleem's memory, personal as it may be, may not only be wrong but also correctable given more information. If this is the case, some kinds of truth are *not* relative, or not completely so.

With the reintroduction of the idea of truth through the back door of its opposite, *Midnight's Children* also investigates the complex fissures and distinctions between fictions and untruths. Certainly, Saleem's narration of Gandhi's assassination falls into both categories. While it is undoubtedly part of the fiction that is *Midnight's Children,* its effort to lay claim to historical personages and events allows it to be read as "untrue" as well, once the mistake is revealed. Few critics note the importance of these distinctions, but Neil ten Kortenaar takes a step in this direction, when he asks, "[I]f history is a fiction, why should any one version be preferable to another?" ("*Midnight's Children*" 53), noting similar ethical pitfalls to those offered by critics of constructivist historiography. However, Rushdie shows not only that some fictions are preferable to others, but also that fiction is not, in itself, a lie. Saleem draws this distinction most clearly when he argues that in India he is "beset by an infinity of alternate realities, while in" Pakistan he is "adrift . . . amid an equally infinite number of falsenesses, unrealities, and lies" (373).

The distinction is established in order to allow Saleem to critique the election-day manipulations of his Pakistani uncle, General Zulfikar, as "lies," not fictions or metaphors. Post-Orwell, it is not surprising to find a critique of an authoritarian government's domination and control of what is considered to be "true," but most such critiques come from a position of relative epistemological certainty, in which manipulation of information is unacceptable precisely because there is a truth underneath to be revealed. Saleem does not here offer a clear and single truth that refutes the falsehoods propagated by the Pakistani government. Instead, he offers an infinite number of alternative realities to oppose infinite lies. The mere identification of this infinity seems to deny the truth/falsehood binary and, in doing so, is in danger of invalidating the critique of lies. At the very least, the notion of multiple (even infinite) truths radically resituates such a critique. Nevertheless, while truth/falsehood is no longer a simplistic dualism in the context of the novel, "fictions" in their multiplicity *are* rhetorically separated from lies. Despite the complication of the truth/falsehood divide, Rushdie's refusal to allow realities and lies the same epistemological status indicates an adherence to materiality that his work is rarely afforded by critics.

In fact, Rushdie's recent nonfiction writings have insisted on the retention of the category of truth, if not in any simplistic positivist fashion. Rushdie's claim "that the world is real" and his efforts to retain notions of the "*thing in itself*" (*Step* 172; emphasis in original) take a central place in his later essays, particularly those collected in *Step Across This Line* (2003). In "Farming Ostriches," for instance, Rushdie notes the importance of an allegiance to truth in both "factual and fictional writing," (13), while he elsewhere praises Arthur Miller for his "insistence on the reality of the real and on the moral function of writing" (46). A brief essay on the Taj Mahal similarly focuses on the distinctions between the original and the second-order representation to the benefit of the former. Of course, Rushdie's nonfiction musings on the nature of truth in the 1990s do not necessarily shed light on his fictional output of the early 1980s, especially given the shift in perspective that undoubtedly occurred in the years following the *Satanic Verses fatwa*. Nevertheless, these straightforward arguments for the retention of the real should, at the very least, encourage a reading of Rushdie that is not so eager to position his work as that which specifically denies all possibility of truthful, or historical, reference.

In fact, there are crucial moments throughout his earlier work wherein it is clear that Rushdie is not merely interested in deconstructing Western histories, but is equally, if not more, interested in asserting a more accurate version of history in their place. This is particularly true in his treatment of the 1919 Amritsar Massacre at Jallianwala Bagh and the 1975–77 Emergency administered by Indira Gandhi. In the case of the Emergency, whereas the positive side had often been highlighted in historical texts, in *Midnight's Children* Saleem insists that the Emergency "had a black part as well as a white" (492). In particular, the paying of taxes and the trains running on time (499) are accomplished through fear, tyranny, suspension of civil rights, and forced sterilizations.[7] For Saleem (and Rushdie) this "black part" is not merely an alternative fiction to the one painted by Indira in official statements, but a truer one.[8]

Likewise, whereas several critical readings of *Midnight's Children* suggest that the novel offers the possibility of multiple interpretations of the Amritsar Massacre, Rushdie clearly asserts the truth of one type of interpretation over another. Sabrina Hassumani argues that the novel suggests that history "is always an interpretation that depends on the subjective perspective of the interpreter" (36). Rushdie, however, consistently makes a distinction between subjective interpretation and ideological deception. In particular, Hassumani suggests that Rushdie offers epistemological equivalency to diametrically opposed versions of the massacre, wherein the "colonizers viewed this as putting order to chaos" and "the colonized viewed it as a cold-blooded massacre" (36). In fact, Rushdie clearly asserts the latter as truth. When Rushdie's General Dyer calls the massacre "a jolly good thing" (34), the scene serves as an ironic condemnation of an imperial system built upon violence and racism, not as a value-neutral difference of opinion.[9]

Metaphor, Metonymy, and *Omeros*

Given Rushdie's political/ethical need for and explicit claims about the categories of truth, reality, and history, it is somewhat surprising that his work has been so consistently read as relativist, deconstructive, or "postmodern." Nevertheless, this view of his work has developed into a massive critical consensus (with occasional, if important, dissenters). Aruna Srivastava, for example, asserts that in *Midnight's Children*, "reality and truth are not quantifiable and not ascertainable. They are constructs of imagination and experience, and of language" (65). Likewise, Sabrina Hassumani notes that in Rushdie's world "there are no absolute versions of history and, in fact, all the versions are constructs" (27), while David Price argues that Saleem "presents history as a performance of narration, as opposed to a representation of events that took place in the past" ("Salman Rushdie's" 93). In the same vein, Nancy Batty has suggested that the confusion of history and fiction is *Midnight's Children*'s primary purpose (80), and Michael Reder makes an even broader claim about Rushdie's beliefs, arguing that "Rushdie believes that history is not scientific or objective; history is the same as 'fiction'" (239).[10]

Most accounts of Rushdie's postmodernism rely heavily on an examination of certain formal strategies used throughout his oeuvre. Just as the sprinkling of errata in *Midnight's Children* have been read as promoting a thoroughgoing mistrust of any one version of the "truth," Rushdie's use of intrusive and self-referential narrators suggest the subjective, and therefore unreliable, nature of the histories they tell. Foremost, however, among the strategies associated with Rushdie's postmodernism is his peculiar brand of magical realism. While similar to progenitors like Gabriel García Márquez,[11] Rushdie's magical realism seems designed to draw attention to the linguistic mediation of historical discourse, specifically by making commonly used metaphors literal. That is, while Western historians, like Stanley Wolpert,[12] might assert that "the Indian business community was turning white" to express the degree to which subcontinental economics was beginning to resemble Western capitalism, such a metaphor is made literal in *Midnight's Children* when Ahmed Sinai and his friends actually begin to change color (204). From Nadir Khan literally being "swept under the rug," to the epidemic "outbreak of optimism," and Ahmed Sinai's frozen "assets," nearly all fantastical elements of the novel derive from a literal adherence to the linguistic tropes present in everyday, and historical, discourse. While we would typically assume that "magic" deviates widely from the historical real, in *Midnight's Children* it arises precisely out of "history," or the language through which it is conveyed. Through "magical realism," then, the novel foregrounds how history is reliant on figurative language to such a degree that it cannot be "literally" true.

The critical attention to this strategy leads almost inevitably to the reasonable argument that Rushdie echoes and reiterates Hayden White's claims that narrative and language prevent an accurate account of history and that, in fact, any sense we have of the reality of history is built on language in all of its semiological slipperiness. As Kortenaar writes, "*Midnight's Children* exposes the fictionality, the constructedness, of the metaphors and narrative conventions implied in national history" ("*Midnight's Children*" 51). That is, by literalizing the metaphors common to historical discourse, Rushdie exposes how a supposedly mimetic medium is actually merely tropology, telling us fantastic things that could never have "actually" happened.

To clarify the ways in which *Midnight's Children* develops metaphor's function, it is helpful to invoke Paul de Man's "The Epistemology of Metaphor." In this essay, de Man begins precisely with the troubling relationship between history's claim to referentiality and its use of metaphors, tropes, and figural language. As de Man attempts to prove over the course of his career, the problems of the referentiality of metaphor are "a recognized source of embarrassment for philosophical discourse . . . , including historiography and literary analysis" (34). The embarrassment is not, however, inherent to metaphor but to the discourses, all of which make implicit claim to referentiality, whether to philosophical truth, to actual events, or to other stable texts. As such, they all must establish the possibility of their discourse referring "rigorously" to their object of study. Metaphor, however, is always referring to something other than its perceived object, through comparisons and signifying chains, making stable and rigorous analysis impossible. As de Man suggests, then, these discourses either have "to give up [their]constitutive claim to rigor . . . or . . . free [themselves] from figuration altogether" (34).

The attempt to free language from figuration is not limited to discourses typically known for their "rigor," however. Even poetry, in an instructive, if paradoxical, example, has proposed the attempt. Derek Walcott's epic poem, *Omeros*, is particularly relevant, paralleling as it does *Midnight's Children*'s engagement with the postcolonial condition and its preoccupation with history. As in *Midnight's Children*, Walcott's central characters live in a postcolonial present (on the island of St. Lucia) but are preoccupied with and explore a colonial past. As part of an effort to uncover and reconnect with Caribbean history, various characters become "historians" of sorts. The British Major Plunkett researches the 1782 Battle of the Saints, the black Achille goes on a spiritual quest for his African past, and the Walcott-narrator figure explores other geographical/historical influences upon his native land.[13] Just as these characters look for some access to the past, however, the threat of figuration continuously recurs. Parallels between *Omeros* and Homer's *Iliad* and *Odyssey* evolve, with the St. Lucian love triangle between Hector, Achille, and Helen compared, metaphorically, to the competition between their ancient Greek namesakes. At first, the comparison seems merely to be a cross between an ironic game and a bold play for the poem's canonicity, but as the poem unfolds, it becomes clear that Walcott introduces the comparison to question and reject figuration more than to validate his own work.

Oddly, since Walcott's verse is often hinged on elaborate metaphors, the epic slowly comes to a figural crisis in which the poet-narrator disavows metaphor itself both for its failure in representation and for the political/social repercussions these failures may generate. In one of numerous moments of self-doubt, the narrator asks, "When would the sails drop / from my eyes, when would I not hear the Trojan War / in two fishermen cursing" (271). In this, he questions metaphor and the comparison of the heroic Greek figures with their latter-day Caribbean echoes. The rejection of metaphor is made explicit in the narrator's praise of the ocean, configured as "natural" and therefore "a wide page without metaphors" (296). If the ocean can do without metaphors, wonders the narrator, why must he rely upon them, and what is gained by doing so?

As the poem continues, it becomes clear that very little is gained and that what is lost is the materiality of the present moment and its island inhabitants. In his comparison of the St. Lucian Helen to the Greek, the narrator finally decides that, "Names are not oars / that have to be laid side by side" (313), and that the mere sharing of names is not only little grounds for metaphorical comparison, but in fact such figuration reduces the "real" Helen, her life and struggle, to but a shadow of the Helen of the mythical past. "You were never in Troy, and, between two Helens / yours is here and alive; . . . / These Helens are different creatures, one marble, one ebony" (312–13). As these lines' focus on racial difference makes clear, part of Walcott's attack on metaphor is an attack on the particular ways in which Afro-Caribbean history and culture has come to be defined only from the perspective of and in relation to the Western culture that imaginatively originates in Greece. That is, while in some ideal sense it is true that both Helens are being compared to and understood in light of one another, in practice the black Helen is made to conform to the "type" of the Greek progenitor, just as St. Lucia itself has been made to conform to the imperatives of Western economy. In the rejection of this metaphorical comparison and the praise of the ocean's resistance to metaphor, it is clear that the poem associates figuration with colonization, attempting to reject both (albeit with an acknowledgment of the impossibility of doing so). While Walcott's poem is not "history" in any traditional sense, it displays a similarity to the "rigor" of historiographic discourse in its inevitably failed attempt to present the referent itself and not be misled by secondary objects of comparison.[14]

In preemptive opposition to *Omeros'* desires to avoid figuration, de Man reminds us that "the use and abuse of language cannot be separated" (41). That is, the representational capacity of language cannot be separated from its figurative content, and when referring to such innocent things as "the legs of the table or the face of the mountain," already a "catachresis" or "abuse of language" takes place, as "one begins to perceive a world of potential ghosts and monsters," or, at the very least, walking tables and talking mountains (de Man 42). As such, de Man suggests that the "noble dream" of tropeless objectivity expressed in *Omeros* must remain a dream because of the very nature of language. Words are not the objects or actions to which they refer and, as such, are already symbolic substitutes even before more complex tropes are introduced.

Even if figuration is, in some sense, inevitable as de Man suggests, *Omeros'* antagonism to metaphor reflects a strain in postcolonial studies that rejects metaphor as inherently oppressive, while expressing a preference for metonymy as an aesthetic mode of liberation. Metaphor is said by several important postcolonial theorists to subjugate colonized or formerly colonized cultures to the Western cultures to which they are frequently compared. Homi Bhabha, Aijaz Ahmad, and the authors of *The Empire Writes Back* (Ashcroft, Griffiths, and Tiffin) note how focusing on the ways in which two cultures are metaphorically "alike" obscures the importance of their difference, effacing their uniqueness. Fredric Jameson, for instance, has been criticized for his tendency to flatten all "third-world" space into one undifferentiated mass typified by a "Hegelian metaphor of the master-slave relation" (Ahmad 105; Fenwick 65n3). To read "metaphorically," as Jameson does, is to understand an "other" culture only in a dominant culture's terms, just as *Omeros'* narrator grapples with St. Lucia from the perspective of Homeric Greece.

According to this critical logic, metonymy, in which one word or phrase is substituted for another with which it is closely associated (or of which it is a part), is preferable to metaphor. Metaphor operates on the basis of "resemblance," making one thing understood through its "resemblance" to something else, while metonymy operates through "contiguity" or proximity: two things that are next to, or associated with, one another, but not necessarily "similar." As such, metonymy may point readers to that "part" of a culture that cannot be understood in terms of its resemblance to another.

As Mac Fenwick notes, "Metonymy is thus privileged [in much postcolonial theory...] as the inscription of radical difference" (48). Bhabha, for instance, valorizes the "partial presence" of metonymy as unsettling to efforts to suture the Other into dominant subjectivity. As Fenwick observes, however, despite theoretical objections, metaphor continues to be a constitutive part of postcolonial literary and theoretical discourse, even in texts that, like *Omeros*, self-consciously reject it.

Nowhere is the pervasiveness of metaphor more evident than in *Midnight's Children*, wherein metaphors are made literal, and where Saleem himself is an all-encompassing metaphor for India itself. Saleem functions both metaphorically and metonymically, however, since he both resembles the nation as a whole and retains some of his own "partially present" particularities that leave him in proximity to India without always reflecting it.[15] The dynamics of form and fragmentation discussed earlier can quite easily be seen to be a version of the metaphor/metonymy debate, wherein totalizing comparisons are sometimes valued, only to be countered by a multitude of contiguous, and partial, fragments.

The division of metaphor and metonymy is itself problematic, as Fenwick is quick to note, since the kind of comparison that purportedly subsumes one compared object to another must also retain their separation if any understanding of either side of the equation is to be maintained. That is, if I assert, "India is (like) England," I must retain a list of qualities that are specifically "English" if I am to see the metaphor as contributing to my understanding of India. If the two are viewed as actually equivalent, I have produced a tautology, not a metaphor, and no knowledge emerges. Metaphor does not, then, eradicate "difference," as some critics suggest. Metonymy likewise relies on our capacity to recognize similarities between contiguous parts, blurring the distinction between the two figures further. From this perspective, *Omeros'* narrator's fears of the effacement of St. Lucian culture are unfounded, since the comparisons to Homeric Greece cannot exist without the retention of the island in at least some of its specificity. Rushdie shows an intense awareness of these contradictions, however, and rather than distance itself from metaphor, as *Omeros* does, *Midnight's Children* draws it ever closer.

Literal Metaphors, Metaphorical Truth, and Fictional Worlds

Where de Man declares that historical discourse must either give up its claims to referentiality or divorce itself from figuration altogether, *Midnight's*

Children refuses both of these options by insisting both on the referentiality of historical discourse and on taking figuration to its unexpected (il)logical extreme. In *Midnight's Children*, Rushdie rejects the idea of "imitating" the world, as such, and instead makes his world imitate language. If referentiality is supposedly guaranteed by the elimination of figuration, Rushdie succeeds in reversing this assertion by creating an alternate world in which the tropological and the literal are coterminous.

In Saleem's India the linguistic slippage invoked by Walcott, de Man, and poststructuralist thought in general is eliminated: the linguistic and the metaphorical refer precisely to reality. The fear, then, of one term of a comparison being unfairly subsumed by another is irrelevant, since the comparison results in a literal equivalence. Indeed, Rushdie successfully undercuts John Locke's argument against the error of "mistak[ing] words for things" (104; vol. 2, bk. 3, ch. 10), by making such a mistake impossible. When Saleem tells us that his father is turning white, this is not a mistake on Saleem's part because in this world, language and reality are not separable. Saying that Ahmed is turning white makes it, magically, true.

In this light, it is curious that critics have affiliated Rushdie's use of literalized metaphor with the poststructuralist exposé of language's failure to refer rigorously to reality. In doing so, they have ignored how the novel insistently associates metaphor not with deviations from and deformations of reality but with truth telling itself. In a world where metaphors are literally true, it makes sense that metaphor would be consistently associated with truth, but Saleem's (and Rushdie's) allegiance to metaphor exceeds the "magical" world of *Midnight's Children* and applies also to our own. Indeed, Saleem's explicit references to metaphor imply that they have the potential to reveal reality, not obscure it. This is most forcefully expressed when Saleem insists to Padma upon the reality of his clairvoyance, although it is clear that it is a metaphor for Rushdie's own authorial access to his characters' minds. "I am not speaking metaphorically; what I have just written . . . is nothing less than the literal, by the hairs of my mother's head truth. . . . Reality can have metaphorical content; that does not make it less real" (229–30).[16]

Here Saleem suggests that although the existence of the "midnight's children" is metaphorical, it is, nevertheless, real and true. That is, while figurative, it is not a wholesale invention, or lie. While it may require considerable interpretational license, there are several senses in which the "midnight's children" to whom Saleem refers do exist, even in the real world, and are not merely inventions of a fevered mind. Saleem says that there were 1,001 children born in the first hour of India's existence as a sovereign nation, and that each of these children had magical gifts or abilities. Although this certainly deviates from any kind of conventionally verifiable historical record, their functional purpose within the novel's world has a clear parallel in our own reality. In fact, "midnight's children" has become a term that is commonly used in historical discourse to refer to the first generation of Indians who never lived under the Raj.[17] So, while the 1,001 fantastical children do not exist *per se,* the people they metaphorically represent undoubtedly do. Like those metaphorical children, the generation that grew up in a newly independent India carried the hope associated with new beginnings, and like those children, much of that optimism was never realized. Importantly, the children in the novel are also linked to the narrative form. The 1,001 children recall the 1,001 tales of the *Arabian Nights,* suggesting that each child is a possible narrative, or story, linking the "hope" associated with the children both to narrative *and* to metaphor, a point to which I shall return.

Rushdie's sense of metaphor as a medium for truth telling is a fairly conventional one, but it is a view maintained throughout the novel. In *Midnight's Children,* metaphor does not so much invalidate historical discourse as elucidate it. Saleem's insistence that fictions, stories, and legends are not always and everywhere the opposite of facts, truth, and reality is not, in fact, limited to this discussion of the children but extends to various other episodes in the novel. Similarly, as Rushdie asserts in an interview, "those elements which are clearly untrue are central to the notion of fiction—but that doesn't mean that they don't tell you the truth" (Chauhan 63). So, when Mian "The Hummingbird" Abdullah, in an effort to create a secular India, fails to form an Islamic Convocation that resists the Muslim League's efforts at Partition, Saleem invokes the "legend" surrounding this event in order to point to its importance, arguing, "Sometimes legends make reality" (47). This legend details Abdullah's assassination by six men in black and the supernatural humming Abdullah unleashes, attracting thousands of stray dogs to avenge him. Certainly, these details cannot be historically/factually "accurate," but their exposition brings attention to an event most often (like Nadir Khan) "swept under the rug" of history.

It has been common, particularly with the increasing power of Hindu nationalism in the 1980s and 1990s, to paint the role of Muslims in Indian political history as ardently separatist and uncooperative. Rushdie's extrapolation of the Hummingbird from the historical truth of Sheikh Abdullah and the Muslim National Conference (Parameswaran 23; R. Clark 66) reminds the reader of the historical marginalization of moderate Islam. In his claim that "legends make reality," Saleem suggests that even if not all coordinates of the story of Abdullah are verifiable,[18] his account keeps alive the historical truth of the existence both of the Conference and of the substantial part of the Muslim community that is neither ardently anti-Hindu nor anti-India.[19]

Consistent with Rushdie's efforts to pinpoint the truth-telling potential of metaphor is his separation of figuration, as such, from lies and intentional deception. This separation of metaphor and lie takes on even greater significance in *The Moor's Last Sigh* (1995). In the later novel, Moraes Zogoiby (the Moor) is convinced to abandon his family by his lover, Uma Sarasvati, due largely to the stories she tells about her past. In fact, Uma presents a different life story to each member of the Moor's family in her effort to supplant his mother and bring herself to artistic and social prominence. While the capacity to occupy multiple subjectivities, to create many life narratives, and to reinvent one's identity is part and parcel of the postmodernism with which Rushdie's work is often associated, here there is a careful limit to such play. That is, while there is a power, a truth, and a political and social utility to metaphor, as discussed above, Rushdie carefully delineates distinctions between metaphors and lies, even when some of his characters do not. When the Moor confronts Uma about her claim that her parents are dead and that her uncle abused her, Uma builds a defense around this difference, or lack thereof. When the Moor reminds her that "the uncle was a husband" and that her parents are alive, Uma insists that the story was merely a "metaphor of how wretched my life was." The Moor's reply, however, is instructive: "It wasn't a metaphor, Uma. . . . It was a lie. What's scary is, you don't know the difference" (269–70).[20] Uma's status as changeling, as limitless source of representations without any true "referential" self beneath the performances, functions as a warning against the extremes of postmodern relativism, "unmooring hybridity from desirability" (Hai 42). While metaphors can carry a kind of truth, ethical resistance to lies remains necessary.

We have seen, then, that *Midnight's Children* creates an alternate world in which the metaphorical and the literal are not opposed terms but are identical. We have likewise seen that, in creating that world, the novel is not merely exposing and parodying historical discourse's failure to convey "truth" because of its reliance on metaphor. Instead, metaphor itself is held up as a kind of truth both in the alternate world of the novel and in our own. To look at the world Rushdie has designed, then, is to find a type of utopia in which the linguistic telling of a story is consistent and equivalent with the events narrated. Despite this referential utopia, however, it soon becomes clear that this world is not free of lies, untruths, and/or errors. As we have already observed, there are the liberal sprinkling of errata to consider, which, when seen in this light, are certainly not on a continuum with the literalized metaphors but contradict their function. Likewise, there is an extensive collection of lies and untruths, like those told by Uma in *The Moor's Last Sigh* and those attributed to Pakistan in *Midnight's Children*. The referential utopia does not, then, have the transparent mimeticism and easy accessibility to facts we might expect, illustrating a clear distinction between the errors against which Locke inveighs, and various others. What becomes clear from this is that Rushdie embraces metaphor so completely in order to more thoroughly expose more damaging distortions of truth. Unlike the postcolonial theory that critiques figuration for its obfuscation of cultural difference, Rushdie embraces it as a means of exploring and exposing less "metaphorical" types of oppression.

The purposes of Rushdie's magical realism come into sharper focus within the discourse of fictional worlds (also called "possible worlds") theory, discussed in relation to *Midnight's Children* by Richard Walsh. Walsh provides a useful shorthand definition of fictional worlds theory and identifies some of its problems. As Walsh explains, this kind of theory developed, at least in part, as a response to poststructuralist accounts of the "problem of fictional reference." Fictional worlds theory seeks to avoid the problem of "reference" altogether, by arguing that the worlds presented in fictional texts should be "understood as non-actual other worlds, rather than as an imitation of this one." From this perspective, the real world is only important insofar as readers use it to supplement their understanding of the "textual construct" (Walsh 114).

Much of Thomas Pavel's book, *Fictional Worlds,* is devoted to explaining how readers fill in gaps left in various "fictional worlds" with their knowledge of the real one. Our reality, then, becomes a supplementary author to fictional texts, but these texts never "refer" to that real world directly. While this approach is useful in establishing the unique nature of Saleem's world, it fails in the face of *Midnight's Children*'s clear attempt to represent the real India of the twentieth century (see Kane 116). The theory is, however, compelling for reading Rushdie, given his repeated fictional depictions of an alternate world that is not, or not quite, our own.

In fact, all or most of Rushdie's fiction seems to take place in the *same* fictional world. Nowhere is this more evident than in Saleem's son Aadam's dramatic reappearance in *The Moor's Last Sigh* (*sans* one "a"), but various other characters also appear in more than one Rushdie novel. Ormus Cama's glimpse of a world not his own, but suspiciously like ours, in *The Ground Beneath Her Feet* further establishes Rushdie's attempts to delineate a "fictional world" that does not precisely "refer" to the real one.[21] Likewise, in *Shame,* Rushdie writes that: "The country in this story is not Pakistan, or not quite. There are two countries, real and fictional, occupying the same space, or almost the same space. . . . [M]y fictional country exists, like myself, at a slight angle to reality" (22). In *Shame,* Rushdie constructs a fictional world, but manages to also clearly refer, in this and other disnarrated asides, to our real world, telling details of his own life and noting its distance from the narrative proper (19–22). As with the errata in *Midnight's Children,* the use of a fictional world illustrates the difficulty of historical reference while still insisting on a reality outside of novelistic discourse. Rushdie's real life may not be part of *this* Pakistan, but it is included in *Shame,* installed alongside its fictional counterpart.

In this regard, Rushdie's "The Location of *Brazil,*" a review of Terry Gilliam's film, is instructive. Rushdie points to how *Brazil* configures an alternative world in which the crushing pessimism, bureaucracy, and foreclosed dreams of the real world are combated. In the film, says Rushdie, "the world of the imagination . . . is . . . at war with the 'real world' . . . in which things inevitably get worse and in which centres cannot hold" (*Imaginary Homelands* 122). This description of *Brazil* applies precisely to *Midnight's Children,* in which Rushdie creates an alternative world in which metaphors come true and hope exists. As in *Brazil,* however, this alternative world meets reality, and its power is there exposed as limited at best. Rushdie reminds us, however, that the idea of *Brazil,* of the "opposition of imagination to reality . . . is of great importance, because it reminds us that we are not helpless; that to dream is to have power" (122). This is, again, precisely the function of the fictional world created in *Midnight's Children,* which reminds us that even the most elaborate and unlikely fantasies may have application to our daily life. The alternative world of literalized metaphor is then configured neither as an imitation of the real one, nor as inviolably separate. Rather, it has a rhetorical relationship to its counterpart, offering an argument on how to change the world, even when such change seems impossible.

This is, in fact, ultimately the claim Walsh makes for fictional worlds, denying both the poststructuralist account of historical reference as "failed imitation" and the fictional worlds model of a textual world disconnected from its real counterpart in any substantive way. In opposition to both schools of thought, Walsh focuses on what he calls a text's "fictionality": its positioning of itself *as* fiction in order to rhetorically comment upon the "real world" without being restricted by its laws. *Midnight's Children* does not, then, merely reveal or expose the figurative (and therefore "unreal") content of historical discourse. Rather, it asserts the functional fictionality of metaphor, highlighting its role in creating a more objective history.

As Michael Riffaterre argues, the layering of figurative language in all literary fiction functions to alert the reader that this is "a circuitous artificial version of the story that could have been told more simply." That is, the reader must mentally reconstruct a "pretransformation text," a version of the story not so colored by figurative language and narrative convention (xv). *Midnight's Children*'s allegiance to both metaphor and history makes this notion even more relevant since the pretransformation text is the past itself, and the layering of metaphor, while providing a certain kind of truth, should not and cannot lie about that text. Instead, the reader is rhetorically invited to restructure history itself from the text they are given.

The crucial function of a world where metaphors are made literal, then, is not to pinpoint the failures of referentiality inherent to metaphor but to emphasize the distinctions between metaphors, errors, and lies, the first of which may carry some historical truth, while the last, particularly in historical discourse, functions as a means of oppression. While many of the references to lies and untruths in *Midnight's Children* are part of a withering critique of the Pakistani government, at other times lies are included principally to establish their separation from metaphor. The most significant instance of this kind of lie in the novel is when Saleem first admits to an intentional falsehood. Importantly, this lie is explicitly contrasted with metaphorical description. "To tell the truth, I lied about Shiva's death. My first out-and-out lie—although my presentation of the Emergency in the guise of a six-hundred-and-thirty-five-day-long midnight was . . . certainly contradicted by the available meteorological data" (510).

As we learn, Saleem has no clear idea of what has become of Shiva. Rather, his lie is motivated by the fear of what may happen to him if Shiva does survive. He hopes that by wishing for and narrating Shiva's death, it may be true. In this he falls "victim to the temptation of every autobiographer, to the illusion that since the past exists only in one's memories and the words which strive vainly to encapsulate them, it is possible to create past events simply by saying they occurred" (510). In this passage, Saleem openly contradicts one of the standard "postmodern" interpretations of *Midnight's Children*, that the novel suggests that referential nonfiction does create events simply by their narration and that there is no significant difference between these arts and lying.[22] In this case, by pointing to one incident in which a lie does occur, Rushdie asserts the crucial distinction between "fibbing" and narrating, as such. Further, the passage encourages a comparison between this particular lie and literalized metaphor, to the detriment of the former. Whereas the claim that Shiva died at the murderous hands of Roshanara Shetty turns out to be an outright falsehood, the metaphor Saleem provides us for the Emergency, while "excessively romantic" and one of the more outlandish examples of literalized metaphor, is not, or not quite, a lie. Rather, the statement contains quite a bit of metaphorical truth. What's more, when Saleem offers that his claims about the dark night of the Emergency do not match with actual weather reports, he refers to the weather in the pretransformation text, the real world, for in Saleem's India as we know it, such strange meteorological events would not necessarily be so strange. Even in that world, however, a lie is a lie and not a metaphor, literal or otherwise.[23]

According to Saleem, Roshanara Shetty, one of the many upper-class socialites who partake in sexual slumming with Shiva, slips into Shiva's prison cell and kills him (507–8). This turns out to be a complete falsehood, and despite Saleem's assertion that "in all literature, what actually happened is less important than what the author can persuade his audience to believe" (310), it becomes clear that, even for Saleem, it is an illusion to believe that it is "possible to create past events simply by saying they occurred." Events occur or they do not, and although our efforts to recall or recreate them may be difficult at best and futile at worst, words do not create the actions they describe.

"What's Real and What's True"

The remorse Saleem shows for lying to his reader(s) suggests not only a conventional ethics, but more specifically, an ethics of narration. Like his errata, Saleem's lies are identified as a violation of the unwritten contract that joins the reader to the writer/historian. While Saleem and Padma, the figure of the reader in the novel, may disagree on the preferable mode of storytelling, they do agree that Saleem will not lie about his life and will make as few errors as possible. When Saleem violates this unspoken agreement, he feels pangs of guilt that he does not when indulging in his literal/metaphorical brand of storytelling or in his nonlinear approach to narrative. Here, again, it is clear that the deviation from material experience that metaphor and narrative create is not equivalent to intentional falsification.

Again, the political commentary accomplished through the distinction between tropology and lies is hinged on the comparison of India to Pakistan. Saleem proposes India to be a land of metaphor, narrative, and figural representation, while Pakistan is seen to be the land of intentional lies and state falsehoods.[24] Like Gilliam's land of dreams, India thus becomes the land of infinite possibility, as in this fictional world the metaphors we invoke, and the narratives we generate, are precisely those that have the possibility of coming true. On the other hand, the unrealities or falsehoods embodied in the novel by Pakistan are clearly those things that are not true, even when they are asserted by the powerful. As such, metaphor and narrative, literally in the world of the novel and metaphorically in our own, open up possibilities and opportunities, political, social, and otherwise, while lies and falsehoods foreclose those opportunities. Metaphor and narrative are, in this context, the stimuli to the sociopolitical imagination that make change possible, while lies merely contribute to the oppressive *status quo*. This distinction helps to untangle one of the most enigmatic statements Saleem makes in the novel: "'What's real and what's true aren't necessarily the same.' *True*, for me, was from my earliest days something hidden inside stories Mary Pereira told me" (87).

Again, this passage could be interpreted as a relativist deconstruction of the nature of reality and of truth, taking something away from each, especially when truth is collated with narrative skill. Inherent in this separation of the real and the true, however, is their mutual separation from the false. While the real correlates with the kind of literal representation of events that it is impossible to reproduce in textual form, the true is the artful telling of those events with a metaphorical correspondence to the actual. Despite the near identity of the real and the true within the world of literalized metaphor, they are never precisely the same. They are, however, tied together by their mutual distance from the false, a distance highlighted in the discussion of India and Pakistan. Rushdie's critique of both nations is essentially a condemnation of a lack of imagination, as neither the leaders nor the citizens of either nation have the capacity to make the truth of narrative and metaphor a reality, as *Midnight's Children* endeavors to do.

In fact, the novel's critique of Pakistan is soon extended to India, blurring the initially clear distinctions between the two nations. At first, the India/Pakistan division is asserted through the deployment of the "midnight's children." The children are, there is little doubt, to be seen as a metaphorical microcosm of India as a whole. As noted above, their original number reflects the number of proposed tales for the *1,001 Nights*, itself a shorthand for an infinity of possible fictions.[25] Likewise, in the *Nights*, storytelling becomes the means by which Scheherazade can forestall her eventual death. This plot is transferred to the fate of India in *Midnight's Children*, as the children become representative of an abundance of national "stories" whose cessation will mean the death of India.

After Saleem's bulging temples crash into the hollows in Sonny Ibrahim's forehead, he is able not only to see and hear the surface noise of all the minds in India but also to access the "pure language" beneath the confusing babble of tongues of the midnight's children (214). Not coincidentally, the moment Saleem breaks through the language barrier separating the children coincides with Nehru's division of India into linguistic territories. Rushdie's capacity to imagine the coming together of those linguistically separated is contrasted with the inability of politicians to do the same. In addition, the revelation that Saleem is only one of many midnight's children diffuses his metaphorical connection to India. The Midnight's Children Conference (MCC) provides a much broader cross-section of race, caste, and class than Saleem himself ever could independently, providing a more comprehensive microcosm of the nation.[26] Saleem remains a metaphor for India, but he is only one possible India, with the other midnight's children representing other potentialities for the nation. Some of these opportunities have already been foreclosed, however, as it is revealed that 420 of the children die before the MCC's first meeting.

Despite this setback, Saleem consistently configures the children as the hope for the future of India, as "a thousand and one possibilities" (230), even if these possibilities are, by real world standards, impossibilities: children who can step into and out of mirrors, multiply fish, become werewolves, change their sex, divine water, etc. It is established, however, that there are no similar children in Pakistan (or Saleem, at least, cannot see them) (225). When there, he discovers that "the offspring of Independence were not all human. Violence, corruption, poverty, generals, chaos, greed and pepperpots . . ." (333). From this, it seems that the real offspring of Partition live in Pakistan, while the magical and the narratable inhabit India.

Similarly, while Saleem's sister was once a font of narrative possibilities, burning shoes and talking to animals, a move to Pakistan changes her nature, "adopting expressions of demureness and submission which must, at first, have seemed false even to her" (334). Saleem's sister is "partitioned," like the subcontinent, into two distinct pieces, the "Brass Monkey" of India, and the Jamila Singer of Pakistan, with the former definitively preferable to the latter (see Kane 111). Consistent with the previously established associations of India and Pakistan, the Brass Monkey is associated with storytelling and Jamila with falsehoods, or lies. However, while the false is initially associated only with Pakistan, it soon becomes clear that lies, political domination, and the violent administration of power occur on both sides of the border.

While Saleem argues that in Pakistan there is a "[d]ivorce between news and reality" (382), such a separation also exists on All India Radio, which reports the dropping of "actual or mythical bombs" on Pakistan and Saleem's family (390). Again, the distinction between India and Pakistan is initially established, as the facts of the bombing are not transformed into the lies they might be from the Pakistani side, but into "myth" or "fiction." Nevertheless, the ironic tone indicates a discrepancy between the truth of what occurred in the Indian bombing of Pakistan and the myth that no bombing occurred. Here, as in Woolf's description of the war victims in *Three Guineas*, the reality of the dead victims of Indian bombing cannot be palliated by fiction. Instead, it is clear that India too is capable of lies: "In the first five days of the war Voice of Pakistan announced the destruction of more aircraft than India ever possessed; in eight days, All-India Radio massacred the Pakistan Army down to, and considerably beyond, the last man" (388). These deceptions, propagated by both governments and their media outlets are part and parcel of the war machinery that perpetuates nationalist hatred, destroying the possibility of growth and cooperation.

The division between the possibilities of India and their lack in Pakistan is not, then, as unassailable as it originally appears, and neither is that between the fictional world and its real alternative. First, according to the logic explored above, it would seem that the transformation of metaphor into reality should only occur within India's borders, but Saleem retains his magical powers of smell in the Land of the Pure and likewise suffers from a metaphorical amnesia that becomes literal. While Saleem initially suggests that only India contains imaginative possibilities, it is clear that Pakistan does as well. Likewise, while only Pakistan seems to foreclose these possibilities, we soon learn that India does the same. Saleem first loses contact with the MCC during his first trip to Pakistan, but he loses the connection permanently, regardless of geography, when he undergoes sinus surgery. The decline of the hope associated with the MCC is not determined by what Saleem knows, or has access to, however. In fact, the tenuous unity of the conference begins to dissolve even before the operation, as does the possible unification of India's diverse peoples.

During the Chinese invasion, the members of the MCC find reasons to leave the conference: the predictor of the future tires of being ignored, the alchemist is lured away by the possibility of gold, and the Brahmin children decide that they do not want their thoughts to have any contact with those of the untouchables. The divisions in India increasingly apply to the conference: greed, lust, gender, race, religion, caste, and class. It is then no surprise that the imaginative possibility of transcending these divisions begins to wane. Once a nation of narrative and metaphor, India becomes a nation of lost narratives and opportunities: the real world itself.

Saleem hopes for a way out of this predicament by insisting upon a "third principle" that will allow the midnight's children to "fulfill the promise of our birth" (292). In fact, Rushdie's creation of a fictional world, designed to comment upon and critique our own, functions as a "third principle," explicitly outside of our own experience, but with the capacity to comment upon it. However, no third principle appears in Saleem's India.[27] Instead, the difficulties encountered by the MCC provide a critique of such a concept and the limits of its usefulness.

This critique is advanced most devastatingly by Shiva, who argues that "there is no third principle; there is only money-and-poverty, and have-and-lack, and right-and-left; there is only me-against-the-world! . . . the world is no place for dreamers or their dreams; the world . . . is things" (292–93). Remarkable throughout Shiva's contributions to the MCC debates is the degree to which, through him, Rushdie predicts and provides the arguments of his materialist critics. Like Saleem, Rushdie is often seen as a dreamer, indulging in flights of fancy and historical pipe dreams rather than presenting the world of things and acknowledging that the only way to approach such a world is to fight. Like Rushdie's critics, Shiva notes that there is nothing outside the world of things, the material world, and that the only resistance to oppression must be violent resistance. That is, dreams of alternative realities and magical metaphors are only dreams, and we are best served by dealing with things as they are. Rushdie's choice of Saleem as narrator and his production of abundant narratives may suggest that Shiva, and his alternate point of view, is meant to be frowned upon.[28] To look at the fate of the MCC, however, is to see that Rushdie has more in common with his materialist critics, and with Shiva, than it initially appears.

While the division between the imagination and promise of India and the lies and social control of Pakistan seems clear at first, as the novel progresses towards the regime of Indira Gandhi, India begins to resemble the Pakistani failure of imagination more than it differs from it. While the lies perpetrated by All India Radio occur under the watch of Prime Minister Shastri, in very short order, "The Widow," as Saleem calls Indira, is elected, and during the Emergency she imprisons all of the extant members of the MCC, surgically removing their magical powers, and sterilizing them. Only Shiva escapes. The 1,001 stories and the imaginative possibilities for the nation that the children represent come to an abrupt end. Of central importance here is the way in which Rushdie provides an unequivocal critique of Indira and the Emergency. Indira is analogized with her Pakistani counterparts, as a dictator who forcibly establishes what is true and even what is narratively possible, shutting down all of the alternatives represented by the MCC.

While this critique stands, the symbolic weight of the MCC prevents their demise from merely functioning as a local and specific political critique of a particular regime. Within the logic of the novel, in fact, Shiva's critique of Saleem predicts the MCC's demise, because the world is built not on dreams and imagination but on material reality. Likewise, the Rushdean imagination that allows the MCC to exist must at some point be supplemented and informed by, if not abandoned to, the world of things. It is at the moment that the members of the MCC are deprived of their powers that the fictional world of literalized metaphor intersects with our own. No longer are metaphors real and no longer are magical powers possible. Rather, the only possible resistance to Indira's regime is the resistance of real people oppressed by power. In this, *Midnight's Children* begins to resemble *Omeros* and the more theoretical critiques of metaphor. While the novel begins with an account of metaphorical and narrative hope, it ends with the destruction of the MCC and the subtraction of tropological magic and narratable beginnings.

Indeed, India's configuration as the land of infinite realities as opposed to the lies of Pakistan is dramatically undercut long before this moment, particularly when the leading generals of India and Pakistan's armies meet. Sam Manekshaw (of India) and Tiger Niazi (of Pakistan) congratulate one another on their war efforts and agree to lie about the atrocities of war: "General Sam, 'Listen old sport: one hears such damn awful lies. Slaughters, old boy, mass graves, special units called CUTIA or some damn thing, developed for purposes of rooting out opposition . . . no truth in it, I suppose?' And the Tiger, 'Canine Unit for Tracking and Intelligence Activities? Never heard of it'" (436–37).[29] The exaggerated use of British upper-crust English and the contradictory simultaneous specification of the CUTIA acronym and denial of its existence lend a gallows humor to this exchange. Signaled in it, however, is not only the death of those lying in mass graves but also the death of the distinction between the two nations that held out hope for one of them. Here lies become truth, and truth is nothing but lies. The sterilization of the midnight's children that follows is then largely a symbolic resolution of something that has already occurred. It is perhaps for this reason that Saleem, who initially represents the former nation so clearly, begins to disassociate himself from his homeland, asking, "*Why, alone of all the more-than-five-hundred-million, should I have to bear the burden of history?*" (440; emphasis in original), and declaring that he "no longer want[s] to be anything except what who I am" (440). Rather than take on the mantle of a metaphor for all of India, he becomes a metonym, a synecdochic part of the whole with no further resonance.

Saleem, then, eventually denies his privileged connection to the nation and his status as special font of narrative and meaning. Shiva, finally, seems to have been proven correct. The search for meaning beyond action and reaction, oppression and struggle, is eliminated, and the difference between this fictional world and the real world is as well, along with the hopefulness the distance between metaphor and reality allows. As such, the novel suggests a need to face the real world of things, of facts and lies, and of abandoning the world of metaphor. With this abandonment comes the birth of Saleem's (adoptive) son. Hardly the dreamer that Saleem is, Aadam seems poised to take on the mantle of resistance and struggle promoted by Rushdie's more materialist critics, since he is described as "stronger, harder, more resolute than I" (489).[30]

Politically, socially, and ethically, however, Saleem's newfound realism leads him not to a mode of struggle, and a contestation of power, but to quietism and resignation: "Politics, children . . . is a bad dirty business. We should have avoided it, I should never have dreamed of purpose" (500). The reader is then left to wonder if this is the conclusion that is meant to emerge from Rushdie's opus: a stoic resignation of struggle just when the real world takes center stage. The removal of the special powers of the members of the MCC is, after all, accompanied by a "sperectomy—the draining out of hope" from Saleem and the India he once represented (503).

Over the course of the novel, then, Rushdie introduces a "third principle," by creating a fictional world that merges the normally separated purviews of metaphor and reality. This third principle, although self-consciously outside of our lived experience, has a rhetorical force upon our world, suggesting that metaphor, narrative, and imagination can provide us with truths about it even if those truths do not touch the world at every point. Metaphor and narrative provide possibilities for social change, imagining worlds beyond the one in which we live, worlds which may have some connection to the future which lies ahead of us, but which are only fiction to our present. This unrealistic idealism is, however, tempered by Shiva's critique, which warns us that the real world is populated by things, not metaphors. As India is slowly drained of its fantastic properties, it is evident that Rushdie's enthusiasm for a metaphorical world is, at the very least, tempered by a realistic ambivalence. The novel recognizes that the real world is characterized by falsehood, lies, and abuse of political power, and while a third principle may provide us with hope for the future, that hope can be rapidly removed by the exigencies of the present.

Saleem, Shiva, and Subaltern Studies

The struggle between Saleem and Shiva is the struggle between narrative, imagination, metaphor, and hope on one hand and materialism, realism, and cynicism on the other. While the book clearly offers Saleem as its protagonist and therefore seems to favor the former cluster of associations, Shiva's critique is not only effective but is also, as we have seen, ever more compelling as the book progresses. In this way, *Midnight's Children* stages debates not only important to postmodern historiography but also to fundamental elements of ethically and politically engaged postcolonial theory. In particular, the Saleem/Shiva debate explores ideas central to opposing perspectives in the Subaltern Studies movement, a group of theorists initially dedicated to exploring what it would mean to write and create history from the view of the oppressed in a postcolonial context. In fact, the debates over the practicality and ethics of relativist historiography detailed in the introduction are strikingly reflected and repeated within postcolonial studies generally, and particularly by the Subaltern Studies collective. Rushdie is an oft-mentioned figure in these debates, despite the fact that his work is not explicitly part of historiographic discourse but operates more firmly in the aesthetic realm. Particularly relevant is the affinity Rushdie's work has with the type of historiography advocated by Dipesh Chakrabarty, one of the more important figures in Subaltern Studies. Chakrabarty argues against the deployment of historical discourse that is in keeping with the values of Enlightenment rationalism, specifically because these are the values of Europe, imperialism, and hegemony. This attack on Enlightenment thought consists principally of a critique of its false claims to objectivity and the ways in which such claims have contributed to domination and exploitation.

Because of his opposition to Western rationalism, Chakrabarty insists on efforts to expose the constructed and ideological nature of European historiography. In doing so, he advocates the notion that postcolonial history should consist of "provincializing Europe" and "taking history to its limits" ("Radical Histories" 286). In this, Chakrabarty's work reflects Hayden White's denaturalization of historical objectivity and, like White, Chakrabarty sees the myth of objectivity as a strategy of hegemonic domination. From Chakrabarty's perspective, Rushdie's exposé of the dependency of historical discourse on figurative language might place his work in a radical political position, foregrounding the impossibility of the European Enlightenment's claim to "objective" history, "taking history to its limits" and resisting Europe's influence. Those that praise Rushdie as postmodern typically champion his politics on these grounds.

Not surprisingly, however, there are postcolonial theorists who see Chakrabarty's vision of historiography not as politically and socially liberating but as dangerous relativism, and this critique extends to Rushdie as well. In particular, Arif Dirlik and Vinay Bahl have accused the Subaltern Studies group of abandoning their "original" goal of uncovering and privileging subaltern and resistant voices in favor of a deconstructive history of the colonizer and the hegemonic West. That is, by advocating a history that "provincializes Europe," Dirlik and Bahl contend that Chakrabarty makes the error of denying oppressed peoples their own history, focusing instead on the fissures in European historiography and paradoxically granting that discourse centrality. In fact, the "mission statement" of the Subaltern Studies collective insisted not upon the deconstruction of European histories but upon the excavation and presentation of the material history of the oppressed. Ranajit Guha argues, for instance, that the "historiography of Indian nationalism has for a long time been dominated by elitism—colonialist elitism and bourgeois-nationalist elitism. What is clearly left out of this unhistorical historiography is the *politics of the people*" (Guha xiv–xv; emphasis in original).

In this, it is clear that for the original Subaltern Studies group, an opposition to Enlightenment objectivity was not an issue. Rather, there is a confidence in objectivity to such a degree that there is a belief that a "true" history of the people can be uncovered and delivered.[31] It is this objectivity that Bahl and Dirlik wish to revive, setting the stage for internecine debates wherein both sides claim political radicalism.

Similarly, while many critics have praised Rushdie for his novels' provincialization of Europe, others have taken an approach more akin to Bahl's critique of Chakrabarty. Bahl accuses Chakrabarty of being more concerned with "keep[ing] alive the philosophical question of difference" than in promoting "the equal distribution of wealth" (89), while V. S. Naipaul similarly argues against Rushdean narrative extravagance, insisting that it "dodges all the issues" (22).[32] More pointedly, M. Keith Booker argues that while Rushdie's aesthetic may undermine notions of rationalist historiography, *Midnight's Children* actually promotes Western liberalism and mocks a discourse that would be truly emancipatory, namely Marxism ("*Midnight's Children*").[33] Booker questions Rushdie's resistance to Western historiography within a political context that affirms Enlightenment rationalism, while rejecting liberal democracy and capitalist globalization.

Placing Rushdie's fiction in this constellation of debates is neither accidental nor coincidental since Rushdie stages such debates between his characters and within his novels. In addition to the Saleem/Shiva debates, Saleem's Uncle Hanif insists on the creation of relentlessly "realistic" films, with allegiance to the truth of the plight of the working classes, after initially specializing in more fantastic storytelling techniques. Likewise, the painter Aurora da Gama in *The Moor's Last Sigh* vacillates between artistic styles that might be said to show allegiance to a realist "objective" aesthetic and those more in line with deconstruction or denaturalization (173). Rushdie, then, at the very least, acknowledges this dichotomy and questions his own methods rigorously. Nowhere is this clearer than in the incisive comments of Shiva, whose materialism, like that of Price in *Waterland,* reminds the reader of what is lost if and when reference to material history is ceded completely. *Midnight's Children,* then, draws distinctions between narrative, metaphors, falsehoods, errors, and lies, suggesting the ways in which lies serve oppressive regimes, while narratives and metaphors offer hope to those oppressed by them.

Ectomies and Turds: Narrative and Its Leftovers

The "sperectomy" administered to the midnight's children by the Widow surgically removes the hope that counterbalances Shiva's materialism and cynicism. In fact, the surgery seems to provide a final victory for Shiva's realism and, in all senses but one, concludes the novel. *Midnight's Children* does continue in fits and starts for another chapter, but in a thematic way, the sperectomy is the quintessential conclusion, providing the nonnarratable moment that D. A. Miller identifies as an analogue for closure. As discussed above, Miller defines the nonnarratable by the elimination of the dissatisfaction that engenders narrative. In *Midnight's Children*, however, the reverse is the case, with the narratable middle of the novel being characterized not by dissatisfaction and lack but by hope, promise, and possibility. Likewise, narration in *Midnight's Children* is eliminated not by the achievement of hope's aspirations but by its surgical excision, making the continued search for satisfaction, and thus continued narration, irrelevant. Peter Brooks's configuration of narrative desire is similarly inverted. Where Brooks correlates the end of a narrative with the climactic achievement of male sexual desire, in *Midnight's Children* narrative desire is eliminated through sterilization, both literal and metaphorical. The sterilization of the MCC is a neutering of narrative itself, thanks to the novel's linkage of the MCC to storytelling through the *1,001 Nights*.

The novel's inversion of the Miller/Brooks model has relevance both for the novel's thematics of fragmentation and unity and for the claims of constructivist historiography. Hayden White's model suggests that it is the satisfaction and coherence of meaning endemic to narrative closure that positions it as antithetical to the real. However, in *Midnight's Children*, the close of narration is not associated with coherence and satisfaction but with dissatisfaction and the world of chance, individualism, lost opportunities, and political struggle. Closure becomes the encounter with the real, rather than an encounter with historiographic deception.

Saleem's loss of will in the face of such daunting and overpowering realism is then understandable, if not quite recommended by the novel. What is clear from its extrapolation of a world of literalized metaphor and from that world's remaining traces in the novel's final chapter is that the literal and limited sense of reality offered by this conclusion denies, rather than affirms, the possibility of political action. Much of the final chapter is actually dedicated to Saleem's reluctance to continue narrating, indicating a lost hope that leads him to stoicism.

On more than one occasion in this chapter, Saleem observes incidents that would previously have been occasions for abundant storytelling, but self-consciously rejects them. The second, and strangest, of these occurs after Saleem has been reunited with his ayah, Mary Pereira. Saleem, looking out of his window, observes a mysterious man with an umbrella defecating a prodigious fifteen-inch turd. Saleem's response is instructive: "Once, when I was more energetic, I would have wanted to tell his life-story . . . but now, I'm disconnected, unplugged, with only epitaphs yet to write." When the man queries Saleem as to the size of his largest excretion, Saleem can only respond, "Seven on a good day" (527–28).

This interlude is so strange and self-contained that it seems to refuse interpretation.[34] Crucial to the episode, however, is its articulation of both Saleem's refusal to continue narrating and narrative's stubborn persistence. While Saleem self-consciously rejects his penchant for extravagant storytelling, he nevertheless feels compelled to narrate the encounter, leaving the sense that he is not as "unplugged" as he claims. What is still puzzling, however, is the relative importance of the incident itself. Why does Saleem feel compelled to include it?

The answer may be found in an earlier incident, wherein Saleem meets Durga, Picture Singh's new wife and Aadam's wet nurse. When Picture introduces Saleem to Durga, Saleem is less than happy to make her acquaintance because "she represented novelty, beginnings, the advent of new stories events complexities, and I was no longer interested in anything new" (513). As in the meeting with the umbrella-man, Saleem's reluctance is not because of any personal animosity towards Durga but rather out of an allegiance to nonnarratability. Durga represents the power of narrative and therefore the hope that has been removed from the novel's protagonist. Saleem, however, is forced to admit her to his rapidly concluding story out of an allegiance to historical verisimilitude, "once Pictureji informed me that he intended to marry her, I had no option: I shall deal with her, however, as briefly as accuracy permits" (513). Accuracy of representation, then, takes precedence over an adherence to the "realism" of nonnarratability that has drained Saleem of his hope. That is, the real, as such, must include narrative and narrative possibility, even after these things seem to have been eliminated. Saleem's ultimate defense of his story is based on a similar plea: "it happened that way because that's how it happened" (530). Saleem here offers that the narratable is not necessarily deviant from historical accuracy. His allegiance to narrative is reasserted not as an escapist alternative world but as an unavoidable element of the real itself, in ways similar to his defense of metaphor.

Consistent with this insistence on verisimilitude in *Midnight's Children* is the notion of the narratable leftover, also theorized by Miller, who suggests that there are authors and works whose work "exemplifies a closure at once enforced and effaced" (*Narrative and Its Discontents* 273). Here, Miller refers to complete works that leave room open for sequels, concluding, but leaving behind that which is "demonstrably capable of producing further narrative" (273). In *Midnight's Children,* closure is associated with repressive politics that "enforce" a world of rigidly defined possibilities through manipulation of truth. This enforcement of closure is accompanied by its effacement, however, in the leftovers of the final chapter. Because of the self-conscious attention to the nature of narrative in *Midnight's Children*, such leftovers are clearly identified as such, as Durga is explicitly identified with "new stories events complexities," while the umbrella man produces a more fetid and material "leftover." Similarly, while most of Saleem's history is "enclosed" in the pickle jars at the Braganza factory, there is one empty, or "left over," leaving room for future stories (442–43). These narrative loose ends are also signifiers of historical reference, presented precisely because "that's how [they] happened."

In this case, as in *Waterland*, the real has a double movement. The excision of the fictional world of literalized metaphor may be necessary to confront the reality of political and social abuse of power, but there is also referentiality in the emerging new stories that lead the reader out of the more "realistic" dead end. Saleem may no longer have the strength to follow Durga's narrative, but Rushdie suggests that we as readers (and writers) must do so, both here and in the revival of this fictional world in future novels. While the crushing loss of hope that is associated with the reality of modern India and the foreclosure of narrative possibility is historically true, so too is the opening of new narratives that may help in the resistance to power. The dialectic of the enclosed and unified with the contingent and leftover is ever present, but it is positioned as an insistence both on the fidelity to the depressing limitation of possibility that reality embodies and to the new opportunities that it also encompasses. In "Imaginary Homelands," Rushdie notes that the content of *Midnight's Children* suggests "despair," but the form is inveterately "hopeful" because it "constantly throws up new stories . . . it 'teems'" (16).

The dialectic nature of history, both despairing and hopeful, both closed and "teeming," both metaphoric and metonymic, is nowhere more clearly expressed than through Shiva, who both insists upon a fidelity to the limited binary world of "masses-and-classes" and provides the most significant narratable leftover in the novel. Shiva is named explicitly after the Hindu god of destruction and (pro)creation (146), marking these concepts as two sides of the same coin.[35] His role as military hero for Indira's India and his crushing of Saleem between his knees is the material realization of his antagonism to Saleem's optimism. Still, despite the role Shiva plays in the elimination of the members of the MCC, he is also instrumental in their (re)creation. When the other members of the MCC are sterilized, Shiva is left to roam free. Upon his return from the Bangladeshi war he enjoys the rewards of his popularity by seducing the wives of rich men and slum-dwelling whores (470, 473). The result is innumerable bastard children.

Shiva's penchant for fathering material children and narrative loose ends is somewhat surprising given his attitude towards pregnancy. Whenever he impregnates a woman, he immediately loses any sexual attraction to her and abandons both mother and child. Nevertheless, while Shiva is an emblem of destruction, he also populates Rushdie's India with a new set of midnight's children, this group encapsulated in Aadam Sinai but containing a variety of hopes, possibilities, and stories like their predecessors. In this, the novel suggests that narrative possibility cannot be eliminated but must come from a grounding in materialism, the "things" that Shiva contends are most important. Certainly, the achievement of nonnarratability encapsulated by the sperectomy is once more undercut by the presence of these narratable "leftovers." Even though the reader never sees the vast majority of Shiva's offspring, their narratable status as genetic and thematic heirs to the members of the MCC is obvious. While Shiva has undergone "voluntary vasectomy" (506), Saleem makes the irrelevance of the operation clear: "Shiva, destroyer of the midnight children, had also fulfilled [his] other role . . . Shiva-the-procreator" (506–7). Saleem insists on the inclusion of the narrative leftovers of Shiva's children, Durga, and the umbrella man on the grounds that "that's how it happened," indicating an allegiance to the materiality of narrative and a concomitant hopeful politics.

"Baby and Afterbirth"

Midnight's Children, then, has a double view of what historical reality is and how we can access it, but it does not dismiss the possibility of such access. While narrativist historiography argues that the achievement of a unified form and coherent explanation generate a discourse of "realism" that deviates from the real, Rushdie's inversion of the trajectories of the narratable and the nonnarratable suggests that a unified form can resist explanation and, in doing so, more closely reference the historical past. At the same time, however, *Midnight's Children* acknowledges White's most essential critique: that adherence to a particular narrative will necessarily exclude important events and shape others. This brings us back to Saleem's errata. Like Saleem's inclusion of narratable leftovers in the final chapter, the errata are real episodes of history that do not fit the unified form of Saleem's narrative. Because they are both important and factually true, however, they must be included in the attempt to accurately portray the past.

The errata themselves may be considered antinarrative leftovers or, as suggested earlier, "disnarrated." They are not part of Saleem's narrative, perhaps, but they are included. While Saleem's narrative asserts that Gandhi died on the same date as the premiere of *The Lovers of Kashmir,* the correction to this error occurs outside of that narrative, as a leftover made present in the text. In the errata, the real world's events encroach upon and interject into the fiction's narrative, as something approximating the real world begins to crack into the fictional world in *The Ground Beneath Her Feet.* They do so, however, without replacing the fictional world's version of events. This creates a shadow narrative that haunts the story, with the real world's facts and dates threatening to invalidate the "entire fabric" of Saleem's narrative. The tension between the world of literalized metaphor and the shadow narration of its real counterpart defines a dialectics of history in *Midnight's Children.* The novel suggests that we need not abandon narrative or figuration in order to represent historical reality, as long as we acknowledge their limitations, supplementing them with their disnarrated elements.

It is no accident that the largest mistake in *Midnight's Children* surrounds Gandhi, for it is on his personage that most histories of modern India linger and which Saleem virtually ignores. Kortenaar makes the provocative claim that Rushdie's near exclusion of Gandhi is a political polemic against the Mahatma's influence upon Indian politics. In doing so, he argues that Rushdie promotes a liberal secular democratic ideal by replacing Gandhi with Shiva, unfairly biasing readers towards Saleem's own Nehruvian politics and away from "the Gandhian and the transcendental" (*"Midnight's Children"* 60). Eric Strand similarly configures Rushdie as anti-Gandhi, particularly in his embrace of "bourgeois materialism" (976). Both critics are correct in labeling Rushdie as humanist, secular, and democratic in his political sympathies, explicitly advocating such classic liberal values as "liberty; equality; fraternity" elsewhere in his work (*Shame* 267). However, the characterization of *Midnight's Children* as anti-Gandhi largely misses the point.

While Saleem never seems to consider the Mahatma as relevant to the history of India, the novel does, particularly when it overtly points to the fact that his exclusion threatens the coherence of Saleem's narrative. However, it is not only at the moment of Gandhi's death that his absent presence haunts Saleem's story. In addition, the Amritsar Massacre, presented through the eyes of Aziz, is committed in response to a Gandhi-inspired protest and strike. While Aziz is the central figure of the episode and is clearly associated with Nehru, Gandhi's influence towers over the event even though he is mentioned only briefly. Similarly, when Saleem remarks that Indira Gandhi is no relation to the Mahatma, it seems to merely provide historical context for Western readers, while indicting Indira's policies (484).[36] What the comparison emphasizes, however, is Rushdie's view of the Mahatma as fundamentally opposed to the type of rule enacted in the Emergency, one administered by force and maintained through the manipulation of religious schism. The Mahatma, the novel suggests, is the furthest thing from Indira. In this context, it is important to recall that Indira is Nehru's daughter, even if she abandons his principles, complicating the simplistic view of Rushdie as a Nehru disciple.

This common view of Rushdie is curious considering his strenuous objections to the consideration of Nehru as a Gandhi disciple in the essay, "Attenborough's *Gandhi*." Here Rushdie insists that India's greatest conflict in defining itself is in the choice between "Nehru, the urban sophisticate who wanted to industrialize India . . . and the rural, handicraft-loving, sometimes medieval figure of Gandhi" (*Imaginary Homelands* 104). However, Rushdie does *not* choose this image of Nehru over and against this image of Gandhi. Rather, he rejects both images as reductive and, in so doing, clarifies his vision of historical reference.[37]

The venom unleashed in Rushdie's review of *Gandhi* is in reaction to more than the film but is certainly not directed against Gandhi himself. Rather, Rushdie objects to the Western tendency to paint the East as a font only of spiritual wisdom as opposed to modern knowledge and political savvy. This facet of Orientalist discourse[38] places the East in a position of economic and political dependency, while removing its positive attributes into a fictional world of metaphysics and spirituality that is difficult to access and has little practical utility. By subjugating Nehru to Gandhi, Attenborough's film, argues Rushdie, participates in Orientalism, and the film's widespread critical and popular acclaim confirms the appeal of such discourse in the West. While it is true that Rushdie opposes the widespread application of Gandhi's doctrine of nonviolence (*Imaginary Homelands* 105), what he principally opposes is the transformation of Gandhi into a Christ figure. Instead, Rushdie insists that Gandhi was a human being with complex motives whose killing "was a political, not a mystical act" (104).[39] Once again, this leads Rushdie to assert the crucial distinction between fiction/mythmaking and lies: "Attenborough's distortions mythologize, but they also lie" (104). Rushdie does not object to mythologizing, *per se*, except to the degree that such myths come at the expense of referential accuracy.[40]

Likewise, Rushdie's final attack on Attenborough's film is based not only on the possibility, but also on the necessity, of accurate historical referentiality within a storytelling medium. Importantly, he argues that referentiality can be recovered in the inclusion of much of what Attenborough has excluded: the national debate between Nehruvian and Gandhian politics, the motivation behind Gandhi's assassination, Gandhi's secular *and* religious sides, and more rounded portrayals of other leaders of the independence struggle. What Rushdie objects to is an inaccurate portrayal of the past that allows only one side of a national debate to be seen.

In this regard, Rushdie is not merely a proponent of Nehruvian politics. If he were, he would be asserting only one side of the Nehru/Gandhi divide and be just as guilty of simplistic reduction as Attenborough. Instead, he insists that showing only one side of this debate and obscuring historical facts to do so is the kind of lie that cannot be tolerated. Similarly, in his critique of contemporary film portrayals of the East, he notes how "Brits" are inevitably at the center of such depictions, while Indians are "bit-players in their own history." His objection is that such films suggest that only Westerners matter "and that is so much less than the whole truth that it must be called a falsehood" (*Imaginary Homelands* 90). Here again, Rushdie exhibits an ethics of inclusion, insisting that only a wide-ranging, all-inclusive representation can hope to contain a measure of truth. It is for this reason that Rushdie writes and promotes a certain kind of novel: "novels in which you try to include everything, what Henry James would call the 'loose, baggy monsters' of fiction" ("*Midnight's Children*" 10).[41]

Rushdie clearly does prefer a Nehruvian secular nation to a religious communalist one, but he is also committed to a historical sense that includes past events that do not necessarily fit easily into his own ideology. Rushdie's policy of historical representation follows the lead of Saleem's family who brings him home from the hospital and refuses to discard any of the evidence of his birth. "Nothing was thrown away; baby and afterbirth were both retained" (140). In this case, while it is possible that mistakes are made (the Sinai family brings home Saleem, not Shiva, after all), it is clear that an effort is made to retain as much as possible. As *Midnight's Children* illustrates, history may then take a narrative form, as long as that form is supplemented with the nonnarrative episodes not easily integrated to it.

In regard to Gandhi, Saleem *does* marginalize his presence, but his consistent reference to his various errors nevertheless places a significant focus on the Mahatma. In addition, by pointing overtly to his mistakes, Rushdie encourages readers to fill in the gaps of Saleem's linear, exclusive narrative in order to more closely encounter the historical past. Although Rushdie focuses on twentieth-century political and social history, he also acknowledges the importance of a larger, more transcendental history, when he refers to his existence within the Kali-Yuga, the Maha Yuga cycle, and the Day of Brahma (223). Likewise, and perhaps more importantly, while critics like Kortenaar and Strand accuse Rushdie of excluding the "Gandhian and the transcendental" (Kortenaar, "*Midnight's Children*" 60), they overlook the form of Rushdie's novel in doing so. If the Mahatma, for some, represents an ideal of hope and promise for India through allusions to a world beyond our own and through the application of extreme political practice, the fictional world of literalized metaphor that lies at the heart of *Midnight's Chil-*

dren serves much the same function. Rushdie's novel does not then exclude the transcendental element of Indian history but includes it as an integral part of its magical realist form. To accuse Rushdie of correlating Shiva and Gandhi is then absurd, for it is Saleem whose narrative powers provide the transcendental hope that Shiva refuses in his focus on the "world of things." Through the literalization of metaphor and the nonnarratable presence of the errata, Rushdie insists on the inclusion of Gandhian ideals alongside Saleem's secularism and Shiva's materialism.[42]

I do not wish to suggest that Rushdie somehow succeeds in presenting an all-inclusive history, but rather that he is able to suggest what is accurate about his account, as well as what is excluded. So, while it is true that Saleem's bourgeois history and perspective can only show one facet of subcontinental history, Rushdie's emphasis on the contingent nature of what is important enough to receive historical representation also gestures to that which is excluded. In particular, the baby-switch of Shiva and Saleem makes the reader note precisely what is missing. It is, after all, at least an even proposition that Shiva should receive Nehru's letter and, if that occurs, an alternative synecdochic "part" would have to be considered central to the nation as metaphoric "whole." Instead, Shiva, the inarticulate adopted son of the beggar, Wee Willie Winkie, is kept silent. In this way, the novel invokes Spivak's well-known question of "Can the Subaltern Speak?" pointing to the contingent and ideological nature of what is typically considered history.

Rushdie here makes an implicit argument that the traditional fare of narrative historiography is not sufficient in itself to represent the truth of the past. In particular, while Saleem's life is a reflection of bourgeois historiography in its tracing over of easily identifiable national histories like Stanley Wolpert's, it is also filled with irrelevant and occasionally inconsistent events that pinpoint Saleem's life as merely one among many. While Saleem focuses on his heroic and representative status throughout most of the novel, he does finally retreat from this stance. In this, Rushdie suggests to his readers that the tracing of Shiva's life might just as easily be a key to uncovering truths of the past. In fact, other alternatives also exist, as both Padma and Parvati, postcolonial working-class women, exemplify the voices that Gayatri Spivak suggests have been not only obscured in historical discourse, but perhaps completely lost.

While Shiva, Padma, and Parvati are never afforded the opportunity to present their own stories in *Midnight's Children,* Saleem's conclusion that the "small individual lives of men, are preferable to all this inflated macrocosmic activity" (500), suggests that all lives deserve greater attention, especially considering the contingent and/or ideological manner in which certain types of lives are chosen to represent history, as such.[43] Padma, too, helps to voice this point of view when she accuses Saleem of being "too intellectual, too skeptical, too out of touch" (Brennan, "Cultural Politics" 123). Rushdie's social and class proximity to his protagonist also positions him as a target of this accusation. Although Saleem accuses Padma of "ignorance and superstition," he does acknowledge that she is a counterbalance to his own biased point of view (37–38). Likewise, it is significant that renewed hope comes from the working classes: Shiva, Durga, and the umbrella man. The novel's deployment of a "provincialized history" of male bourgeois India is then supplemented by an injunction to, like the Subaltern Studies collective, recover the lost voices of the "other" India. It is for this reason that David Price asserts that often the "focus is on the common, everyday experience of average people," which "comprises a more accurate history" ("Salman Rushdie's" 104).[44] While this is only partially true, it is an important part.

Unlike *Waterland* and *Between the Acts,* however, Rushdie's novel does not assert the historical irrelevance of traditional history and narrative in order to epistemologically value the nonnarrative, the lack of progress and action, and the working class as opposed to their bourgeois counterparts. Rather, in the lives of both Saleem and Shiva, we have the suggestion that the macrocosmic, the metaphorical, and the narrative may provide us with ideals of progress, universalism, and meaning that are essential not only to our accessing of the historical past but also to our movement towards the future. At the same time, Saleem has a quotidian, even nonnarratable, side that, when coupled with the exclusion of similar details in Shiva's life, stands in metonymically for the individual lives not represented in narrative histories. This quotidian side of Saleem must be included if historical "baby and afterbirth" are to be retained.

Midnight's Children, then, suggests that a combination of literary techniques can help us represent the past accurately. While Rushdie plays with the forms used to present history, he also insists that there is a real to be accessed and that the cost of obscuring that real is substantial. Whether it is the Amritsar Massacre, the Emergency, the Indo-Pakistani conflict, or simply the lives of those not given the opportunity to represent themselves, Rushdie points to events and personages buried in history and in rhetoric that must be recovered if political and social progress in the present is to be gained. In "Outside the Whale," Rushdie notes that complete objectivity is "an unattainable goal," but it is one for which, he insists, we must struggle (*Imaginary Homelands* 101). Likewise, Rushdie insists upon an ethics based upon the possibility of truth: "It seems to me imperative that literature enter . . . arguments, because what is being disputed is nothing less than what is the case, what is truth and what untruth" (100). Far from being an exercise in historical relativism, *Midnight's Children* is an effort to enter into that argument.

CHAPTER 4

"It's Enough Stories"

Truth and Experience in Art Spiegelman's Maus

> The postmodern and the post-Holocaust become mutually intertwined issues that are best addressed in relation to each other.
> —Dominick LaCapra, *Representing the Holocaust* (188)

> Sublime experience is to be defined in terms of what you are rather than in terms of what you *know*.
> —Frank Ankersmit, *Sublime Historical Experience* (225)

The first volume of Art Spiegelman's comic-book Holocaust (auto)biography/memoir, *Maus*, closes with an expression of anger and despair at a lost connection with the past. When Spiegelman's textual surrogate, Artie, expresses an interest in recovering his mother's diary, his father Vladek has to admit that such a recovery is now impossible: "These notebooks [. . .] one time I had a very bad day . . . and all of these things I destroyed [. . .] These papers had too many memories. So I burned them" (158–59). Artie is already attempting to recover and chronicle his father's Holocaust memories through a series of interviews, but the loss of this additional document prompts an angry response, "God damn you! You—You Murderer! How the hell could you do such a thing!!" (159). Although Artie soon puts on an apologetic face, in the final panel, in which Artie walks away from Vladek, he mutters "murderer" again (159). Artie here sees documents as tantamount to the thing itself. Anja, who committed suicide years earlier, dies again through the burning of her diary, investing the textual with an intense materiality.[1]

The scene succeeds in encapsulating the double movement of the book commented on by most critics. On one hand, *Maus* is supremely invested in recovering the past in all of its plenitude, to connect with its materiality, and, as far as possible, to mimetically reproduce the lives and histories of the Spiegelman family within their Holocaust context. Indeed, most early reviewers insist that the general thrust of the book is one of unflinching realism, claiming not only that the past can be accessed, but that it must be. This is especially the case with reviews of the first volume, released in 1986. In *The New Republic,* Adam Gopnik calls *Maus* a work of "hyperrealist detail" (30), while in *The Nation* Robert Grossman refers to the "hideous truth" (23) *Maus* conveys. Paul Grant notes that the focus of the book is on "telling the truth" (100) and David Gates's *Newsweek* review focuses on its "unblinking realism." Even the reviews of *Maus II* focus more on its realism than on its denaturalizing tactics, despite the broader emphasis on these strategies in the second volume. Reviewers describe it as "accurate" (Finn), as "an honest and direct expression" of the Holocaust (Jones), and as "true," "realistic," and naturalistic (Mordden 92). These reviewers express what is certainly the popular response to *Maus,* that it is a book compelling precisely for its capacity to convey the horror of the Holocaust in a truthful manner, with few palliating or sentimentalizing features. As Miles Orvell writes, "Above all, *Maus* is committed to its function as an authentic, factual record of the Holocaust" (118).

It is, however, difficult to reconcile this assessment with what Artie himself consistently voices within its pages: an ever-increasing despair at achieving accuracy, referentiality, or truth. This despair is highlighted by his realization that Anja's history is "murdered," gone forever with her diaries, but is far from limited to this moment. Elsewhere, the book focuses not only on particular barriers to the historical recovery process but also on the more philosophical notion that no matter how many documents, interviews, or archives are read, conducted, or uncovered, the past will always remain irretrievably removed from the present. Likewise, Artie begins to despair of his own capacity to turn his documents and interviews into a representation that can approximate reality. In talking to his wife, Françoise, Artie says, "I feel so inadequate trying to reconstruct a reality that was worse than my darkest dreams. And trying to do it in a comic strip! I guess I bit off more than I can chew. . . . There's so much I'll never be able to understand or visualize. I mean reality is too complex for comics. So much has to be left out or distorted" (*Maus II* 16). Like Hayden White, Artie expresses suspicion of his medium of historical transmission, emphasizing how it is impossible to tell a history without selecting, eliding, or erasing a substantial number of actual events, and how his attempts at mimesis are inevitably, then, "inadequate."

This, in turn, casts suspicion on Anja's diary, which itself can only show slices of the past and thus may also be insufficient. Still, Artie's anger at the diary's loss cannot merely be linked to Oedipal psychology.[2] It must also be tied to Spiegelman's simultaneous insistence on fidelity to the past and a denial of the possibility of such fidelity.

I am not the first to notice this contradiction at the heart of *Maus*. Critics have read the book in widely contradictory ways. Some, like the reviewers, read it as a rigorously mimetic witnessing of horrific events that fulfills its ethical duty to confirm the Holocaust. Others, however, read it as a "postmodern" denaturalization of the historical process, in which it is confirmed that representing the past is impossible. Still others insist that both movements exist and cannot be reconciled.[3] However, the claims for *Maus's* postmodernism rely heavily on reading the memoir as a meditation on the possibility of "knowing" the Holocaust, rather than as an experience that bears the imprint of its subject matter. In this chapter, I argue that these contradictory readings may be resolved by suggesting the ways in which we might read both movements of the book as bearing the imprint of history. Doing so requires both a division of the spheres of truth and experience as Frank Ankersmit has done in his recent work and a look at the distinction between fiction and nonfiction.

Thus far in this book I have focused on novels and authors that present their own historiographic theories. Woolf's "moments of being," Swift's "Here and Now," and Rushdie's literal metaphors and "narrative leftovers," are, I argue, attempts to consider and present possible solutions to thorny questions of historical reference. In this chapter, however, I supplement that model in order to suggest how a broader range of postmodernist historical narrative may be read as illustrative of recent historical theorizing that challenges constructivist historiography, even if it may not "intentionally" articulate its own theory.[4] That is, while *Maus* may not present us with its own coherent theory of historical reference, it usefully illustrates the ways in which postmodernist historical writing may be reread as bearing the imprint of history even as it despairs at the possibility of transmitting knowledge of the past.

In this discussion, I suggest that Frank Ankersmit's recent move from exemplar of the more extreme camp of postmodern historiography (particularly in *Narrative Logic*) to his insistence on the possibility of accessing historical "experience" in textual representations is productive for a reorientation of historiographic theory and a rereading of postmodernist historical narrative. If we view postmodern self-reflexivity not as a means of highlighting what we do not "know" but as a means of expressing the *experience* of postmodernity, and particularly of post-Holocaust history, it becomes possible to reevaluate the possibility of encountering the past through texts and in our present. *Maus* is then an ideal candidate for reading through an Ankersmitian prism. *Maus* provides a representation of the event most frequently cited as "unrepresentable," and therefore most evidentiary of the paradoxical ethics and "truths" of postmodernism. Through its dual narration, *Maus* suggests the ways in which notions of historical truth may be separated from those of experience, maintaining an allegiance to both of these categories and fulfilling the ethical injunction to remember.

The Ethics of Holocaust Representation

The introduction of this book highlights the ethical objections to postmodern theories of epistemology and ontology. While the theorization of the postmodern "withdrawal of the real" may seem merely to confront epistemological questions about the (im)possibility of knowing the truth and ontological questions about the absence of being, these questions unavoidably confront ethical, moral, and political dilemmas. If truth, reality, and the past are irretrievably absent, the ethical imperative to remember past traumas and to do our best to prevent their repetition is preemptively defeated. Likewise, if representation is conceived of as mere social construction without referential component, the ethical duty to "witness" that past and represent what one has learned in the present is reconfigured as deception coupled with an abuse of power. Nowhere is this intersection of the epistemological and the ethical clearer than in Holocaust representation.

Ethically, it is an article of faith in much of the Jewish community that the Holocaust must be maintained as an objective fact and that losing touch with that fact can only lead to both a possible repetition of the Holocaust's horrors and/or a dissolution of the Jewish community. As Kenneth Stern of the American Jewish Committee argues, "If the Holocaust is denied, relativized, recedes from memory with the passing generations . . . a braking force against the two-thousand-year world tradition of anti-Semitism will be diminished" (24). Stern cites the threat of Holocaust denial to erase the undeniable historical truth, to diminish the importance of the past event, and to therefore lead to unethical future behavior. He is confident that "knowing" past events serves as a stable launching pad for an ethical position in the present. For Stern, epistemology translates into ethics despite the similarly positivist perspective of the deniers.[5]

The Jewish community's injunction to "never forget" the Holocaust and to insist on its irrefutable and concrete factuality is not, however, linked only to fears of a renewed anti-Semitism but also to a communal identity that has made the Holocaust one of its central features. Indeed, Phillip Lopate has gone so far as to suggest that the memory of the Holocaust has come to replace or obscure many other traditional elements of Jewish faith. While Lopate is critical of how the Holocaust's centrality has reduced the "religion itself" into a "marginally necessary preamble for this negative miracle" (55–65), others agree with Lopate about the Holocaust's centrality to Jewish identity but read such an allegiance to the recent past as positive (Gilman 34–36). Most commentators agree that the Holocaust is now a central defining feature of Jewishness and that denying the event strikes at the heart of what it means to be a Jew.

In practical terms, however, the anxiety displayed by Stern and others in the face of Holocaust denial is hardly worthwhile, at least according to Peter Novick, who notes that the number of people who take any stock in Holocaust denial remains infinitesimal. Novick describes the deniers as "fruitcakes," "screwballs," and "nuts," emphasizing the connection of Holocaust denial to the lunatic fringe (*Holocaust* 270–72). Novick's dismissal of the deniers does not, however, account for all of the fears expressed by Stern, and it is worth taking these concerns somewhat more seriously than Novick. Lurking alongside Stern's positivist fear of losing contact with the "object" that is the past is the more "postmodern" fear that such contact is impossible and that no document, no series of documents, no archives, no evidence, can refer to or restore the past in all of its plenitude. Stern, after all, is not only concerned that the Holocaust may be denied but also that it may be "relativized," a term that subtly links Holocaust denial to poststructuralist philosophical discourse. In this, the objectivist version of Holocaust denial that looks for and fails to find incontrovertible evidence from the gas chambers is improbably connected with the theoretical position that contends that all knowledge is inevitably socially determined and ideological. Stern's invocation of "relativism" suggests that these two visions, while philosophically opposed, pose the same danger to the Jewish community, and that the extreme application of poststructuralist views would amount to something similar to Holocaust denial: the impossibility of verifying this central event.

I do not wish to claim that subscribing to poststructuralist theory is tantamount to Holocaust denial, as Deborah Lipstadt suggests in *Denying the Holocaust*.[6] Rather, I wish to suggest the ethical problems such philosophy invites, if taken to its logical conclusions. While Novick characterizes Holocaust deniers accurately, Stern's notion of relativizing the event holds more resonance than its outright denial given the influence of poststructuralism, particularly in the academy. While the Holocaust-denying proposals of Arthur Butz and Robert Faurisson may draw more popular attention,[7] the indirect link between deconstructionist Paul de Man and Nazism has held equal fascination in academic circles, wherein those who oppose poststructuralism note the ways in which the philosophy is related to a Nietzchean nihilism that borders on Nazism. De Man's tenuous links to the Nazis long precede his poststructuralism, but to some the link is not coincidental. To these, denying our capacity to access past events is dangerously close to denying the events themselves. If confirming the existence of the traumatic event is, in itself, ethical, the challenge to epistemology and ontology is an ethical challenge.

It would be foolish to suggest that the "linguistic turn" is a turn towards Holocaust denial, but it is worthwhile to note the ways in which it may be a turn away from "ethics," or at least ethics as traditionally conceived, as I discussed in the introduction. At the very least, it is worth emphasizing the paradoxical position the Holocaust occupies in the ethical/moral debates surrounding postmodernism. While it is the single most cited twentieth-century trauma that we cannot allow to be "relativized" by postmodern theory, it is also frequently seen as the key event that dramatically encapsulates, even proves, such theory. If postmodernism is about the failure of representation, the Holocaust is the foundational test case of an event that is impossible to represent. The most well-known version of this claim is Theodor Adorno's argument that it would be barbaric to write lyric poetry after Auschwitz (*Negative Dialectics* 362). This fairly limited claim has subsequently been expanded dramatically, however. Raul Hilberg writes that it is "equally barbaric to write footnotes after Auschwitz" (25). Indeed, Hilberg and others insist that such an attempt is not only barbaric (an ethical position)[8] but also doomed to failure because of the impossibility of representing the traumatic nature of the event (an epistemological position). Arthur Cohen notes that thought itself "is alien to the enormity of the death camps" (1), while Emil Fackenheim asserts that the more the psychologist, the historian, or the "psychohistorian" attempts to explain the Holocaust the more he is forced to admit its "inexplicability" (233; Seeskin 110). Similarly, George Steiner argues that Auschwitz lies outside speech and reason (123), while Elie Wiesel argues that it negates all systems and doctrines (7).

This catalogue of things that Auschwitz defeats, exceeds, or denies is just as easily read as a description of things that poststructuralist (and some kinds of postmodern) theory refutes. For Barthes, footnotes are mere "reality effects" with no ties to the referent of the past. For Derrida, speech is no longer seen as prior to, or more "present" than, the elusiveness of writing. For Lyotard and Foucault, reason is no longer a natural or universal truth but an ideologically complicit language game that serves to dominate, while for Lyotard all systems and doctrines are reduced to that which we now have "incredulity" towards. It is the parallel between these theoretical assessments of the Holocaust and those of postmodernity that leads Dominick LaCapra to link the two irrevocably in the epigraph to this chapter. Ironically, the impossibility of representing the Holocaust because of its unique capacity to horrify and stupefy becomes, in the discourses of postmodernity, the impossibility of representing anything. The "unique" Holocaust becomes the example that lays bare its similarity with everything else.

The Holocaust is then that which *must* be remembered and represented if we are to prevent its repetition, just as it is archetypically that which cannot be represented or recovered. This fundamental contradiction leads to various arguments in the historical community about the best ways to represent the Holocaust, if such an effort is to be made. Saul Friedlander and Berel Lang, for instance, argue for a straightforward, stripped-down, nonstylistic transcription of events, while others praise a "postmodern," self-referential, denaturalizing, and alienating aesthetic that acknowledges the futility of representing the Holocaust even as it undertakes that task. Lang argues for "nonrepresentational representation," "without mediation but also without bringing the events themselves once again to life" (*Holocaust Representation* 13), while Friedlander advocates a "dissociation from the . . . postmodern phase of contemporary sensibility" (Sicher 351–52). That is, both give priority to an aesthetic that presents the facts of the past in a straightforward fashion and without any of the self-conscious and self-canceling gestures of postmodernism.

It is, however, characteristic of this "postmodern phase" to deny the possibility of any attempt at transparent representation on the grounds that a presentation of events "without mediation" is impossible and that a style that presents itself as objective only conceals its own mediation and ideology. The characteristics of the Holocaust that make it seem unrepresentable make a more postmodern approach seem preferable to many, including Hayden White, whose preference for modernist form is well established. Likewise, because of the Holocaust's exemplary status as a unique event whose characteristics are considered to be *the* characteristics of postmodernity, these same debates are frequently transferred to historical study more generally, wherein historians like White call for a reexamination of historical representation because of the impossibility of capturing *any* past event in straightforward fashion.

At the core of such debates is the notion that one must choose between the two possibilities posed, both in the Holocaust representation debates and in *Maus*. First, we have the option to believe that knowledge of the Holocaust, if not the intensity of its experiences, *can* be transmitted textually and therefore these facts can speak for themselves. Alternatively, it is possible to believe that such transmission is impossible, and while we may *try*, as we have always tried, to express what happened in the past, we must also make the requisite self-reflexive gestures that illustrate that we know our efforts are futile. Understandably, those who believe that a connection to the past, and to the Holocaust, is an ethical necessity disavow the latter position, but it is equally understandable that those who see the possibility of transparent representation as impossible have objections to "nonrepresentational representation." Neither side, however, is typically willing to consider the possibility that this is a false dichotomy, that the "postmodern phase" of Holocaust representation bears the imprint of the past just as surely as "nonrepresentational representation" and that both are necessary to accurately represent past experience.

Truth and Experience

Generalizing the inexplicability of the Holocaust to all of human history, as some postmodern theory does, is problematic at best and allows for sweeping statements that have little bearing on the specific challenges of historical representation.[9] While the Holocaust may share some traits with other technologically engineered genocides of the twentieth and twenty-first centuries, it is quite dissimilar from the lives of the suburban middle class in 2010 South Florida, to take a personal example. To say that both are inexplicable and devoid of logic may be true in some abstract theoretical sense, but they are inexplicable for different reasons and in different ways, if indeed the latter is inexplicable at all. The experience of the two differs, and the question should not be if we can ever "know" if the Holocaust occurred (which, by nearly all accounts, we do) but whether historical discourse can transmit its experience in such a way that it can have an ethical impact. For this reason, it is important to focus debates over historical representation not only on questions of knowledge but also on questions of experience.

Frank Ankersmit's efforts to separate notions of truth and experience are most clearly articulated in *Sublime Historical Experience* (2005), although the origins of the project go back (at least) to *History and Tropology* (1994). In the earlier book, Ankersmit notes how contemporary philosophy, beginning with the Cartesian *cogito*, "created an almost unbridgeable gap between mind and knowledge on the one hand and the world on the other," while philosophy was given the task " . . . of building an epistemological bridge over an essentially ontological cleft between subject and object" (25). That is, with Descartes's "I think therefore I am," human thought becomes philosophically separated from the brute world of ontological being and "sense data" and human "experience" are read as "signs" of reality, rather than reality in its own right. Saussure's "bracketing" of language from referent is merely one version of this philosophical project. According to Ankersmit, the whole of post-Cartesian philosophy is predicated upon a division of subject and object that can, or cannot, be overcome.

While there are problems with viewing some forms of poststructuralism in this light,[10] Ankersmit's lumping together of diverse thinkers like Descartes and Derrida has the unexpected benefit of unveiling Aristotle as a surprising alternative. Ankersmit configures Aristotle as one of the last important thinkers who assumes the continuity between subject and object. Aristotle, says Ankersmit, insists that "sense data" is not merely a "sign" or "trace" of the world's presence but is, in fact, that which connects mind and world, making them continuous. Aristotle's metaphor is that the mind functions like a ring pressed against wax: "we must understand that sense is that which is receptive of sensible forms apart from their matter, as wax receives the imprint of the signet ring apart from the iron or gold from which it is made" (69; *De Anima* II:12, 424a). For Aristotle, the world makes its impressions upon the senses and the senses retain it. The mind actually *becomes* the object of thought, not merely a second-order prosthesis that follows it. Therefore, "forms, experience, and knowledge do not separate us from the world . . . but unite us with" it (Ankersmit, *History and Tropology* 25–26).

Freud's conception of the "mystic writing pad" applies similar ideas to memory, as Ankersmit notes. Freud suggests that we can conceive of memory as wax that receives the impressions of past experience and, in the unconscious, never loses them. Freud imagines two plastic sheets layered over the wax, associating them with the conscious mind. While these may lose the information written on them, the wax itself (or the unconscious mind) will always retain the information or experience (Freud 232). Repressed experiences or memories may return when we least expect, indicating their continuing presence even when not recalled by the conscious mind. Memories, for Freud, are not mere "signs" that gesture toward the world without ever touching it. Instead, they *are* the form of the world impressed upon the mind. When memories return they are not merely the system of signs we use to re-present the past (the wax material), but are also the past itself (the shape the wax takes from past experience).

Crucial in Ankersmit's revival of Aristotle, however, is his assertion that Aristotle's notion of the world's impression upon the mind may not always transmit precise factual "knowledge" about the truth of what happened in the past but may instead give us an experience of the past best articulated in the realm of feelings. "How we *feel* about the past is no less important than what we know about it" (*Sublime Historical Experience* 10). For Ankersmit, feelings are not a mere subjective, and therefore unreliable, expression of an individual, as they are quite often seen. Rather, they are an index to historical experience that goes beyond "knowledge." When viewed in this light, the contradictions expressed in *Maus* are an expression of the feelings impressed upon its author by the inheritance of Holocaust trauma and not (or not only) an expression of epistemological doubt. Likewise, various types of poststructuralist and/or postmodern theory may convey the experience of the Holocaust, as opposed to merely expressing the epistemological difficulties in confirming its existence.

Gabrielle Spiegel's insightful examination of Derrida's poststructuralism helps link Ankersmit's insights with Holocaust representation. Spiegel notes how Derrida's biographical and geographical position on the outskirts of the Holocaust in part determines and governs his philosophy. Spiegel suggests that Derrida has much in common not with Holocaust survivors themselves but with their "second-generation" children, whose lives were irrevocably shaped, transformed, and traumatized by the Holocaust, but who did not experience it directly. Derrida, born in 1930 in Algeria, was, of course, a Jew and, as such, experienced "the war and the anti-Semitism of the Pétain regime" (Spiegel 224n20). Nevertheless, he narrowly missed the direct experience of the concentration camps. Spiegel argues that for Derrida, as for the children of Holocaust victims, the Holocaust is itself an "absent origin," something that is at the center of his life and work, but which he did not directly experience. "Derrida belongs . . . to that 'second generation' of the post-Holocaust world, on whose psyche has been indelibly inscribed an event in which it did not participate" (37). What Spiegel suggests is that the Holocaust itself is the psychic impression that makes Deconstruction possible. If one recalls the "impression" of the historical ring on Aristotle's metaphorical wax, one can see how the past, far from impossible to access in Derrida's philosophy, is always present on its surface. In this context, the most important of Derrida's experiences is that which he did not undergo: the experience of lack.

Spiegel explores this possibility by observing how, for both first- and second-generation survivors, the Holocaust is generally acknowledged to "exceed the representational capacity of language and to cast suspicion on the ability of words to convey reality" (Spiegel 39). This "suspicion" is of course the central element of poststructuralist philosophy and as such, the Holocaust itself can be seen as the absent origin of the philosophy of absent origins, just as the experience of lack may be seen as the fundamental beginning for a philosophy that denies plenitude. Far from revealing how the past can never be made present in its representations, Derrida's philosophy illustrates how the past *is* undeniably present.

While Spiegel's account is insightful, it has a somewhat limited utility.

From her logic, nearly any deconstructive reading or postmodern narrative bears the imprint of Holocaust "experience," if not its epistemological truths. Ankersmit's allegiance to the transmission of historical "experience," cannot, then, be a substitute for "truth" but must instead function as a supplement to more traditional accounts of historical accuracy. Importantly, *Maus* expresses the experience of the Holocaust in ways that are similar to poststructuralist philosophy, while also confirming the veracity of events that constitute its epistemological truth. In refusing to domesticate the facts into a meaning-making narrative, *Maus* conveys the experience of meaninglessness while paradoxically also confirming the possibility of epistemological accuracy.

Maus as/and Postmodern History

Art Spiegelman is an actual, rather than metaphorical, second-generation Holocaust survivor, and within Spiegel's context it is no surprise that *Maus* partakes amply of a postmodern aesthetic, noted frequently by critics, if downplayed by early reviewers. Barry Laga asserts that "typical of many postmodern writers, Spiegelman is distrustful of all claims to truth and hypersensitive to the view that reality and objectivity are not givens but social and linguistic constructs" (66–67). For Laga, Spiegelman is preoccupied with pinpointing what we cannot know, rather than in recapturing the facts of his father's life. To a degree, Laga is correct, as *Maus* does display remarkable skepticism towards the possibility of representing truth. While *Maus's* postmodern credentials have been recorded amply before, I will recount some of them here in order to illustrate how they might be reread in light of Ankersmit's ideas.

First, Spiegelman places heavy emphasis on the medium of his history, emphasizing its formal qualities in order to suggest how this version of the past is not transparent or identical with the past itself. The primary trope of the book, the use of anthropomorphic cartoon animals to portray historically real human beings is only the most obvious of these formal strategies. In *Maus*, Jews are mice, Nazis are cats, Poles are pigs, and Gypsies are, of course, moths. In this way, Spiegelman both literalizes common metaphors (*à la* Rushdie) and denaturalizes the stereotypical Nazi discursive construction of Jews as vermin.[11] That is, by drawing Jews as mice, Spiegelman concretizes the ways in which contemporary discourses about Jews might have looked had they been transparently true, ironically revealing their inherent falsehood. The visual distance between the cartoon mice and the real Jews of Europe is a way of highlighting how the medium of transmission governs what we perceive to be true, even as *Maus* refuses to provide an alternative, more "real" visual representation, except in certain isolated cases.

Not content to make the Nazi construction of Jews as animals transparent, however, *Maus* also points the reader to its own complicity in the circulation of representational power. While the Nazis had the power to portray, and make others see, Jews as vermin, *Maus* self-reflexively reveals the power of the allegorical iconography that Spiegelman deploys. Nowhere is this clearer than in a humorous scene in which Artie discusses with Françoise, a French converted Jew, how she should be depicted. Here, Artie experiments with several sketches, literally illustrating the power of imagistic representation. Through his choices, Artie illustrates to what degree he controls the ways in which we perceive Françoise (and others), much as anti-Semitic discourse controlled perception of Jews in Nazi Germany.

If Françoise is to be drawn as a bunny, she will be read as "sweet and gentle" (*Maus II* 11), but if she is portrayed as a frog, she will be conferred the stereotypical traits of the French. As it stands, the scene serves to emphasize just how contingent race and ethnicity are. While Jewishness was once seen as an "essential" racial category, Spiegelman illustrates not only how someone can "convert" to this "race" simply by viewing it as a religion, but also how that which we tend to view as external distinguishing racial features may be conferred from without, by those with the power to represent.[12] Françoise is a mouse, not because she self-identifies as Jewish but because those with the power to depict confer that category upon her. In this context, Marianne Hirsch suggests that Spiegelman "come[s] close to duplicating the Nazi racist's refusal of the possibility of . . . cultural integration" (56). The reason Spiegelman only "comes close" to rigidly "fixing" racial categories is because he shows us Artie's decision-making process. In so doing, he reveals that race is neither essential nor objective but rather subjective and ideological, encouraging his readers to interrogate and reject these depictions.[13]

This dynamic of identity, race, and ethnicity is continually emphasized throughout *Maus,* wherein characters are sometimes depicted as anthropomorphic animals but are also, particularly in the outermost diegetic frame, sometimes depicted as humans in animal masks. While, from time to time, this may seem to confer a kind of liberating agency on those who get to choose their own race, religion, or identity, more often than not the reverse is the case, and the animals' species originate from an external source. The parallel between Spiegelman's own text and Nazi practice is emphasized when the Nazis decide who is Jewish and who is not, regardless of the person's self-identification. When a prisoner in the camp tries to define himself as German, he has no success. As Vladek notes, " . . . for the Germans, this guy was Jewish!" (*Maus II* 50). Although Spiegelman portrays the man first

Figure 1: From *Maus II: A Survivor's Tale: And Here My Troubles Began* by Art Spiegelman, copyright © 1986, 1989, 1990, 1991 by Art Spiegelman. Used by permission of Pantheon Books, a division of Random House, Inc.

as a mouse and then as a cat in succeeding panels, in this case it is the Nazi's power of representation that matters and the man is killed. In an interview Spiegelman emphasizes, " . . . the people sent to their slaughter as Jews didn't necessarily identify themselves as/with Jews; it was up to the Nazis to decide" (Ewert, "Reading Visual Narrative" 101). In this scene, as in his construction of Françoise, Spiegelman admits complicity, representing the man as a mouse/Jew, as the Nazis do, despite his protests to the contrary. While Spiegelman does not use his representational powers for violence, that possibility is always present in the pages of *Maus*.

In all of this, a Foucauldian[14] attitude towards historical reference is evident from both an ethical and an epistemological perspective. If there is any "history" on display here, it is the history of discourse, wherein the reader is discouraged from asking the question of which version of the man is "true," the Jew or the German. In fact, the "real" itself is in perpetual withdrawal, while discourse determines what will be given that label. When Artie asks if the man was "really a German," Vladek replies, "Who knows," indicating the folly of trying to "find the real." In the panel that depicts his death, the man reverts to an anthropomorphic "mouseness," illustrating the finality of Nazi discursive power, although much of his body is not visible (*Maus II* 50). The dual principles of a radically postmodern view of history are here combined. First, it is implied that the past (the "fact" of the man's ethnicity) is gone and cannot be recovered. Beyond this, however, is the notion that representations, far from presenting us with the truth about the past, are always and inescapably both creating "truth" and asserting ideology. Only the factuality of the man's death seems to exceed this relativistic view.

Spiegelman's meditation on the mimetic limits and ideological power of representation extends beyond his own drawings, however, to the politics of Holocaust representation as a whole. Nowhere is this more apparent than in a scene in which Vladek balks at the prospect of picking up a black hitchhiker, instead inscribing him with racist stereotypes. In this scene, it is clear that the memory of the Holocaust does not provide Vladek with insight into the nature of racism, or innate sympathy for others who are oppressed. Instead, Vladek insists, "It's not even to compare, the schvartsers and the Jews" (*Maus II* 99). Spiegelman's denaturalization of racial identities is clearly not supported by Vladek. Instead, Vladek's view of Jewish identity, built largely on the Holocaust itself, reconstructs the Jew as white, the black man's "other." This reflects the shift on a broader societal level, wherein Jews themselves, once configured as black in nineteenth-century racialist discourse,[15] are now discursively transformed, allowing the Arab in Palestine to become a "dark other," rather than a sibling in racial oppression. As Edward Said has noted, Arabs are seen as "outlandish, strange, hostile" ("Zionism"

216), much as Vladek sees the hitchhiker, solidifying the degree to which identification with the Holocaust may lead to the passing on of ideological oppression, while insulating Jews from such treatment.[16] The scene highlights the problems with the notion that "objectively" confirming a traumatic event may somehow provide an ethical bulwark against future oppression. Instead, Vladek's oppression confers a perceived moral high ground from which he mistreats others with impunity.

Holocaust commentators like Novick and Marc Ellis have suggested that Vladek's attitude toward the Holocaust is not atypical of the post-Holocaust Jewish community. Ellis observes that it was only in the wake of the Six-Day Israeli War of 1967 that the Holocaust became a central element of Jewish identity, linked to notions of "Jewish empowerment in Israel," Jewish self-identification as "innocent victims," and Israeli identification with "messianic redemption" (Rothberg 680). That is, Ellis suggests, the Holocaust's importance to Jewish subjectivity only arose when it became ideologically convenient, giving Israel political and moral capital in its extended conflict with the Arab world.

Israeli philosopher and survivor of the death camps, Yehuda Elkana, likewise argues that the increasing importance of the Holocaust is linked to its contemporary political capital. In "A Plea for Forgetting," Elkana argues that the Holocaust lesson that "the whole world is against us [Israel, the Jews]" and that "we are the eternal victim" was the "tragic and paradoxical victory of Hitler." Elkana goes on to suggest that "this lesson . . . had contributed to Israeli brutalities in the West Bank and to the unwillingness to make peace with the Palestinians." Ultimately, Elkana claims that the Jewish injunction to remember the Holocaust is not only misleading, but also damaging: "It may be that it is important for the world at large to remember. . . . For our part, we must *forget*" (Novick, *Holocaust in American Life* 164; emphasis in original). This argument too reflects a Foucauldian logic that insists that any knowledge, any memory, is already part and parcel of a "will to power," and that the remembrance of the Holocaust inevitably leads to the use of that memory to assert power over others. From this perspective, the Holocaust becomes a "legitimating apparatus for Jewish chauvinism and for the Jewish state" (Rothberg 680–81).

Despite the importance of these ethical concerns, it is possible to argue that a past event's redeployment for present politics does not necessarily mean that the event is in itself historically inaccessible. Rather, we might try to separate "history" as the events of the past from "history" as it is retold for personal or social advantage. *Maus*, however, both pinpoints the ethical pitfalls of historical representation and articulates our epistemological distance from the past itself.

If *Maus*'s use of "funny animals" is its most clearly and easily articulated assertion of the inevitable mediation between the historical real and its later representation,[17] then the occasional and strategic use of human figures in animal masks at least gives the initial impression that there may be a reality beneath the representation. Likewise, Spiegelman's inclusion of photographs of himself, his brother Richieu, Anja, and Vladek, seems to drop the veil of mediation, if only briefly. However, more often than not, the photographs themselves are revealed to be instances of mediation, not an example of where a representation can tell the truth of the past.

Spiegelman's "Prisoner on the Hell Planet," first published in *Short Order Comix #1* seven years before the first installment of *Maus*, is reprinted in the later book as a means of conveying the details of Anja's suicide and Artie's perceived culpability in her death. While Vladek, Anja, and Artie are the central figures in this drama, in "Prisoner" they are depicted as human beings, not as mice. In this context, the photograph of Anja included on the first page seems initially to function as a "reality effect," confirming the connection between the representation and the real world. Despite this initial mimeticism, however, there is a stylized sketched hand that holds the photograph, contributing to the sense that this is more a "fantasy of realism" than a clear "touching of the world." If an illustrated human hand is holding the picture, which is in turn part of a comic held by an anthropomorphic mouse (in *Maus*) in a book that is held by a human reader, the layers of construction become vertiginous. The photograph does not provide a guarantee of referentiality, especially given the family's happiness in the photo, which is belied by the mother's suicide and the son's recent release from a mental hospital.

Likewise, a photo of Vladek included near the close of *Maus II* shows him in a concentration camp uniform, but it is revealed in the course of the narrative that it is not his own but a mock one used at a "photo place" for "souvenirs" (134). That is, the "realistic" picture of the Vladek of the camps can only be produced afterwards, staged for the purposes of memory: a simulacrum of a past that is already, thankfully, gone. *Maus*, then, uses photographs not simply as a means of establishing a mimetic attachment to the historical past but also to suggest the ways in which all media are subject to staging and manipulation, distancing us from the referent they claim to reproduce.[18] While cartoon mice are quite obviously not "true" copies of their human surrogates, *Maus* illustrates how photographs may be no closer to their referent. As Marianne Hirsch writes, "Spiegelman lays bare the levels of mediation that underlie all visual representational forms" (11). The occasional and increasing use of drawn photographs that remain true to the animal metaphor alongside the "real" photographic reproduction of human figures only serves to blur whatever boundaries may remain between

Figure 2: *Maus I: A Survivor's Tale: My Father Bleeds History* by Art Spiegelman, copyright © 1973, 1980, 1981, 1982, 1984, 1985, 1986 by Art Spiegelman. Used by permission of Pantheon Books, a division of Random House, Inc.

the purportedly real photograph and the definitively constructed drawing (*Maus* 17, *Maus II* 114–15).

From all of this, it is clear that although Artie dramatically excoriates Vladek for distancing him from Anja's past, Spiegelman performs a similar task for the reader, indicating to us how any representation of the past is more mediated, and therefore distant, than it may initially appear. In fact, not only are Spiegelman's representations far from the reality they initially appear to reflect, but they continually run the risk of asserting ideological control. Like the Nazis' depiction of Jews and Vladek's redeployment of his Holocaust memories to justify his racism, Spiegelman is sure to implicate himself when he depicts Artie at the outset of chapter 2 of *Maus II*. Sitting at his drawing table, in front of television interviewers, Artie discusses the commercial success of the first volume of his book while sitting atop a pile of anthropomorphic mouse corpses. He is depicted not as a mouse but as a man wearing a mouse mask, performing Jewishness for commercial gain. The simultaneously humorous and threatening depiction of the American advertiser offering a license deal for Artie vests ("*Maus*. You've read the book now buy the vest!" [42]) indicates how Artie (and Spiegelman himself) uses the past not merely to recall it in the present but for his own profit and on the backs of the Jews his book is purportedly "remembering." Artie displays a questionable connection to the past in order to participate in the circulation of power and profit.[19]

It is for these reasons that Artie questions his whole project when, on a visit to his therapist, he quotes Samuel Beckett in saying, "Every word is like an unnecessary stain on silence and nothingness" (*Maus II* 45). Here, Artie notes how any attempt at speaking, witnessing, or portraying history runs into not only the impossibility of finding the historical real but also into the ethical difficulties that suggest that any representation is an act of power and oppression. The therapist, Pavel, inspires Artie's observation when he says, " . . . look at how many books have already been written about the Holocaust. What's the point? People haven't changed. . . . Maybe they need a newer, bigger Holocaust" (*Maus II* 45). Here, Artie and Pavel seem to reject representation in two ways. First, Artie promotes a complete withdrawal from signification, preferring silence and nothingness. Second, while Pavel is clearly commenting on the dark side of human nature, his remark also suggests that a return of the referent (a newer, bigger Holocaust) would be preferable, since a repetition of the event itself would no longer be a representation of it, but the thing itself, independent of the ethical and epistemological dilemmas Artie raises. Elsewhere, Artie also voices a desire to have been at Auschwitz himself, "so I could really know what they lived through" (*Maus II* 16).[20] While Artie eventually withdraws this wish, it is indicative of the kind of paralysis that a poststructuralist view of representation can induce. Artie's epistemological and ethical despair leads him to wish for silence or renewed genocide, neither of which seems artistically or ethically productive. Nevertheless, *Maus's* representational despair is supplemented and complicated both by its commitment to traditional historical accuracy and by its capacity to convey Ankersmitian experience through memory and history. Given all of these doubts and recriminations about the possibility of historical representation, one wonders why such care is taken by Spiegelman in "getting it right," or how it is possible that so many readers praise *Maus* precisely for its truthfulness.

Maus as/and Memory

Pavel's rhetorical wish for a "new Holocaust" indicates a desire, even a desperate yearning, for the materiality of the referent that is not uncommon in contemporary theory. This possibility is not limited, however, to Pavel's fantasies about the referent's literal return, but is often, particularly in the context of the Holocaust, configured in terms of the opposition between history and memory. As Jonathan Boyarin observes, the postmodern attempt to delegitimate "universal history" has, at times, led to the reification of memory and the effort to understand history and memory as "fundamentally different modes of relating to the past" (93). In the previous section, I discuss *Maus's* treatment of the past without making a significant distinction between these two "modes," but given the fact that Vladek personally remembers the Holocaust while Artie comes to the same material belatedly, like a historian, collating, arranging, and fact-checking documentary evidence, it is a crucial distinction and one that bears further examination.

If traditional history presents us with unified events, "sponging ... all diversity off of them" in an effort to create "coherent comprehension" (Certeau 78), memory, due to its individual nature, seems to resist this unifying effort at social definition.[21] That is, because memories are typically (if not always) conceived of as individual and unique, they are by their nature not integrated into a larger institutional or cultural narrative that defines the "self" of the culture and marginalizes or oppresses its "others." The power of memory is likewise linked by its proponents with the capacity to make the referent of the past present, as opposed to merely creating a representation of the missing. For theorists like Pierre Nora, then, memory overcomes the debates over Holocaust representation. It is seen as something else entirely.

> Memory and history, far from being synonymous, appear now to be in fundamental opposition. Memory is life, borne by living societies founded in its

name. It remains in permanent evolution, open to the dialectic of remembering and forgetting, unconscious of its successive deformation, vulnerable to manipulation and appropriation, susceptible to being long dormant and periodically revived. History ... is the reconstruction, always problematic and incomplete, of what is no longer. Memory is a perpetually actual phenomenon, a bond ... to the eternal present; history is a representation of the past. (8)

Maurice Halbwachs similarly notes that memory focuses on that which is continually present, repeated, and "essentially unaltered," while history focuses on the rupture between the past and present (85–86). For Nora and Halbwachs, the past is not gone in an ontological sense as long as it is remembered and memory keeps alive any slivers of the past that remain in its grasp. If a historian writes an account of the Holocaust, it is merely a representation of the past, separated from its "presence," or essential being. If a survivor, like Vladek Spiegelman, remembers the Holocaust, however, it is, in some sense, present ("eternally") and real ("perpetually actual"). While both memory and history are, then, prone to error, manipulation, and appropriation, only one transmits the referent of the past, while the other "refers" to it with the compromised tools of signification. It is for this reason that personal memory retains some authority over the proliferation of textuality and electronic media so pervasive in contemporary society. Ankersmit's account of Aristotelian impressions on the wax of the mind, or Freud's "mystic writing pad" seem, in fact, to support this notion. The mind that remembers retains the impression of the past, carrying it into the present. This may help to explain the collective Jewish impulse to "witness" through memory the events of the Holocaust. Indeed, firsthand accounts are typically called "testimonies," a name tied closely to the "legal process of establishing evidence in order to achieve justice" (Young, *Writing* 28). That is, the sense of "testimony" as authoritative is linked to the notion that the truth of the past is integral to the possibility of justice in the present. Such a belief is amply reflected in both the Yale Fortunoff and Survivors of the Shoah Foundation collections of videotaped survival testimonies.[22]

Michael Staub pinpoints the contradictions within the impulse to collect memory-work, however, indicating that the faith entrusted to these memories more accurately reveals fears about the loss of a connection to the past than an effective means of accessing it: "[T]hey reflect a general anxiety over the impending death of all concentration camp survivors and their living memories. When they are gone, we will have mountains of written texts, videotapes, films, recordings, and other evidence. But the actual voices will be lost forever. How, then, to approximate the authority of the oral in a world increasingly suspicious of ... written evidence?" (35). Staub's "authority of the oral" identifies an attempt by many to hold on to Nora's notion of a "continuous present" carried through individual memory. History, from this perspective, can only be a secondhand, prosthetic addendum to memory's witnessing of the past. While "writing" may be the most-cited prostheses that intercedes between the source of the past and its immanent memory, Staub notes how our contemporary age is replete with alternative prostheses, or texts: videotapes (and now DVDs and YouTube files), audio tapes (and now CDs and sound files), films, etc. Each of these, it is suggested, can only approximate the oral and the remembered, which are implied versions of the referent itself.[23] This division between the oral and the written is, of course, one of the earliest targets of Derridean deconstruction in "Plato's Pharmacy," some twenty years before Nora offers the distinction, and it is useful to consider how poststructuralism blurs the distinction between these modes of relating to the past.

In the *Phaedrus*, Plato privileges memory, the "real," and the internal retention of the past over and against any prosthetic version that might be aided by writing. Derrida, however, rigorously illustrates that this distinction can only be arbitrary since "[t]he outside is already *within* the work of memory.... A limitless memory would in any event be not memory but infinite self-presence. Memory always ... already needs signs in order to recall the non-present with which it is necessarily in relation" (*Dissemination* 109; emphasis in original). That is, memory is not a prelinguistic internal recreation of past events but is already a process by which "signs" are used to approximate the "real" of the past, and always unsuccessfully so. Memory *is* writing in the sense that it is the use of signs to "represent" that which is no longer there. A "limitless self-presence" would entail a timeless subject whose past was also its present and therefore also its future. Such a subject does not exist outside of theoretical physics or science fiction. Likewise, if memory did not partake of signs, a memory of the Holocaust would reenact it, reviving a referent better left behind, despite Artie's occasional wishes in *Maus*.

Memory, then, according to poststructuralist logic, is not what Nora claims but is what he defines as history, a "representation of the past" with no claim to a "presence" that we can know without mediation. In fact, writing and history's prosthetic character is not its most threatening attribute, according to Derrida. Rather, it is threatening because it can breach the perceived internal self-presence of the subject. Plato voices the concern that writing will sap the internal capacity of the thinker to remember without its aid, indicating that writing is not actually irremediably external to the truth of the past, but that it can invade the inside, weaken, or destroy it. As Derrida points out, writing is then already inside, since memory is a process of signification, not a reproduction of the past. It is for this reason that the "line between memory and its supplement [writing], is more than subtle; it is hardly perceptible" (*Dissemination* 111). For Derrida, the distinction between memory and history proposed by Nora and Halbwachs dissolves. While it is hopeful to conceive of memory as a "present" alternative to the re-vision that history offers, the notion of memory's "presence" is a false one, since both are merely signifiers of a referent long gone. The only thing "present" in the mind of s/he who remembers is the "absence" characterized by signification, a trace of the past: "a pseudo-trace, a detritus, a re-ferent, a carrying back to/from a past that is so completely decontextualized, so open to recontextualization, that it ... becomes ... an emblem of a past evacuated of history" (Crapanzano 137). From a poststructuralist perspective, memory is no different from history.

Maus as/and Narrative

At first blush, *Maus* performs the same deconstruction of the memory/history binary as Derrida does in "Plato's Pharmacy." Initially, we are given the firsthand witness and the seemingly immanent memory of Vladek in opposition to the secondhand and prosthetic history of Artie. However, while Artie and Vladek's versions of the past are competitive, they are similar in terms of their distance from the historical referent. Read through an Ankersmitian prism, however, the similarity of memory and history does not have to mean that *neither* has the capacity to convey the truth and/or experience of the past. Rather, it may mean that *both* do. A look at *Maus's* treatment of narrative and nonnarrativity helps elucidate this possibility.

Interestingly, Spiegelman's attitude towards, and public statements about, narrative are filled with ambivalence. In many of his early works ("Ace Hole, Midget Detective," "The Malpractice Suite," "Don't Get Around Much Any More" [*Breakdowns*]), Spiegelman is largely uninterested in telling a "story." Instead, these comics serve more as commentary on the medium, pushing the boundaries of the comics' page's paradoxical and simultaneous presentation of multiple sequential temporal images (narrative) and a single static atemporal one (nonnarrative). In a 1982 interview in *The Comics Journal*, Spiegelman and his wife, Françoise Mouly, observe that plot is largely just a "conventional formula," a "comfortable matrix," and "manipulation" (Groth, Thompson, and Cavalieri 45–47). Nevertheless, Spiegelman admits that he doesn't "think comics can be non-narrative" (55), principally because that which separates comics from painting, still photography, and other visual art is precisely the juxtaposition of *sequential* images. Without sequentiality and temporality, the medium of comics does not exist. Despite this observation and his consistent admission that *Maus* is "narrative in every sense of the word" (Groth, Thompson, and Cavalieri 36), *Maus* retains an antipathy for elements of plot. While the book(s) certainly tells a story and formally embraces narrativity in ways that Spiegelman's previous work did not, it retains a critique of narrative, and particularly its tendency to "comfort," to make meaning out of the meaningless, and to obscure the historical truth.

In *Maus*, then, Artie partakes of various textual prostheses (tapes, photographs, history books) in order to connect with the past. It soon becomes evident, however, that Vladek too is distanced from his own experience by a less concrete prosthesis of signification: narrative. While it is true that poststructuralist philosophy might focus more closely on language as that "text" that neither Vladek nor Artie can escape in their search for a referent, narrative is more clearly the problem that *Maus* addresses, as it is for Hayden White and postmodern historiography more generally. Ankersmit, for instance, even in his earlier, more radically relativist, period, is willing to concede that while individual statements about the past can be true, narratives present thornier problems and yield greater results since they present us not with a collection of statements about the past but with a proposal about what those statements mean.[24] It is this meaning-making quality that White argues arises from "emplotment," the transformation of events into a narrative. This problem is most clearly articulated in *Maus* in Vladek's efforts to provide closure to his Holocaust experiences after being reunited with Anja.

On the final pages of *Maus II*, Vladek recounts his return to Sosnowiec, Poland, and his reunification with Anja after their time in concentration camps. As Vladek describes the encounter, "It was such a thing that everybody around was crying together for us. . . . More I don't need to tell you. We were both very happy, and lived happy. Happy ever after" (*Maus II* 136). While the moment is poignant, reflection on the rest of the book reminds the reader of the fallacy of Vladek's statement. While he may well have been happy at the moment of the reunion, all readers know that they do not live "[h]appy ever after," given Anja's 1968 suicide and all that follows. The presentation of that suicide in "Prisoner on the Hell Planet" gives the reunion a different meaning when made a part of *Maus*.[25] Spiegelman's explicit rejection of "fatuous attempts to give [the Holocaust] a happy ending" (Dreifus 35) must, in this context, be read as a rejection of his father's Romance "plot," and perhaps of "plot" generally conceived.

As Arlene Fish Wilner points out, Vladek's oral narrative is specifically configured not only as memory but also as "story," subject to the perils of emplotment. The idea of the "authority of the oral" is belied by the ways in which the oral too is dependent upon narrative structures that assert meaning where none inherently exists. Vladek's account also indicates the problematic role closure plays in narrative representation. While the reunion itself undoubtedly occurred, its placement within a narrative, and particularly at the end of a narrative, gives it a meaning that is conspicuously misleading. In *Metahistory,* White points out the ways in which historians not only make events into stories but into particular types of "plots" familiar from fictive writing: Romance, Tragedy, Comedy, and Satire (37). While it may be true that this list is too limited for more general purposes, it is clear that Vladek is making an effort to emplot his Holocaust experience as "Romance," making it "mean" the happiness and joy of true love that overcomes all obstacles, even when the most significant of those obstacles is the Holocaust. The fact that Vladek's narration closes here indicates an effort on his part to exert the power of narrative closure over the power of the camps.[26] For White, it is closure that makes narratives "mean," in that they satisfy the desire (by reader, writer, teller, or listener) to put everything in its place and to fit together. As I discuss throughout this book, narratives *are* narratives by virtue of their closure, allowing the retrospective gaze that makes sense of all that precedes it.[27]

What makes Vladek's closure interesting, however, is that it is neither inconclusive (a staple of twentieth-century modernism) nor tidily explanatory (a staple of nineteenth-century realism). Instead, the conclusion is resolutely incongruous. It *does* provide a tidy conclusion, but it is manifestly unsatisfactory in its efforts to do so. When the reader recalls Vladek's eyewitness account of prisoners being forced to jump into piles of burning bodies, with the body fat being "scooped and poured again so everyone could burn better" (*Maus II* 72), his "happy ever after" not only fails to provide an explanation but highlights its failure to do so. Likewise, earlier in the book, Vladek attempts to control the *beginning* of his "Romance" by excluding his messy affair with Lucia Greenberg. While Vladek does tell Artie this story, he makes him promise not to include it in *Maus* (*Maus* 23). Spiegelman's inclusion of the episode, in order to make the book "more real—more human" (*Maus* 23) indicates the degree to which he resists the conventional plot into which Vladek tries to wrestle his experiences (even as it implicates Artie for betraying his father's trust). While "happy ever after" is a conventional end to a conventional romance plot, the unedited beginning, when combined with the traumatic middle of Vladek's tale, and the "future" events recounted in Artie's competing narrative, renders such a conclusion not only unsatisfactory but also inaccurate.

This romance plot is not, as we have seen, Vladek's only attempt to make narrative sense of his experiences. At times, he wants to make himself an exemplar of the postwar Jewish/ Israeli narrative of innocence and redemption, a narrative that prevents him from seeing himself in the role of racist, or oppressor, in the incident with the black hitchhiker. He also uses his Holocaust experiences as a means of returning half-eaten groceries and gaining discounts on their replacements, transforming his inexplicable trauma into a way of garnering sympathy from the store manager (*Maus II* 90). Traumatic and antinarrative experiences are thus transformed into simple narratives for personal gain. While these narratives may provide momentary comfort, clarity, understanding, or explanation to Vladek, they cannot, in the end, satisfactorily account for or integrate the events of Vladek's past. While Vladek's Holocaust experiences *are* part of an emplotted romance, they also resist their role in that story.

Indeed, Vladek's Holocaust experiences exemplify Ankersmit's observation that we should "expect the translation of the world into language to meet with some resistance now and then.... Is it not only at such occasions that we can become aware of reality *itself,* as possessing autonomy?" (*Historical Representation* 143; emphasis in original). It is clear, in fact, that the reader particularly feels reality's autonomy when Vladek attempts to transform his survivor's account into a conventional narrative. As White insists, events, and particularly the Holocaust, do not make sense, and this reality shows resistance to the systems of signification applied to it, narrative foremost among them.

Although several critics note the implicit critique of Vladek's narrative compulsion in *Maus*, it is important to see this critique not merely as an attack on Vladek's personal failings, but on the form of narrative itself insofar as it attempts (and fails to achieve) mimesis. The "happy ever after" panel that concludes Vladek's narrative is succeeded by several more that conclude Artie's "present-day" account. Vladek says to Artie: "So ... let's stop, please your tape recorder ... I'm tired from talking, Richieu, and it's enough stories for now" (*Maus II* 136). Vladek reclines upon his bed, exhausted, and Spiegelman ends the book (outside the narrative) with the drawing of a tombstone with the names of Vladek and Anja, accompanied by their birth and death dates. Finally, Spiegelman's signature is included, along with the dates of the composition of *Maus* (1978–1991). While Vladek's narrative is closed within a version of a conventional "marriage plot," Artie's is concluded with another typical version of closure: death. While we do not witness Vladek's death in the narration, we have witnessed his progressive decline, and the tombstone dates his death to 1982, four years after Spiegelman began work on *Maus*, but long before its 1991 completion. The deaths of Anja and Vladek are not, however, merely arbitrary endings to a story. Rather, in *Maus*, they are also metaphors for the end of all stories, or the idea of stories. The last words spoken, " . . . it's enough stories for now," echo Pavel's " . . . maybe it's better not to have any more stories" (*Maus II* 45).

While the inclusion of a work's dates of composition is not uncommon, Spiegelman's juxtaposition of *Maus*'s with those of his parents' lives indicates that the telling of the story is itself a kind of death, perhaps of one version of Art Spiegelman, but also of Holocaust "stories" more generally. Vladek mistakenly calls Artie Richieu, the name of Spiegelman's elder brother, killed by relatives in an attempt to save him from the Nazis (*Maus* 109). This cements the relationship between the two hinted at earlier, in which Artie discusses his sense of competition with Richieu. "The photo [of Richieu] never threw tantrums or got in any kind of trouble. . . . It was an ideal kid and I was a pain in the ass. I couldn't compete" (*Maus II* 15). By calling Artie by his brother's name, Vladek unconsciously attempts to recall or revive this (idealized) portion of his past that is forever gone. At the same time, however, he declares the close of his narrative impulse, indicating that his efforts at recovering the past through narrative are over and that Artie will never, of course, be Richieu, no matter what stories Vladek (or Artie) may invent.

The inclusion of the two sets of parallel dates also invokes the familiar "kinship between writing and death," discussed by both Derrida and Foucault. Foucault emphasizes how writing is only necessary if the originator of the story is "absent" or "the writing subject endlessly disappears" (Foucault, "What Is an Author?" 1623). This lack of the author's "presence" indicates not only death but also the impossibility of connecting with the referent. For Derrida, the *pharmakon* of writing wields "power, *over* death but also in cahoots with it," since it allows the author to live after death in representation, but at the same time contributes to the "forgetting" or loss of the "original" (*Dissemination* 104–5). In the latter sense, the completion of *Maus*, accompanied by the tombstone and the composition dates, may be read as merely another account of the failure to revive the referent: the Holocaust itself.

In drawing attention to the text as representation, as writing, these dates reiterate the counternarrative that *Maus* has kept alive throughout. While Vladek's account is a narrative of the Holocaust, trying to revive its events and make sense of them, Artie's "present-day" narrative is always (and increasingly) an account of the failure to do so. If the tombstone and signature combine to be a model of narrative closure, the meaning they convey is a lack of meaning, of the impossibility of Holocaust representation, and of the necessity of silence. Artie's despair is, like Vladek's romance plot, a narrative that makes a kind of inverted sense of his mother's suicide and his father's Holocaust experiences. In this case, the "meaning" is a lack of meaning.

Artie's account of the failure of language and representation to convey the truth of the past is itself predicated on reading its events *as* a narrative in which time progresses in a linear fashion from the past to the present and dramatic change occurs that spurs a narrative desire for explanation. It is, after all, only through articulating a rupture that separates present from past that we can begin to say that the past is irretrievable and inaccessible. This rupture, or change, is precisely that which spurs narrative itself, according to such influential models as those of Tzvetan Todorov, Peter Brooks, and D. A. Miller, as discussed in previous chapters. The introduction of this change is that which separates the present telling from past events and which, paradoxically, introduces the impossibility of completely capturing those events, even as they become narratable. From this point of view, the present is of a fundamentally different nature from the past, and language, representation, and narrative merely (and futilely) try to bridge the gap. Paradigmatically, the Holocaust's "difference" from those events that precede it is so dramatic that it demands to be narrated. It simultaneously introduces problems for representation precisely because of the dramatic rupture between it and the past (and future). For Artie, the oxymoronic narrative of meaninglessness or silence becomes necessary.

Just as Vladek's romance plot is contradicted and invalidated by the true events of the Holocaust, however, Artie's narrative of failure and insufficiency is contradicted by Vladek's experiences. Even as Artie repeatedly throws up his hands at the impossibility of recapturing history, his transmission of Vladek's account allows some of history's truths to "bleed" through its mediation. The narrative of insufficiency is belied by Artie/Spiegelman's intense preoccupation with rendering the past accurately. In fact, Spiegelman highlights the amount of reconstruction in his father's account not merely to indicate the inevitable distortion involved in any depiction of the past but also to supplement Vladek's version of events with more accurate alternatives. Nowhere is this clearer than in the depiction of Vladek's recollection of his daily departure from the work camp. Artie's research uncovers that an orchestra "played as [Vladek] marched out the gate," while Vladek asserts that he remembers "only marching, not any orchestras." Spiegelman visually depicts the musical instruments anyway (*Maus II* 54). Spiegelman is willing to express Vladek's perspective, but not at the expense of a more fully documented referentiality.[28] James Young comments on how this dual narration, Vladek's oral and Spiegelman's visual, allows us a view of "two stories being told simultaneously" ("Holocaust" 676), and how we might read these "two stories" as a competition between a "narrative" strain that tells the story and an "antinarrative" one that "deconstructs" the first (673). In this case, however, the deconstruction not only questions the narrative but gestures towards a greater historical accuracy.

In this, there is some similarity to Rushdie's use of disnarrated errata. A narrative is provided but is not the limit of the information given, sacrificing coherence for accuracy in ways that invert White's complaints about narrative historiography. In an interview, Spiegelman describes this dynamic: "Now my father's not necessarily a reliable witness, and I never presumed that he was. So, as far as I could corroborate anything he said, I did—which meant, on occasion, talking to friends and to relatives and also doing as much reading as I could" (Brown 93). Similarly, in *Maus*, Artie asks Pavel, also a survivor, for corroboration of details after Vladek dies (*Maus II* 47) and includes representations of Vladek's sketches to clarify oral testimony. Vladek's sketch of his family's "bunker" in Srodula, built to avoid capture, fulfills the purpose of Holocaust testimony according to Stern and others: to prevent the event's repetition. Vladek wants to show Artie "exactly how was it—just in case," implying that the drawing is not merely a "reality effect" for Artie's book but might be needed in case he too has to hide for his life in some nightmare future (*Maus* 110). While Artie may not be able to present all of the events accurately, the fragments of his account that *are* true may become lifesavers someday.

If Vladek tries to emplot the Holocaust as Romance, then Artie tries to emplot it with an ironic tropology "in which the author signals in advance a real or feigned disbelief in the truth of his own statements" (White, *Metahistory* 37). Certainly, the scenes in which Artie expresses the insufficiency of his ability to represent the Holocaust, or Françoise, fall into this category, as do the variety of scenes wherein he discusses the difficulties he is having in writing the second volume. Vladek's accounts of the camps, however, succeed in making these events present to the reader in ways that belie the claim that the past is irretrievably passed. The mere fact that Vladek's romance can be invalidated by the brute intractability of the events he describes indicates their autonomy and actuality despite Artie's construction of a narrative of insufficiency.

In fact, *Maus* consistently and visually resists the notion that the past is not present. As various critics have shown, *Maus* continually highlights not only Artie's frustration at his distance from the past but also the insistent presence of the past in the narrative present. Erin McGlothlin, for one, details how Vladek is commanded to "Face Left!" by Dr. Mengele in the camps and reenacts his movements for Artie's benefit (*Maus II* 58). The reader sees four panels in a horizontal "strip." The first three show Vladek demonstrating to Artie in the present, with the fourth showing Vladek in the past being commanded by Mengele. As McGlothlin notes, "This last panel effects a visual

"It's Enough Stories" | 173

break in the block of panels, for it suddenly transports the reader from a visual depiction of a present of verbal narration of the past to a visual depicton of the narrated moment of the past itself" (178). While at first the distinction between past and present seems clear from the visual disjunction between the third and fourth panels, in fact there is more temporal continuity between the four panels than it initially appears. McGlothlin observes that Vladek occupies the same space in the fourth panel as he does in the first three, and the place of the observer, Artie, is replaced by the Nazi, Mengele, who, like Artie, records Vladek's movements and responses. McGlothlin argues that this establishes a "visual analogue between the original scene of victimization and trauma and the retelling of the event, insisting that the two are not distinct, mutually exclusive processes (179). Beyond this, however, it is possible to see *Maus'* resistance to a narrative form that relies on some version of chronology, recounting what is past in the present. Instead, the past is present, not merely in the psychological scars born by both Vladek and Artie but also in the material body of Vladek. This series of panels insists on our seeing that the same body in the camp "selection" process is the one recounting his story to his son, and as long as that body is present the past is materially accessible, written upon it.

The comics form is, in fact, inherently suited to such an observation since it is the only medium in which time is both linear and spatial. One must read temporally to progress from panel to panel, but at the same time a reader can view the pictures in several panels (or in a whole page) simultaneously, allowing her to see both narrative past and narrative present in her own present while reading.[29] This formal feature indicates how a model of narrative in which time progresses forward, separating the past that occurred from the present that explains, is unsatisfactory. Here, Spiegelman subverts temporal expectations by placing the "past" in the far right of the series of panels. In a medium wherein the reader is expected to assume that the panel to the right will take place in the "future" of the panel to its left, this inversion of expectation brings the past momentarily into the future. As Joshua Charlson writes, in *Maus* "[s]tory is never a smooth, self-contained progression . . . ; it is interrupted by the present, just as the present is continually assaulted by the past" (107). *Maus* consistently illustrates the continuity between past and present in this manner, often subtly sliding from Vladek as (present) narrator to Vladek as (past) character with visual cues (McGlothlin 182), allowing the reader to see both past and present simultaneously and experience the relays between them.

Even within the single panel, Spiegelman refuses a simple separation of past events as contrasted with present narration. In particular, when Vladek recounts the hanging of four young girls who were friends of Anja, they are depicted not in their "past" environment in the camps but as hanging from the trees in the Catskills while Vladek and Artie drive by (*Maus II* 79). As Rick Iadonisi points out, "temporal seepage" is a crucial element of the text, in which events in past time "bleed" into the present. Most typically, critics see these moments as narratological metalepses and as evidence of the psychological impact of the camps on both Vladek and Artie. At the same time, however, these moments must be read as resisting Artie's narrative of historical belatedness. While Artie quite frequently expresses despair at the impossibility of recapturing the past, at other times it impresses itself upon the present with such force that it can be seen and heard. Whether it is in the rotating body of Vladek or in the legs of the hanging victims, the material past is embodied in these panels and exceeds the notion of the past as a mere ghost or trace in the shadow of present signification. The poststructuralist narrative in which past experience disappears and is transfigured into nonreferential representations is challenged by this version of antinarrative, wherein the procession from past to present is replaced by a page, and a world, in which the two exist simultaneously.[30]

"A Problem of Taxonomy"

In focusing on the ways in which Vladek's reliance on narrative distorts the truth of his historical account, Spiegelman may be seen to be deconstructing the division Nora, Halbwachs, and others erect between memory and history. If history is a belated instrument that relies upon representation to reconfigure the past, then Vladek's own engagement with the compromised tools of signification indicates how memory may be defined in similar ways. Derrida's claim that the distinction between writing (absence/history) and speech (presence/memory) is "barely perceptible" is particularly apt here. This is not merely to say, however, that there is no such thing as memory and that all we have is history, signification, and belatedness. Rather, while it does suggest that the attributes typically applied to history must be applied to memory, it also implies the reverse, that the attributes typically applied to memory may be applied to history.

If, as Derrida asserts, the danger of writing, from Plato's point of view, is that it threatens the interior and the immanent with infection from the outside, then the permeability of external signification with the interior world (of memory/presence) is established. If one adopts Ankersmit's notion of experience impressing itself upon the mind, this permeability works both ways, wherein experience may not only impress itself upon mind/memory, but it may also be transferred to more prosthetic means of representation, like writing, and historical texts. That is, if representation can get *in,* then surely (past) experience can get *out,* both into the texts regarded as "documents" for historical research (or first-person accounts like Vladek's) *and* into the texts that arise from those texts (or third-person historical accounts, like that of Art Spiegelman).

Appropriating Aristotle, Ankersmit argues that the best analogy for the practice of historical representation is, therefore, "nostalgia." That is, rather than adhere to the binary division of history and memory, Ankersmit wishes to see them as essentially the same, or, at the very least, inextricable. He does so not in order to lump memory in with history as non-referential representations, but to position history as potentially partaking of the experiential presence often associated with memory. He observes that "nostalgia . . . has nothing to do with inferences on the basis of evidence; it really *is* an experience of the past— . . . in the sense of our experiencing *again* the same feelings we . . . had in a remote part of our personal past" (*History and Tropology* 203; emphasis in original). Contrary to poststructuralism's objections to "nostalgia for lost origins," Ankersmit proposes a reimagination of historical inquiry around "nostalgia," defined as experiential memory of a past experience, not merely a romantic glossing-over of such experience. Where Art Spiegelman would undoubtedly be fundamentally opposed to histories revolving around conventional definitions of nostalgia, *Maus* embodies Ankersmit's more charitable sense of it as "experiential memory." Ankersmit insists on "nostalgia" as the important term, because it implies emotional investment in the past, not detached recollection. While *Maus* is certainly not nostalgic in the usual sense of the term, neither is it emotionally detached. For Ankersmit, it is nostalgia that will recall not the "facts" of what happened, but the emotional experience, and it is this explicitly subjective "experience" that can be transferred into the historian's representation. Ankersmit's emphasis is on the transfer of the "same feelings," or sensations, from past to present, not necessarily on accuracy.

Ankersmit likewise argues that the definition of experience is closely linked to "sensation" as theorized by Lodewijk van Deijssel, who, like Aristotle, says that "the result of . . . sensation is that the customary demarcations between the self and external reality momentarily disappear" (*Sublime Historical Experience* 132). More importantly, however, Van Deijssel's "account of sensation" defines it as a "disruption of temporal continuity and of the normal sequence of before, now, and afterward." It generates "the conviction that its content is a repetition of something that has happened in precisely this same way maybe centuries ago. . . . [T]he past and the present are momentarily united in a way that is familiar to us all in the experience of déja vu" (132). As such, Ankersmit argues against historiography that insists on a detached "objective" style. It is objectivity, from this perspective, that drains historical representation of that which might actually attach it to the past: sensation, feeling, and nostalgia.

While it would be fundamentally incorrect to call Vladek, or Artie, or Art Spiegelman "nostalgic" for the days of the Holocaust in the usual sense of the term, the ways in which Vladek recalls his experiences and allows readers to experience them emotionally is an illustration of the capacity for memory to recapture the past despite its dependency on representational techniques. Because of the permeability of mind and world, these techniques might be said to bear the world's imprint. Unlike other theorists of memory's "presence," however, Ankersmit extends the idea of experiential nostalgia to history, noting how Petrarch was "nostalgic" for classical antiquity, Ruskin for the Middle Ages, and Michelet for the great Revolution (*History and Tropology* 204).[31] Like the psychoanalytic return of the repressed, Ankersmit suggests that the experience of these events can be revisited through historical representation.

Ankersmit is not, however, naïve enough to suggest that merely being nostalgic for past experience allows one to represent it accurately and without factual error. He does, however, argue that emotional investment is an absolute necessity if historical experience is to be conveyed. He acknowledges, then, the necessity of rigorous methods, use of archives, and traditionally defined historical research as a means of making and verifying various individual statements about the past. Nevertheless, he advocates the search for an experiential representation that is more than a collection of the various true factual statements one might make about it. That such experience must necessarily be different from living through the event is inevitable, but Ankersmit nevertheless insists that it is at least possible to undergo an "experience of the *difference* or *distance* between the present and the past" (*History and Tropology* 201; emphasis in original).

It is here that Ankersmit might be said to finally admit to a partially "postmodern" view in which the material object of the past cannot be reified, and all that can be experienced is the difference between the real and the experienced. Still, Ankersmit's notion of nostalgia articulates history in a way that is different from the by-now-familiar notion of narrative emplotment that explains the past without ever experiencing it. As Ankersmit argues, sounding much like Hayden White, "Narrative coherence may guarantee the easiest access to the past, but it obscures the authenticity of our experience of it. What has been ... mastered narratively is no longer accessible to historical experience" (*History and Tropology* 210).

Ankersmit's insistence that history may be seen as equivalent to memory/nostalgia is not merely a version of the Derridean deconstruction of the differences between memory and history. Instead, it allows for the possibility that history too can articulate the presence of the past, not through narrative coherence but through alternative means. From this perspective, we may once again employ Richard Terdiman's argument that memory functions both as *"the absolute reproduction of unchanging contents"* and also as *"the mobile representation of contents transformed"* (288; emphasis in original). That is, the past world *is* contained in the Aristotelian impression it makes upon the mind (reproduction) but is also unavoidably accompanied by a redeployment of these elements in representation. It is only where the former exceeds the capacity of the latter to explain it that the real becomes evident. Vladek's memories contain the truth of his experiences in the Holocaust as well as his efforts to wrestle them into (narrative) meaning, but to suggest that the only thing present in his account is a gesture to the lost is to underestimate the presence of his memories. The fact that memories can often be "involuntary" illustrates the tension between memory as the impression of the world upon the mind and memory as a purely imaginative process. If the past is not being consciously recalled, but asserts itself regardless, one can hardly label those memories as complete construction. It is possible to argue, in accordance with White, that the romance plot falsifies Vladek's horrible experiences, but it would be more accurate to say that Vladek's experiences invalidate the romance plot, revealing a connection to a past that has not been mastered. The experiences surely hold as much power as the formal apparatus constructed to convey them.

For this reason, Spiegelman's own claim that he has "mastered" his emotional connection to the *Maus* material rings only partially true. In an interview, Spiegelman notes that "the parts that are in the book are now in neat little boxes. I know what happened by having assimilated it that fully" (Witek 101). Despite this claim, the experiences undergone by both writer and reader cannot be completely explained by any of the text's narratives. While Vladek and Artie's lives may literally be in "little boxes," or panels, on the page, clearly their experiences exceed these boxes, given Spiegelman's continued efforts to grapple with them in the *Maus* museum exhibit, the *Complete Maus* CD-ROM, and the reappearance of mouse faces and masks in later projects like *In The Shadow of No Towers* and "Portrait of the Artist as a Young %@ξ*!"(*Breakdowns* 4–22) (not to mention t-shirts, posters, and coffee mugs at New York's Strand bookstore). As in *Midnight's Children*, these "leftovers" of the *Maus* project indicate the degree to which the real cannot be contained by its representations. If *Maus* is history, it is not simply retrospective, prosthetic, and detached. Like memory, it also experientially transmits the real.

Maus makes this clear by giving us a historian who is as emotionally invested as the person carrying first-person memories. The horrifying sensations Vladek experiences during the Holocaust are revisited and repeated by Artie, even as he denies his capacity to convey the events accurately. For Ankersmit, this emotional investment is the only way to make contact with past experience, since it is only sensation that breaks down the chronology of past, present, and future. While Ankersmit tends to avoid the Holocaust in his examples,[32] theorists like Marianne Hirsch and Dominick LaCapra have noted how second-generation Holocaust survivors do "experience" its effects, despite the critical tendency to divide them from the previous generation. LaCapra too notes how memory and history cannot be "opposed in binary fashion" (*History in Transit* 67). One reason for this is the possibility that the experiences of an individual or community may be inherited by the next generation. LaCapra revives the long discredited Jean-Baptiste Lamarck, who believed in the genetic inheritance of acquired characteristics, as a metaphor for the experience of trauma: "This 'inheritance,' more precisely repetition or reproduction, occurs through some combination of . . . conscious processes such as education as well as critical practices, including . . . signifying practices, which may enact changes on what is inherited, and unconscious . . . processes such as identification or mimeticism, including . . . compulsive repetition of posttraumatic events" (107). This proposal, arrived at through psychoanalytic theory, refuses the poststructuralist narrative that relegates "experience" to the past (if it exists at all) and positions "signifying practices" in the present. Rather, LaCapra allows for the notion that representation may change or distort the experiences that are inherited, but that they can nevertheless be transmitted from person to person even through signification, and may repeat themselves, often in the form of neurotic behaviors. The notion that experience is transmitted not through genetic link, but through signifying practices and empathic identification, allows for the possibility that Ankersmit advocates, that the experience of the real is not impossible to reproduce in second-hand historical testimony. Rather, it is that for which history should be aiming.

LaCapra uses *Maus* as an example of this possibility in his rebuttal of Novick's claims about the renewed Jewish-American interest in the Holocaust, post-1967. As explored briefly above, Novick reads the assertion of the importance of the Holocaust in the Jewish community as merely part of a political appropriation that ultimately justifies aggressive Zionism. LaCapra, however, sees the possibility that the experience of the Holocaust is reasserting itself in the children of its victims. If the experience is, in some sense, inherited, it is no surprise that while the event may be repressed by those who literally survive it, its impression on the mind returns in the next generation. As LaCapra notes, Novick's version of the Holocaust revival is one in which "the relation of present to past is a one-way street paved with narrow self-interest and symbolic capital" (*History in Transit* 95). While it is certainly true that memories can be, and are, deployed for politically suspect purposes, this does not mean that all such representations are completely removed from past experience.

Marianne Hirsch's proposed term, "post-memory," is also useful in this context, as it suggests that memory may exceed the life of a single individual. Hirsch asserts that "post-memory . . . is distinguished from memory by generational distance and from history by deep personal connection" (8), but she also characterizes post-memory as "as full and as empty as memory itself" in its susceptibility to "narration and mediation." While Hirsch's concept refuses the distinctions between the "presence" of memory in the individual and the belated mediations that follow, it does not go far enough in observing the degree to which history too is both representation and reproduction. As Ankersmit insists, history too can evolve out of a deep personal connection to the past and can convey past experience, despite the unavoidable mediation that accompanies it. While *Maus* is typically associated with memory, it supplements Vladek's memories and Artie's post-memories with Spiegelman's research, providing both an experiential depiction of the past and one that is "truthful" in its fidelity to the available facts.

This, indeed, is what separates a text like *Maus* both from Holocaust histories like those advocated by Lang and Friedlander, and from more clearly postmodern documents like Derrida's philosophy or Samuel Beckett's trilogy (*Molloy, Malone Dies, The Unnameable*). The former texts present what Ankersmit might associate with the "truth" of the Holocaust without conveying the "experience" of the event, while the latter may convey the experience, without referring to its factual truths. In advocating "nonrepresentational representation," Lang and Friedlander suggest a form that would convey the facts without any pretense to making the experience of those events present. While *Maus* certainly conveys a series of facts, this is not the limit of its efforts. While *Maus* carefully presents us with the "truth" of the orchestra at Vladek's work camp, with illustrations of how some Jews built bunkers to hide from the Nazis, with concentration camp exchange rates (*Maus II* 64), and even with hand-drawn "blueprints" of the gas chambers (*Maus II* 70), the book is not designed as a series of facts about the Holocaust. Rather, *Maus* also bears the imprint of subjective and emotional Holocaust experience.

If we recall Spiegel's account of Derridean philosophy, we must also note how Derrida's work bears the imprint of the Holocaust. Like *Maus*, deconstruction conveys the "second-generation" experience of the Holocaust in its preoccupation with lost origins, epistemological aporia, and despair over lost meaning. In Ankersmit's Aristotelian sense, the Holocaust makes its impression on both of these "second-generation" texts, but again with one significant difference. Both *Maus* and deconstruction, to varying degrees, formally reflect what Ankersmit would associate with the "experience" or the sensation of the Holocaust, but, in its content *Maus* also makes an effort to present what we epistemologically "know." While it conveys the feelings of loss and displacement that the Holocaust engenders, particularly through Artie's narrative of postmodern despair, it also provides a representation of that which engenders those feelings, linking actual events and historical personages with the belated effects they have on the present. In this it suggests the differences between specific past events and their reiteration in present experience/representation, while theoretical deconstruction provides *only* the experience. While *Maus* illustrates a variety of representational problems, it also asserts that representations are representations of *something*, and that while the past may be impossible to fully understand, it may be experienced through the texts it leaves in its wake.

The debate over Holocaust representation has been starkly divided between those who advocate an "unadorned" style and those supporters of a "postmodern phase" that advocates self-canceling gestures. *Maus* makes little sense when viewed through the prism of this dichotomy. While Spiegelman's text does insist on historical accuracy in an unadorned style,[33] it also consists of self-reflexive gestures that seem to deny the possibility of the accuracy it studiously achieves. This is only problematic, however, if we read *Maus's* postmodernism as a "withdrawal of the real" and not as a version of the very mimeticism it is said to repudiate. That is, while Spiegelman's compiling of sources and meticulous fact-checking speak to his desire to meet the requirements of a historical philosophy that privileges "knowledge," his use of epistemologically and ontologically destabilizing techniques function as a means of allowing both writer and reader to experience or "feel" past events for which they were not present.

The division of "truth" and "experience" perhaps accounts for the "problem of taxonomy" that Spiegelman notes in a 1991 letter to *The New York Times Book Review*. The *Times* had been placing *Maus* on the "fiction" side of its bestseller lists, a position that made Spiegelman "queasy" for both epistemological and ethical reasons. Spiegelman jokingly suggests that the *Times* should add a "nonfiction/mice" category to their lists, but the *Times* instead moved the book to the nonfiction side of the ledger. The decision was based both on Pantheon Books' categorizing of *Maus* as "history; memoir" and the Library of Congress' "nonfiction" label, but Spiegelman's own argument is not that there are *no* fictional elements in the book, but that the fidelity to facts outweighs the book's distancing elements. In contrast,

Ankersmit's theory suggests that *Maus's* mice are important elements in the transmission of historical "experience," even if they deviate from what we know to be factual truth.

Nevertheless, the notion of historical truth, as confirmed by documentary evidence, archives, and firsthand accounts, remains important, just as the categories of fiction and nonfiction remain at least provisionally so. There is, ultimately, a difference between an account like Vladek Spiegelman's that relates the experiences of someone who witnessed a traumatic event and an account like Benjamin Wilkomirski's *Fragments*, which *claims* to witness those events, but, in terms of factual truth, does not. Despite this shortcoming, it is possible to see *Fragments* as a fiction that conveys something of the experiential truth of the Holocaust. It is likewise possible that *Fragments*, through research, could contain *some* accurate facts about the Holocaust. *Fragments* is not, ultimately, considered nonfiction, however, because of the various "truth" claims it makes that turn out to be false, even lies. Wilkomirski's claims are a breach of the ethical relation between writer and reader. Nevertheless, while *Fragments* may fail ethically in its betrayal of the reader's trust, it can still *lead* to ethics if its experiential transmission of the past is powerful enough to impact and guide readers' attitudes towards the Holocaust and its contemporary reflections. Undoubtedly, however, a fidelity to truth facilitates the transmission of historical experience, since readers are unlikely to take seriously texts that lie about their relationship to the past factually, even if the account is powerful experientially. For this reason, texts like *Maus* that attempt to wed truth and experience are valuable: their fidelity to the facts of the past allow their experiential component to be consumed without the skepticism that occurs when central facts turn out to be misleading.

As Barbara Lounsberry notes, "when the factual accuracy of a work is questioned, or when authorial promises are violated, a work of literary nonfiction is either discredited or transferred out of the category" (xiv). The recent spate of discredited memoirs (like James Frey's *A Million Little Pieces*) confirms Lounsberry's claim, supported by critics like Daniel Lehman, who, like Spiegelman, insist that the fiction/nonfiction distinction matters. Lehman notes how nonfiction texts have the unique capacity to be simultaneously "reflexive," referring to the world and characters inside the text, and "referential," referring to the real world outside (17). The latter of these requires both writer and reader to "experience their implication in history" (Lehman 165), to consider what responsibility they may have in the lives, deaths, suffering, and trauma of real people, as opposed to the abstract conceptions (or "characters") present in a novel. Certainly, placing *Maus* on the fiction side of the bestseller lists refuses the palpable sense of Spiegelman's "implication" (and our own) in his real father's suffering and in the suffering of several generations of European Jews. To the degree that texts can not only "reflect" (if imprecisely) real-world experiences, but also impact those experiences (and vice versa), the difference between fiction and nonfiction matters.

The introduction of the kind of self-reflexive, framebreaking, "postmodern" narrative strategies discussed in this book make the fiction/nonfiction divide more problematic, however. As Lehman notes in his discussion of Tim O'Brien's Vietnam narratives, these strategies may be used for what seem to be diametrically opposed purposes, both to "foreground the fictivity or constructedness of fiction" and to "force readers to confront the factuality . . . that grows out of . . . historical . . . experience" (181). By continually reminding the reader that the real Art Spiegelman is writing *Maus,* readers become unavoidably aware of the constructedness of the textual artifact, but they are also reminded that a real person has constructed it from the details of real lives that take place "over the edge" (to use Lehman's terminology) of the text.

While Lehman sees these two tendencies of postmodernism to be opposed, they only appear so if one examines the fiction/nonfiction divide from the perspective of historical truth, or factual accuracy. Certainly, emphasizing a text's constructedness may seem to distance it from the kind of fidelity to objective facts that we expect of traditional history or nonfiction. If a text reveals its formal and subjective construction, it seems to acknowledge its inability to transparently present the truth about the world. At the same time, as I have illustrated over the course of this chapter, one could read these same alienating techniques as an expression of the *experience* of the past, particularly in the case of traumatic experiences like the Holocaust or Vietnam, where the meaning of the facts assembled never coalesces, no matter how many of them we have to hand. From this perspective, the metafictional content of *Maus* can be seen both as an expression of the experience of the Holocaust and as a reminder of the critical distance needed to uncover its factual truths. Lehman's division of fiction from nonfiction depends on the notion of "implication," but the idea of implication itself depends on the subjective emotions and experiences of the readers, writers, and personages depicted in a text, not merely on the facts it reveals. The despair at the inevitable constructedness of any account of the past is part of this experience, not a disavowal of it. As such, the foregrounding of constructedness is constitutive of, not opposed to, these postmodern narratives' efforts to force an encounter with the world.

Those who normally label fiction and nonfiction pay little or no attention to the idea of historical experience I have explored in this chapter. Rather, such labels tend to derive purely from notions of truth (and/or from market or legal concerns). Although I do not propose an absolute abolition of such categories, I do suggest that we acknowledge that the conveyance of historical experience may be as important as fidelity to truth and that even texts that we normally label fictions may have significant historical implications from the point of view of experience.

As Spiegelman points out in his letter to the *Times*, "The borderland between fiction and nonfiction has been fertile territory for some of the most potent contemporary writing," and Lehman likewise observes that part of the impact of O'Brien's Vietnam narratives is in their capacity to "defeat . . . generic certainty" (181). Indeed, this borderland is typically associated with a postmodernism that attempts to expose or reveal the fictionality of factual writing or, as White suggests, the "historical text as literary artifact." It is perhaps more useful, however, to see this borderland as a place where factual "truths" and historical "experience" may intersect in ways still not authorized by academic or popular historical study. With academic institutions and publishing houses still much more likely to approve historical treatises that project an air of objectivity, texts that portray a nostalgic passion for the past, or that formally bear the impression of the events they convey, are more likely to be seen by critics and readers as "fiction" or "postmodern" or both and their allegiance to historical accuracy as self-cancelling at best. It is, I suggest, more productive to attempt to explore the relationship of truth and experience in such texts and to see in what ways they may convey history in both modes without peremptorily classifying them as "fiction" or "nonfiction."

Within current categories, many postmodernist historical texts provide "problems of taxonomy." Both *Waterland*'s and *Between the Acts*' main characters never existed, and even the "true" historical events that they do discuss are treated in a fairly cursory manner. Nevertheless, both texts are committed not only to discussing and theorizing the transmission of history and historical trauma but also to reflecting the traumas and horrors of contemporary history in their form. *The Book of Laughter and Forgetting* and *Midnight's Children* are even trickier to consider in this regard. While they too transmit historical experience, they also convey (usually) accurate historical facts and include real people in real situations among their "characters." While Kundera's Tamina and Rushdie's Saleem, for instance, never existed, Gustav Husak, Milan Kundera, and Indira Gandhi did and do. These texts tell us facts about Communist Bohemia and twentieth-century India, but they are not completely limited by them. To merely call these texts "fiction" and to consider only their reflexivity (and not their referentiality) is to ignore the ethical impact they have precisely because of their allegiance to both truth and experience.

Dorrit Cohn's sketch of the functional distinctions between fiction and nonfiction in *The Distinction of Fiction* pinpoints the stylistic limits of both "genres." As she points out, it is fiction's status as "nonreferential" (15) that allows an author to provide access to characters' minds, even when operating mostly from a third-person point of view (often in free-indirect discourse). Since no real people have the power to read minds, nonfiction is not typically authorized to show any person's thoughts other than the author's. Instead, the nonfiction author must rely on speculations about motivations, using inferential (or "must have") statements that inform the reader that the inner rationale for the actions of historical personages must remain matters of inference (27). As Hayden White continually observes, historical plots resemble fictional ones on the level of story, but as Cohn points out, on the level of discourse, there are usually significant differences, based on the nonfiction author's reluctance to pose *as* truth those things that can only be a matter of speculation (116–17). Cohn therefore asserts that story and discourse may be a useful division for fictional narratives, but for nonfiction narratives one must also add "reference" as a third category that dictates important qualities of the other two (112).

What is clear from Cohn's discussion is how the appearance of fidelity to historical truth may actually distance the reader from Ankersmitian experience. By not allowing any access to the thoughts or feelings of the historical personages in nonfiction narrative, a writer may effectively indicate that they will only tell us what they (and we) can "know" about these historical events. This emphasis on knowledge prevents the reader from accessing the subjective feelings of those involved, sacrificing the Ankersmitian "experience" of the past for an account of its facts. Even when feelings are presented, they are couched in a distancing style that reminds the reader of what s/he can and cannot know rather than creating an empathetic identification between reader and character. Carefully couched assertions like, "Napolean *must have* been trepidatious on the morning of the attack" replace the intimacy of free-indirect style. *Maus*'s schizophrenic quality, wherein fidelity to historical facts collide with stylistic devices that both distance the reader epistemologically and draw him closer emotionally, attempts to overcome this difficulty, presenting both the truth and the experience of historical events.

Postmodern histories, then, may be classified either as fiction (*Waterland, Between the Acts*) or as nonfiction (*Maus*) from the perspective of epistemological truth, but such stark divisions may not be useful given the possibility that historical experience may be conveyed in fictional guise and that "nonfiction" histories may be accurate on the truth front but lacking in their transmission of experience. *Maus*'s attempt to convey *both* truth and experience resulted in a text that stymied the *Times*' listmakers. Such confounding of the truth/experience divide may well be necessary if historical narratives are to have ethical and/or political impact.

Coda

On one level, my conclusions in this chapter may be read as retrograde. To suggest that literary works, because they are paradoxical and contradictory, may be read as revelatory of historical experience may strike some as reminiscent of New Critical notions discarded by most scholars years ago. I am not, however, advocating *Maus*, or other literary texts, as purveyors of "universal" truths that both convey and transcend individual experience. Rather, I am suggesting that it is important to maintain the category of local and historical truths for the ethical reasons enumerated throughout this book and that it is important to see historical documents (including "fiction") as capable of conveying elements of the real without discarding poststructuralist insights into the complexity of representation. Ankersmit and LaCapra turn to unfashionable thinkers like Aristotle and Lamarck in order to try to escape the critical orthodoxy that has reduced all texts to systems of ideologically oppressive signs that never bear the imprint of reality. Like them, I am not advocating a return to a notion of simple and transparent mimesis, but I believe it is necessary to look beyond this world of inescapable textuality to the possibility that reality, in making its imprint on texts, can exceed the form in which it is conveyed. While *Maus* may have "no moral center" (Witek 117), it makes an ethical response to the Holocaust possible by confirming its experiential and factual existence.

As Ankersmit notes, "Only in a thoroughly historicized world, only after the past itself and the historical subject have lost their contours and have been reduced to mere moments . . . only then will it be possible to break through the thick crusts of [categorized/mediated] history and meet history in its quasi-noumenal nakedness. You need these crusts to be able to break them off" (*Sublime Historical Experience* 277). That is, as postmodernism has continued to prove, it is impossible to locate a past event without viewing it through the media in which it is presented. This is not to say, however, that we cannot *see* these mediations and see where they fail to encapsulate and explain reality, as they attempt to do. These "crusts" reveal their own failure, suggesting the possibility of the real attaching itself to signifying practices despite their capacity to obscure it.

As Ankersmit also observes, there is a contemporary tendency to see texts, representations, and signifying practices as on another level than the reality in which we live. In this view, reality is a three-dimensional world of things, "middle-sized dry goods" (Ankersmit, *Sublime Historical Experience* 245), while texts are two-dimensional approximations that masquerade as the real. In truth, representations (books, painting, sculptures, films) are three-dimensional objects that occupy the same world of everyday existence that we do. As such, these physical objects occupy space over a given period of time. This is not to advocate for a fetishization of "old" objects, representational or otherwise, but to continue to discourage the Cartesian separation of subject and object. Subjects are, in fact, also three-dimensional objects and are, in that sense, real, as are the products of representation that emerge from them. To dismiss a representation as having little or no relation to reality because it is the product of a "subject," a communal meaning-system, or a language is to suggest that none of these things are, in and of themselves, "real." When presented this way, it becomes almost banal to observe that, indeed, they are real, in any sense one can imagine that word being used, and so, with Ankersmit, it is worth reviving the historiographic fortunes of the subjective and the emotional. If the world makes an impact on individuals, what those individuals produce may teach us about the world, as long as we are willing to navigate the signifying crusts along the way.

CONCLUSION

Conclusion

Expanding the Field

> History . . . is a nightmare from which I am trying to awake.
> —James Joyce, *Ulysses* (34)

While it might be tempting to do so, I do not wish to assert that all texts commonly labeled as postmodern insist upon a level of the historical real that both resists and precedes discourse. Rather, I wish to suggest that the critical homogenization of these texts has made this strain of thought difficult to see. The expansive scope of a hugely influential work like Linda Hutcheon's *A Poetics of Postmodernism* gives a sense of sameness to the discourse of postmodernism that inhibits the analysis of the specificity of any one text. My own expansive treatment of individual texts can, on the other hand, inhibit the analysis of the degree to which transferability from one text to others is possible. Briefly, then, I wish to suggest that the ideas presented in this book are relevant for other texts, both fiction and nonfiction, that may, if analyzed expansively, give further insight into the nature of historical reference. While I have started to do so with brief readings of Woolf's and Swift's wider *oeuvres*, Jeanette Winterson's *Lighthousekeeping*, Derek Walcott's *Omeros*, and John Fowles's *The Magus* and *The French Lieutenant's Woman*, it is worthwhile to expand the palette of texts in reconsidering postmodernism in terms of ethics and historical reference.

By thinking about a variety of texts through the prism of those already discussed, it is possible to see how they too may be more interested in finding the real than in denying the possibility of doing so. For example, Woolf's interest in nonsequential (or simultaneous) temporality and moments that exceed their place in a temporal series can be seen in diverse texts like Winterson's *Sexing the Cherry* (1990) and Carlos Fuentes's *Terra Nostra* (1976). Winterson's engagement with Einsteinian space-time suggests that the past is literally always present in our unrecognized four-dimensional world. Her narrator's assertion that common claims like "time is a straight line" and "the difference between the past and the future is that one has happened while the other has not" are nothing more than "lies" (90), is part of a rejection both of the sequentiality of narrative and of historical claims that the past is inaccessible. Her bringing together of two seventeenth-century protagonists with their late 1980s mirror images suggests that the past is always accessible because it is actually simultaneous with present and future. *Terra Nostra* likewise presents various historical and fictional eras coexisting, suggesting the possibility of bringing one time in contact with another. Both novels are typically read as critiquing purportedly objective "accepted" versions of history, and rightly so, but it is also worthwhile to consider how they offer not a rejection of "history" *per se*, but rather an alternative based on the capacity for the past to touch the present.

Other recent texts play with time in similar ways, and it is likewise possible, and perhaps necessary, to reevaluate their attitudes towards historical reference. In *Nights at the Circus* (1984), Angela Carter depicts a society that has no sense of past, present, and future in ways that predict and reflect Winterson's discussion of the Hopi Indians in *Sexing the Cherry*, while in D. M. Thomas's *The White Hotel* (1981), the future continually "returns" in the fashion of the repressed Freudian past. The narrative reformulation of "Lisa's" past cannot explain or give meaning to her neuroses or trauma because they originate not there but in the future, suggesting again the nonsequentiality of time. Likewise, Caryl Churchill's play *Cloud 9* (1979) functions, like *Between the Acts*, as a denaturalization of various (colonial, patriarchal) hegemonic discourses in both past and present, but it also embodies past and present subjects in the same actors, suggesting continuity of history and the material tangibility of the past in the present. Tom Stoppard's *Arcadia* combines this strategy with a discussion of fractal mathematics, simultaneous time, and the second law of thermodynamics, suggesting the ways in which past and present touch one another. Even as the play's "present day" characters are frustrated by the impossibility of confronting the past, the audience sees it on the stage.

As numerous critics have noted, *Midnight's Children* owes much to texts like Gabriel García Márquez's *One Hundred Years of Solitude* (1967) and Günter Grass's *The Tin Drum* (1959), and with this in mind, it may be necessary to think of these texts more in terms of their allegiance to historical truth than in terms of their deconstruction of it. In particular, Márquez's delineation of the 1928 Colombian banana massacre as a truth obscured by traditional histories predicts Rushdie's concerns in regard to the Emergency and the Amritsar Massacre. Grass's novel traces the history of pre- and post-WWII Danzig/Gdansk in ways strikingly similar to Rushdie's treatment of India, and to read Rushdie as postmodernist historical fiction that insists both on referentiality and ethics indicates how Grass may be read in similar ways.

Even texts as strange and fanciful as Angela Carter's *The Infernal Desire Machines of Doctor Hoffman* (1972) and Phillip K. Dick's *The Man in the High Castle* (1962) offer theorizations of the real. Carter's thematization of narrative as desire, along with the death of Dr. Hoffman and the destruction of his desire machines suggests the possibility of a real beyond narrative in ways similar to the surgical excision of narrative desire in *Midnight's Children*. Dick's alternate history of a world in which the results of World War II are reversed installs the real within it, as the titular character is the one person in the book with access to our own reality (or one remarkably similar to it), writing a book in which the Allies do win the war. The installation of an object, or idea, that represents reality, like the Man's book, can also, perhaps, be seen in a novel like Don Delillo's *Underworld* (1997), in the Bobby Thompson home run ball, or in Julian Barnes's *History of the World in 10 1/2 Chapters* (1989). In the half chapter, Barnes writes that "we must believe" in both love and truth "or we're lost" (244), casting not only a deconstructive eye on traditional, progressive, and hegemonic histories, but asserting the necessity of at least provisionally defining an alternative. As Hutcheon observes, many texts that typically garner the "postmodern" label depict historical events and/or comment on the nature of history. While it is possible that such texts like Maxine Hong Kingston's *Woman Warrior* (1976), John Banville's *Doctor Copernicus* (1976), E. L. Doctorow's *Book of Daniel* (1971), Delillo's *Libra* (1988), and J. M. Coetzee's *Foe* (1986) invoke history in order to finally invalidate it, we would do well to consider the possibility that they may instead suggest productive ways of representing, and accessing, the past.

It is not my contention that a close and expansive reading of each of these texts would reveal that they theorize the real in the same ways, or even that nonnarrativity would necessarily be the strategy deployed in each of them. Rather, it is important to rely on their own specificity to discover what they can teach us about historical reference. With this goal in mind, I would like to consider somewhat more closely a pair of texts with similar structural features that might be misread as denying historical reference, when in fact they insist upon it. Ian McEwan's *Atonement* (2001) and Yann Martel's *Life of Pi* (2001) exhibit a structure in which a series of events are presented as, more or less, real, before a final postscript, epilogue, or chapter pulls the rug out from under the reader, suggesting that everything (or much) once considered "true" in the novel must be reconsidered or rejected. They, on a global scale, reenact Samuel Beckett's more local and repeated practice, particularly in *Molloy*, of asserting an idea or event before immediately asserting its opposite or withdrawing the first.

McEwan provides a novel that is intensely realistic, presenting events that could have happened between 1935 and 1999 in a style that almost always allows the reader to believe that s/he is being told a "true story," despite our knowledge of its fictionality. In a final epilogue, however, it is revealed that these events, and particularly the reunification of two lovers after World War II, is not real in the context of the book but merely part of a nested novel written by one of its other characters. *Life of Pi* depicts a boy, Pi, who is shipwrecked on a small boat with a tiger before undergoing a number of adventures, many of which, in magical realist fashion, could not literally be true, despite the convincing way in which Pi tells the story. While the events of *Life of Pi* are less realistic and less linked to history than those in *Atonement*, the structure of the two works are similar. At the close of *Life of Pi* as well, we learn that Pi's tale is not true even in the context of his own fictional world. Instead, Pi's adventures serve to mask a much more traumatic and horrifying reality that neither Pi nor the reader wishes to face.

Despite the generally realistic elements of *Atonement*, part 3 closes with the reunification of lovers after World War II that is similar to the "happy ever after" joining of Vladek and Anja in *Maus*. In the final 1999 postscript, however, the conventional romantic ending is withdrawn, not only revealing that the story we have read thus far was merely a story but also providing information about the "actual" end of these lovers. In this section, a conventional play written by thirteen-year-old Briony Tallis some sixty-four years earlier is performed on the occasion of her seventy-seventh birthday. This play, *The Trials of Arabella*, ends with the unification of lovers and a rhyming couplet that emphasizes the complete and conventional closure of the tale. *The Trials* is clearly meant to mockingly parallel the conclusion Briony has given to the autobiographical novel that we have just read, in which her sister Cecilia is reunited with Robbie Turner after his traumatic service at Dunkirk. The novel, we learn, serves as a kind of (ineffective) atonement for Briony, who causes both Robbie's wrongful imprisonment and the lovers' separation in the same summer in which *The Trials* was written. Now, through the medium of her writing, she is able to bring them back together again. Although previous drafts of the novel told the sobering truth of the matter,

Briony can "no longer think what purpose would be served, if . . . I tried to persuade my reader . . . that Robbie Turner died of septicemia at Bray Dunes on 1 June 1940, or that Cecilia was killed in September . . . by the bomb that destroyed Balham Underground Station" (350). She observes that the only purpose of such an ending would be "bleakest realism" and notes that once the novel is published, "we will only exist as my inventions" (350) and therefore she may as well invent a happy ending.

Certainly, it is possible to read this conclusion as a means of denaturalizing the principally realistic novel that comes before it, suggesting that all we know and all we can ever know are texts that may influence us in particular ways, or serve our purposes (as Briony's novel helps assuage her guilt), but which do not accurately represent the real world. Because the novel seems so rigorously realistic for most of its 300+ pages, the way in which the final section denaturalizes all that has come before seems to function as a "postmodern" deconstruction of sorts. That is, it makes us reevaluate everything we took to be "real," and therefore makes us question the possibility of encountering the real. At the same time, the mere presence of this final section introduces us to a level of narrative that encourages us to look beyond the "happy ending" narrative initially presented and to confront us with the "bleakest realism" of war, bombs, and septicemia. While it is true that even this postscript is mere construction (McEwan's this time) without mimetic component, by creating frames around Briony's narrative, it also allows readers to see the text they are reading as an interior frame that has, in its turn, an external frame that is the real world in which we live. When Briony thinks to herself, "how can a novelist achieve atonement when, with her absolute power of deciding outcomes, she is also God?" (350), the novel makes us think not only of Briony's novel but also of the novel we are completing, *Atonement*. In doing so, it makes us consider the ethical quandary at the heart of both novelists' decisions. Is it more ethical to conclude the horrors of Dunkirk and the Blitz with a lovers' reunion that implies that all that has come before it functions as mere impediments to the "happy ending," or is it more ethical to end the tale with a more "realistic" death, emphasizing the traumatic reality of Dunkirk and the Blitz? In "real" life, after all, there were many lovers who died, but also many who were reunited. The reference to the novelist as God is reminiscent of *The French Lieutenant's Woman*. Like that novel, the connection of author to deity encourages the reader to articulate both the similarities and the differences between a textual world that is governed by a controlling presence and a real world that is likely not.

Neither of the endings of *Atonement* is true in any conventional sense, of course, since the people involved are characters, not real people. At the same time, however, when Briony observes that "the letters the lovers wrote are in the archives of the War Museum" (350), there is a reference to the real-world Imperial War Museum, from which McEwan used "letters, journals, and reminiscences of soldiers and nurses serving in 1940" (n.p.) for his source material. While, in a historical sense, it may not be possible to confirm or deny the final disposition of Cecilia and Robbie, McEwan here gestures to a world beyond those in the novel's pages, a world where specific facts can be confirmed, and where one's ethical responsibilities may exceed that of the novelist's. That is, while *Atonement*'s postscript acknowledges a postmodernity in which reality is always mediated by texts, it does not merely settle for this observation, but instead also questions what responsibility the artist, creator, or historian has to history and its documents.

The final section, then, moves the novel beyond a simple realistic transcription that never acknowledges its own mediation, but it also moves it beyond a simply "postmodern" notion that the truth can never be known. By revealing a level of the real underneath the seemingly realistic, *Atonement* encourages us to do the same in regards to history itself. It is too easy and self-serving for Briony to abandon "bleakest realism" in the name of "atonement." While Cecilia and Robbie are not of our real world, they are of hers and deserve the truth from which ethical responses can arise. McEwan's novel encourages his readers to think seriously about their own responsibilities to the truth, whether they have a novelist's God-like capacity to control representations or not. Briony's efforts to get the details of the Battle of Dunkirk right (339) are paralleled by McEwan's own fidelity to wartime documents in *Atonement*, or to the practice of neurological surgery in his later novel, *Saturday* (2005). While on one level Briony does not seem to consider her rewriting of her sister's history as any kind of transgression, she does refer to her "offenses against veracity" (336), a phrase that would be impossible to deploy if there were not some base level of the real that she, and the novel, were not configuring as more true than Briony's own novel. Briony's acknowledgment that she could not retain the "courage of [her] pessimism" (350) likewise implies that her retreat from the truth is a kind of cowardice, as are her efforts to suggest that her revisions are meaningless because Cecilia and Robbie are mere texts, not truths. In fact, in her world, they are both. As in Rushdie's errata, *Atonement*'s postscript provides a disnarrated segment of the text that does not fit into Briony's narrative, but which nevertheless insists upon historical accuracy. That this postscript is subsumed into McEwan's narrative does not invalidate its insistence on the historical real.[1]

Winner of the 2002 Man Booker Prize, *Life of Pi* has a similar structure and leads to somewhat similar conclusions. Like Briony, Pi reveals that the stories he has been spinning are not true in the context of his own world, and like Briony, he suggests that despite this lack of truth the stories he has been telling are preferable to "bleak realism." In the more exotic tale, Pi is shipwrecked on a lifeboat with a tiger, a hyena, an orangutan, and a zebra. The tiger, named Richard Parker, is the lone survivor among the animals after internecine battles, and Pi then has a series of adventures with him over the better part of a year, before being recovered by Japanese officials.[2] When these officials do not believe his story, he offers them another (much shorter) one, in which the lifeboat is peopled by Pi, his mother, the ship's cook, and a wounded sailor. Here, the other inhabitants amputate the sailor's leg for fishing bait, leading to the cook's cannibalism, the murder of Pi's mother by the cook, and Pi's subsequent killing of the cook and consumption of his heart. The Japanese officials take on the role of the reader, interpreting the first story in light of the second. They identify the zebra as a symbol for the sailor, the orangutan as Pi's mother, the hyena as the cook, and the tiger as Pi himself. The two stories, then, are not two stories at all but (largely) the same story, with metaphorical content provided to make the first more entertaining and more religiously meaningful, as Pi "turned to God" as a means of survival (311). Since neither story provides an explanation for the sinking of the ship, Pi asks the officials which story they prefer, and they choose the "story with the animals" (317).

As Pi points out to the officials, "you can't prove the question either way," (317) and "[t]he explanation for the sinking of the *Tsimtsum* is at the bottom of the Pacific" (316). Pi succeeds in convincing them that neither story can be "proven" as true, and since this is the case we may as well choose the more enjoyable and entertaining story. If this is the case, however, one wonders why Pi (and Martel) does not give us only the first story and not the second. While some elements of the longer story have no clear analogue in the more realistic one, and others, like the sinking of the ship, simply have no explanation, it is clear that the second story, despite its own unrealistic elements, is meant to be seen as "more real" than the first. While Pi loses his parents in both stories, the witnessing of his own mother's murder and Pi's own treatment of the cook in the second story give the first emotional weight. Because of the second story, Pi's fanciful adventures in the first begin to take on elements of trauma, loss, transgression, and redemption that serve to explain Pi's turn to God more adequately. In this, the novel makes a shambles of Pi's premises. He claims he wants the officials to choose the first story for their official report because it is "better," but, as in *Waterland* and *Atonement,* it might be more productively seen as a narrative that therapeutically salves his trauma. The second story is too close to the real and perhaps explains his tears of relief when the officials choose the first.

From this perspective, the first story is not "better" than the second, but supplemented by it. The real trauma on board the lifeboat produces the extravagances of the Richard Parker story, just as the Richard Parker story makes it possible to cope with the real trauma. These are not merely two stories from which we can choose (as a more traditionally "postmodern" reading of the novel might suggest), but an exploration of the dialectic relationship of mimetic reproduction and signifying representation. While the novel acknowledges certain limits to historical recovery, it also explores the pervasive power of the real to generate stories, and of stories to transmit the real. *Atonement* and *Life of Pi* both insist on a world more real than the fictions that occupy the majority of their pages, and even though this more real world is just another fiction, it, in turn, reminds us of the distinctions between those worlds and our own.

My attention here to two twenty-first century texts foregrounds the substantial period of history covered by this book. *Between the Acts* is, no doubt, distant in perspective from *Atonement* and *Life of Pi*, as the sixty years between their publication dates would indicate. That is, while the texts considered in this study have some similar theorizations of the notion of "history," there is little doubt that history itself, the actual events and discourses in the world that surrounded their production, impacted their writing and their attitudes toward history more theoretically conceived. While my conscious decision to focus on relatively few texts in great detail makes any generalizations about how history itself generated the ideas in these texts suspect, there is little doubt that different circumstances and discourses influenced and directed Woolf's writing of *Between the Acts* than those that provided similar impetus to the early-1980s *Midnight's Children* and *Waterland*. Likewise, it seems hardly coincidental that two texts with such striking structural similarities as *Atonement* and *Life of Pi* arrived in the same year of the new century.

Virginia Woolf's critique of a purportedly objective patriarchal "realism" may perhaps be linked to similar anti-objectivist discourses circulating in the 1920s and 1930s, both in historical discourse and elsewhere. Einstein's theories of relativity and Heisenberg's Uncertainty Principle are widely acknowledged as important (if widely misinterpreted) influences on a nascent "relativism" during the period. Woolf's knowledge of and similarities to Henri Bergson's notion of the subjective experience of time indicates how her critique of objective history arises out of contemporary discourses and not independently of them. In fact, American historians in the interwar period like Charles Beard and Carl Becker were already questioning the Rankean objectivity that had dominated the profession. Interestingly, Peter Novick notes that World War I "posed a fundamental and sweeping challenge to the profession's posture of disinterested objectivity," since it was often "optimism and faith in progress which . . . had grounded their faith in objectivity" in the first place (*That Noble Dream* 111). That is, the faith in Enlightenment rationalism to solve the world's problems was irrevocably shaken by the First World War, and the natural result was a questioning of rationalism itself, which in turn could not help but negatively impact faith in science and history. Woolf's own view of the trauma of World War I is available in *Jacob's Room, Mrs. Dalloway, To the Lighthouse,* and the fractured stream-of-consciousness narratives therein may easily be read as a rejection of some kind of objective "third-person" historian's view, although not necessarily of the capacity to access the past.

The effort to build a new cultural consensus in response to the threat of the Axis powers made Woolf's challenge to patriarchal histories and objectivity unfashionable rather quickly, as discussed earlier, and the discourses that challenged her later work are similar to those that reasserted objectivity as a possibility and a goal for the historical profession in the years that followed. To oppose Hitler, the West had need of the kind of cultural consensus that notions of "objective truth" suggested, and relativist thinkers like Becker and Beard were largely disregarded in favor of a reasserted objectivity in the 1950s and early 1960s. While these decades do find some writers later labeled as "postmodern" emerging, the decay of consensus seen in the objections to the Vietnam War, the feminist movement, "reverse colonization," and the "black power" movement of the later 1960s and 1970s undoubtedly contributed to the more widespread critique of "objectivity" in philosophy, historical discourse, literature, and popular culture that followed in the 1970s and 1980s. The student revolts in France of 1968 undoubtedly generated and influenced poststructuralist philosophy, just as that philosophy became influential on the historical profession, as discussed in the introduction. Certainly, texts like *Waterland* and *Midnight's Children* seem part of a discursive field that includes Hayden White, Michel Foucault, Thomas Kuhn, and Edward Said, rather than independent of them. All of these thinkers, of course, focus on how "discourses" or theoretical paradigms create our perceptions of reality or "facts," rather than the possibility of their transparent transmission. Novick suggests that it is Foucault who was the most "broadly influential" of these thinkers (*That Noble Dream* 535), and it is little surprise that ideas propagated by Foucault surface in fictional texts in the years that follow, whether he was a direct influence or not. Likewise, it is not difficult to ascertain that Foucault's own political commitments are generated by his historical moment, not independent of it.

It may be too soon to try to determine cultural or historical influences on twenty-first century texts, although there is little doubt that recent backlash against "postmodernism" may be linked to efforts to generate a new cultural consensus post-9/11. It is possible that texts like *Atonement* and *Life of Pi* may someday be seen as the last gasp of a dying movement no longer relevant in a world forced once again to "choose sides" between Enlightenent rationalism and fundamentalist fanaticism. What this book attempts to articulate, however, is how this binary, like so many others, is an untenable one to apply to postmodernist texts. To configure postmodernism as a kind of irrational radical relativism is to ignore the ways in which its discourses, literary and otherwise, insist on a complex rationalism, an allegiance to historical fact, and a rejection of the relativism of which it is often accused. A rejection of consensus is not, after all, the same as a rejection of truth. Certainly, these texts, and postmodern theory itself, cannot help but be a product of history, but this does not mean that they cannot help us theorize what history is and can be.

Throughout this book I have suggested that postmodernism, literary and theoretical, is frequently more dependent upon notions of history, reality, and truth than is generally acknowledged. Both Hayden White and Frank Ankersmit, widely considered to be two of the more extreme exemplars of postmodern historiography, admit at various times to the intractability of certain historical events to discursive deformation. Reading these theorists closely may yield insight into the relationship of representation and reality, rather than the radical relativism so often ascribed to their names. Similarly, postmodern authors provide a plethora of approaches to the representation of reality, not a blanket rejection of that possibility.

Kundera's "guerilla" histories, Woolf's "Moments of Being," Swift's "Here and Now," Rushdie's use of antinarrative errata, and Spiegelman's encounters of past and present in the single comics panel all suggest that despite barriers of textuality and signification, reality can be encountered. I hope to have suggested both why such an assertion is ethically necessary and why it is theoretically possible. While it is common to read postmodernism as antimimetic and therefore inimical to ethical investigation, it is perhaps now time to confront the postmodern as a version of mimeticism and as a confrontation with the ethical, whatever its historical origins.

NOTES

Introduction

1. For treatments of Kundera as postmodern, see Eagleton, Chvatik, Lodge, Molesworth, Kleberg, and Patchay. Perhaps the most polemical resistance to such characterizations is by Straus.

2. There are, of course, definitions of postmodernism that do not, perhaps, rely on the notion of the "withdrawal of the real" quite so heavily, if at all. John Barth's "Literature of Exhaustion" (1967) and "Literature of Replenishment" (1980) are preoccupied enough with "form" to forego discussion of literature's mimetic role almost completely. The status (or absence) of reality is usually central to discussions of the postmodern, however.

3. This movement in historiographic theory goes by several names (metahistory, narrativism, postmodern historiography, constructivist historiography, etc.). For the moment, however, I will refer to them as "postmodern" for the sake of making some general observations. I will later sort through these terms as it becomes necessary.

4. Peter Novick's *That Noble Dream* chronicles the rise of Ranke's ideas to prominence in the United States. As Novick points out, Ranke's statement may be translated to mean "as it essentially happened" and Ranke, like Hegel, had a tendency to see history as a reflection of an overarching spiritual plan (Novick 28). This, of course, lends some ambiguity to his purported argument for "objectivity." In fact, while Ranke was celebrated in the United States for his empiricism, in Germany his indebtedness to the idealist tradition was emphasized (Novick 28). "*Wie es eigentlich gewesen*" is oft-quoted, but surprisingly rarely cited and its origins are obscure. Ranke's claim that he desires to "extinguish himself" from history comes from the preface to *The Secret of World History*.

5. Robert Berkhofer calls this collective dream of a comprehensive and unified history "The Great Story."

6. My use of "Foucauldian" here does not cover, of course, the full trajectory of Foucault's philosophical development. This account of history and discourse as disciplinary constructions relies principally on "Nietzsche, Genealogy, History," which may be Foucault's most "constructivist" denial of the presence and/or accessibility of past events. The early Foucault of *Madness and Civilization* and even of *The Order*

of Things would not, perhaps, make such extreme claims about the constructedness of the historical referent, although this attitude is present in those texts. Likewise, the later Foucault of the last two volumes of *The History of Sexuality* and the late interviews would be unlikely to elide human agency in quite the ways Foucault does in this essay. The "middle period" Foucault I describe here is, however, an important touchstone for the "postmodern" historiography I describe in this introduction, and is perhaps the most prevalently known.

7. Although historians Carl Becker and Charles Beard generated substantial objections to Rankean objectivity in the 1930s, their opposition was soon pushed aside because of the nationalist exigencies of the Second World War (Novick, *That Noble Dream* 133–67). Likewise, despite the 1973 publication date of *Metahistory,* White's influence, substantial in other fields, was not felt fully within his own discipline for quite some time. Richard Evans's 1999 book, *In Defense of History,* for instance, defends the discipline's traditional Rankean assumptions and methods against the philosophers of the linguistic turn. In doing so, he reveals an anxiety about postmodern historiography that had been relatively rare previously. The same can be said of Appleby, Hunt, and Jacob's *Telling the Truth about History* (1995). Recent books that detail the history of the linguistic turn in the historical profession indicate the degree to which it can no longer be merely ignored (see Fulbrook, E. Clark, and Spiegel).

8. Barthes argues that narrative was "elaborated in the crucible of fictions" and is therefore inherently problematic for historically referential use because it constructs "myths" ("Discourse of History" 140). Consistent with Barthes's use of the term "myth" in *Mythologies,* he accuses historical narrative of ideological complicity.

9. Although White's *Metahistory* is generally agreed to be the key text in the rise of postmodern historiography, there are other important publications that predate it. Among these are Morton White's *The Foundations of Historical Knowledge* (1965), A. R. Louch's "History as Narrative" (1969), Maurice Mandelbaum's "A Note on History as Narrative" (1967), W. B. Gallie's *Philosophy and the Historical Understanding* (1964), and the essays contained in Louis Mink's *Historical Understanding*. These texts also discuss history's relationship to narrative, and fiction.

10. White defines the annal as a list of events in chronological order, while the chronicle "starts out to tell a story but breaks off *in media res* eliminating the possibility of a conclusion" ("Value of Narrativity" 5). Because conclusions are often that which provide an explanation and meaning to a narrative, annals and chronicles can be seen to refuse that explanation (5). As White acknowledges, however, sequentiality can lead to the assumption of causality, and therefore both annals and chronicles can be read as protonarratives of a sort.

11. At times, however, even Tamina's memories might be read as oppressive of others since she attempts to impose the image of her husband on the face of every man she meets (116).

12. In the end, Tamina does not succeed in her quest to find these memories, but it is not because she tries and fails but because she is never given the opportunity. Raphael places her upon the boat and takes her to the children's island before she is able to articulate her desire to undertake her journey through the past.

13. White's amendments to this basic account of his ideas, derived principally from "The Value of Narrativity in the Representation of Reality" (1981) are many and further contributions of followers and opponents are legion. I will discuss some

of these throughout the book. It is worthwhile to mention that White's introduction to *Metahistory* (1973) emphasizes how narrative has the capacity to dictate morality by molding the events that are its raw material into different "modes of emplotment." White's appropriation of these modes from Northrop Frye's *Anatomy of Criticism* contributes to the sense that White sees history and fiction as intimately linked.

14. Although the "modernisms" that White advocates have not yet taken center stage in historical discourse, there has been a movement in the past thirty years away from narrative models and towards forms that challenge the problems White identifies. Among these are the *histoire des mentalités* in France and the similar *microstories*, exemplified by the work of Carlo Ginzburg (see Ankersmit, *History and Tropology* 154–58). Also interesting is the work of the French Annalistes, who focus less on "human" narratives of political/military history and more on long-term trends in economics and culture. This focus on causes and changes, even over the long term, can be seen to be merely a different kind of narrative, but it does indicate an alternative approach to historiography.

15. In a postcolonial context, Gayatri Spivak voices similar concerns in "Can the Subaltern Speak?" which questions both the practical possibility and the ethical desirability of rendering unspeakable moments speakable.

16. For an excellent discussion of further possible divisions to the nonnarratable, see Warhol ("Neonarrative"). Warhol identifies what I am calling the nonnarratable as "subnarratable," or that which "needn't be told because it's normal" (222). My "antinarrative " is similar to Warhol's "supranarratable," defined as "what can't be told because it's ineffable" (223). Warhol also adds what she calls "antinarratable" ("what shouldn't be told because of social convention") and "paranarratable" ("what wouldn't be told because of formal convention") (224–27). While I see the utility of these terms, they are not relevant to this study, and I therefore employ my own terms published previously elsewhere ("Swamps of Myth").

17. Along with Cathy Caruth's *Unclaimed Experience,* Slavoj Žižek, in particular, draws LaCapra's attention as someone who focuses unduly upon the sublime, especially in *The Sublime Object of Ideology.*

18. It is worth noting that Derrida, while interested in, even preoccupied with, Levinas, seeks to "deconstruct" the most radical ramifications of Levinas's ethics in "Le mot d'accueil," noting how all selves are also "Others," how the Other is always multiple, and how a third term necessarily mediates the self/Other relationship, codifying its results in ways inimical to Levinas's resistance to codification (see Bennington 39–41). As such, Derrida does not "reject" traditional *or* Levinasian ethics, but instead reveals how each is contaminated by the other.

19. See Parker for a more complete account of how deconstruction began to turn toward the ethical, as well as for a summary of contemporary discourses that contributed to this "ethical turn" (32–42).

20. While there is little doubt that Derrida explicitly discusses ethics (and politics) with more frequency in the wake of the de Man and Heidegger affairs, I do not believe these works can be properly labeled as a "turn to ethics." I read them more as a "deconstruction" of ethics, refusing notions of "rules of behavior," or even the possibility of making ethical choices. His primary example in *The Gift of Death* is of Abraham's decision of whether or not to sacrifice Isaac. Derrida insists that this is an impossible decision, but that it is not *unique* in its impossibility. Rather, it is "the most common thing" (68), and, in fact, *all* ethical decisions are impossible, even

"mad" (66) and therefore not subject to ethical codes or rules. This is not ethics in a conventional sense, but an unraveling of it as Derrida's explicit rejection of anything resembling Kantian ethics indicates (68).

21. While there is certainly a concurrent "neo-humanist" movement that approaches ethics in more traditional ways, the "deconstructive" ethics linked to Levinas is undoubtedly that which has pulled the mainstream of literary studies towards the ethical (see Craps 6–9).

22. For similar Levinas-influenced claims, see Gibson (63) and Critchley. Lyotard's definition of the postmodern is also seen as "ethical" by many because of its rejection of the metanarratives of modernity that oppressed the "others" of Western society. However, Lyotard's notion of the "withdrawal of the real" indicates that while such metanarratives may not be true, rejection of them also cannot be based upon ontological "fact." From this a *différend* is created, an argument that is irresolvable because of no common ground that can mediate between them. The "ethics" of the *différend* derives from the impossibility of reducing the conflict to questions of truth or "knowledge" in ways similar to the Levinasian "face." The powerful influence of Levinas (and Lyotard) can be seen in recent collections that attempt to theorize ethics (see Gabriel and Ilcan and Madison and Fairbarn).

23. In a well-known concession, Gayatri Spivak acknowledges the political utility of such "essentialisms" when she advocates "strategic essentialism," to be used in particular political circumstances ("Subaltern Studies").

24. The distinction between morality and ethics is an important one in philosophical circles, and one of which Jenkins avails himself (in unconventional ways) in historical debates. Due to space constraints, it is beyond my purview to discuss the distinction thoroughly here, although I agree with Nancy Fraser's attempt to reject any categorical distinction between the two on the basis of "right" vs. "good" or on the basis of "redistribution" vs. "recognition" (97).

Chapter One

1. The *Outline of History* is modeled after either H. G. Wells's *Outline of History* or G. M. Trevelyan's *History of England*. Most critics cite Wells, but Patricia Joplin argues that "the actual source" is Trevelyan (103n4). Joplin does not, however, explain the source of her confidence in the attribution.

2. This notion of modernism is, of course, perpetually under question and has various sources. T. S. Eliot's "*Ulysses*, Order, and Myth," in which he argues that Joyce's use of mythological parallels "is simply a way of controlling, of ordering, of giving a shape and a significance to the immense panorama of futility and anarchy which is contemporary history" (681) is perhaps the best known. Closer to home, Woolf and the Bloomsbury circle were influenced by Roger Fry's focus on "significant form" in the visual arts. Another treatment of modernism that separates art from life is Theodor Adorno's notion of "autonomous art" (see "Commitment"). Woolf's own unorthodox political commitments indicate the problematic nature of these definitions of modernism.

3. In McLaurin's defense there is ample evidence for Woolf being an aesthete, a misconception she occasionally propagates herself. In "Modern Fiction," for instance, she castigates "materialist" writers like Wells, Bennett, and Galsworthy for

discharging "the work" of "government officials" (105). It is this kind of self-representation that led a new generation of artists in the 1930s to critique Woolf for producing art that no longer met the needs of the world (see H. Lee 602-4, 647-705; Bell 2:185-91). When, however, Woolf writes in a letter to her nephew, Julian, that "all politics be damned" (*Letters* 5:436), we cannot take this to be merely a statement of a detached formalism. Rather, it should also be read as a critique of contemporary politics.

4. Woolf makes this point explicitly both in *A Room of One's Own* and in "Women and Fiction." "This is an important book, the critic assumes, because it deals with war. This is an insignificant book because it deals with the feelings of women in a drawing-room" (*Room* 74; "Women" 145).

5. McWhirter calls *Between the Acts* perhaps the first "postmodern historical novel" (805-8). See also Hussey, Caughie, Joplin, Daugherty, Waugh, and Christie for readings of the novel as postmodern.

6. This scene is noted and cited almost universally by critics of the novel. It is central to most of the postmodern readings I cite in note 5 in order to establish its meta-fictiveness. See also Hafley (187).

7. See Zwerdling (*"Between the Acts"*) and Ames ("Carnivalesque") for discussions of the balance between La Trobe's desire for artistic unity and her simultaneous commitment to dispersal and fragmentation.

8. *Three Guineas* precedes *Between the Acts* closely in the bibliography of Woolf's major works. She was reading the proofs of the former on April 11, 1938, and began composing the latter fifteen days later. *Roger Fry* was ultimately published between the two.

9. Simon Critchley correctly points out that there are, in fact, two distinct iterations of this principle. "[T]he first claims that there is no 'outside-text,' no text outside [*Of Grammatology* 158], whereas the second claims that there is *nothing* outside of the text [*Of Grammatology* 163], that the text outside is nothing, implying by this that any reading that refers the text to some signified outside textuality is illusory" (Critchley 25; emphasis in original). Both are variations on the central notion that reality is not separate from signification, but is constituted by it.

10. See Wiley, Marder, and Joplin for further discussions of the novel's "frames" in Brechtian terms.

11. Such a parallel is most explicitly expressed in the first chapter of *Three Guineas*. In referring to two publications banishing women to the house and giving men exclusive purview in the public sphere, Woolf writes, "One is written in English, the other in German. But where is the difference?" (53).

12. Woolf delineates a credo for women as "outsiders" in England. "'For,' the outsider will say, 'in fact, as a woman, I have no country. As a woman I want no country. As a woman my country is the whole world'" (*Three Guineas* 109). For Woolf, nationalism itself is a patriarchal idea, bound inextricably to violence and enslavement. She establishes women as "outsiders" by counting them among the enslaved (108). Despite the rhetorical power of this statement, the comparison of all women, and especially Woolf herself, to slaves may stretch the analogy too far at this moment in history, exposing Woolf's somewhat lesser sensitivity to issues of class and race.

13. A similar point is made symbolically through the geographical commentary in *Figgis's Guide Book* (1833). "The Guide Book still told the truth. 1833 was true in 1939" (52).

14. It is here that both deconstruction and Hutcheon's version of postmodern parody differ from the standard notion of parody (or non-postmodern parody). Typically, parody is an attempt to mock a particular person, discourse, or politics through imitation. This imitation takes a position "outside the text" it parodies, however, implying a "meaning" of critique and an alternative point of view. Jameson's delineation of parody as opposed to (postmodern) pastiche is one attempt to highlight this difference (*Postmodernism* 17).

15. The focus on human life as ideologically influenced "repetition" is also central to *The Years* (1937). In that novel, Woolf depicts successive generations of the Pargiter family and the ways in which they repeat their "forefathers'" achievements and mistakes. By the end of the novel, taking place in "the present day," characters are repeating entire conversations from twenty years (and more) previous, again suggesting how little things change in the historical "long term" under the influence of patriarchal discourse (see esp. 315–16, 369). Characters' professed optimism for a "new world" is, as in *Between the Acts,* balanced by the reader's (and several characters') knowledge that even the wish for a "new world" is just a repetition of previous wishes (329–30). The other possible cause and derivation of such unavoidable repetition in *Between the Acts* is the notion of a primitive, natural, and/or essential nature to the roles played by men and women. Woolf's invocation of primitive societies and behaviors in Lucy's daydreams and La Trobe's vision lend credence to this point of view (see Marcus, "Liberty, Sorority, Misogyny" 77). Nevertheless, the complicated deployment of narrative frames suggests that these primitive and "natural" repetitions are actually constructions, repeated because of the "general text" or symbolic power of culture.

16. The choice of Whitehall is significant, as Rachel Blau DuPlessis points out: "Whitehall is a synecdoche for British civil service and administrative agreements that endure beyond changes in specific governments, and thus is a metaphor for broad sociocultural agreement" (39). That is, it is a virtual synonym for British patriarchal hegemony. As both McWhirter (795) and DiBattista (197) note, Whitehall was also the place where the British war council met, tying the violence of the rape to the broader violence of oncoming war.

17. The incident, according to Gillian Beer, is "startlingly, not invented" (137).

18. For more in-depth discussions of photographs in Woolf, see Sarker and Humm. For a discussion of newspapers in the novel, see Westman.

19. Woolf notes that every newspaper "is financed by a board .. each board has a policy ... each board employs writers to expound that policy" (*Three Guineas* 95). She also observes that if one is to get "the facts," reading at least three newspapers is necessary to "come ... to your own conclusion" (95).

20. Most critics acknowledge the continuity between Woolf's views on pacifism in *Three Guineas* and in *Between the Acts,* as I do here. For a contrary viewpoint, see Mackay (238–39).

21. For a discussion of Woolf's similarity to Cage, see Cuddy-Keane ("Virginia Woolf" 91), Laurence, and Caughie (*Virginia Woolf and Postmodernism* 55–56).

22. See Richardson (56–62) for a brief but useful overview.

23. See Banfield ("Time Passes") for a discussion of the transformation of two "moments" into narrative in *To the Lighthouse.* For Banfield, the deployment of "moments" may be read as a critique of the temporality and sequentiality of narrative (476), and as an insistence on the "reality" of crystallized moments (493–95),

something I further explore over the course of this chapter.

24. For one of the first discussions of *The Waves*' critique of imperialism, see Marcus (*Hearts of Darkness* 59–85).

25. All of this might be seen to contribute to what Roland Barthes refers to as "reality effects," or static included merely to convince the reader that what is happening is "real." For Barthes, however, this tends to be an element of "realistic" fiction, which wishes its readers to read it as transparently mimetic (as in his reading of *Sarrasine* in *S/Z*). Woolf's static is not part of a realist aesthetic and serves different purposes.

26. This is not peculiar to Woolf, of course, since many modernist works are dedicated to the minutia and "unimportant details" of existence. However, Woolf's concentration on narrative's role in creating traditional history and oppression makes a reevaluation of the "static" in this novel worthwhile.

27. See Friedman and Wallace for the connection between antinarrativism, lyricism, and pre-Oedipal modes of narration in Woolf. As both authors explain, psychoanalytic models of masculine desire are based on the concept of a male infant's initial desire for the mother, which is then redirected towards alternative objects, none of which can ever completely substitute. This leads to a desire that can never be completely satisfied, but which is forever delayed, consummated, resituated, and pursued anew. This is then reflected in models of narrative like those of Scholes, Brooks, and the Barthes of *The Pleasure of the Text*. The pre-Oedipal focus on lyric, as discussed by Friedman and Wallace, posits a feminine desire for the mother that is not necessarily foreclosed as it is in the Oedipal scenario. This model rejects the notion that all desire must mimic masculine Oedipal progression and in doing so suggests an alternative to narrative itself. As both Friedman and Wallace observe, Kristeva's semiotic register, as opposed to the symbolic, reflects this vision of the lyric. While Friedman sees Woolf's reliance on the lyric as a statement of feminism versus male-dominated traditional plot, Wallace is less convinced, noting how an overreliance on lyricism does not allow for entry into the social world as it currently exists, avoiding the problems and concerns of real-world feminism. Particularly interesting as countertexts to critics who see lyricism as opposed to Oedipal desire are Abel and de Lauretis. Also, see Dubrow, who rejects the claim that interplay between narrative and lyric must necessarily be antagonistic, exploring the ways in which they build upon and supplement one another. She also provides a useful overview of previous readings of lyric.

28. For useful overviews of Bergsonian philosophy, see Kolakowski, Mullarkey, and Deleuze. Also see the collection *Key Writings* and its introduction by Pearson and Mullarkey.

29. The accusation that Bergson allows for two incompatible worlds is common among his critics. Nevertheless, Bergson attempts "to show that realism and idealism both go too far, that it is a mistake . . . to make of [matter] a thing able to produce in us perceptions, but in itself of another nature than they" (*Matter and Memory* 9).

30. It is this element that is underplayed in the somewhat similar reading of Woolf via Bergson provided by James Hafley, who discusses the "freedom" of the present without reference to its important materiality (185).

31. Russell asserts that Bergson's fears are unfounded because knowledge of the future does not determine it, just as present knowledge of what happened in the past does not cause that past (Banfield, "Tragic Time" 53).

32. See Zwerdling (both sources) for this type of reading.

33. Historical progression toward a prolonged "Present Day" section is also present in *The Years*, following ten years after *Orlando*. Here too, the novel covers a lengthy period of time in a fairly chronologically progressive fashion. This "present" section is again the longest, providing a glimpse of "frozen time" to counter the narrative progression of the rest of the novel. "I want the present," says Eleanor Pargiter, reflecting, perhaps, Woolf's own desire to arrest that singular moment (336).

34. I am only passingly familiar with the film and will not engage with the distance between Žižek's reading and *Stromboli* itself. The model for the notion of symbolic suicide for Žižek is Antigone, whom Woolf references as a model for passivity and the Society of Outsiders in *Three Guineas* (18) and which plays a significant role in *The Years* in Edward Pargiter's translation. See also DiBattista (193) and Wiley (5).

35. In actuality, there is some difficulty in attributing the latter passage cited to La Trobe. It may, in fact, be Isa, as the lines occupy a paragraph between one clearly expressing La Trobe's mind and one that does the same for Isa. The overlap serves to formally cement the connection between the two women.

36. For a useful parallel reading of this scene, see Sears, who compares it to a sixties "happening" designed to shock the audience for "therapeutic or terroristic ends" (227).

37. There have been several readings of the novel as embodying a new language, although not in precisely these terms. See Ames ("Carnivalesque"), Brownstein, Eisenberg, Scott, and Vandivere.

38. Several critics of the novel note the importance of this diary entry. In particular, see Hussey (248–49n8), Joplin (91), Watkins (358), DiBattista (221), and Zwerdling ("*Between the Acts*" 226). Lucio Ruotolo's reading of this section of the novel is an important precedent for my own (226–27). See also Cuddy-Keane ("Politics" 281).

39. The irony of this moment is personal for Woolf, whose husband Leonard was intensely committed to the League (Zwerdling, *Virginia Woolf* 283, 292; MacKay 233)

40. The purpose of Lacanian psychoanalysis is to bring the patient attached to "Imaginary" ideal images of himself properly into the Symbolic by allowing him to transform self-descriptive statements from "empty speech" into "full speech" or into an "intersubjectively intelligible narration of his past" (J. Lee 42). That is, the dialogue between the analyst and analysand need not necessarily capture the past with factual accuracy, but it must convert the fragmented and alienated identity into a coherent, shared, and *narratable* story, bringing the analysand into an intersubjective community and out of a narcissism linked to the Imaginary.

41. For more traditionally Lacanian readings of the novel, see Brownstein and Busse.

42. This brief discussion of Lacan's and Derrida's treatment of time is not meant to configure either thinker as politically inactive or retrograde. Rather, what I wish to indicate here is how Woolf's resistant politics is based upon a complex allegiance to materiality, historical reference, and (therefore) presence, and how Derrida's is based on the "non-presence" of the present moment (see Bennington 128–40, esp. 137).

43. For an overview of the practices and discourses of feminism that precede and accompany Woolf's writing of *A Room of One's Own*, see Zwerdling (*Virginia Woolf* 210–42).

44. Dasenbrock's sense of Kuhn as a radical relativist is not unchallenged. For an overview and discussion of Kuhn's philosophical position, see Nickles. Likewise, as noted above, the later Foucault is more interested in human agency than he is in *Power/Knowledge*, *The Archaeology of Knowledge*, or *Discipline and Punish*.

45. See Zwerdling (both sources) for an example of the pessimistic view. More optimistic readings often focus on the novel's status as "comedy," which provides a final unity that resolves the novel's deep and insistent conflicts. In these readings, the continuity between these peasants and the villagers in the present day provides a source of festive continuity and unity (see DiBattista, Little, Barrett, and [in slightly different ways] Esty and Cuddy-Keane ["Politics"]).

Chapter Two

1. Among those who mention White specifically, and postmodern historiography more generally, are Brewer and Tillyard, Acheson, Tange, Irish, and Cooper ("Imperial Topographies").

2. Tamás Bényei notes that there are two dominant strands of Swift criticism. The first focuses on *Waterland* and reads Swift as a postmodern purveyor of historiographic metafiction, while the second looks at Swift's work *in toto* and reads it in a more realist and ethical light. In the first group are Hutcheon, A. Lee, Irish, Cooper ("Imperial Topographies"), Wells, Price (*History Made*), Landow, Schad, Higdon, Acheson, Bedggood, Brewer and Tillyard, and Todd. In the second are Poole, Wheeler, and Bényei himself. Most similar to my own reading are those by Decoste, Craps, and Lea who, to my mind, combine the two strands.

3. For a definition of "classical" history, see Foucault ("Nietzsche"). Foucault argues that "classical" history attempts to present history as unified and comprehensible. In doing so, it erases the past rather than preserving it.

4. For a brief look at how *Waterland* appropriates and parodies Victorian narratives of progress through the Atkinsons, see Landow (204–5). My own extended discussion follows.

5. See Foucault's *Madness and Civilization* and *The History of Sexuality*.

6. The idea that Victorians saw their own age as one of historical progress is a common one but was challenged then as it is now. Nevertheless, many contemporary theorists find that the Victorians tended to have a faith in history itself as a realization of historical process and progress, which is met by increasing skepticism in the twentieth and twenty-first centuries. Hegel's notion of the Spirit of History is, of course, central here. For an interesting account of how the Victorian view of historical "progress" was constructed, see Crosby.

7. For a reading of the novel from a Freudian perspective, see Wells (67–80).

8. White makes little distinction between the "literary" and the "fictional." Indeed, at one point, White refers to the capacity to make meaning from history as a "literary, that is to say fiction-making, operation" ("Historical Text" 85). Literature and fiction are not, of course, mere synonyms, given the modes of literature that are potentially nonnarrative (like lyric poetry) or which may make explicit truth claims. These distinctions are not important to White in this essay, but they do play a role later in this book.

9. Swift's need to *use* a metaphor to express the notion of the historical real

leaves his novel (and my argument) open to the standard poststructuralist critique that any notion of reality is itself a trope, or imbricated in tropology. While I do wish to challenge such a claim eventually (see chapter 4), my primary goal here is to note that, while it may be possible to "deconstruct" *Waterland,* the novel is not itself (or not merely) a deconstruction of history as many critics have suggested.

10. See Price (*History Made* 220–30) for an extensive discussion of the ways in which *Waterland* refuses the dichotomy of the two different ways of "making history."

11. For additional Lacanian readings of the novel, see both Lea and Murphy.

12. See Wells for an alternative account of these moments, deriving from Benjamin, via the quotation that serves as an epigraph to this chapter. Žižek also links the psychoanalytic model of "the return of the repressed" with Benjamin (*Sublime Object of Ideology* 141). Wells's application of these ideas to *Waterland* has some similarities with my own, but she offers narrative as the means by which these moments can occur, rather than that which impedes them (84–85).

13. There is some ambiguity as to whether or not Dick is, indeed, "too big." Crick is not actually present for Mary's sexual tutoring of Dick. He then, not surprisingly, gets suspicious and jealous of their encounters. He is quick to note that the "too big" story is merely Mary's version of events (261). Crick's suspicion is passed to the reader because he is the narrator and we have no outside corroboration of Mary's story. This confusion does not, however, necessarily obviate the significance of Dick's impotency, since the confusion itself leads to the abortion of the child, lending symbolic truth to Dick's impotence, even if Mary's explanation is suspect.

14. I do not here suggest that the Freudian model is a natural and/or essential one. Rather, it is clear that Swift self-consciously explores and exploits Freud to comment on the nature of mysteries, secrets, and narratability.

15. Several readings of *Waterland* see Dick to be a representative of the Real, in his brute physicality and connections to the natural world (see Price, *History Made* 244 and Lea 90). I agree with these readings only insofar as we acknowledge the real's link to the failure of narrative. See DeCoste for a reading of Dick congenial to my own.

16. Here, the etymological link of "boxes" and "books" is important in tying together their mutual capacity to reveal secrets. See D. A. Miller (*Novel and the Police* 216). For more on the gothic in *Waterland,* see McKinney (822).

17. It is Mary's womb that is described as an "empty vessel" and which, like the "wide empty spaces" of the fens, is continually associated with reality. The contradiction of "nothing" being associated with the real has been noted by several critics as evidence of the novel's refusal of historical reference. It is fairly clear, however, that the "nothing" referred to in the book refers to lack of meaning, not the lack of material existence. As Crick asserts, "Women are equipped with a miniature model of reality: an empty but fillable vessel" (239). The "fillable" nature of "nothing" suggests how people attempt to inflict meaning upon reality, but the reality of the real remains. See Price (*History Made* 236–58).

18. See Warhol, Winnett, and Farwell for objections to models of masculine narrative desire. See also the work of Hélène Cixous and Luce Irigaray for critiques of Freud's masculinist tendencies.

19. This scene is often taken by critics to be an expression of the novel's typically postmodern refusal of clear-cut origins, providing an alternative explanation for

Mary's barrenness. The fact that the eel episode chronologically precedes the pregnancy indicates, however, how Swift contrasts the "fairy tale" explanation of the eel on the lap, with the reality of the abortion. The latter is clearly the cause of Mary's later inability to conceive.

20. Damon Decoste also insightfully sees the distinction between curiosity and desire as central to the novel's initial definition of "history"—not merely narrative but also, more fundamentally, "inquiry," a pursuit of truth that never ceases (395).

21. Swift's writing shows a near obsession with the idea of adoption and other forms of "surrogate parenting" and their relative reality. In addition to the novels discussed in this chapter, *Last Orders* (1996) explores the relationship of an adoptive son to his recently-deceased father. More recently, *Tomorrow* (2007) revolves around the revelation to a pair of twins that their father is not "real" and that they are instead the products of *in vitro* fertilization.

22. For a more complete discussion of historical reference in its relation to the Holocaust, see chapter 4.

23. For the possibility of encountering the real, even in narrative, it is useful to consider Fredric Jameson's *The Political Unconscious,* wherein he argues that "language manages to carry the Real within itself as its own intrinsic or immanent subtext" (81). Nevertheless, Jameson does insist on history itself as "outside the text," "for it is fundamentally non-narrative and nonrepresentational" (82). Because of this contradiction, Jameson admits that we can only encounter the Real ("asymptotically") "by way of prior (re)textualization" (82). The referent of history, then, is not a mere articulation of textual functions, but may only be encountered through representation. It can never be reexperienced in its totality, but it *can* be encountered.

24. For a complementary, and insightful, view of *Waterland* that explores convincingly the dialectical nature of reality and representation in *Waterland,* see Craps (and particularly his discussion of Catherine Bernard's earlier treatment) (79–85). Bernard's discussion of the contrast between the "realistic," chronological narrative element of the novel and the formal elements that deny the easy transparency of the former are similar to my own appropriation of Terdiman. Craps's conclusion that the ethics of the novel lie in its effort to "bear[. . .] witness to a traumatic history in the hope of preventing it from returning with a vengeance" (103) is, however, problematic. Rather, it is the inevitability of history's return that makes an ethical examination of the past possible.

25. Foremost among "postmodern" readings of *Ever After* is that of Holmes. Lea, Malcolm, and Craps all provide more nuanced accounts but still insist upon various versions of the novel's postmodernism.

26. More generally, the Victorian era is a site of frequent postmodern visitation. A. S. Byatt's *Possession* (1990) is also a case wherein the Victorian past is a signifier of the reality that can still "possess" us in the present.

27. Again, Hutcheon and Alison Lee label Fowles's work as "historiographic metafiction." Malcolm Bradbury also reads *The Magus* as postmodern, as do Salami and Cooper (*Fictions of John Fowles*).

28. It is (again) possible to argue that Fowles's novels, in this way, perform their own interpellation of the reader, but it would nevertheless be inaccurate to portray Fowles as a postmodern deconstructor of history.

29. This line in *The Magus* is virtually repeated in *The French Lieutenant's Woman,* wherein Charles's first encounter with his daughter is described as "history reduced

to a living stop, a photograph made flesh" (458). These moments, like the frozen moments in *Between the Acts,* can be read as "moments of being" where past reality (history) is made materially present.

Chapter Three

1. See also Warhol ("Neonarrative").

2. Robyn Warhol argues that labeling something a "dream" or "imagination" might not be disnarration if these events happen in the mind of a character ("Neonarrative" 229). The label would still apply to Fowles's novel if he were to retain "the last few pages . . . are not what happened" without adding the subsequent qualifier.

3. For other readings of form and fragmentation in the novel, see Gorra, Rege, Brigg, and Wilson.

4. Eventually we learn that neither Aziz nor Naseem (later called the Reverend Mother) are biologically related to the narrator, due to Mary Pereira's swap of Shiva's cradle for Saleem's. Aziz is, of course, named after the doctor in E. M. Forster's *A Passage to India,* one of a number of literary "grandparents" to Rushdie's novel.

5. Even before his final explosion, Saleem begins to "fall apart." He loses a tonsure of hair to his teacher, Emil Zagallo, and the tip of a finger to some Cathedral school bullies (265–69). Both incidents reflect the division and re-division of India by Partition, the Bangladesh war, and the separation into linguistic states.

6. Critics have taken this injunction seriously, uncovering additional errata, some made by Rushdie himself. See Gorra, Brennan (*Salman Rushdie*), and Kortenaar (*Self* 229–51).

7. As Stanley Wolpert writes, "Fear motivated millions of Indians to greater efficiency. Police were free to do as they liked. . . . A chill climate of silent terror gripped many Indian homes" (qtd. in Kuchta 213–14). Later editions of Wolpert tone down the implicit critique of the Emergency (Wolpert 397–404). For a more complete discussion of the Emergency and its intersections with *Midnight's Children,* see Kuchta (211–14).

8. The "black and white" nature of Indira's Emergency is linked also to the positive and negative effects of the British Raj through the metaphor of Indira's "centre-parted" hair (460), which matches that of the novel's symbolic English colonist, Methwold.

9. Rushdie's essay "Attenborough's *Gandhi*" is similarly a critique of a "false history" perpetuated by the film *Gandhi.* One key coordinate of this deception is the effort in the film to distance Britain as a whole from the horror of the Amritsar Massacre. In *Gandhi,* General Dyer is treated with only horror and disdain upon his return to England, suggesting that while Dyer's actions were unforgivable, England itself had a more enlightened view of India. In truth, Dyer received a hero's welcome, indicating the extent of British racism. For this reason, Rushdie argues, "artistic selection has altered the meaning of the event. It is an unforgivable distortion" (*Imaginary Homelands* 103).

10. For more readings of *Midnight's Children* as postmodern history, see Birch, Hutcheon (*Politics of Postmodernism* 63–76), Booker ("Beauty and the Beast") Shepherd, Kane, Goonetilleke, and Kortenaar (*Self* 167–189). For counterarguments, see François, Ghosh, Merivale, Barnaby, and Brennan ("Cultural Politics").

11. Rushdie's magical realism is different from that of Márquez in that Saleem is always apologizing for the extravagances of his narrative, while Márquez almost always presents "magical" occurrences as normal (Kortenaar, *Self* 26, 230). Márquez's version is also heavily indebted to the oral tradition, while Rushdie's seems to be more textually based, despite his own claims for the influence of orality (Rushdie, "*Midnight's Children*" 7–8).

12. Wolpert's *A New History of India* is frequently cited as either a source text for *Midnight's Children* or as an example of the kind of historical account that Rushdie parodies. See Lipscomb and Kortenaar ("*Midnight's Children*").

13. Walcott's claims that the Caribbean has nothing to do with history in "The Muse of History" and "The Caribbean Culture of Mimicry" is initially belied here, but *Omeros*'s ultimate rejection of metaphor is accompanied by a rejection of history in keeping with these essays.

14. My reading of *Omeros* and metaphor can be productively supplemented by Melas.

15. See Sanga (4) and especially Fenwick for a further reading of metaphor and metonymy in Rushdie.

16. This cry for literal interpretation occurs several times throughout the novel. The degree to which the audience is supposed to take Saleem himself literally is, however, questioned at various points. It is possible to read all of the fantastical elements of the novel as emanating from Saleem's diseased mind. Rushdie discusses this possibility in "Adapting *Midnight's Children*" (*Step Across This Line* 72). See also Kortenaar (*Self* 229–51).

17. See Guha, particularly the introduction.

18. For instance, Sheikh Abdullah survived long after Independence and Partition, only the idea of an undivided India died (Parameswaran 23; R. Clark 66).

19. For Rushdie's sustained attacks on Hindu communalism and the effacement of Muslim efforts at cooperation and support of a unified India, see the "Riddle of Midnight" (*Imaginary Homelands* 26–33), Chauhan (209–12), "God in Gujarat" (*Step Across This Line* 345), and *The Moor's Last Sigh*. See also Trousdale.

20. As usual, there is some ambiguity to Rushdie's assertions of a limit to the changeling side of human subjectivity. The Moor elsewhere asserts the value of precisely these principles in his commentary against the Hindu cult of Ram (351). Likewise, Aurora da Gama functions as a positive counterbalance to Uma, as she comes to see artistic hybridity as an ideal in itself. Still, while Rushdie's aversion to monolithic personality and community is well commented upon, his aversion to the infinite delights of proteanism is less widely acknowledged.

21. Characters from early Rushdie novels increasingly recur in later ones, raising the question of the importance of these interconnections. Likewise, Rushdie comments on Gabriel García Márquez's fictional world of Macondo, stressing that it should not be seen as "an invented self-referential closed system" (*Imaginary Homelands* 301–2), contradicting some elements of fictional worlds theory. He points out that Márquez is not writing about a fantasy world but "about the one we inhabit" (*Imaginary Homelands* 128). The same is true of Rushdie.

22. For a reading of this passage similar to and supplementing my own, see Su (560–61).

23. For a diametrically opposed interpretation of this passage, see Booker, "Beauty and the Beast" (983). Booker claims that Saleem's confession of his lie

invokes the (in)famous "liar's paradox," although my understanding of this paradox involves someone who claims to *always* lie (not who claims to lie just once).

24. India (especially Bombay) is also configured as a land of hybridity, while Pakistan is one of "purity," but in accord with the other associations of Pakistan, this "purity" can only be a lie (see Rushdie, *Imaginary Homelands* 67 and "*Midnight's Children*" 4). As such, the two nations are better seen as competing versions of hybridity (Kortenaar, *Self* 220).

25. See Harrison (58) and especially Batty for discussions of Rushdie, storytelling, and the *1,001 Nights*.

26. Strand argues that the MCC's status as representative of Indian multiplicity is undercut by Saleem's decision not to delineate the separate voices of the conference (262). Strand claims that this "paradoxically gives the children a *homogeneous* quality" (999), but his critique is too broad. Saleem delineates not only the powers of the children but also their genders, classes, castes, and geography, if not each child's name and individual history.

27. Rushdie's interest in a third principle also crops up in *The Ground Beneath Her Feet*, in which the Anglophile Darius Cama proposes something similar.

28. See especially Kortenaar, who argues that "the reader is free to prefer Shiva to Saleem as the mirror of India. But the concern for order is valuable . . . and we readers cannot but opt for order over chaos. There is no absolute reason to choose Saleem, but no reader will choose Shiva. The historian offers order and narrative. His enemy . . . seeks only chaos" ("*Midnight's Children*" 57, *Self* 199). This claim is not quite accurate, as I will show.

29. Here is another historical error. Jajit Singh Aurora, not Manekshaw, accepted Niazi's surrender.

30. It is worth noting that the optimism that could be associated with the assignment of these attributes to Aadam Sinai is undercut by his reappearance in *The Moor's Last Sigh*. Adam, the spelling of his name Westernized, departs from the novel into prison, convicted on a variety of counts including "corruption, drug-smuggling, arms dealing, money laundering, and procuring" (Moss 126; *Moor's* 370).

31. It is this "naïve" belief in the possibility of objectively speaking for the subaltern voices of India that draws Gayatri Chakravorty Spivak's ire in "Can the Subaltern Speak?"

32. See Brennan (*Salman Rushdie*) and Gorra for readings that, to varying degrees, agree with Naipaul.

33. See Strand and Brennan ("Cosmopolitans and Celebrities") for similar critiques of Rushdie's bourgeois sympathies.

34. Wilson does attempt a brief interpretation of this passage.

35. The pairing of the Widow (or the goddess Kali) and Parvati-the-Witch (or the goddess Parvati) establishes a similar parallel, as they too together represent creation and destruction.

36. For an extended discussion of this passage, see Price ("Salman Rushdie's"). For Rushdie's own discussion of Indira's opportunistic deployment of her last name, see "Dynasty" (*Imaginary Homelands* 50).

37. Strand rather forcefully misreads this passage when he argues that Rushdie himself configures Gandhi as "rural, handicraft-loving, etc." (979). See also Rushdie's more recent essay, "Gandhi, Now" (*Step* 165–70).

38. My use of this term obviously relies on the groundbreaking work of Edward

Said in *Orientalism*.

39. Rushdie makes a similar, less convincing, case for his portrayal of the prophet Mohammed in *The Satanic Verses* in several interviews (see Chauhan).

40. Here, I keep Frank Kermode's distinction between myth and fiction in mind. Kermode suggests that fiction is always acknowledged as untrue in the conventional sense, while myth, although often more outlandish, is often seen as containing elements of truth or reality that are transhistorical. Rushdie's work suggests that history and myth can coexist despite Kermode's (and Barthes's similar) claims that histories are fiction and History is a myth.

41. See Needham for a similar account of Rushdie's devotion to "bagginess" in the context of *Shame*.

42. Critics have attacked Rushdie's use of "magical realism" as part of the exoticizing of the East, collaborating with the Orientalism he critiques. Rushdie replies to this accusation in "Adapting *Midnight's Children*," noting that "Western critics tended to focus on its more fantastic elements, while Indian reviewers treated it like a history book" (*Step* 72). That is, the view of the book as "exotic" derives more from the reader's position than from anything intrinsic. This does not quite address the charge, leveled influentially by Brennan, that the novel panders to the Western audience, self-consciously selling its own cosmopolitanism. While these critiques have some validity, Rushdie's opposition to Orientalism and his mockery of overtly "mystical" efforts to tackle political problems makes me more inclined to see how Rushdie's form contributes to those politics.

43. While Saleem refers specifically to men, Rushdie's fictional practice indicates not only an avowed feminism but also a correlation between the position of the postcolonial subject and the position of women. Still, Rushdie's deployment of gender and his construction of women over the course of his oeuvre are contradictory. For an excellent overview of these issues in Rushdie, see Hai. See also Grewal, Krishnaswamy, and Mann.

44. Price's essay is typical in its assertion of Rushdie's efforts to deconstruct positivist accounts of history. In doing so, however, he positions Rushdie as antagonistic towards a type of history that seeks to "preserve the 'historical truth,'" favoring instead the mode of the artists who "explore the myriad dimensions of past experience" ("Salman Rushdie's" 104). In ceding the former type of discourse, Price indirectly suggests that Rushdie cannot assert anything about historical accuracy. It is thus a bit of a surprise when he claims that Rushdie's focus on the common and the everyday is somehow more accurate than other types of history. Price does qualify this claim by asserting that this view is solely from Saleem's perspective, but we would do well not to cede the discourse of accuracy to those with a naïve trust in transparent referentiality.

Chapter Four

1. There are some complexities to Anja's diaries. They are not, in fact, what she wrote during her time at Birkenau. Rather, while such diaries existed, they were destroyed, and so the notebooks Vladek destroyed were already a retrospective replacement and might be considered to be even more "distant" from the events themselves (*Maus* 84).

2. For discussions of the Oedipal and/or the "absent mother" in *Maus*, see Laga (80–83), Bosmajian, Hirsch, Elmwood, Glejzer, LaCapra (*History and Memory* 172, 178), Levine, and especially Nancy Miller.

3. Deborah Geis refers to *Maus's* postmodernism several times (2–3). Likewise, without using the term, Joshua Brown notes how *Maus* offers itself not as a "chronicle of undefiled fact but a constitutive process . . . a construction of the past" (95). Staub also notes how the book focuses on "the uselessness of representations" (35) but distances his reading from postmodernism, per se. Miles Orvell sees the primary objective of *Maus* to be historical accuracy but associates its outer diegetic frame with "postmodernism" (125), before noting how the book as a whole exceeds that label (126). Michael Rothberg also refers to how *Maus* is "haunted by the inadequacy of representation" (669), while Arlene Fish Wilner refers to the book's "postmodernism" (174), before noting how it contradicts its own claim that "reality's too complex for comics." Joshua Charlson notes the contradictions of realism and postmodernism in the book, suggesting that *Maus* does not resolve the contradiction (94).

4. The problem of author intent is a notoriously tricky one over the course of the history of literary criticism and one I fully intend to skirt here. As may be clear, however, I do find it useful to try to determine a governing theoretical point of view in literary texts, particularly as it pertains to the ways in which these texts address my own preoccupations. Whether we call this governing point of view the "implied author," the "career author," or simply the "author" is not central here except insofar as I take a slightly different tack in this chapter.

5. Lyotard discusses the paradoxical positivism of the Holocaust denier by noting that a Holocaust denier's argument is not that we *cannot* know what happened in the past but that we *do* know given the evidence we have available to us: "to identify a site as a gas chamber, [the Holocaust denier] shall accept as a valid witness only a victim of a gas chamber; now, according to [their] adversary, such victims can only be dead; otherwise the gas chamber would not be what it is claimed to be; thus there are no gas chambers" (Lyotard, *Le Différend* 16).

6. Lipstadt blames the willingness of college newspaper editors in the early 1990s to publish Holocaust denial advertisements on the influence of Derrida, Foucault, Barthes, et. al. As Novick points out, however, these philosophers were never cited by editors themselves and likely had little to do with the decision (*Holocaust* 271).

7. Faurisson's "The Problem of the Gas Chambers" (1978) was one of the initial attempts to deny the Holocaust's existence in France (Vidal-Naquet ix). Butz's *The Hoax of the Twentieth Century* (1976) helped inspire the Institute for Historical Review, which was devoted to uncovering the Holocaust as a hoax in the United States. This touched off a brief firestorm of controversy, including the publication of a series of books that denied the deniers (see Stern, Lipstadt, and Vidal-Naquet). For a brief account of these events, see Novick, *Holocaust* (270–72). Faurisson and Butz were preceded by David Hogan's *The Myth of the Six Million* and David Irving's *Hitler's War* (1977).

8. As Joseph Witek observes, the position taken by Adorno is that "to aestheticize . . . the profound evil of the Holocaust is to appropriate for one's own ends the unique experience of the victims of the gas chambers." This becomes even more problematic in the case of a comic-book representation, which "might appear as a grotesque degradation of the Holocaust" (97) because of comics' status as a "low"

form of popular culture. Those few who have read *Maus* as degrading criticize the use of animal masks/metaphors as potentially collaborative with Nazi stereotypes (see Harvey 241–45) or as implying a "natural" predator/ prey relationship (see Halkin 55).

9. See much of Dominick LaCapra's work for an extended critique of the tendency to both hyperbolize the Holocaust's traumatic inaccessibility and to generalize its sublimity into a postmodern universal.

10. Poststructuralists rarely configure their philosophy as Cartesian in the way Ankersmit describes. In fact, rather than suggest that it is impossible for the "subject" to know the "object," poststructuralist thought more often argues that that which we assume to be the "object" or the "essential" truth is actually a product of language or discourse, a social production, not an individual (or "subjective") one. As such, the "object" tends to disappear as mere discursive articulation. As in Ankersmit's account, then, the "thing itself" is not evident. This is not necessarily because of the failings of the subject, however, but because of the "depth" of language.

11. The primary reason for Spiegelman's deployment of the comic-book form is because it had always been his medium of choice. It is, however, also an appropriate one in the sense that Jews were often portrayed as mice, rats, and vermin in cartoon form in Julius Streich's Nazi weekly *Der Sturmer*. The other commonly cited source for Spiegelman's choice of mice is Fritz Hippler's equally anti-Semitic film *Der ewige Jude* (1940), which crosscuts between ghetto rabbis and sewer rats (Doherty 74–75). The history of "cat and mouse" conflict in comics is also relevant, beginning perhaps with George Herriman's *Krazy Kat*. For a discussion of *Maus*'s interaction with the "funny animal" tradition, see Witek (109–12) and Orvell. For a discussion of the use of human bodies with animal heads in traditional Jewish art, see Young ("Holocaust" 687) and Gopnik (33–34).

12. For my more extended discussion of *Maus* and race, see Berlatsky ("Memory as Forgetting" 126–29).

13. Spiegelman transgresses his own metaphor at times, depicting more animalistic rats (*Maus* 147), four-legged cats, and questions about whether these animals "louse up" his metaphor (*Maus II* 43). These deviations serve to draw attention to his metaphor, revealing it as a construction that can be violated (see Staub 39).

14. Again, I speak here of middle period Foucault. See note 6 of the Introduction for an explanation.

15. For an account of the racial ascription of the Jews in the nineteenth century, see Gilman (99–101, 234–43). For example: "Jews bear the . . . stigma of the black skin of the syphilitic," and "Jews are black, according to nineteenth-century racial science, because they are not a pure race, . . . that comes from Africa" (99).

16. See Rothberg for a discussion of how Spiegelman links Vladek's treatment of the hitchhiker with Israeli/Palestinian relations. While it is not clear to me that Spiegelman is explicitly treating Israeli politics here, it is clear that *Maus* points out how remembrance of a traumatic event can be redeployed for oppressive purposes.

17. It is worth noting that while I tend to read the use of the animal metaphor as a principally postmodern strategy, Spiegelman insists that the masks actually help us to see the truth in his depiction. "To use these ciphers, the cats and mice, is actually a way to allow you past the cipher at the people who are experiencing it" (Witek 102).

18. For further discussion of photographs in *Maus*, see Charlson (109–11), Hirsch, Hatfield, and Elmwood.

19. The contrast of *Maus* with traditional funny animals like Mickey Mouse necessarily rests on the distinction between the Disney capitalist/corporate machine that exploits everything and anything for profit and Spiegelman's text, which either draws the line between profit and "art" somewhere (at *Maus* vests, for instance), or, at the very least, expresses some guilt about it. Vladek, portrayed as an amoral capitalist in the pre-war years, believes he is giving Artie a compliment when he compares him to the "big-shot cartoonist" Walt Disney (*Maus* 133), but Artie obviously feels differently. Nevertheless, Spiegelman does articulate parallels between his own mice and those of Disney in the epigraph to *Maus II*, which quotes a mid-1930s German newspaper article's condemnation of Mickey Mouse and Jews, with both linked to debased amoral capitalism.

20. Bosmajian notes how the desire to have been present at Auschwitz is not atypical for children of survivors. Bosmajian posits that this "insane wish" comes about as a result of the knowledge that the "gap between the experience of the disaster and any mimetic or symbolic construct of it is unbridgeable" (33).

21. The division of memory and history is undercut by some versions of poststructuralist theory, as discussed in this chapter, and is also problematic given Maurice Halbwachs's notion of "collective memory," which asserts that no memory is individual but can only be constructed in relationship to communities.

22. In *History and Memory After Auschwitz*, Dominick LaCapra puts the number of Fortunoff testimonies at 3,700 and the Survivors of the Shoah Foundation's at approximately 50,000 (11). In the ten years that have passed since that book's publication, at least several hundred more have been added to the Fortunoff testimonies and perhaps several thousand to the Survivors of the Shoah. To link either or both of these collections to a true or transparent touching of the past to the present is, as always, problematic, particularly in the case of the latter, funded by Steven Spielberg and directed with Hollywood logic and production values (Novick, *Holocaust* 275–76).

23. Nancy K. Miller makes a similar claim about *Maus* when she notes that listening to Vladek's recorded voice at the *Maus* museum exhibit gives the listener the sense that "the father performs unmediated—to the world" (55). Miller does acknowledge, however, that the *impression* of the unmediated is, of course, problematic (59n13).

24. Ankersmit distinguishes between a "description" of the past that aims at truthfulness and the "representation" (particularly narrative) of the past that is an argument for how a particular slice of the past is to be defined. Descriptions distinguish between a portion that is referring to reality and a portion that is a property of that referent. So, in "the cat is orange," the "cat" refers to a real-world object and "is orange" describes one of its properties. Because of the simplicity of the statement, it can be empirically confirmed or denied and is therefore either "true" or "false." Nevertheless, because of its simplicity, the statement tells us very little about the cat, its origins, its history, its relationships (*Narrative Logic*, chapters 1–3). Ankersmit concludes that because history aims not only to tell us the factual "truth" of past events but also to orient us towards them and to help us understand their complexities, this model has little utility. It is possible, of course, to imagine a more radical response to Ankersmit that would focus on how a single word in this description ("orange") can only be corroborated within agreed social and linguistic boundaries, making such corroboration not a confirmation of the statement's "objective" truth but of social/

linguistic agreement. While there is little doubt that "facts" depend on what social groups consider factual, it is also true that the discrepancies between such groups are likely to be more limited when treating such a simple declarative statement. Statements of this kind infrequently create the kinds of social and political problems so central to middle-period Foucauldian thinking, for instance. The orangeness of cats has rarely been a significant bone of political contention. Other short statements may be much more difficult to extract from their discursive context, however. Freud's "a child is being beaten" or Spivak's "white men are saving brown women from brown men" might seem initially to be the kind of factual statement Ankersmit sees as confirmable, but they are embroiled in larger cultural narratives that circulate power. Ankersmit's broader point, however, is that these larger discourses are precisely that which we should investigate, both because they create more problems for notions of transparent representation and because they have greater educational potential (*Historical Representation* 39–48). Ankersmit further argues that narratives/representations can be "true" even if some of their individual statements are false (*Narrative Logic* 58–78).

25. Interestingly, as the *Complete Maus* CD-ROM reveals, these lines are not a direct quote from Vladek, but are edited and rewritten by Spiegelman. Vladek actually said "finally I found her. The rest I don't need to tell you, because we both were very happy" (Bosmajian 41). While the "happy ending" of the story is still palpably false, Spiegelman's addition of "ever after" emphasizes (even provides) the fairytale feel of Vladek's conclusion.

26. For a discussion of the problems of providing closure in any Holocaust narrative, see Levine (70).

27. There are some examples of critics relying on outcomes to interpret *Maus* in ways similar to Vladek's emplotment. In particular, Tabachnick suggests that Vladek's survival is somehow meant to happen by God, something "proven" by various fulfilled prophecies in the text. While there is an emphasis on prediction and fulfillment in these episodes, there is also an emphasis in *Maus* on the role chance plays in who survived the camps. Pavel asserts, "It wasn't the best people who survived, nor did the best ones die. It was *random!!*" (*Maus II* 45; emphasis in original). Given Pavel's wisdom throughout *Maus*, it is more likely that we are meant to see the random nature of survival than the fated triumph of Vladek.

28. For further commentary on the orchestra scene, see Ewert (both sources) and Iadonisi (51–52).

29. Nearly all comics theorists note this feature unique to the medium. Scott McCloud, for example, discusses how comics transform time into space in *Understanding Comics*: "[I]n comics, the past is more than just memories for the audience and the future is more than just possibilities! Both past and future are real and visible all around us! Wherever your eyes are focused, that's now. But at the same time your eyes take in the surrounding landscape of the past and future!" (104). The surfeit of exclamation points does not invalidate the claim.

30. Of course, all of these drawings are *representations* of the past, not the thing itself, even if they occupy the same diegetic level as the person who creates them. The blurring of diegetic levels suggests that the past can be made present, but it does not actualize that suggestion unless we acknowledge that representations can retain some material portion of that which they represent, a possibility I explore in the next section of the chapter.

31. Nora ultimately makes a similar claim. While memory and history have become fundamentally separate, he argues that they need to be (re)united in histories that partake of the emotion and the "presence" of memory.

32. Ankersmit argues against the Holocaust being classified as "sublime" or as "collective trauma" because "the perpetrators of this unprecedented crime were vanquished in World War II and because their actions did not and could not become part of our collective future" (*Sublime Historical Experience* 351). Ankersmit idiosyncratically argues that "Western historical consciousness" was not forced to redefine itself in the case of the Holocaust, allowing the West to "discard" or "neutralize" the event by classifying it only as part of the past and *not* of the present (351). Ankersmit therefore suggests that the Holocaust is somehow "narratable" because it does not define our society in the present. I disagree strongly with Ankersmit here. Just because the Allies ultimately won the war does not mean that the Holocaust has not been cause for a restructuring of the West's collective psyche. Rather, I believe it has.

33. Obviously, *Maus is* "adorned" with pictures and pervasive animal metaphors, but its relative simplicity in terms of drawing style and artistic presentation emphasizes the "mimetic" element of the text and deemphasizes the stylistic complexity and artistic pyrotechnics that can sometimes characterize graphic narratives, including Spiegelman's earlier works. Witek argues that the "plain understated visual style" (100) reflects Vladek's narration, but it more closely mirrors Spiegelman's effort to transmit the facts of the past without the barrier of formal complexity. Joshua Brown further details Spiegelman's compositional methods and how they lead to a sense of transparent simplicity. Most comics artists draw pages at twice the final publication size, in an effort to get more detail into each panel, to obscure mistakes, and to make the "finished product appear tighter and sharper" (102). Spiegelman avoids this technique and draws *Maus* at the same size at which it is read. Spiegelman suggests that this is to make the work "more vulnerable" and to "leave me without as many intermediaries between me and somebody reading *Maus*" (Brown 102). That is, despite the various techniques in *Maus* highlighting mediation, the drawing and compositional style actually push in the other direction, toward an attempted transparency.

Conclusion

1. For an investigation of the ethics of the postscript in *Atonement,* see Phelan ("Narrative").

2. The conceit of the book was admittedly "borrowed" from Brazilian author Moacyr Scliar's *Max and the Cats,* in which a Jewish boy is shipwrecked and left adrift on a boat with a panther. Martel's borrowing led to a brief controversy over *Pi*'s "plagiarism" (see, for example, Blackstock).

WORKS CITED

Abel, Elizabeth. "Narrative Structure(s) and Female Development: The Case of *Mrs. Dalloway*." In *Virginia Woolf: A Collection of Critical Essays*, edited by Margaret Homans, 93–114. Englewood Cliffs, CA: Prentice Hall, 1993.

Acheson, James. "*Historia* and Guilt: Graham Swift's *Waterland*." *Critique* 47.1 (Fall 2005): 90–100.

Adorno, Theodor. "Commitment." In *The Essential Frankfurt School Reader*, edited by Andrew Arato and Eike Gebhart, translated by Francis McDonagh, 300–318. New York: Urizen Books, 1978.

———. *Negative Dialectics*. Translated by E. B. Ashton. New York: Seabury Press, 1973.

Ahmad, Aijaz. *In Theory: Classes, Nations, Languages*. New York: Verso, 1992.

Ames, Christopher. "Carnivalesque Comedy in *Between the Acts*." *Twentieth-Century Literature* 44.4 (Winter 1998): 394–408.

———. "The Modernist Canon Narrative: Woolf's *Between the Acts* and Joyce's 'Oxen of the Sun.'" *Twentieth Century Literature* 37.4 (Winter 1991): 390–404.

Ankersmit, Frank R. *Historical Representation*. Stanford, CA: Stanford University Press, 2001.

———. *History and Tropology*. Berkeley: University of California Press, 1994.

———. *Narrative Logic*. The Hague: Martinus Nijhoff, 1993.

———. *Sublime Historical Experience*. Stanford, CA: Stanford University Press, 2005.

Appleby, Joyce, Lynn Hunt, and Margaret Jacob. *Telling the Truth about History*. New York: W. W. Norton, 1995.

Aristotle. *De Anima*. Translated by R. D. Hicks. Buffalo, NY: Prometheus Books, 1991.

———. *Aristotle's Poetics*. Translated by James Hutton. New York: W. W. Norton, 1982.

Ashcroft, Bill, Gareth Griffiths, and Helen Tiffin. *The Empire Writes Back: Theory and Practice in Post-Colonial Literatures*. London: Routledge, 1989.

Bahl, Vinay. "Situating and Rethinking Subaltern Studies for Writing Working-Class History." In *History after the Three Worlds: Post-Eurocentric Historiographies*, edited by Arif Dirlik, Vinay Bahl, and Peter Gran, 85–124. Lanham,

MD: Rowman & Littlefield, 2000.
Banfield, Ann. *The Phantom Table: Woolf, Fry, Russell, and the Epistemology of Modernism.* Cambridge: Cambridge University Press, 2000.
———. "Time Passes: Virginia Woolf, Post-Impressionism, and Cambridge Time." *Poetics Today* 24.3 (Autumn 2003): 471–516.
———. "Tragic Time: The Problem of the Future in Cambridge Philosophy and *To the Lighthouse*." *Modernism/Modernity* 7.1 (2000): 43–75.
Banville, John. *Doctor Copernicus.* New York: Vintage International, 1976.
Barnaby, Edward. "Airbrushed History, Photography, Realism and Rushdie's *Midnight's Children.*" *Mosaic* 38.1 (March 2005): 1–16.
Barnes, Julian. *A History of the World in 10 1/2 Chapters.* New York: Vintage International, 1989.
Barrett, Eileen. "Matriarchal Myth on a Patriarchal Stage: Virginia Woolf's *Between the Acts.*" *Twentieth Century Literature* 33.1 (Spring 1987): 18–37.
Barth, John. *The Friday Book: Essays and Other Nonfiction.* New York: Putnam, 1984.
Barthes, Roland. "The Discourse of History." In *The Rustle of Language*, translated by Richard Howard, 127–40. New York: Farrar, Straus, and Giroux, 1986. Originally published in *Social Science Information* 6.4 (1967): 65 as "Le Discours de l'histoire."
———. "An Introduction to the Structural Analysis of Narrative." Translated by Lionel Duisit. *New Literary History* 6.2 (Winter 1975): 237–72. Originally published in *Communications* 8 (1966) as "Introduction á l'analyse structurale des récits."
———. *Mythologies.* Translated by Annette Lavers. New York: Hill and Wang, 1972.
———. *The Pleasure of the Text.* Translated by Richard Miller. New York: Hill and Wang, 1975.
———. *S/Z: An Essay.* Translated by Richard Miller. New York: Hill and Wang, 1974.
Batty, Nancy. "The Art of Suspense: Rushdie's 1001 Midnights." In *Reading Rushdie Perspectives on the Fiction of Salman Rushdie*, edited by M. D. Fletcher, 69–81. Amsterdam: Rodopi, 1994.
Baudrillard, Jean. *Simulacra and Simulation.* Translated by Sheila Faria Glaser. Ann Arbor: University of Michigan Press, 1994.
Beckett, Samuel. *Three Novels: Molloy, Malone Dies, The Unnameable.* New York: Grove Press, 1955, 1956, 1958.
Bedggood, Daniel. "(re)Constituted Pasts: Postmodern Historicism in the Novels of Graham Swift and Julian Barnes." In *The Contemporary British Novel since 1980*, edited by James Acheson and Sarah C. E. Ross, 203–16. New York: Palgrave Macmillan, 2005.
Beer, Gillian. *Virginia Woolf: The Common Ground.* Edinburgh: Edinburgh University Press, 1996.
Bell, Quentin. *Virginia Woolf: A Biography.* 2 vols. London: The Hogarth Press, 1990.
Benjamin, Walter. "Theses on the Philosophy of History." In *Illuminations*, edited by Hannah Arendt, translated by Harry Zohn, 253–64. New York: Schoen Books, 1968.
———. "The Work of Art in the Age of Mechanical Reproduction." In *Illuminations*, edited by Hannah Arendt, translated by Harry Zohn, 217–52. New York: Schoen Books, 1968.
Bennington, Geoffrey. *Interrupting Derrida.* New York: Routledge, 2000.
Bényei, Tamás. "The Novels of Graham Swift: Family Photos." In *Contemporary British Fiction*, edited by Richard J. Lane, Rod Mengham, and Philip Tew, 40–55.

Cambridge: Polity Press, 2003.
Bergson, Henri. *Henri Bergson: Key Writings*. Edited by Keith Ansell Pearson and John Mullarkey. New York: Continuum, 2002.
———. *Matter and Memory*. 1896. New York: Zone Books, 1988.
———. *Time and Free Will: An Essay on the Immediate Data of Consciousness*. 1889. Translated by F. L. Pogson. New York: Macmillan, 1959.
Berkhofer, Robert. *Beyond the Great Story*. Princeton, NJ: Princeton University Press, 1995.
Berlatsky, Eric. "Memory as Forgetting: The Problem of the Postmodern in Kundera's *The Book of Laughter and Forgetting* and Spiegelman's *Maus*." *Cultural Critique* 55 (Fall 2003): 101–51.
———. "'The Swamps of Myth . . . and Empirical Fishing Lines': Historiography, Narrativity, and the 'Here and Now' in Graham Swift's *Waterland*." *Journal of Narrative Theory* 36.2 (Summer 2006): 254–92.
Bernard, Catherine. "Dismembering/Remembering Mimesis: Martin Amis, Graham Swift." In *British Postmodern Fiction*, edited by Theo d'Haen and Hans Bertens, 121–44. Amsterdam: Rodopi, 1993.
Bernasconi, Robert. "The Truth That Accuses: Conscience, Shame, and Guilt in Levinas and Augustine." In *The Ethics of Postmodernity: Current Trends in Continental Thought*, edited by Gary B. Madison and Marty Fairbairn, 24–34. Evanston, IL: Northwestern University Press, 1999.
Bhabha, Homi. *The Location of Culture*. London: Routledge, 1994.
Birch, David. "Postmodernist Chutneys." *Textual Practice* 5.1 (Spring 1991): 1–7.
Blackstock, Colin. "Booker Winner In Plagiarism Row: Author Admits Idea Came from Brazilian Novel." *The Guardian*, 8 November 2002. Accessed 17 December 2009. http://www.guardian.co.uk/world/2002/nov/08/bookerprize2002.awardsandprizes.
Booker, M. Keith. "Beauty and the Beast: Dualism as Despotism in the Fiction of Salman Rushdie." *ELH* (1990) 977–97.
———. "*Midnight's Children*, History and Complexity: Reading Rushdie after the Cold War." In *Critical Essays on Salman Rushdie*, edited by M. Keith Booker, 283–314. New York: G. K. Hall & Co., 1999.
Booker, M. Keith, ed. *Critical Essays on Salman Rushdie*. New York: G. K. Hall & Co., 1999.
Bosmajian, Hamida. "The Orphaned Voice in Art Spiegelman's *Maus*." In *Considering* Maus: *Approaches to Art Spiegelman's 'Survivor's Tale' of the Holocaust*, edited by Deborah Geis, 26–43. Tuscaloosa: University of Alabama Press, 2003.
Boyarin, Jonathan. *Storm from Paradise: The Politics of Jewish Memory*. Minneapolis: University of Minnesota Press, 1992.
Bradbury, Malcolm. *No, Not Bloomsbury*. New York: Columbia University Press, 1988.
Brennan, Timothy. "Cosmopolitans and Celebrities." *Race and Class* 31.1 (1989): 1–19.
———. "The Cultural Politics of Rushdie Criticism: All or Nothing." In *Critical Essays on Salman Rushdie*, edited by M. Keith Booker, 107–28. New York: G. K. Hall & Co., 1999.
———. *Salman Rushdie and the Third World*. New York: St. Martin's Press, 1989.
Brewer, John, and Stella Tillyard. "History and Telling Stories: Graham Swift's *Water-*

land." *History Today* (January 1985): 49-51.
Brigg, Peter. "Salman Rushdie's Novels: The Disorder in Fantastic Order." In *Reading Rushdie: Perspectives on the Fiction of Salman Rushdie*, edited by M. D. Fletcher, 173-85. Amsterdam: Rodopi, 1994.
Brooks, Peter. *Reading for the Plot: Design and Intention in Narrative*. Cambridge, MA: Harvard University Press, 1984.
Brown, Joshua. "Of Mice and Memory." *Oral History Review* 16.1 (Spring 1988): 91-109.
Brownstein, Marilyn. "Postmodern Language and the Perpetuation of Desire." *Twentieth Century Literature* 31.1 (Spring 1985): 73-88.
Busse, Kristina. "Reflecting the Subject of History: The Return of the Real in *Between the Acts*." *Woolf Studies Annual* 7 (2001): 75-101.
Butler, Judith. "Ethical Ambivalence." In *The Turn to Ethics*, edited by Marjorie Garber, Beatrice Hanssen, and Rebecca L. Walkowitz, 15-28. New York: Routledge, 2000.
Butler, Judith, Ernesto Laclau, and Slavoj Žižek. *Contingency, Hegemony, Universality: Contemporary Dialogues on the Left*. New York: Verso, 2000.
Byatt, A. S. *Possession: A Romance*. New York: Vintage International, 1990.
Caldwell, Ann Stewart. "The Intrusive Narrative Voice of Milan Kundera." *The Review of Contemporary Fiction* 9.2 (Summer 1989): 46-52.
Carr, David. "Narrative and the Real World: An Argument for Continuity." In *History and Theory: Contemporary Readings*, edited by Brian Fay, Philip Pomper, and Richard T. Vann, 137-54. Malden, MA: Blackwell, 1998.
———. *Time, Narrative, and History*. Bloomington: Indiana University Press, 1986.
Carr, David, Thomas R. Flynn, and Rudolf A. Makkreel, eds. *The Ethics of History*. Evanston, IL: Northwestern University Press, 2004.
Carroll, David. *The Subject in Question: The Languages of Theory and the Strategies of Fiction*. Chicago: University of Chicago Press, 1982.
Carter, Angela. 1972. *The Infernal Desire Machines of Doctor Hoffman*. New York: Penguin Books, 1994.
———. *Nights at the Circus*. New York: Penguin, 1984.
Caruth, Cathy. *Unclaimed Experience: Trauma, Narrative, and History*. Baltimore: Johns Hopkins University Press, 1996.
Caughie, Pamela L. *Virginia Woolf and Postmodernism: Literature in Quest and Question of Itself*. Urbana: University of Illinois Press, 1991.
Caughie, Pamela L, ed. *Virginia Woolf in the Age of Mechanical Reproduction*. New York: Garland Publishing, 2000.
Certeau, Michel de. *The Writing of History*. Translated by Tom Conley. New York: Columbia University Press, 1988.
Chakrabarty, Dipesh. "Postcoloniality and the Artifice of History: Who Speaks for Indian Pasts." In *A Subaltern Studies Reader, 1986-1995*, edited by Ranajit Guha, 263-94. Minneapolis: University of Minnesota Press, 1997.
———. "Radical Histories and the Question of Enlightenment Rationalism: Some Recent Critiques of Subaltern Studies." In *Mapping Subaltern Studies and the Postcolonial*, edited by Vinayak Chaturvedi, 256-80. New York: Verso, 2000.
Charlson, Joshua. "Framing the Past: Postmodernism and the Making of Reflective Memory in Art Spiegelman's *Maus*." *Arizona Quarterly* 57.3 (Autumn 2001): 91-120.

Chatman, Seymour. *Story and Discourse: Narrative Structure in Fiction and Film.* Ithaca, NY: Cornell University Press, 1978.
Chauhan, Pradyumna. *Salman Rushdie Interviews: A Sourcebook of His Ideas.* New York: Greenwood, 2001.
Christie, Stuart. "Willing Epigone: Virginia Woolf's *Between the Acts* as Nietzschean Historiography." *Woolf Studies Annual* 8 (2002): 157–74.
Churchill, Caryl. *Cloud 9.* 1979. Revised American Edition. New York: Routledge, 1991.
Chvatik, Kvetoslav. "Milan Kundera and the Crisis of Language." *The Review of Contemporary Fiction* 9.2 (Summer 1989): 27–36.
Clark, Elizabeth A. *History, Theory, Text: Historians and the Linguistic Turn.* Cambridge, MA: Harvard University Press, 2004.
Clark, Roger Y. *Stranger Gods: Salman Rushdie's Other Worlds.* Montreal: McGill-Queen's University Press, 2001.
Coetzee, J. M. *Foe.* New York: Penguin, 1986.
Cohen, Arthur. *The Tremendum.* New York: Crossroad, 1981.
Cohn, Dorrit. *The Distinction of Fiction.* Baltimore: Johns Hopkins University Press, 1999.
Cooper, Pamela. *The Fictions of John Fowles: Power, Creativity, Femininity.* Ottawa: University of Ottawa Press, 1991.
———. "Imperial Topographies: The Spaces of History in *Waterland*." *Modern Fiction Studies* 42.2 (Summer 1996): 371–96.
Crapanzano, Vincent. "The Postmodern Crisis: Discourse, Parody, Memory." In *Bakhtin in Contexts: Across the Disciplines,* edited by Amy Mandelker, 137–50. Evanston, IL: Northwestern University Press, 1995.
Craps, Stef. *Trauma and Ethics in the Novels of Graham Swift: No Short Cuts to Salvation.* Brighton: Sussex Academic Press, 2005.
Critchley, Simon. *The Ethics of Deconstruction: Derrida and Levinas.* 2nd ed. West Lafayette, IN: Purdue University Press, 1999.
Crosby, Christina. *The Ends of History: Victorians and "The Woman Question."* New York: Routledge, 1991.
Cuddy-Keane, Melba. "The Politics of Comic Modes in Virginia Woolf's *Between the Acts*." *PMLA* 105.2 (March 1990): 273–85.
———. "Virginia Woolf, Sound Technologies, and the New Aurality." In *Virginia Woolf in the Age of Mechanical Reproduction,* edited by Pamela Caughie, 69–96. New York: Garland Publishing, 2000.
Dasenbrock, Reed Way. *Truth and Consequences: Intentions, Conventions, and the New Thematics.* University Park: The Pennsylvania State University Press, 2001.
Daugherty, Beth Rigel. "Face to Face With 'Ourselves' in Virginia Woolf's *Between the Acts*." In *Virginia Woolf: Themes and Variations: Selected Papers from the Second Annual Conference on Virginia Woolf,* edited by Mark Hussey and Vara Neverow-Turk, 76–82. New York: Pace University Press, 1993.
de Lauretis, Teresa. *Alice Doesn't: Feminism, Semiotics, Cinema.* Bloomington: Indiana University Press, 1984.
de Man, Paul. "The Epistemology of Metaphor." In *Aesthetic Ideology,* edited by Andrzej Warminski, 34–50. Minneapolis: University of Minnesota Press, 1996.
Debord, Guy-Ernest. *The Society of the Spectacle.* 1965. Translated by Ken Knabb. Edinburgh: AK Press, 2006.

Decoste, Damon Marcel. "Question and Apocalypse: The Endlessness of 'Historia' in Graham Swift's *Waterland*." *Contemporary Literature* 43.2 (Summer 2002): 377–99.
Deiman, Werner. "History, Pattern, and Continuity in Virginia Woolf." *Contemporary Literature* 15.1 (Winter 1974): 49–66.
Deleuze, Gilles. *Bergsonism*. New York: Zone Books, 1988.
Delillo, Don. *Libra*. New York: Penguin, 1988.
———. *Underworld*. New York: Scribner, 1997.
Delorey, Denise. "Parsing the Female Sentence: The Paradox of Containment in Virginia Woolf's Narratives." In *Ambiguous Discourse: Feminist Narratology and British Women Writers*, edited by Kathy Mezei, 93–108. Chapel Hill: University of North Carolina Press, 1996.
Derrida, Jacques. "The Deconstruction of Actuality." *Radical Philosophy* 68 (1994): 28–41.
———. *Dissemination*. Translated by Barbara Johnson. Chicago: University of Chicago Press, 1981.
———. "Force of Law: The Mystical Foundation of Authority." In *Deconstruction and the Possibility of Justice*, edited by Drucilla Cornell, Michel Rosenfeld and David Gray Carson, translated by Mary Quaintance, 3–67. New York: Routledge, 1992.
———. *The Gift of Death* and *Literature in Secret*. Translated by David Wills. Chicago: University of Chicago Press, 1995, 2008.
———. *Limited Inc*. Translated by S. Weber. Evanston, IL: Northwestern University Press, 1988.
———. *Of Grammatology*. Translated by Gayatri Chakravorty Spivak. Baltimore: Johns Hopkins University Press, 1974.
———. "Ousia and *Grammé*: Note on a Note from *Being and Time*." In *Margins of Philosophy*, translated by Alan Bass, 29–68. 1982.
———. *The Politics of Friendship*. Translated by George Collins. New York: Verso, 2006.
———. "Violence and Metaphysics: An Essay on the Thought of Emmanuel Levinas." In *Writing and Difference*, translated by Alan Bass, 79–153. Chicago: University of Chicago Press, 1978.
DiBattista, Maria. *Virginia Woolf's Major Novels: The Fables of Anon*. New Haven, CT: Yale University Press, 1980.
Dick, Philip K. *The Man in the High Castle*. New York: Vintage Books, 1962.
Dirlik, Arif. "Is There History after Eurocentrism? Globalism, Postcolonialism, and the Disavowal of History." In *History after the Three Worlds: Post-Eurocentric Historiographies*, edited by Arif Dirlik, Vinay Bahl, and Peter Gran, 25–48. Lanham, MD: Rowman & Littlefield, 2000.
———. "Whither History?: Encounters with Historism, Postmodernism, Postcolonialism." In *History after the Three Worlds: Post-Eurocentric Historiographies*, edited by Arif Dirlik, Vinay Bahl, and Peter Gran, 241–58. Lanham, MD: Rowman & Littlefield, 2000.
Dirlik, Arif, Vinay Bahl, and Peter Gran, eds. *History after the Three Worlds: Post-Eurocentric Historiographies*. Lanham, MD: Rowman & Littlefield, 2000.
Doctorow, E. L. *The Book of Daniel*. 1971. New York: Penguin, 1986.
Doherty. Thomas. "Art Spiegelman's *Maus*: Graphic Art and the Holocaust." *American Literature* 68.1 (March 1996): 69–84.

Dreifus, Claudia. "Art Spiegelman: The *Progessive* Interview." *Progressive* (November 1989): 34–37.

Dubrow, Heather. "The Interplay of Narrative and Lyric: Competition, Cooperation, and the Case of the Anticipatory Amalgam." *Narrative* 14.3 (October 2006): 254–71.

DuPlessis, Rachel Blau. *Writing Beyond the Ending: Narrative Strategies of Twentieth-Century Women Writers*. Bloomington: Indiana University Press, 1985.

Eagleton, Terry. "Estrangement and Irony." *Salmagundi* 73 (Winter 1987): 25–32.

Eisenberg, Nora. "Virginia Woolf's Last Words on Words: *Between the Acts* and 'Anon.'" In *New Feminist Essays on Virginia Woolf*, edited by Jane Marcus, 253–66. Lincoln: University of Nebraska Press, 1981.

Eliot, T. S. "Myth and Literary Classicism." In *The Modern Tradition: Backgrounds of Modern Literature*, edited by Richard Ellmann and Charles Feidelson, Jr., 679–81. New York: Oxford University Press, 1965. Rpt. of "*Ulysses*, Order, and Myth." *The Dial* 75 (1923): 480–83.

Elkana, Yehuda. "A Plea for Forgetting." *Ha'aretz*, 2 March 1988.

Elmwood, Victoria A. "'Happy, Happy Ever After': The Transformation of Trauma Between the Generations in Art Spiegelman's *Maus: A Survivor's Tale*." *Biography* 27.4 (Fall 2004): 691–721.

Ermath, Elizabeth Deeds. *Sequel to History*. Princeton, NJ: Princeton University Press, 1992.

Esty, Joshua D. "Amnesia in the Fields: Late Modernism, Late Imperialism, and the English Pageant-Play." *English Literary History* 69.1 (2002): 245–76.

Evans, Richard J. *In Defense of History*. New York: W. W. Norton, 1999.

Ewert, Jeanne C. "Art Spiegelman's *Maus* and the Graphic Narrative." In *Narrative Across Media: The Languages of Storytelling*, edited by Marie-Laure Ryan, 178–93. Lincoln: University of Nebraska Press, 2004.

——. "Reading Visual Narrative: Art Spiegelman's *Maus*." *Narrative* 8.1 (January 2000): 87–103.

Fackenheim, Emil. *To Mend the World*. New York: Schocken Books, 1982.

Farwell, Marilyn. *Heterosexual Plots and Lesbian Narratives*. New York: New York University Press, 1996.

Fenwick, Mac. "Crossing the Figurative Gap: Metaphor and Metonymy in *Midnight's Children*." *Journal of Commonwealth Literature* 39.3 (2004): 45–68.

Finn, Molly. "A Comic Book That Sears Your Heart." *Commonweal*, 28 February 1992, 23.

Fish, Stanley. *Is There a Text in This Class?* Baltimore: Johns Hopkins University Press, 1982.

Fletcher, M. D., ed. *Reading Rushdie: Perspectives on the Fiction of Salman Rushdie*. Amsterdam: Rodopi, 1994.

Forster, E. M. *Aspects of the Novel*. New York: Harcourt Brace Jovanovich, 1927.

Foucault, Michel. *The Archaeology of Knowledge*. Translated by A. M. Sheridan Smith. New York: Harper & Row, 1976.

——. *Discipline and Punish: The Birth of the Prison*. 1977. Translated by Alan Sheridan. New York: Vintage, 1995.

——. *The History of Sexuality: Volume I: An Introduction*. Translated by Robert Hurley. New York: Vintage Books, 1990.

——. *Madness and Civilization: A History of Insanity in the Age of Reason*. Translated by Richard Howard. New York: Vintage, 1965.

———. "Nietzsche, Genealogy, History." In *The Foucault Reader*, edited by Paul Rabinow, 76–100. New York: Pantheon Books, 1984.

———. *The Order of Things: An Archaeology of the Human Sciences*. 1970. Translated by Alan Sheridan. New York: Vintage, 1973.

———. *Power/Knowledge: Selected Interviews and Other Writings*. Edited by Colin Gordon. New York: Pantheon, 1980.

———. "What Is an Author?" In *The Norton Anthology of Theory and Criticism*, edited by Vincent B. Leitch, 1622–36. New York: W. W. Norton, 2001.

Fowles, John. *The French Lieutenant's Woman*. 1969. Boston: Back Bay Books, 1998.

———. *The Magus: A Revised Version*. 1966. London: Picador, 1988.

François, Pierre. "Salman Rushdie's Philosophical Materialism in *The Satanic Verses*." *Reading Rushdie: Perspectives on the Fiction of Salman Rushdie*. Ed. M. D. Fletcher. Amsterdam: Rodopi, 1994. 305–19.

Fraser, Nancy. "Recognition without Ethics?" In *The Turn to Ethics*, edited by Marjorie Garber, Beatrice Hanssen, and Rebecca L. Walkowitz, 95–126. New York: Routledge, 2000.

Freud, Sigmund. "A Note Upon the Mystic Writing Pad." In *The Standard Edition of the Complete Psychological Works of Sigmund Freud, Volume XIX (1923–1925)*, translated by James Strachey, 227–32. London: The Hogarth Press, 1961.

Friedlander, Saul, ed. *Probing the Limits of Representation: Nazism and the "Final Solution."* Cambridge, MA: Harvard University Press, 1992.

Friedman, Susan Stanford. "Lyric Subversion of Narrative in Women's Writing: Virginia Woolf and the Tyranny of Plot." In *Reading Narrative: Form, Ethics, Ideology*, edited by James Phelan, 162–85. Columbus: Ohio State University Press, 1989.

Fuentes, Carlos. *Terra Nostra*. Translated by Margaret Sayers Peden. New York: Farrar, Straus, and Giroux, 1976.

Fulbrook, Mary. *Historical Theory*. New York: Routledge, 2002.

Gabriel, Barbara and Susan Ilcan, eds. *Postmodernism and the Ethical Subject*. Montreal: McGill-Queen's University Press, 2004.

Gates, David. "The Light Side of Darkness." *Newsweek*, 22 September 1986, 79.

Geis, Deborah, ed. Considering *Maus: Approaches to Art Spiegelman's 'Survivor's Tale' of the Holocaust*. Tuscaloosa: University of Alabama Press, 2003.

Geras, Norman. "Language, Truth and Justice." *New Left Review* 209 (1995): 110–35.

Garber, Marjorie, Beatrice Hanssen, and Rebecca L. Walkowitz. *The Turn to Ethics*. New York: Routledge, 2000.

Ghosh, Bishnupriya. "An Invitation to Indian Postmodernity: Rushdie's English Vernacular as Situated Cultural Hybridity." In *Critical Essays on Salman Rushdie*, edited by M. Keith Booker, 129–53. New York: G. K. Hall & Co., 1999.

Gibson, Andrew. *Postmodernity, Ethics, and the Novel: From Leavis to Levinas*. New York: Routledge, 1999.

Gilman, Sander. *The Jew's Body*. New York: Routledge, 1991.

Glejzer, Richard. "*Maus* and the Epistemology of Witness." In *Witnessing the Disaster: Essays on Representation and the Holocaust*, edited by Michael Bernard-Donals and Richard Glejzer, 125–37. Madison: University of Wisconsin Press, 2003.

Goonetilleke, D. C. R. A. *Modern Novelists: Salman Rushdie*. New York: St. Martins Press, 1998.

Gopnik, Adam. "Comics and Catastrophe; The True History of the Cartoon and the Meaning of Art Spiegelman's *Maus*." *The New Republic*, 22 June 1987, 29–33.

Gorra, Michael. "'This Angrezi in which I am forced to write': On the Language of *Midnight's Children*." In *Critical Essays on Salman Rushdie*, edited by M. Keith Booker, 188–204. New York: G. K. Hall & Co., 1999.

Gotanda, Neil. "A Critique of 'Our Constitution is Color Blind.'" In *Critical Race Theory: The Key Writings That Formed the Movement*, edited by Kimberlé Crenshaw, Neil Gotanda, Gary Peller, and Kendall Thomas, 257–75. New York: The New Press, 1995.

Grant, Paul. Review of *Maus: A Survivor's Tale* and *Brought to Light: A Graphic Docudrama*. *Race and Class* 31 (1989): 99–101.

Grass, Günter. *The Tin Drum*. Translated by Ralph Manheim. New York: Vintage International, 1961. Published originally in German as *Die Blechtrommel* in 1959.

Grewal, Inderpal. "Salman Rushdie: Marginality, Women, and *Shame*." *Genders* 3 (Fall 1988): 24–42.

Grossman, Robert. "Mauschwitz." *The Nation*, 10 January 1987, 23–24.

Groth, Gary, Kim Thompson, and Joey Cavalieri. "Slaughter on Greene Street: Art Spiegelman and Françoise Mouly Talk About *Raw*." In *Art Spiegelman: Conversations*, edited by Joseph Witek, 35–67. Jackson: University Press of Mississippi, 2007.

Guha, Ranajit, ed. *A Subaltern Studies Reader, 1986–1995*. Minneapolis: University of Minnesota Press, 1997.

Hafley, James. "A Reading of *Between the Acts*." In *Virginia Woolf Critical Assessments*, vol. 4, edited by Eleanor McNees, 184–92. Mountfield, UK: Helm Information, Ltd., 1994. Rpt. from *Accent* 13 (Summer 1953): 178–87.

Hai, Ambreen. "'Marching in From the Peripheries': Rushdie's Feminized Artistry and Ambivalent Feminism." In *Critical Essays on Salman Rushdie*, edited by M. Keith Booker, 16–50. New York: G. K. Hall & Co., 1999.

Halbwachs, Maurice. *The Collective Memory*. Translated by Francis J. Ditter, Jr. and Vida Yazdi Ditter. New York: Harper Colophon Books, 1980.

Halkin, Hillel. "Inhuman Comedy." *Commentary* 93.2 (February 1992): 55–56.

Harrison, James. *Salman Rushdie*. New York: Twayne Publishers, 1992.

Harvey, Robert C. *The Art of the Comic Book: An Aesthetic History*. Jackson: University Press of Mississippi, 1996.

Hassumani, Sabrina. *Salman Rushdie: A Postmodern Reading of His Major Works*. Madison, NJ: Fairleigh Dickinson University Press, 2002.

Hatfield, Charles. *Alternative Comics: An Emerging Literature*. Jackson: University Press of Mississippi, 2005.

Hegel, Georg Wilhelm Friedrich. *Hegel's Philosophy of Mind: Being Part Three of the Encyclopedia of the Philosophical Sciences (1830) Together with the Zusätze in Bourmann's Text (1845)*. Translated by William Wallace and A. V. Miller. London: Clarendon Press, 1971.

Higdon, David Leon. "Double Closures in Postmodern British Fiction: The Example of Graham Swift." *Critical Survey* 3.1 (1991): 88–95.

Hilberg, Raul. "I Was Not There." In *Writing and the Holocaust*, edited by Berel Lang, 17–25. New York: Holmes & Meier, 1988.

Hirsch, Marianne. "Family Pictures: *Maus*, Mourning, and Post-Memory." *Discourse* 15.2 (Winter 1992–93): 3–29.

Holmes, Frederick. "The Representation of History as Plastic: The Search for the Real Thing in Graham Swift's *Ever After*." *ARIEL* 27.3 (July 1996): 25–44.
hooks, bell. "Postmodern Blackness." In *The Norton Anthology of Theory and Criticism*, 2478–84. New York: W. W. Norton, 2001.
Humm, Maggie. "Virginia Woolf's Photography and the Monk's House Albums." In *Virginia Woolf in the Age of Mechanical Reproduction*, edited by Pamela Caughie, 219–46. New York: Garland, 2000.
Hussey, Mark. "'I' Rejected; 'We' Substituted: Self and Society in *Between the Acts*." In *Virginia Woolf Critical Assessments*, vol. 4, edited by Eleanor McNees, 242–53. Mountfield, UK: Helm Information, Ltd., 1994. Rpt. from *Reading and Writing Women's Lives: A Study of the Novel of Manners*, edited by Bege K. Bowers and Barbara Bowers, 141–52. Ann Arbor: University of Michigan Press, 1990.
Hutcheon, Linda. *A Poetics of Postmodernism: History, Theory, Fiction*. New York: Routledge, 1988.
———. "The Politics of Postmodern Parody." In *Intertextuality*, ed. Heinrich F. Plett, 225–36. New York: W. de Gruyter, 1991.
———. *The Politics of Postmodernism*. London: Routledge, 1989.
Iadonisi, Rick. "Bleeding History and Owning His (Father's) Story: *Maus* and Collaborative Autobiography." *The CEA Critic* 57.1 (Fall 1994): 41–56.
Irish, Robert K. "About Desire and Narrativity in Graham Swift's *Waterland*." *Modern Fiction Studies* 44.4 (Winter 1998): 916–34.
Jameson, Fredric. *The Political Unconscious: Narrative as a Socially Symbolic Act*. Ithaca, NY: Cornell University Press, 1981.
———. *Postmodernism, Or, The Cultural Logic of Late Capitalism*. Durham, NC: Duke University Press, 1991.
———. *Sartre: The Origins of a Style*. New York: Columbia University Press, 1984.
———. "Third-World Literature in the Era of Multinational Capitalism." 1986. In *The Jameson Reader*, edited by Michael Hardt and Kathi Weeks, 315–39. Malden, MA: Blackwell, 2000.
Jenkins, Keith. *Why History? Ethics and Postmodernity*. New York: Routledge, 1999.
Jenkins, Keith, ed. *The Postmodern History Reader*. New York: Routledge, 1997.
Johnson, Barbara. *A World of Difference*. Baltimore: Johns Hopkins University Press, 2006.
Jones, Bill. "Boundless Schizophrenic World." *American Book Review* 14.6 (February–March 1993): 6–7.
Joplin, Patricia Klindienst. "The Authority of Illusion. Feminism and Fascism in Virginia Woolf's *Between the Acts*." *South Central Review* 6.2 (Summer 1989): 88–104.
Joyce, James. *Ulysses*. New York: Vintage International, 1934.
Kane, Jean M. "The Migrant Intellectual and the Body of History: Salman Rushdie's *Midnight's Children*." *Contemporary Literature* 37.1 (Spring 1996): 94–118.
Katz, Tamar. *Impressionist Subjects: Gender, Interiority, and Modernist Fiction in England*. Urbana: University of Illinois Press, 2000.
Kellner, Hans. "However Imperceptibly: From the Historical to the Sublime." *PMLA* 118.3 (May 2003): 591–96.
Kermode, Frank. *The Sense of an Ending: Studies in the Theory of Fiction with a New Epilogue*. Oxford: Oxford University Press, 2000.
Kingston, Maxine Hong. *Woman Warrior: Memoir of a Girlhood among Ghosts*. 1976.

New York: Vintage, 1989.
Kleberg, Lars. "On the Border: Milan Kundera's *The Book of Laughter and Forgetting*." *Scando-Slavica* 30 (1984): 57–72.
Kolakowski, Leszek. *Bergson.* New York: Oxford University Press, 1985.
Kortenaar, Neil ten. "*Midnight's Children* and the Allegory of History." *ARIEL* 26.2 (April 1995): 41–62.
———. *Self, Nation, Text in Salman Rushdie's* Midnight's Children. Montreal: McGill-Queen's University Press, 2004.
Krishnaswamy, Revathi. "Mythologies of Migrancy: Postcolonialism, Postmodernism, and the Politics of (Dis)location." *ARIEL* 26.1 (January 1995): 125–46.
Kuchta, Todd M. "Allegorizing the Emergency: Rushdie's *Midnight's Children* and Benjamin's Theory of Allegory." In *Critical Essays on Salman Rushdie,* edited by M. Keith Booker, 205–24. New York: G. K. Hall & Co., 1999.
Kuhn, Thomas. *The Structure of Scientific Revolutions.* 2nd ed. Chicago: University of Chicago Press, 1970.
Kundera, Milan. *The Art of the Novel.* Translated by Linda Asher. New York: Harper & Row, 1986.
———. *The Book of Laughter and Forgetting.* Translated by Aaron Asher. New York: HarperCollins, 1996.
———. *Testaments Betrayed: An Essay in Nine Parts.* Translated by Linda Asher. New York: HarperCollins, 1993.
Lacan, Jacques. *Ecrits: A Selection.* Translated by Alan Sheridan. New York: W. W. Norton, 1977.
LaCapra, Dominick. *History and Criticism.* Ithaca, NY: Cornell University Press, 1985.
———. *History and Memory After Auschwitz.* Ithaca, NY: Cornell University Press, 1998.
———. *History in Transit: Experience, Identity, Critical Theory.* Ithaca, NY: Cornell University Press, 2004.
———. *Representing the Holocaust: History, Theory, Trauma.* Ithaca, NY: Cornell University Press, 1994.
———. *Writing History, Writing Trauma.* Baltimore: Johns Hopkins University Press, 2001.
Laclau, Ernesto. "Deconstruction, Pragmatism, Hegemony." In *Deconstruction and Pragmatism,* edited by Chantal Mouffe, 47–68. London: Routledge, 1996.
Laga, Barry. "*Maus,* Holocaust, and History: Redrawing the Frame." *Arizona Quarterly* 57.1 (Spring 2001): 61–90.
Landow, George P. "History, His Story, and Stories in Graham Swift's *Waterland.*" *Studies in the Literary Imagination* 23.2 (Fall 1990): 197–212.
Lane, Christopher. "The Poverty of Context: Historicism and Non-Mimetic Fiction." *PMLA* 118.3 (May 2003): 450–69.
Lang, Berel. *Holocaust Representation: Art within the Limits of History and Ethics.* Baltimore: Johns Hopkins University Press, 2000.
Lang, Berel, ed. *Writing and the Holocaust.* New York: Holmes & Meier, 1988.
Lanser, Susan Sniader. *Fictions of Authority: Women Writers and Narrative Voice.* Ithaca, NY: Cornell University Press, 1992.
Laurence, Patricia. *The Reading of Silence: Virginia Woolf in the English Tradition.* Stanford, CA: Stanford University Press, 1992.

Lea, Daniel. *Graham Swift*. Manchester: Manchester University Press, 2006.
Lee, Alison. *Realism and Power: Postmodern British Fiction*. London: Routledge, 1990.
Lee, Hermione. *Virginia Woolf*. New York: Alfred A. Knopf, 1997.
Lee, Jonathan Scott. *Jacques Lacan*. Boston: G. K. Hall & Co., 1990.
Lehman, Daniel W. *Matters of Fact: Reading Nonfiction over the Edge*. Columbus: Ohio State University Press, 1997.
Levinas, Emmanuel. "Bad Conscience and the Inexorable." In *Face to Face with Levinas*, edited by Richard A. Cohen, 35–40. Albany: State University of New York Press, 1986.
——. *Nine Talmudic Writings*. Translated by A. Aronowicz. Bloomington: Indiana University Press, 1990.
——. *Otherwise than Being or Beyond Essence*. Translated by Alphonso Lingis. Boston: Kluwer, 1978.
Levine, Michael G. "Necessary Stains: Art Spiegelman's *Maus* and the Bleeding of History." In *Considering* Maus: *Approaches to Art Spiegelman's 'Survivor's Tale' of the Holocaust*, edited by Deborah Geis, 63–104. Tuscaloosa: University of Alabama Press, 2003.
Lipscomb, David. "Caught in a Strange Middle Ground: Contesting History in Salman Rushdie's *Midnight's Children*." *Diaspora* 1.2 (Fall 1991): 163–89.
Lipstadt, Deborah E. *Denying the Holocaust: The Growing Assault on Truth and Memory*. New York: The Free Press, 1993.
Little, Judy. "Festive Comedy in Woolf's *Between the Acts*." *Women and Literature* 5 (Spring 1977): 26–37.
Locke, John. *An Essay Concerning Human Understanding*. 2 vols. Edited by John W. Yolton. New York: Dutton, 1961.
Lodge, David. "Milan Kundera and the Idea of the Author in Modern Criticism." *Critical Quarterly* 26.1–2 (1984): 105–21.
Lopate, Phillip. "Resistance to the Holocaust." *Tikkun* (May–June 1989): 55–65.
Lounsberry, Barbara. *The Art of Fact: Contemporary Artists of Nonfiction*. New York: Greenwood, 1990.
Lyotard, Jean-François. *Le Différend*. Paris: Minuit, 1983.
——. *The Postmodern Condition: A Report on Knowledge*. Translated by Geoff Bennington and Brian Massumi, 71–82. Minneapolis: University of Minnesota Press, 1984.
——. *The Postmodern Explained to Children*. London: Turnaround, 1992.
Mackay, Marina. "Putting the House in Order: Virginia Woolf and Blitz Modernism." *Modern Language Quarterly* 66.2 (June 2005): 227–52.
Madison, Gary B., and Marty Fairbarn, eds. *The Ethics of Postmodernity: Current Trends in Continental Thought*. Evanston, IL: Northwestern University Press, 1999.
Malcolm, David. *Understanding Graham Swift*. Columbia: University of South Carolina Press, 2003.
Mann, Harveen Sachdeva. "'Being Borne Across': Translation and Salman Rushdie's *The Satanic Verses*." *Criticism* 37.2 (Spring 1995): 281–308.
Marcus, Jane. *Hearts of Darkness: White Women Write Race*. New Brunswick, NJ: Rutgers University Press, 2004.
——. "Liberty, Sorority, Misogyny." In *Virginia Woolf and the Languages of Patri-*

archy, 75–95. Bloomington: Indiana University Press, 1987.
———. *Virginia Woolf and the Languages of Patriarchy*. Bloomington: Indiana University Press, 1987.
Marcus, Jane, ed. *New Feminist Essays on Virginia Woolf*. Lincoln: University of Nebraska Press, 1981.
———. *Virginia Woolf and Bloomsbury: A Centenary Celebration*. Bloomington: Indiana University Press, 1987.
———. *Virginia Woolf: A Feminist Slant*. Lincoln: University of Nebraska Press, 1983.
Marder, Herbert. "Alienation Effects: Dramatic Satire in Between the Acts." *Papers on Language and Literature* 24.4 (Fall 1988): 423–35.
Márquez, Gabriel García. *One Hundred Years of Solitude*. 1970. Translated by Gregory Rabassa. New York: HarperPerennial Classics, 1998. Published originally in Spanish as *Cien Años de Soledad* in 1967.
Martel, Yann. *Life of Pi*. Orlando, FL: Harcourt, 2001.
McCloud, Scott. *Understanding Comics: The Invisible Art*. New York: HarperCollins, 1993.
McEwan, Ian. *Atonement*. New York: Doubleday, 2001.
———. *Saturday*. New York: Nan A. Talese, 2005.
McGlothlin, Erin. "No Time Like the Present: Narrative and Time in Art Spiegelman's *Maus*." *Narrative* 11.2 (May 2003): 177–98.
McHale, Brian. *Postmodernist Fiction*. New York: Methuen, 1987.
McKinney, Ronald. "The Greening of Postmodernism: Graham Swift's *Waterland*." *New Literary History* 28.4 (Autumn 1997): 821–32.
McLaurin, Allen. *Virginia Woolf: The Echoes Enslaved*. Cambridge: Cambridge University Press, 1973.
McWhirter, David. "The Novel, The Play, and the Book: *Between the Acts* and the Tragicomedy of History." *English Literary History* 60 (1993): 787–812.
Melas, Natalie. "Forgettable Vacations and Metaphor in Ruins." *Callaloo* 28.1 (2005): 147–68.
Merivale, Patricia. "Saleem Fathered by Oskar: *Midnight's Children*, Magic Realism, and *The Tin Drum*." In *Magical Realism: Theory, History, Community*, edited by Lois Parkinson Zamora and Wendy B. Faris, 329–46. Durham, NC: Duke University Press, 1995.
Miller, D. A. *Narrative and Its Discontents: Problems of Closure in the Traditional Novel*. Princeton, NJ: Princeton University Press, 1981.
———. *The Novel and the Police*. Berkeley: University of California Press, 1988.
Miller, J. Hillis. *The Ethics of Reading: Kant, de Man, Eliot, Trollope, James, and Benjamin*. New York: Columbia University Press, 1987.
Miller, Nancy K. "Cartoons of the Self: Portrait of the Artist as a Young Murderer—Art Spiegelman's *Maus*." In *Considering* Maus: *Approaches to Art Spiegelman's 'Survivor's Tale' of the Holocaust*, edited by Deborah Geis, 44–62. Tuscaloosa: University of Alabama Press, 2003.
Mink, Louis O. *Historical Understanding*. Edited by Brian Fay, Eugene O. Golob, and Richard T. Vann. Ithaca, NY: Cornell University Press, 1987.
Molesworth, Charles. "Kundera and *The Book:* The Unsaid and the Unsayable." In *Milan Kundera and the Art of Fiction*, edited by Aron Aji, 231–47. New York: Garland Publishing, 1992.
Mordden, Ethan. "Kat and Maus." *The New Yorker*, 6 April 1992, 90–96.

Moss, Laura. "'Forget those Damnfool Realists!' Salman Rushdie's Self-Parody as the Magical Realist's 'Last Sigh.'" *ARIEL* 29.4 (October 1998): 121-40.
Mullarkey, John. *Bergson and Philosophy*. Notre Dame, IN: University of Notre Dame Press, 2000.
Murdoch, Iris. *Existentialists and Mystics: Writings on Philosophy and Literature*. New York: Penguin, 1998.
Murphy Sean. "In the Middle of Nowhere: The Interpellative Force of Experimental Narrative Structure in Graham Swift's *Waterland*." *Studies in the Humanities* 23.1 (June 1996): 70-83.
Naipaul, V. S. "My Brother's Tragic Sense." *Spectator* 258 (January 1987): 22-23.
Needham, Anurandha Dingwaney. "The Politics of Post-Colonial Identity in Rushdie." In *Reading Rushdie: Perspectives on the Fiction of Salman Rushdie*, edited by M. D. Fletcher, 145-57. Amsterdam: Rodopi, 1994.
Nickles, Thomas, ed. *Thomas Kuhn*. Cambridge: Cambridge University Press, 2002.
Nietzsche, Friedrich. "On the Uses and Disadvantages of History for Life." In *Untimely Meditations,* edited by Daniel Breazeale, translated by R. J. Hollingdale, 59-123. New York: Cambridge University Press, 1997.
———. "On Truth and Lie in An Extra-Moral Sense." In *The Portable Nietzsche*, 42-47. 1873. Translated by Walter Kaufmann. New York: The Viking Press, 1954.
Nora, Pierre. "Between Memory and History: Les Lieux de Mémoire." *Representations* 26 (Spring 1989): 7-25.
Novick, Peter. *The Holocaust in American Life*. Boston: Houghton Mifflin, 1999.
———. *That Noble Dream: The "Objectivity Question" and the American Historical Profession*. Cambridge: Cambridge University Press, 1988.
Nussbaum, Martha. *Love's Knowledge: Essays on Philosophy and Literature*. New York: Oxford University Press, 1990.
Orvell, Miles. "Writing Posthistorically: *Krazy Kat, Maus,* and the Contemporary Fiction Cartoon." *American Literary History* 4.1 (Spring 1992): 110-40.
Oxindine, Annette. "Rhoda Submerged: Lesbian Suicide in *The Waves*." In *Virginia Woolf: Lesbian Readings*, edited by Eileen Barrett and Patricia Cramer, 203-21. New York: New York University Press, 1997.
Parameswaran, Uma. *The Perforated Sheet: Essays on Salman Rushdie's Art*. Delhi: Affiliated East-West Press, 1988.
Parker, David. *Ethics, Theory, and the Novel*. Cambridge: Cambridge University Press, 1994.
Patchay, Sheena. "Re-Telling Histories in *The Unbearable Lightness of Being* and *The Book of Laughter and Forgetting*." *Journal of Literary Studies* 14.3-4 (December 1998): 245-52.
Pavel, Thomas. *Fictional Worlds*. Cambridge, MA: Harvard University Press, 1989.
Pawlowski, Merry M., ed. *Virginia Woolf and Fascism: Resisting the Dictators' Seduction*. New York: Palgrave, 2001.
Pearson, Keith Ansell, and John Mullarkey. "Introduction." In *Henri Bergson: Key Writings*, 1-48. New York: Continuum, 2002.
Petrovic, Lena. "Hear the Voice of the Artist: Postmodernism as Faustian Bargain." In *Beyond Postmodernism: Reassessments in Literature, Theory, and Culture*, edited by Klaus Stierstorfer, 51-76. New York: Walter de Gruyter, 2003.
Phelan, James. "Narrative Judgment and the Rhetorical Theory of Narrative: Ian McEwan's *Atonement*." In *A Companion to Narrative Theory*, edited by James

Phelan and Peter J. Rabinowitz, 322–36. Malden, MA: Blackwell, 2005.

———. *Reading People, Reading Plots.* Chicago: University of Chicago Press, 1989.

Píchová, Hana. *The Art of Memory in Exile: Vladimir Nabokov and Milan Kundera.* Carbondale, IL: Southern Illinois University Press, 2002.

Poole, Adrian. "Graham Swift and the Mourning After." In *An Introduction to Contemporary Fiction*, edited by Rod Mengham, 150–67. Cambridge: Polity Press, 1999.

Price, David W. *History Made, History Imagined: Contemporary Literature, Poiesis, and the Past.* Urbana: University of Illinois Press, 1999.

———. "Salman Rushdie's 'Use and Abuse of History' in *Midnight's Children*." *ARIEL* 25.2 (April 1994): 91–108.

Prince, Gerald. *A Dictionary of Narratology.* Lincoln: University of Nebraska Press, 1987.

———. "The Disnarrated." *Style* 22.1 (1987): 1–8.

Proust, Marcel. *Swann's Way.* 1913. Translated by Lydia Davis. New York: Penguin, 2004.

Ranke, Leopold von. *The Secret of World History: Selected Writings on the Art and Science of History.* Edited by Roger Wines. New York: Fordham University Press, 1981.

Reder, Michael. "Rewriting History and Identity: The Reinvention of Myth, Epic, and Allegory in Salman Rushdie's *Midnight's Children*. In *Critical Essays on Salman Rushdie*, edited by M. Keith Booker, 225–49. New York: G. K. Hall & Co., 1999.

Rege, Josna E. "Victim into Protagonist? *Midnight's Children* and the Post-Rushdie National Narratives of the Eighties." In *Critical Essays on Salman Rushdie*, edited by M. Keith Booker, 250–82. New York: G. K. Hall & Co., 1999.

Richardson, Brian. *Narrative Dynamics: Essays on Plot, Time, Closure, and Frames.* Columbus: Ohio State University Press, 2002.

Rickard, John S. *Joyce's Book of Memory: The Mnemotechnic of Ulysses.* Durham, NC: Duke University Press, 1999.

Ricoeur, Paul. *Time and Narrative.* 3 Vols. Translated by Kathleen Blarney and David Pellauer. Chicago: University of Chicago Press, 1988.

Riffaterre, Michael. *Fictional Truth.* Baltimore: Johns Hopkins University Press, 1990.

Rigney, Ann. *Imperfect Histories: The Elusive Past and the Legacy of Romantic Historicism.* Ithaca, NY: Cornell University Press, 2001.

Rorty, Richard. *Contingency, Irony, and Solidarity.* Cambridge: Cambridge University Press, 1989.

———. "Nineteenth-Century Idealism and Twentieth-Century Textualism." In *Consequences of Pragmatism: Essays, 1972–1980*, 139–59. Minneapolis: University of Minnesota Press, 1982.

Rothberg, Michael. "'We Were Talking Jewish': Art Spiegelman's *Maus* as 'Holocaust' Production." *Contemporary Literature* 35.4 (Winter 1994): 661–87.

Ruotolo, Lucio P. *The Interrupted Moment: A View of Virginia Woolf's Novels.* Stanford, CA: Stanford University Press, 1986.

Rushdie, Salman. *The Ground Beneath Her Feet.* New York: Henry Holt and Co., 1999.

———. *Imaginary Homelands: Essays and Criticism, 1981–1991.* London: Granta Books, 1991.

———. *Midnight's Children.* 1981. New York: Penguin Books, 1991.

———. "*Midnight's Children* and *Shame*." *Kunapipi* 7.1 (1985): 1–19.
———. *The Moor's Last Sigh*. New York: Vintage Books, 1995.
———. *Satanic Verses*. New York: Henry Holt and Co., 1988.
———. *Shame*. New York: Henry Holt and Co., 1983.
———. *Step Across This Line: Collected Nonfiction 1992–2002*. New York: The Modern Library, 2003.
Said, Edward. *Orientalism*. New York: Random House, 1978.
———. "Zionism from the Standpoint of Its Victims." In *Anatomy of Racism*, edited by David Theo Goldberg, 210–46. Minneapolis: University of Minnesota Press, 1990.
Salami, Mahmoud. *John Fowles' Fiction and the Poetics of Postmodernism*. Rutherford, NJ: Fairleigh Dickinson University Press, 1992.
Sanga, Jaina C. *Salman Rushdie's Postcolonial Metaphors: Migration, Translation, Hybridity, Blasphemy, and Globalization*. Westport, CT: Greenwood Press, 2001.
Sarker, Sonita. "*Three Guineas*, the In-corporated Intellectual, and Nostalgia for the Human." In *Virginia Woolf in the Age of Mechanical Reproduction*, edited by Pamela Caughie, 37–66. New York: Garland Publishing, 2000.
Schad, John. "The End of the End of History: Graham Swift's *Waterland*." *Modern Fiction Studies* 38.4 (Winter 1992): 911–26.
Scholes, Robert. *Fabulation and Metafiction*. Urbana: University of Illinois Press, 1979.
Scott, Bonnie Kime. "The Word Split Its Husk: Woolf's Double Vision of Modernist Language." *Modernist Fiction Studies* 34.3 (Autumn 1988): 371–85.
Sears, Sallie. "Theater of War: Virginia Woolf's *Between the Acts*." In *Virginia Woolf: A Feminist Slant*, edited by Jane Marcus, 212–35. Lincoln: University of Nebraska Press, 1983.
Seeskin, Kenneth. "Coming to Terms with Failure: A Philosophical Dilemma." In *Writing and the Holocaust*, edited by Berel Lang, 110–21. New York: Holmes & Meier, 1988.
Shepherd, Ron. "*Midnight's Children* as Fantasy." In *The Novels of Salman Rushdie*, edited by G. R. Taneja and R. K. Dhawan, 33–43. New Delhi: Indian Society for Commonwealth Studies, 1992.
Sicher, Efraim. *Breaking Crystal: Memory and Writing After Auschwitz*. Champaign: University of Illinois Press, 1997.
Spiegel, Gabrielle. *The Past as Text: The Theory and Practice of Medieval Historiography*. Baltimore: Johns Hopkins University Press, 1997.
Spiegelman, Art. *Breakdowns*. 1977. New York: Pantheon Books, 2008.
———. *Maus: A Survivor's Tale: My Father Bleeds History (Mid-1930s to Winter 1944)*. New York: Pantheon Books, 1986.
———. *Maus II: A Survivor's Tale: And Here My Troubles Began (From Mauschwitz to the Catskills and Beyond)*. New York: Pantheon Books, 1991.
———. "A Problem of Taxonomy." *New York Times Book Review*, 29 December 1991, 4.
Spivak, Gayatri Chakravorty. "Can the Subaltern Speak?" In *Marxism and the Interpretation of Culture*, edited by Cary Nelson and Lawrence Grossberg, 271–312. Urbana: University of Illinois Press, 1988.
———. "Subaltern Studies: Deconstructing Historiography." In *Subaltern Studies IV*, 330–63. Delhi: Oxford University Press, 1986.

Srivastava, Aruna. "'The Empire Writes Back': Language and History in *Shame* and *Midnight's Children.*" *ARIEL* 20.4 (October 1989): 62–78.
Staub, Michael E. "The Shoah Goes On and On: Remembrance and Representation in Art Spiegelman's *Maus.*" *Melus* 20.3 (Fall 1995): 33–46.
Steiner, George. *Language and Silence: Essays on Language, Literature, and the Inhuman.* New York: Atheneum, 1967.
Stern, Kenneth S. *Holocaust Denial.* New York: The American Jewish Committee, 1993.
Stone, Lawrence. "The Revival of Narrative." *Past and Present* 85 (1979): 3–24.
Stoppard, Tom. *Arcadia.* London: Faber and Faber, Limited, 1993.
Strand, Eric. "Gandhian Communalism and the Midnight Children's Conference." *ELH* 72 (2005): 975–1016.
Straus, Nina Pelikan. "Erasing History and Deconstructing the Text: *The Book of Laughter and Forgetting.*" *Milan Kundera and the Art of Fiction,* edited by Aron Aji, 248–66. New York: Garland Publishing, 1992.
Su, John J. "Epic of Failure: Disappointment as Utopian Fantasy in *Midnight's Children.*" *Twentieth Century Literature* 47.4 (Winter 2001): 545–68.
Swift, Graham. *Ever After.* New York: Vintage International, 1993.
——. *Last Orders.* New York: Vintage, 1997.
——. *Out of This World.* London: Penguin, 1988.
——. *Shuttlecock.* London: Allen Lane, 1981.
——. *The Sweet Shop Owner.* London: Heinemann, 1980.
——. *Tomorrow.* New York: Vintage, 2008.
——. *Waterland.* New York: Vintage, 1983.
Tabachnick, Stephen E. "The Religious Meaning of Art Spiegelman's *Maus.*" *Shofar: An Interdisciplinary Journal of Jewish Studies* 22.4 (Summer 2004): 1–13.
Tange, Hanne. "Regional Redemption: Graham Swift's *Waterland* and the End of History." *Orbis Litterarum* 59 (2004): 75–89.
Terdiman, Richard. *Present Past: Modernity and the Memory Crisis.* Ithaca, NY: Cornell University Press, 1993.
Thomas, D. M. *The White Hotel.* New York: Simon & Schuster, 1981.
Todd, Richard. "Narrative Trickery and Performative Historiography: Fictional Representation of National Identity in Graham Swift, Peter Carey, and Mordechai Richler." In *Magical Realism: Theory, History, Community,* edited by Lois Parkinson Zamora and Wendy B. Faris, 305–28. Durham, NC: Duke University Press, 1995.
Todorov, Tzvetan. *Introduction to Poetics.* Translated by Richard Howard. Minneapolis: University of Minnesota Press, 1981.
Trevelyan, George Macaulay. *History of England.* 2nd ed. New York: Longman's, Green and Co., 1942.
Trousdale, Rachel. "'City of Mongrel Joy': Bombay and the Shiv Sena in *Midnight's Children* and *The Moor's Last Sigh.*" *Journal of Commonwealth Literature* 39.2 (2004): 95–110.
Vandivere, Julie. "Waves and Fragments: Linguistic Construction as Subject Formation in Virginia Woolf." *Twentieth Century Literature* 42.2 (Summer 1996): 221–33.
Vidal-Naquet, Pierre. *Assassins of Memory: Essays on the Denial of the Holocaust.* Translated by Jeffrey Mehlman. New York: Columbia University Press, 1992.

Walcott, Derek. "The Caribbean: Culture or Mimicry." *Journal of Interamerican Studies and World Affairs* 16.1 (February 1974): 3–13.

———. "The Muse of History." In *Is Massa Day Dead? Black Moods in the Caribbean*, edited by Orde Coombs, 1–27. New York: Doubleday, 1974.

———. *Omeros*. New York: Farrar, Strauss, and Giroux, 1990.

Wallace, Honor McKitrick. "Desire and the Female Protagonist: A Critique of Feminist Narrative Theory." *Style* 34.2 (Summer 2000): 176–85.

Walsh, Richard. "Fictionality and Mimesis: Between Narrativity and Fictional Worlds." *Narrative* 11.1 (January 2003): 110–21.

Warhol, Robyn. "Guilty Cravings: What Feminist Narratology Can Do for Cultural Studies." In *Narratologies: New Perspectives on Narrative Analysis*, edited by David Herman, 340–55. Columbus: Ohio State University Press, 1999.

———. "Neonarrative; or, How to Render the Unnarratable in Realist Fiction and Contemporary Film." In *A Companion to Narrative Theory*, edited by James Phelan and Peter J. Rabinowitz, 220–231. Malden, MA: Blackwell, 2005.

Watkins, Renée. "Survival in Discontinuity—Virginia Woolf's *Between the Acts*." *The Massachusetts Review* 10 (Spring 1969): 356–76.

Waugh, Patricia. *Feminine Fictions: Revisiting the Postmodern*. London: Routledge, 1989.

Wells, Lynn. *Allegories of Telling: Self-Referential Narrative in Contemporary British Fiction*. New York: Rodopi, 2003.

Westman, Karin. "'For Her Generation The Newspaper Was A Book': Media, Mediation, and Oscillation in Virginia Woolf's *Between the Acts*." *Journal of Modern Literature* 29.2 (Winter 2006): 1–18.

Wheeler, Wendy. "Melancholic Modernity and Contemporary Grief: The Novels of Graham Swift." In *Literature and the Contemporary: Fictions and Theories of the Present*, edited by Roger Luckhurst and Peter Marks, 63–79. Harlow: Longman, 1999.

White, Hayden. "The Burden of History." In *Tropics of Discourse*, 27–50. Baltimore: Johns Hopkins University Press, 1978.

———. *The Content of the Form*. Baltimore: Johns Hopkins University Press, 1987.

———. *Figural Realism: Studies in the Mimesis Effect*. Baltimore: Johns Hopkins University Press, 1999.

———. "Historical Emplotment and the Problem of Truth." In *Probing the Limits of Representation*, edited by Saul Friedlander, 37–53. Cambridge, MA: Harvard University Press, 1992.

———. "The Historical Text as Literary Artifact." In *Tropics of Discourse*, 81–100. Baltimore: Johns Hopkins University Press, 1978.

———. *Metahistory: The Historical Imagination in Nineteenth-Century Europe*. Baltimore: Johns Hopkins University Press, 1973.

———. "The Modernist Event." In *Figural Realism: Studies in the Mimesis Effect*, 66–86. Baltimore: Johns Hopkins University Press, 1999.

———. *Tropics of Discourse*. Baltimore: Johns Hopkins University Press, 1978.

———. "The Value of Narrativity in the Representation of Reality." In *On Narrative*, edited by W. J. T. Mitchell, 1–23. Chicago: University of Chicago Press, 1981.

Wiesel, Elie. "The Holocaust as Literary Inspiration." *Dimensions of the Holocaust*. Evanston, IL: Northwestern University Press, 1977.

Wiley, Catherine. "Making History Unrepeatable in Virginia Woolf's *Between the*

Acts." *Clio* 25.1 (Fall 1995): 3–20.
Wilkomirski, Benjamin. *Fragments: Memoirs of A War-Time Childhood.* New York: Schocken Books, 1995.
Wilner, Arlene Fish. "'Happy, Happy Ever After': Story and History in Art Spiegelman's *Maus.*" *Journal of Narrative Technique* 27.2 (Spring 1997): 171–89.
Wilson, Keith. "*Midnight's Children* and Reader Responsibility." *Critical Quarterly* 26.3 (Autumn 1984): 23–37.
Winnett, Susan. "Coming Unstrung: Women, Men, Narrative, and the Principles of Pleasure." *PMLA* 105.3 (May 1990): 505–518.
Winterson, Jeanette. *Lighthousekeeping.* Orlando, FL: Harcourt, 2004.
———. *Sexing the Cherry.* New York: Grove Press, 1989.
Witek, Joseph. *Comic Books as History: The Narrative Art of Jack Jackson, Art Spiegelman, and Harvey Pekar.* Jackson: University Press of Mississippi, 1989.
Wolpert, Stanley. *A New History of India.* 4th ed. New York: Oxford University Press, 1993.
Woolf, Virginia. *Between the Acts.* 1940. New York: Harvest, 1970.
———. *The Complete Shorter Fiction of Virginia Woolf.* 2nd ed. Edited by Susan Dick. Orlando, FL: Harcourt, 1989.
———. *The Diary of Virginia Woolf: Volume V: 1936–1941.* Edited by Ann Olivier Bell. London: The Hogarth Press, 1984.
———. *The Letters of Virginia Woolf.* Eds. Nigel Nicolson and Joanne Troutman. 6 vols. London: The Hogarth Press, 1975–1980.
———. "Modern Fiction." *Collected Essays.* Vol. II, 103–10. New York: Harcourt, Brace & World, Inc., 1967.
———. *Moments of Being.* 2nd ed. Edited by Jeanne Schulkind. New York: Harvest, 1985.
———. "Mr. Bennett and Mrs. Brown." *Collected Essays.* Vol. I, 319–37. New York: Harcourt, Brace & World, 1967.
———. *Mrs. Dalloway.* 1925. New York: Harcourt, 1953.
———. "The Narrow Bridge of Art." *Collected Essays.* Vol. II, 218–29. New York: Harcourt, Brace & World, 1967.
———. *Orlando: A Biography.* 1928. Orlando, FL: Harcourt, 1956.
———. "Phases of Fiction." *Collected Essays.* Vol. II, 56–102. New York: Harcourt, Brace & World, 1967.
———. *Pointz Hall: The Earlier and Later Typescripts of* Between the Acts. Edited by Mitchell A. Leaska. New York: University Publications, 1983.
———. *A Room of One's Own.* 1929. Orlando, FL: Harcourt, 1989.
———. *Three Guineas.* 1938. Orlando, FL: Harcourt, 1966.
———. *The Voyage Out.* 1915. New York: The Modern Library, 2001.
———. *The Waves.* 1931. New York: Harcourt, 1959.
———. *To the Lighthouse.* 1927. New York: Harcourt Brace & Co., 1951.
———. "Women and Fiction." *Collected Essays.* Vol. II, 141–48. New York: Harcourt, Brace, & World, 1967.
———. *The Years.* 1937. Orlando, FL: Harcourt, 1965.
Wyschogrod, Edith. *An Ethics of Remembering: History, Heterology, and the Nameless Others.* Chicago: University of Chicago Press, 1998.
Young, James. "The Holocaust as Vicarious Past: Art Spiegelman's *Maus* and the Afterimages of History." *Critical Inquiry* 24.3 (Spring 1998): 666–99.

———. *Writing and Rewriting the Holocaust: Narrative and the Consequences of Interpretation.* Bloomington: Indiana University Press, 1988.
Žižek, Slavoj. "Class Struggle or Postmodernism? Yes Please!" *Contingency, Hegemony, Universality: Contemporary Dialogues on the Left.* New York: Verso, 2000.
———. *Enjoy Your Symptom! Jacques Lacan in Hollywood and Out.* New York: Routledge, 1992.
———. *The Sublime Object of Ideology.* New York: Verso, 1989.
Zwerdling, Alex. "*Between the Acts* and the Coming of War." *Novel* 10 (1977): 220–36.
———. *Virginia Woolf and the Real World.* Berkeley: University of California Press, 1986.

INDEX

1,001 Nights. See *Arabian Nights*
Abdullah, Sheikh Mohammed, 122, 209n18
Adorno, Theodor, 150, 200n2, 212n8,
Ahmad, Aijaz, 119
Ames, Christopher, 46, 69, 201n7, 204n37,
Amritsar Massacre, 115, 140, 144, 189, 208n9
Ankersmit, Frank, 10, 13, 25, 37, 145, 147–48, 152–55, 163–64, 166–67, 169, 174–76, 178–81, 184–86, 196, 199n14, 213n10, 214–15n24, 216n32. See also *History and Tropology*; *Sublime Historical Experience*
annals. *See* nonnarrative, modes of history
Antigone (Sophocles), 204n34
antinarrative, 22, 26, 37–38, 64, 72, 80, 90–94, 100, 102, 109, 139, 169, 171, 174, 196; defined, 23–24. See also here and now; moments of being; nonnarrative; trauma
Arabian Nights, 122, 128, 136, 210n25
Arcadia (Stoppard), 188
The Archaeology of Knowledge (Foucault), 11, 73, 205n44
Aristotle, 52–53, 56, 75–76, 153–54, 164, 175, 177, 180, 185
Aspects of the Novel (Forster), 12–14
Atonement (McEwan), 190–94, 196, 216n1
Attenborough, Richard, 141, 208n9
"Attenborough's *Gandhi*" (Rushdie), 141–42, 208n9, 210n37
Aurora, Jagjit Singh, 210n29
Auschwitz, 150, 162, 214n20

Bahl, Vinay, 134–35
Banfield, Ann, 60–62, 202–3n23
Banville, John, 189
Barnes, Julian, 189. See also *History of the World in 10 ½ Chapters*
Barth, John, 197n2
Barthes, Roland, 86, 212n6; and history 9–12, 150, 211n40; and myth 86, 198n8, 211n40; and narrative (plot), 23, 53, 96, 198n8, 203n27; and "reality effects" 203n25. See also "The Discourse of History"; *Mythologies*; *The Pleasure of the Text*; *S/Z*
Batty, Nancy, 116, 210n5

Baudrillard, Jean, 5-6
Beard, Charles, 194-95, 198n7
Becker, Carl, 194-95, 198n7
Beckett, Samuel, 162, 179, 190. See also *Molloy*
Beer, Gillian, 202n17
Bell, Julian, 201n3
Benjamin, Walter, 5-6; and history, 77, 82-83, 206n12. See also "The Work of Art in the Age of Mechanical Reproduction"; "Theses on the Philosophy of History"
Bennett, Arnold, 200n3
Benyei, Támas, 205n2
Bergson, Henri, 39, 59-65, 71-72, 194, 203nn28-31. See also *Matter and Memory; Time and Free Will*
Berkhofer, Robert, 197n5
Bernard, Catherine, 207n24
Bernasconi, Robert, 33
Between the Acts (Woolf), 24, 37, 39-53, 56-60, 62-78, 81, 102, 107, 109-10, 144, 183-84, 188, 194, 200n1, 201nn5-8, 201n10, 201n13, 202nn15-18, 202nn10-21, 203nn25-27, 203n30, 204n32, 204nn35-39, 204n41, 205n45, 207-8n29
Bhabha, Homi, 119-20
Birkenau, 211n1
Bloomsbury, 40, 200n2
The Book of Laughter and Forgetting, 1-3, 7-9, 11, 16-22, 34-36, 183, 196, 197n1, 198nn11-12
Booker, M. Keith, 135, 208n10, 209-10n23
Borges, Jorge Luis, 29
Bosmajian, Hamida, 212n2, 214n20, 215n25
Boyarin, Jonathan, 163
Brazil (Gilliam), 125
Brecht, Berthold, 108, 201n10
Brennan, Timothy, 144, 208n6, 208-9n10, 210nn32-33, 211n42
Brooks, Peter, 23, 53, 80, 94-98, 136, 171, 203n27

Brown, Joshua, 172, 212n3, 216n33
"The Burden of History" (White), 21-22
Butler, Judith, 26-27, 29, 33-34. See also "Ethical Ambivalence"
Butz, Arthur, 149, 212n7
Byatt, A. S., 207n26. See also *Possession*

Cage, John, 50, 202n21
"Can the Subaltern Speak?" (Spivak), 143, 199n15, 210n31, 215n24
capitalism, 80-83, 116, 118, 135, 162, 214n19; and postmodernism, 5, 202n21. See also colonialism; Marxism
Carr, David, 28, 53, 75, 79
Caroll, David, 113
Carter, Angela, 188-89. See also *The Infernal Desire Machines of Doctor Hoffman; Nights at the Circus*
Caruth, Cathy, 199n17
Caughie, Pamela, 51, 201n5, 202n21
Certeau, Michel de; and history, 10-11, 28, 88-90
Chakrabarty, Dipesh, 134-35
Charlson, Joshua, 173, 212n3, 213-14n18
Christianity, 94-95, 97, 99-100, 104-5, 130, 140-42
Chronicles. See nonnarrative, modes of history
Churchill, Caryl, 188. See also *Cloud 9*
class, social, 33, 37, 78, 80, 83, 86, 88, 99, 103, 107, 127-28, 130, 134-35, 138, 140, 143-44, 152, 210n26, 210n3. See also Marxism
Clementis, Vladimír, 1-2, 11-12, 16-17
closure; death as, 169-70; narrative, 22-24, 54, 82, 110, 136-38, 167-70, 190, 215n26. See also narrative; process; teleology
Cloud 9 (Churchill), 188
Coetzee, J. M., 189
Cohen, Arthur, 150
Cohn, Dorritt, 184. See also *The Distinction of Fiction*

colonialism, 45–46, 54–55, 69, 74, 80–83, 85–86, 88, 103, 115–16, 134, 188, 195, 203n24, 208n8, 211n38, 215n24; and postcolonialism, 84, 117–20, 122, 124, 133–34, 141–43, 199n15, 211n42
comics, 145–46, 160, 166–67, 173, 196, 212n3, 212–13n8, 213n11, 215n29, 216n33
communism: in Czechoslovakia, 1–3, 11, 16, 22, 34, 183
consciousness, individual. *See* subjectivity
constructivist historiography. *See* historiography, postmodern
Coulanges, Fusel de, 10
Course in General Linguistics (Saussure), 4
Craps, Stef, 200n21, 205n2, 207nn24–25
Critchley, Simon, 48, 200n22, 201n9
curiosity. *See* narrative, as desire

Darwin, Charles, 104–6
Dasenbrock, Reed Way, 73–74, 205n44
Davidson, Donald, 74
Debord, Guy, 5
deconstruction. *See* Derrida, Jacques; poststructuralism
Decoste, Damon, 205n2, 206n15, 207n20
Deiman, Werner, 39
Deleuze, Gilles, 38, 61, 203n28
Delillo, Don, 189. *See also Underworld*
De Man, Paul, 27, 117, 119–21, 149–50, 199n20. *See also* "The Epistemology of Metaphor"
Derrida, Jacques, 4–5, 9, 45, 48, 150, 153–154, 165–66, 170, 174, 176, 179, 212n6; and ethics, 26–27, 31–32, 199n18, 199–200n20, 201n9; and time, 71–72, 204n42. *See also* "Force of Law"; *Of Grammatology*; *The Gift of Death; Limited Inc.*; "*Ousia* and *Grammé*"; "Plato's Pharmacy"; "Violence and Metaphysics"

Descartes, René, 151–52, 186, 213n10
Dick, Philip K. 189. *See also The Man in the High Castle*
Discipline and Punish (Foucault), 11, 205n44
Dictionary of Narratology (Prince), 14
Dirlik, Arif, 134–35
"The Discourse of History" (Barthes), 9–12, 198n8
the disnarrated, 25, 112–13, 124, 139–40, 172, 192, 208n2; defined, 110. *See also* errata; narrative, leftovers of
Disney, Walt, 214n19
The Distinction of Fiction (Cohn), 184
Doctorow, E. L., 189
Dubrow, Heather, 203n27
DuPlessis, Rachel Blau, 202n16
Dyer, Reginald (General), 115, 208n9

Ecrits (Lacan), 69–71
Einstein, Albert, 5, 62, 188, 194
Elkana, Yehuda, 159
Eliot, T. S., 43, 200n2
Ellis, Marc, 159
the Emergency, 115, 126, 131, 140, 144, 189, 208nn7–8
The Empire Writes Back (Ashcroft, Griffiths, and Tiffin), 119
the Enlightenment. *See* rationalism
episteme, 73–75, 83. *See also* Foucault, Michel
epistemology. *See* knowledge, the study of
"The Epistemology of Metaphor" (De Man), 117, 119–21
Ermath, Elizabeth Deeds, 9–10, 12
errata, 25, 110, 112–13, 116, 123–24, 126–27, 135, 139–40, 142–43, 172, 192, 196, 208n6. *See also* disnarrated; narrative, leftovers of
"Errata" (Rushdie), 112–13
"Ethical Ambivalence" (Butler), 26–27, 33–34
ethics 40, 42, 49–50, 52–53, 63–64, 66, 68, 70–71, 74–75, 80, 107, 114, 116,

123, 132–33, 142, 144, 148–50, 159, 162–63, 180–81, 183, 185, 187, 189, 191–92, 196, 199n18, 199–200n20, 200nn21–22, 200n24, 207n24, 216n1; and history, 28–34, 36–38; and/vs. politics, 26, 33–34; and postmodern(ism)/poststructuralism, 7, 26–34, 37–38, 49, 77, 199n19; and/as responsibility, 26–27, 33
The Ethics of History (Carr, Flynn, and Makkreel), 28
Evans, Richard, 198n7
Ever After (Swift), 103–6, 207n25
experience. *See* truth, and/vs. experience

Fackenheim, Emil, 150
fairy tales, 49–50, 85–86, 99, 103, 206–7n19, 215n25
fascism, 32, 49–51. *See also* Nazism
Faurisson, Robert, 149, 212n7
feminism, 26, 30, 33, 39–42, 44–54, 55–59, 63, 65–68, 71–74, 82, 86, 98, 103, 188, 194–95, 201nn11–12, 202nn15–16, 203n27, 204n43, 210n26, 211n43
Fenwick, Mac, 119–20, 209n15
fictional worlds theory, 124–27, 130, 132–33, 209n21
Fish, Stanley, 73–74
Forster, E. M., 12–14, 208n4. *See also Aspects of the Novel; Passage to India*
Foucault, Michel, 4–5, 34, 82, 150, 158–59, 170, 195, 197–98n6, 205n44, 205n3, 205n5, 212n6, 213n14, 215n24; and epistemes, 73–75; and history, 11–13, 29, 45, 79; and lack of agency, 74. *See also The Archaeology of Knowledge; Discipline and Punish; The History of Sexuality; Madness and Civilization;* "Nietzsche, Genealogy, History"; *The Order of Things; Power/Knowledge;* "What Is An Author?"
"Force of Law" (Derrida), 26
Fowles, John, 106–8, 110, 187, 190, 207nn27–28, 207–8n29, 208n2. *See also The French Lieutenant's Woman; The Magus*
fragmentation, 17–18, 63–65, 69–71, 75, 110–11, 120, 136, 172, 201n7, 204n40, 208n3. *See also* errata; disnarrated; subjectivity, fragmented
Fragments (Wilkomirski), 181
Fraser, Nancy, 200n24
freedom, 61–62, 203n30; existential, 66, 107–8. *See also* suicide, symbolic
The French Lieutenant's Woman (Fowles), 106–8, 110, 187, 190, 207n28, 207–8n29, 208n2
the French Revolution, 78–79
Freud, Sigmund, 84–85, 93, 95, 97–99, 153, 164, 188, 205n7, 206n14, 206n18, 215n24
Frey, James, 181
Friedlander, Saul, 151, 179
Friedman, Susan Stanford, 53, 203n27
Fry, Roger, 40, 200n2, 201n8
Frye, Northrop, 198–99n13
Fuentes, Carlos, 188. *See also Terra Nostra*

Galsworthy, John, 200n3
Gandhi (Attenborough), 141, 208n9
Gandhi, Mohandas Karamchand, 140–43, 210n37; assassination of, 22, 113–14, 139–141. *See also Gandhi* (Attenborough)
Gandhi, Indira, 22, 37, 135, 138, 140–41, 183, 210n36; and the Emergency 115, 131, 208n8
Gates, David, 146
Geis, Deborah, 212n3
Geras, Norman, 30
Gilliam, Terry, 125, 127. *See also Brazil*
The Gift of Death (Derrida), 26, 31–32, 199n20
Gilman, Sander, 149, 213n15

Ginzburg, Carlo, 199n14
Gopnik, Adam, 146, 213n11
Gosse, Philip Henry, 105
Gotanda, Neil, 31
Gottwald, Klement, 1-2, 11-12, 16-17
Of Grammatology (Derrida), 5, 45, 201n9
Grant, Paul, 146
Grass, Günter, 188-89. See also *The Tin Drum*
Grillparzer, Franz, 20
Grossman, Robert, 146
The Ground Beneath Her Feet (Rushdie), 124, 140, 210n27
Guha, Ranajit, 134, 209n17

Hafley, James, 201n6, 203n30
Halbwachs, Maurice, 164, 166, 174, 214n21
Hassumani, Sabrina, 115-16
Hegel, Georg Wilhelm Friedrich, 26, 119; and history, 10, 197n4, 205n6; and memory, 18; and time, 72
Heidegger, Martin, 71, 199n20
Heisenberg, Werner, 5, 194
"Here and Now," 24, 80, 91-95, 97, 101, 103-4, 108, 147, 196
Herriman, George, 213n11
Hilberg, Raul, 150
Hindu(ism), 122, 138, 209nn19-20, 210n35
Hippler, Fritz, 213n11
Hirsch, Marianne, 156, 160, 178-79, 212n2, 213-14n18
historiographic metafiction. See postmodern(ism), and history
historiography 40, 101, 117, 119, 134-35, 143, 175, 186, 199n14; postmodern, 9-14, 20-23, 28-29, 31, 26, 43-44, 55, 77, 79, 84-86, 88-89, 92, 101-2, 111, 114, 117, 133-34, 136, 139, 146-47, 151, 167, 172, 196, 197n3, 198n6, 204n1. See also Ankersmit, Frank; White, Hayden
history, 39-40, 115, 119, 121, 122, 131, 163, 178, 180-82, 187-90, 192, 195-96, 202n15, 204n33, 204n42, 205n6, 207n23, 208nn9-10, 209n13, 211n44; as/vs. art, 40-43, 57, 59; defined, 78, 87-88; discursive construction of/reference to, 1-3, 6-7, 10-15, 22-23, 29, 37, 39, 44-45, 71-75, 81-86, 89, 99, 102, 105, 116, 125-26, 151, 158, 177, 179, 194-95; dismissed as a field of study, 9-10; as eros, 28-29; and ethics/politics, 7-9, 28-34, 36-38, 49-50; as literature, 22, 183, 205n8; literary, 42; as meaningless, 15, 20-21; as/vs. memory, 102, 112-14, 163-66, 174-75, 177-79, 214n21, 216n31; method of study, 12-13, 135; as myth, 85-86, 211n40; as/and/vs. narrative, 14-26, 43-44, 50-52, 54, 57-59, 62, 64-65, 68, 70, 77-103, 105, 109-10, 113, 116-17, 126, 136-43, 155, 167-74, 176-77, 192, 198nn9-10, 198-99n13, 199n14, 203n26, 214-15n24; as nostalgia, 175-76, 183; as oppression/power, 11-12, 18, 34, 49-52, 54-55, 126, 134, 148-49, 156, 158-59, 162; as "the past," 15, 89, 102, 105, 139, 145-50, 154, 159-60, 177, 179, 185, 194; as resistance, 34-35; as unifying form, 11, 14-16, 20-21, 24-25, 43-44, 49-51, 64, 70, 98, 109-113, 138, 205n3. See also historiography; memory; reality
History and Tropology (Ankersmit), 10, 13, 152-53, 175-76
The History of Sexuality (Foucault), 11, 198n6, 205n5
History of the World in 10 ½ Chapters (Barnes), 189
Hitler, Adolph, 45, 76, 159, 195. See also the Holocaust, Nazi(sm),
the Holocaust, 22, 29, 37-38, 146-47, 159-60, 162-65, 167-72, 176-78, 180-82, 185, 207n22, 212nn5-7, 212-3n8, 215nn26, 216n32; denial

of, 148–50, 212n5–7; as/and postmodernism, 145, 150–52, 154–55, 213n9; representation of, 151–52, 154, 158, 179–80; survivors of, 154–55, 164, 172, 178, 214n20, 214n22. *See also* Nazi(sm)
Homer, 118–20
hooks, bell, 30–31
Husak, Gustav, 2, 8–9, 183
Hutcheon, Linda, 187; and historiographic metafiction, 6–7, 79, 81, 189, 205n2, 207n27, 208n10; and the definition of postmodernism, 6–9, 42; and postmodern parody, 48–49, 202n14. See also *A Poetics of Postmodernism*; *The Politics of Postmodernism*; "The Politics of Postmodern Parody"
the hypernarratable, 25–26

Iadonisi, Rick, 174, 215n28,
Identity. *See* subjectivity
"Imaginary Homelands" (Rushdie), 109, 112, 138
imperialism. *See* colonialism
India, 46, 55, 82–83, 109, 111–12, 114, 116, 120–22, 124, 126–34, 138–44, 183, 189, 208nn4–5, 208nn7–9, 209n12, 209nn18–19, 210n24, 210n26, 210n28, 210n31, 211n42
The Infernal Desire Machines of Doctor Hoffman (Carter), 189
Irish, Robert, 79, 205nn1–2
Islam, 122, 209n19, 211n39
Israel, 159, 169, 213n16

Jallianwala Bagh. *See* Amritsar Massacre
Jameson, Fredric, 22; and history, 9, 207n23; defines postmodernism, 5–6, 202n14; and the "third world," 119. See also *Postmodernism*; *The Political Unconscious*; "Third World Literature"
Jenkins, Keith, 9–10, 31–33, 200n24.

See also *Why History?*
Jew(s). *See* Judaism
Johnson, Barbara, 27
Joplin, Patricia, 51–52, 200n1, 201n5, 201n10, 204n38
Joyce, James, 1, 19, 43, 187, 200n2. See also *Ulysses*
Judaism, 47, 148–49, 154–56, 158–59, 162, 164, 169, 178–79, 182, 193, 213n11, 213n15, 214n19, 216n2. *See also* race

Kant, Immanuel, 26, 200n20
Kellner, Hans, 24
Kennedy, John F., 22
Kermode, Frank, 211n40
King, Martin Luther, 22
Kingston, Maxine Hong, 189
knowledge, 21–22, 75, 85, 99, 106, 111, 120, 141, 147–49, 151–54, 180, 184, 190, 194, 200n22, 202n15, 203n31, 214n20; and ethics, 32–34, 37–38, 98; as oppression/power, 12, 29, 34, 171; the study of (epistemology), 2, 6, 24, 26, 28, 30, 36–38, 73, 89, 114–15, 117, 148, 150, 152, 154–55, 158–59, 162–63, 179–80, 184. *See also* truth
Kolakowski, Leszek, 61, 203n28
Kortenaar, Neil ten, 114, 117, 140, 142, 208n10, 209nn11–12, 209n16, 210n24, 210n28
Kristeva, Julia, 203n27
Kuhn, Thomas, 73, 195, 205n44
Kundera, Milan, 1–3, 7–9, 11, 16–22, 34–36, 183–84, 196, 197n1, 198nn11–12. See also *The Book of Laughter and Forgetting*; *Testaments Betrayed*

Lacan, Jacques, 4, 83, 85, 204n41, 206n11; and fragmented subjectivity, 69–70; and "the mirror stage," 69–71, and narrative, 70–71, 204n40; and the Real, 92–93,

99–100; and "symbolic suicide," 66–68, and time, 71–72, 204n42. See also *Ecrits*
Lacapra, Dominick, 25, 79, 101, 145, 151, 178–79, 185, 199n17, 212n2, 213n9, 214n22
Laga, Barry, 155
Lamarck, Jean-Baptiste, 178, 185
Lang, Berel, 151, 179
Language, 128, 150; figurative, 22, 51, 62, 110, 114, 116–20, 125, 127, 134, 140, 143, 172, 206n9; as the Lacanian Symbolic, 69–70, 75, 83, 85, 92–93, 99; redefined, 67–68, 204n37; relationship to reality/truth, 4–5, 10–13, 34–35, 51, 56, 74, 78–79, 83–85, 121, 123, 126–27, 154, 165, 167, 169, 171, 186, 207n23, 213n10, 214–15n24. *See also* metaphor; metonymy; poststructuralism
Last Orders (Swift), 207n21
The League of Nations, 69, 204n39
Lee, Alison, 79, 205n2, 207n27
Lehman, Daniel, 181–83
Levinas, Emmanuel, 26–29, 31, 33, 199n18, 200nn21–22
Life of Pi (Martel), 190, 192–94, 196, 216n2
lies, 10, 42, 84, 114, 121, 135, 141, 181, 200, 209n9, 209–10n23; vs. truth, 123, 126–33, 141–42. *See also* truth.
Lighthousekeeping (Winterson), 106, 187
"The Linguistic Turn." *See* historiography, postmodern; poststructuralism
Little, Judy, 75, 205n45
Limited Inc. (Derrida), 45, 48
Lipstadt, Deborah, 149, 212nn6–7
"The Location of *Brazil*" (Rushdie), 125
Locke, John, 121, 124
Lopate, Phillip, 149
Lounsberry, Barbara, 181
Lyotard, Jean-François, 3–6, 9, 31–32, 79, 150, 200n22, 212n5. See also *The Postmodern Condition*

lyric, 53–54, 203n27, 205n8; vs. narrative, 54, 58

Madness and Civilization (Foucault), 197n6, 205n5
magical realism, 65, 116–17, 121, 124, 129–32, 143, 190, 209n11, 211n42
The Magus (Fowles), 107–8, 187, 207nn27–28, 207–8n29
The Man in the High Castle (Dick), 189
Manekshaw, Sam, 132, 210n29
Márquez, Gabriel García, 116, 188–89, 209n11, 209n21. See also *One Hundred Years of Solitude*
Martel, Yann, 190, 192–94, 196, 216n2. See also *Life of Pi*
Marx, Groucho, 34
Marx, Karl, 34
Marxism, 4–5, 33–34, 83, 135. *See also* class, social
Matter and Memory (Bergson), 60–62, 65, 203n29
Maus (and *Maus II*) (Spiegelman), 37, 145–48, 151, 154–85, 190, 196, 211–12n1, 212nn2–3, 212–13n8, 213nn11–13, 213nn16–17, 213–14n18, 214nn19–20, 214n23, 215n25, 215nn27–28, 215–16n30, 216n33
Max and the Cats (Scliar), 216n2
McCloud, Scott, 215n29
McEwan, Ian, 190–94, 196, 216n1. See also *Atonement; Saturday*
McGlothlin, Erin, 172–73
McHale, Brian, 6. See also *Postmodernist Fiction*
McLaurin, Allen, 40, 200n3
McWhirter, David, 41, 47, 75, 201n5, 202n16
memory 40, 60–61, 72, 92, 111, 153, 160, 163, 167; as/vs. forgetting, 2–3, 9, 17–19, 36, 159, 164; as/vs. history, 102, 112–14, 163–66, 174–75, 177–79, 214n21, 216n31; and post-memory, 179; vs. power,

2–3, 8–9, 34; as representation, 102, 166, 177; as reproduction, 102, 166, 177; spontaneous vs. "recollected," 18–19, 177. *See also* history
metahistory. *See* historiography, postmodern
Metahistory (White), 12–13, 168, 172, 198n7, 198n9, 198–99n13
metafiction. *See* postmodern(ism)
metaphor, 10, 22, 56, 90, 106, 114, 128–29, 135, 143–44, 147, 160, 209n14, 212–13n8, 213n13, 213n17, 216n33, 213n13, 213n17, 216n33; made literal, 116–17, 120–21, 123–27, 130–31, 136, 138, 140, 142–43, 155, 206n9, 209n16; vs. metonymy, 119–120, 132, 209n15; opposed, 118–20, 131, 209n13; as truth, 121–26, 128, 133, 136. *See also* language, figurative; metonymy
metanarratives; 50, 82, 100 incredulity towards, 4, 51, 150, 200n12
metonymy, 52, 119–20, 132, 138, 144, 209n15
Michelet, Jules, 176
Midnight's Children (Rushdie), 25, 37, 109–17, 120–144, 177, 183, 188–89, 194–95, 208nn3–8, 208–9n10, 209n11–12, 209n15–16, 209n18, 209nn21–22, 209–10n23, 210nn24–26, 210nn28–30, 210n32–36, 211n40, 211nn42–44
Miller, Arthur, 115
Miller, D. A., 23, 80, 87, 136–37, 171, 206n16
Miller, J. Hillis, 27
Miller, Nancy, 212n2, 214n23
mimesis, 7–8, 12, 16–17, 30, 36, 38, 41, 43–44, 51, 53, 65, 105, 117, 121, 123–25, 146–47, 158, 160, 169, 178, 180, 185, 191, 194, 196, 197n2, 203n25, 214n20, 216n33
"Modern Fiction" (Woolf), 43, 53, 200–1n3
modernism 4, 19, 39–40, 53, 101, 151, 168; vs. postmodernism, 6; vs.

realism (or narrative), 22, 199n14, 200n2, 203n26
"The Modernist Event" (White), 13, 22
Molloy (Beckett), 179, 190
"moments of being," 24, 59, 62–64, 66, 72, 75, 80, 147, 188, 196, 202–3n23, 207–8n29
Monday or Tuesday (Woolf), 54
The Moor's Last Sigh (Rushdie), 123–24, 135, 209nn19–20, 210n30
morality, 1, 4, 20, 26, 30–34, 66, 74, 86, 111, 115, 148, 150, 159, 185, 198–99n13, 200n24. *See also* ethics; politics
Mouly, Françoise, 146, 156–58, 166, 172
Mrs. Dalloway (Woolf), 43, 51, 54, 56, 195
Murdoch, Iris, 1
Muslim. *See* Islam
myth, 43, 85–86, 92, 99, 109, 118, 129, 141, 200n2; defined, 86, 198n8, 211n40
Mythologies (Barthes), 86, 198n8

Naipaul, V. S., 135, 210n32
the narratable, 19, 51, 54, 70, 129, 132, 137, 139, 171, 204n40, 216n32; vs. the nonnarratable, 24–25, 57, 65, 87–90, 95–97, 136, 139. *See also* narrative
narrative, 2, 29, 147–48, 160, 163, 173, 179–80, 195; as actions; 51–52, 65–66, 96; and causality, 14, 87, 102; defined 13–14, 23–24, 51–53, 72, 89; as desire (sexual), 25, 51–52, 58–59, 80, 86–89, 94–99, 136, 168, 171, 189, 203n27, 206n18, 207n20; as explanation, 14, 24, 51, 64, 86–88, 90, 93, 96, 111, 176; as/and/vs. history or reality, 14–26, 35, 37–38, 40, 43–44, 50–59, 62, 64–65, 68, 77–113, 116–17, 122–24, 126–27, 136–43, 155, 167–74, 176–77, 191–92, 194, 198nn9–10, 198–99n13, 199n14, 203n26, 206n17, 214–15n24; as

hope, 122, 127–33, 135–37, 139, 143–44; leftovers of, 17, 25, 137–39, 147, 177; vs. lyric, 53–54, 58; and subjectivity, 70–72; as therapy, 22, 80–81, 84–88, 90, 92–93, 100–2, 104, 167, 193–94; as a unified sequence, 13–14, 18, 20, 23–24, 52–57, 64, 66–67, 69–71, 75–76, 80–83, 100–2, 108–11, 139, 142, 166, 198n10, 202n23, 210n28; as violence 52, 65, 76. *See also* antinarrative; closure; disnarrated; hypernarratable; narratable; nonnarratable; nonnarrative
narrativist historiography. *See* historiography, postmodern
Nazi(sm), 27, 32–33, 45–46, 52, 101, 149–50, 155–56, 158, 162, 170, 173, 179, 201n11, 212–13n8, 213n11. *See also* fascism; the Holocaust
Nehru, Jawaharlal, 112, 128, 140–43
newspaper(s), 50–51, 82, 202nn18–19, 212n6, 214n19
Niazi, Amir Abdullah Khan ("Tiger"), 132, 210n29
Nietzsche, Friedrich, 10, 12, 20, 150. *See also* "On Truth and Lie in An Extra-Moral Sense"
"Nietzsche, Genealogy, History" (Foucault), 11–12, 197n6, 205n3
Nights at the Circus (Carter), 188
nonfiction, 126, 147, 180–84, 187
the nonnaratable 143; defined, 24, 199n16; vs. the narratable, 24, 57, 65, 80, 87–90, 95–97, 100, 136–37, 139, 144. *See also* nonnarrative
nonnarrative, 26, 37–38, 40, 59, 90, 98, 166, 189, 205n8; and access to history/reality, 22–23, 56, 66–68, 77–78, 80, 87–89, 97, 99, 102, 109, 137, 139, 142, 144, 207n23; defined, 23–24; as lyric, 53–54, 58; modes of history (annals, chronicles), 15, 20, 198n10; as pacifism, 52. *See also* antinarrative; disnarrated; the nonnarratable

Nora, Pierre, 112, 163–66, 174, 216n31
Novick, Peter, 149, 159, 178, 194–95, 197n4, 198n7, 212nn6–7, 214n22. See also *That Noble Dream*
Nussbaum, Martha, 27

object(ivity), 7–8, 21, 50, 159, 188, 210n31, 214–15n24; in history, 10–11, 119, 125, 134–35, 144, 149, 155, 194–95, 197n4, 198n7; as impossible, 3–4, 9–11, 28–29, 41, 74; as possible, 10; vs. subjectivity, 3, 9–10, 60–62, 74, 115–16, 152–54, 156, 175–76, 182–83, 186, 194, 213n10
O'Brien, Tim, 182–83
Omeros (Walcott), 117–20, 131, 187, 209nn13–14
One Hundred Years of Solitude (Márquez), 188–89
"On Truth and Lie in an Extra-Moral Sense" (Nietzsche), 10
ontology, 4, 6, 9, 61, 71–72, 75, 78, 97, 148, 150, 152, 164, 180, 200n22
orality, 167–68, 171–72, 174, 209n11, 214n23; vs. writing, 164–66
The Order of Things (Foucault), 4–5, 74, 197–98n6
Orientalism. *See* colonialism
Orlando (Woolf), 50, 77–78, 216n33
Orvell, Miles, 146, 212n3, 213n11
Orwell, George, 114
the Other, 26–27, 29, 33–34, 67, 199n18
"*Ousia* and *Grammē*" (Derrida), 71–72
"Outside the Whale" (Rushdie), 144

pacifism, 33, 50, 52, 56–57, 63, 67–68, 141, 202n20
Pakistan, 114, 123–32, 144, 210n24
parody, 25, 44, 47, 65, 67, 90, 94–95, 112, 123, 205n4, 209n12; defined, 48–49; 202n14
Passage to India (Forster), 208n4
the past. *See* history; the present

patriarchy. *See* feminism
Pavel, Thomas, 124
Petrarch, Francesco, 176
Petrovic, Lena, 30
Phelan, James, 108, 216n1
photograph(y), 5, 50, 103, 160–62, 166, 170, 202n18, 207–8n29, 213–14n18; manipulated, 1–3, 16, 160
Píchova, Hana, 16
Plato, 165–66, 174
"Plato's Pharmacy" (Derrida), 165–66, 170, 174
The Pleasure of the Text (Barthes), 203n27
plot. *See* narrative
A Poetics of Postmodernism (Hutcheon), 42, 79, 187
The Political Unconscious (Jameson), 207
politics, 40, 58, 64, 68, 71, 78, 116, 132, 136–38, 141–42, 148, 159, 179, 185, 200n23, 200–1n2, 204n42; and/vs. ethics, 26, 29–30, 33–34; and postmodernism, 7, 29–30
The Politics of Postmodernism (Hutcheon), 6–7, 56, 208n10
"The Politics of Postmodern Parody" (Hutcheon), 48–49
Possession (Byatt), 207n26
possible worlds theory. *See* fictional worlds theory
postcolonialism. *See* colonialism, and postcolonialism
The Postmodern Condition (Lyotard); 3–6, 150, 200n22
postmodern(ism), 3, 16, 35–36, 73, 107, 147–49, 163, 179, 185, 192, 196, 206–7n19; defined, 3–9, 197n2, 200n22; and ethics/politics, 7–8, 27–34, 49, 77, 199n19; and history, 6–11, 28–29, 31–36, 39, 48–49, 79, 84, 158, 176, 207n27, 209n10; as/and the Holocaust, 145, 150–52, 154–55, 213n9; in literature, 6, 8, 15–16, 21, 23–25, 36, 38–39, 42, 48–49, 89, 101, 103, 105–6, 108, 116, 123, 126, 147, 155, 180, 182–84, 187, 189, 191, 195–96, 200nn5–6, 202n14, 207nn25–28, 212n3, 213n17; vs. modernism, 6, 19. *See also* historiography, postmodern
Postmodernism, Or, The Cultural Logic of Late Capitalism (Jameson), 9, 202n14
Postmodernist Fiction (McHale), 6
postmodernist historical fiction, 8, 15–16, 21, 23–25, 37, 189; or narrative, 147, 183
poststructuralism 8, 10–12, 24–25, 34, 37, 44–45, 48, 72, 73–74, 81, 83–85, 99, 102, 117, 119, 121, 124–25, 128, 135, 149–50, 154–55, 162, 165–67, 174–76, 178–79, 195, 198n7, 200n21, 201n9, 206n9, 213n10, 214n21; and ethics, 26–29, 31, 34; and history, 9, 28–29, 31; and postmodernism, 4–6. *See also* Derrida, Jacques; Foucault, Michel; Kristeva, Julia; Lacan, Jacques
Power/Knowledge (Foucault), 73, 205n44
Prague, 1, 18–19
the present, 11–12, 17, 19, 21, 25, 50, 63, 65, 69–72, 133, 169–70, 178, 204n33, 204n42; defined, 59; grammatical tense, 71–72; materiality of, 60–62, 66–68, 71–72, 75–77, 91; and/vs. the past, 23–25, 31–32, 36–38, 61–64, 77, 88–89, 93–94, 100, 103, 106, 117–118, 146, 148, 154, 162, 163–64, 166, 170–75, 179–80, 188, 196, 203n31, 215–16n30, 216n32
Price, David, 84, 116, 144, 205n2, 206n10, 206n15, 206n17, 210n36, 211n44
Prince, Gerald, 14; and "disnarration," 109–10. See also *Dictionary of Narratology*
"Prisoner on the Hell Planet" (Spiegelman), 160–61, 167
Process, vs. progress (toward closure), 86–90, 205n6
Proust, Marcel, 19; See also *In Search of*

Lost Time
psychoanalysis, 18–19, 22, 58, 71, 84–85, 88, 92–95, 97–99, 100, 147, 153, 176, 178, 188, 203n27, 204n40, 206n12, 212n2. *See also* Freud, Sigmund; Lacan, Jacques

race, 31–33, 116, 118, 128, 130, 156, 158, 162, 169, 195, 201n12, 208n9, 213n12, 213n15; definitions of 31
Ranke, Leopold von, 10, 194, 197n4, 198n7; See also *The Secret of World History*
rationalism, 27, 32, 45, 78, 81, 134–35, 150, 195–96
the real(ity), 40–41, 71–72, 75, 90, 111–12, 114–18, 122, 124–26, 128–29, 152, 160, 162, 165, 177–78, 181–82, 185–90, 192–93, 196, 202n23, 207n23; access to, 8, 16–19, 22–24, 36, 49–51, 62–63, 80, 87–89, 102, 144, 146, 173; vs. art, 40–44; as a discursive/linguistic construction, 4–6, 15, 42–47, 99–100, 105, 155, 195; defined, 87–89; Lacanian, 67, 71, 92–93, 99–101, 206n15; literary reference to (*see* mimesis); as matter/things, 60–61, 64, 72, 104, 130–33, 139, 173, 176, 186; as meaningless, 15, 20–21; and/vs. narrative, 15–26, 35, 50–51, 52, 56, 58–59, 62–64, 66, 77, 87, 91–111, 113, 123–24, 136–40, 155, 168–69, 191, 194, 206n17; in withdrawal, 4–7, 9, 29, 36, 103, 148, 158, 180, 200n22. *See also* history; truth
reason, *see* rationalism
Reder, Michael, 116
relativist historiography. *See* historiography, postmodern
religion, 4, 130, 140–42, 193. *See also* Christianity; Hinduism; Islam; Judaism
Ricoeur, Paul, 53
Riffaterre, Michael, 125

Rigney, Ann, 24
A Room of One's Own (Woolf), 53, 68, 201n4, 204–5n43
Rorty, Richard, 5
Rossellini, Roberto, 66, 204n34
Rothberg, Michael, 159, 212n3, 213n16
Rushdie, Salman, 25–26, 37, 109–17, 120–44, 147, 155, 172, 183, 188–89, 192, 194–96, 208nn3-9, 208–9n10, 209nn11–12, 209nn15–16, 209nn18–22, 209–10n23, 210nn24–30, 210nn32–37, 211nn39–44. *See also* "Attenborough's *Gandhi*"; "Errata"; *The Ground Beneath Her Feet*; "The Location of *Brazil*"; *Midnight's Children*; *The Moor's Last Sigh*; "Outside the Whale"; *Shame*; *Step Across This Line*
Ruskin, John, 176
Russell, Bertrand, 60–62, 203n31

Said, Edward, 158, 195, 211n38
Saturday (McEwan), 192
Saussure, Ferdinand de, 4, 11, 153. See also *Course in General Linguistics*
Scliar, Moacyr, 216n2. See also *Max and the Cats*
In Search of Lost Time (Proust), 19
Sears, Sallie, 204n36
The Secret of World History (Ranke), 197n4
the self. See subjectivity
Sexing the Cherry (Winterson), 188
Shame (Rushdie), 124–25, 140, 211n41
Shastri, Lal Bahadur, 143
"A Sketch of the Past" (Woolf), 37, 62–64, 66
Spanish Civil War, 50
Spiegel, Gabrielle, 154–55, 179, 198n7
Spiegelman, Anja, 145–47, 160–62, 167, 169, 173, 190, 211–12n1
Spiegelman, Art, 37, 145–48, 151, 154–85, 190, 196, 211–12n1, 212nn2–3, 212–13n8, 213nn11–13, 213nn16–17, 213–14n18, 214nn19–

20, 214n23, 215n25, 215nn27–28, 215–16n30, 216n33. See also *Maus* (and *Maus II*); "Prisoner on the Hell Planet"
Spiegelman, Richieu, 160, 169–70
Spiegelman, Vladek, 145, 156, 158–64, 166–79, 181, 190, 211–12n1, 213n16, 214n19, 214n23, 215n25, 215n27, 216n33
Spielberg, Steven, 214n22
Spivak, Gayatri Chakravorty, 143, 199n15, 200n23, 210n31, 215n24. See also "Can the Subaltern Speak?"
Srivastava, Aruna, 113, 116
St. Lucia, 117–20
Stalinism, 9. See also Communism
Staub, Michael, 164–65, 212n3, 213n13
Steiner, George, 150
Step Across This Line (Rushdie), 115, 209n16, 209n19, 210n37, 211n42
Stern, Kenneth, 148–49, 172, 212n7
Stone, Lawrence, 14
Stoppard, Tom, 188. See also *Arcadia*
Strand, Eric, 140, 142, 210n26, 210n33, 210n37
Streich, Julius, 213n11
Subaltern Studies, 133–35, 144, 210n31
subject(ivity), 4, 18, 35, 42, 47, 88, 103, 113, 165, 199n20; communal, 30, 148–49, 159, 163; fragmented or multiple, 69–71, 75, 123, 204n40, 209n20; as impossible, 73–74; through narrative, 70–72, 92, 123, 204n40; and/vs. objectiv(ity), 3, 9–10, 60–62, 74, 115–16, 152–54, 156, 175–76, 179, 182–86, 194, 213n10. See also Freud, Sigmund; Lacan, Jacques; psychoanalysis
the sublime, 4, 24–25, 31, 35, 101, 145, 199n17, 213n9, 216n32
Sublime Historical Experience (Ankersmit), 25, 152–53, 185
suicide, 43, 56, 58, 75, 78, 99, 103, 145, 160, 167, 170; symbolic, 66–68, 107, 204n34
Swift, Graham, 24–26, 36–37, 77–109, 147, 187, 193–96, 205nn1–2, 205n4, 205n7, 206nn9–17, 206–7n19, 207nn20–21, 207nn24–25. See also *Ever After*; *Last Orders*; *Tomorrow*; *Waterland*
the Symbolic. See language, as Lacanian Symbolic
S/Z (Barthes), 203n25

Tabachnick, Steven, 215n27
teleology, 23, 54, 58, 79, 87, 97, 100. See also closure; process
Terdiman, Richard, 102, 105, 177, 207n24
Telling the Truth about History (Appleby, Hunt, Jacob), 198n7
Terra Nostra (Fuentes), 188
Testaments Betrayed (Kundera), 36
That Noble Dream (Novick), 195, 197n4, 198n7
"Theses on the Philosophy of History" (Benjamin), 77, 82–83, 206n12
"Third World Literature in the Era of Multinational Capitalism" (Jameson), 119
Thomas, D. M., 188. See also *The White Hotel*
Thompson, Bobby, 189
Three Guineas (Woolf), 44–47, 50, 57, 68, 129, 201n8, 201nn11–12, 202nn19–20, 204n34
time, 58, 106, 186, 194, 204n42; as atomistic moments, 54–55, 59–64, 71–72, 75–76, 188, 202n23; as flow, 60–61, 64, 71–72; as sequence, 54–55, 60, 62, 81, 166, 173–75, 188, 202n23; as simultaneous/spatialized, 62, 173–74, 188, 215n29
Time and Free Will (Bergson), 60
The Tin Drum (Grass), 188–89
Todorov, Tzvetan, 13, 23, 25, 89, 171
Tomorrow (Swift), 207n21
To The Lighthouse (Woolf), 54, 195, 202n23
trauma, 22, 25, 37, 56, 68, 78–81, 84–85,

88, 91–94, 99–102, 104, 148, 150, 153–54, 159, 168–69, 174, 178, 181–83, 188, 190–91, 193–95, 207n24, 213n9, 213n16, 216n32
Trevelyan, G. M., 200n1
tropology. *See* language, figurative; metaphor; metonymy
truth 1–5, 6–12, 15–16, 19–22, 29–30, 34–37, 39, 43, 47, 49, 51, 65, 73–75, 77, 79, 83–84, 86, 91–92, 96–99, 104–5, 112, 115–117, 120, 135, 138–39, 142–46, 150, 158, 160, 163–65, 171–72, 186, 189–90, 192–93, 195–96, 200n22, 205n8, 206n13, 207n20, 211n40, 211n44, 213n10, 213n17, 214n22, 214–15n24; and/vs. experience, 37, 147, 151–55, 166, 167, 174–85; vs. lies, 114, 123, 126–33, 141–42; metaphorical, 121–26, 128, 133. *See also* history; knowledge; lies; reality

Ulysses (Joyce), 1, 19, 43, 187, 200n2
Underworld (Delillo), 189

"The Value of Narrativity in the Representation of Reality" (White), 10, 14–15, 20, 198n10, 198–99n13
van Deijssel, Lodewijk, 175
"Violence and Metaphysics" (Derrida), 27
Victorian, 46–47, 48, 74, 82–83, 85, 106–7, 205n4, 205n6, 207n26
The Vietnam War, 32, 182–83, 195
The Voyage Out (Woolf), 54

Walcott, Derek, 117–21, 131, 187, 209nn13–14. See also *Omeros*
Wallace, Honor McKitrick, 58, 203n27
Walsh, Richard, 124–25
Warhol, Robyn, 98, 199n16, 206n18, 208nn1–2
Waterland (Swift), 24–26, 36–37,

77–105, 107, 109–10, 135, 138, 144, 183–84, 193–95, 205nn1–2, 205n4, 205n7, 206nn9–17, 206–7n19, 207n20, 207n24
Watkins, Renée, 59, 209n38
The Waves (Woolf), 54–58, 203n24
Wells, H. G., 200n1, 200–1n3
Wells, Lynn, 205n2, 205n7, 206n12,
"What is An Author?" (Foucault), 170
White, Hayden 35, 40, 86, 195, 205n1; and history, 10, 12–15, 20–24, 37, 43–44, 77–79, 83–85, 89, 101, 111, 117, 134, 136, 146, 151, 167–69, 172, 176–77, 183–84, 196, 198n7, 198n9, 198–99n13, 199n14, 205n8; vs. narrative 12–15, 20–24, 37, 43–44, 77–80, 83–85, 117, 136, 139, 151, 167–69, 172, 198n10, 198–99n13, 199n14, 205n8; and psychoanalysis, 84–85, 88. *See also* "The Burden of History"; *Metahistory*; "The Modernist Event"; "The Value of Narrativity . . ."
The White Hotel (Thomas), 188
Why History? (Jenkins), 9–10, 31–33, 200n4
Wiesel, Elie, 150
Wilkomirski, Benjamin, 181. See also *Fragments*
Williams, Raymond, 79
Wilner, Arlene Fish, 167, 212n3
Winterson, Jeanette, 106, 187–88. See also *Lighthousekeeping; Sexing the Cherry*
Witek, Joseph, 177, 185, 212–13n8, 213n8, 213n17, 216n33
Wittgenstein, Ludwig, 4
Wittig, Monique, 68
Wolpert. Stanley, 116, 143, 208n7, 209n12
Woolf, Leonard, 204n39
Woolf, Virginia, 24, 36–37, 39–60, 62–77, 80, 88, 103, 109, 129, 147, 187–88, 194–96, 200n2, 201–2n3, 201nn4–8, 201nn11–13, 202nn15–17, 202nn18–21, 202–3n23,

203nn24–27, 203n30, 204nn33–39, 204nn41–43, 205n45, 207–8n29. See also *Between the Acts;* "Modern Fiction"; *Monday or Tuesday; Mrs. Dalloway;* "moments of being"; *Orlando; A Room of One's Own;* "A Sketch of the Past"; *Three Guineas; To The Lighthouse; The Voyage Out; The Waves; The Years*
"The Work of Art in the Age of Mechanical Reproduction" (Benjamin), 5
World War I, 52, 74, 84, 194–95
World War II, 45–47, 52, 63, 74, 76, 189–92, 195, 198, 216n32
writing. *See* language; narrative; orality
Wyschogrod, Edith, 12, 28–30

The Years (Woolf), 64, 66, 202n15, 204nn33–34
Young, James, 164, 171, 213n11

Zeno of Elea, 60
Žižek, Slavoj, 25, 34, 66–67, 83, 85, 92–93, 99, 101, 199n17, 204n34, 206n12

THEORY AND INTERPRETATION OF NARRATIVE
James Phelan and Peter J. Rabinowitz, Series Editors

Because the series editors believe that the most significant work in narrative studies today contributes both to our knowledge of specific narratives and to our understanding of narrative in general, studies in the series typically offer interpretations of individual narratives and address significant theoretical issues underlying those interpretations. The series does not privilege one critical perspective but is open to work from any strong theoretical position.

Franz Kafka: Narration, Rhetoric, and Reading
  EDITED BY JAKOB LOTHE, BEATRICE SANDBERG, AND RONALD SPEIRS

Social Minds in the Novel
  ALAN PALMER

Narrative Structures and the Language of the Self
  MATTHEW CLARK

Imagining Minds: The Neuro-Aesthetics of Austen, Eliot, and Hardy
  KAY YOUNG

Postclassical Narratology: Approaches and Analyses
  EDITED BY JAN ALBER AND MONIKA FLUDERNIK

Techniques for Living: Fiction and Theory in the Work of Christine Brooke-Rose
  KAREN R. LAWRENCE

Towards the Ethics of Form in Fiction: Narratives of Cultural Remission
  LEONA TOKER

Tabloid, Inc.: Crimes, Newspapers, Narratives
  V. PENELOPE PELIZZON AND NANCY M. WEST

Narrative Means, Lyric Ends: Temporality in the Nineteenth-Century British Long Poem
  MONIQUE R. MORGAN

Understanding Nationalism: On Narrative, Cognitive Science, and Identity
  PATRICK COLM HOGAN

Joseph Conrad: Voice, Sequence, History, Genre
  EDITED BY JAKOB LOTHE, JEREMY HAWTHORN, JAMES PHELAN

The Rhetoric of Fictionality: Narrative Theory and the Idea of Fiction
  RICHARD WALSH

Experiencing Fiction: Judgments, Progressions, and the Rhetorical Theory of Narrative
  JAMES PHELAN

Unnatural Voices: Extreme Narration in Modern and Contemporary Fiction
  BRIAN RICHARDSON

Narrative Causalities
  EMMA KAFALENOS

Why We Read Fiction: Theory of Mind and the Novel
  LISA ZUNSHINE

I Know That You Know That I Know: Narrating Subjects from Moll Flanders *to* Marnie
  GEORGE BUTTE

Bloodscripts: Writing the Violent Subject
  ELANA GOMEL

Surprised by Shame: Dostoevsky's Liars and Narrative Exposure
  DEBORAH A. MARTINSEN

Having a Good Cry: Effeminate Feelings and Pop-Culture Forms
ROBYN R. WARHOL

Politics, Persuasion, and Pragmatism: A Rhetoric of Feminist Utopian Fiction
ELLEN PEEL

Telling Tales: Gender and Narrative Form in Victorian Literature and Culture
ELIZABETH LANGLAND

Narrative Dynamics: Essays on Time, Plot, Closure, and Frames
EDITED BY BRIAN RICHARDSON

Breaking the Frame: Metalepsis and the Construction of the Subject
DEBRA MALINA

Invisible Author: Last Essays
CHRISTINE BROOKE-ROSE

Ordinary Pleasures: Couples, Conversation, and Comedy
KAY YOUNG

Narratologies: New Perspectives on Narrative Analysis
EDITED BY DAVID HERMAN

Before Reading: Narrative Conventions and the Politics of Interpretation
PETER J. RABINOWITZ

Matters of Fact: Reading Nonfiction over the Edge
DANIEL W. LEHMAN

The Progress of Romance: Literary Historiography and the Gothic Novel
DAVID H. RICHTER

A Glance Beyond Doubt: Narration, Representation, Subjectivity
SHLOMITH RIMMON-KENAN

Narrative as Rhetoric: Technique, Audiences, Ethics, Ideology
JAMES PHELAN

Misreading Jane Eyre: *A Postformalist Paradigm*
JEROME BEATY

Psychological Politics of the American Dream: The Commodification of Subjectivity in Twentieth-Century American Literature
LOIS TYSON

Understanding Narrative
EDITED BY JAMES PHELAN AND PETER J. RABINOWITZ

Framing Anna Karenina: *Tolstoy, the Woman Question, and the Victorian Novel*
AMY MANDELKER

Gendered Interventions: Narrative Discourse in the Victorian Novel
ROBYN R. WARHOL

Reading People, Reading Plots: Character, Progression, and the Interpretation of Narrative
JAMES PHELAN

www.ingramcontent.com/pod-product-compliance
Lightning Source LLC
Chambersburg PA
CBHW030133240426
43672CB00005B/118